Management
Competencies
and Incompetencies

Management
Competencies and Incompetencies

WILLIAM P. ANTHONY, PH.D.
*Professor and Chairman of Management
College of Business
Florida State University*

ADDISON-WESLEY PUBLISHING COMPANY
Reading, Massachusetts • Menlo Park, California
London • Amsterdam • Don Mills, Ontario • Sydney

Library of Congress Cataloging in Publication Data

Anthony, William P
  Management.

  Includes bibliographies.
  1. Management. I. Title.
HD31.A593   658.4   79-25171
ISBN 0-201-00085-7

Copyright © 1981 by Addison-Wesley Publishing Company, Inc. Philippines copyright 1981 by Addison-Wesley Publishing Company, Inc.
All rights reserved. No part of this publication may be reproduced, stored in a retrieval system, or transmitted, in any form or by any means, electronic, mechanical, photocopying, recording, or otherwise, without the prior written permission of the publisher. Printed in the United States of America. Published simultaneously in Canada. Library of Congress Catalog Card No. 79-25171.

ISBN 0-201-00085-7
ABCDEFGHIJ-MA-89876543210

Preface

What makes a manager effective? What mistakes should a manager avoid making? How does a manager maximize gains and minimize losses? These questions are asked frequently by university students and professional practicing managers. They have no easy cookbook answers. Management is an extremely complex process which is still not fully understood from a scientific standpoint. It is just as much an art as it is a science.

Yet, we do know some things about managerial effectiveness. Over the last two decades there has been a virtual revolution in management writing and research both by academic scholars and professional practitioners. The purpose of this book is to use this information in presenting a model of managerial effectiveness. The book is written primarily for the professional manager who, like all conscious professionals, is concerned with maintaining managerial competencies, skills, and knowledge. Many of these individuals will likely be enrolled in executive MBA programs or in other executive and professional development programs. However, such classroom activity is not a necessary condition for understanding the material in this book; a conscientious process of self-study should enable any manager to grasp the concepts presented in this book.

Several learning aids are contained in the book. I've used the question and answer framework in structuring the chapters. Most of us think in a question and answer format and usually learn using this approach. Every chapter ends with a series of questions for analysis and review. References for further reading are provided. Key concepts are highlighted throughout the book. Short cases and exercises appear at the end of each chapter where concepts explained in the text can be applied. Examples of various concepts are also presented in the chapters themselves.

This book will not answer all your questions nor solve all your managerial problems. No book alone in management can do that. But by thoroughly studying the material presented in the book, you should have the necessary knowledge and skills to design more efficient ways of solving your problems. You should gain a better appreciation of the problems you face and should be able to develop more effective alternative approaches, and draw on a more diversified problem-solving tool kit. To accomplish this end, I have tried to present practical approaches and solutions which can be immediately used to develop managerial competencies and skills.

Material in the book has been tested with undergraduate and graduate students and with a host of professional managers at all management levels, from supervisor to executive, both in business and governmental organizations. Their evaluation and comments has assisted me greatly in making the material relevant to managerial needs. They have also helped me cut the academic jargon as much as possible. Such jargon is generally avoided, and if it is possible to express the same thought without the jargon, I do. However, there are instances when I feel the academic concept loses a great deal of its meaning if translated into the vernacular. In these instances, I try to provide a short, to-the-point, workable definition of the idea or concept.

Though I have been assisted by many people in writing the book, I would especially like to thank Ms. Diane Dyer and Ms. Rosanne Heard who did such a fine job typing the manuscript.

Tallahassee, Florida W.P.A.
June 1980

Contents

Part I INTRODUCTION   1

1 What Should a Manager Do?   3
The Management Process   4
Conclusion   15
Questions   15
Cases and Exercises   16
References   19

2 What Must a Manager Know?   20
Environment and Market   21
Organization   25
People   28
Task   29
Conclusion   29
Questions   30
Cases and Exercises   30
References   33

3 What Skills Must a Manager Practice?   35
What Are Managerial Skills?   36
Conclusion   43
Questions   43
Cases and Exercises   44
References   47

Part II DEVELOPING MANAGERIAL KNOWLEDGE   49

4 What Should a Manager Know About the Environment?   51
Effects of Components of the Environment   51
Relevancy of the Environment   53
Ways of Knowing   57
Conclusion   58
Questions   58
Cases and Exercises   60
References   62

5 What Should a Manager Know About the Market?   64
Customers versus Consumers   65
Consumer Behavior   69
Competition   73
Ways of Knowing   74
Conclusion   75
Questions   76
Cases and Exercises   76
References   79

6 What Should a Manager Know About the Organization?   81
Purpose and Goals   82
Structure, Policy, Procedure   86
Key Personnel   89
Products and Services   89
Ways of Knowing   90
Conclusion   91
Questions   92
Cases and Exercises   92
References   94

7 What Should a Manager Know About People?   96
Needs, Demands, Expectations, and Requests   97
Top Management   99
Immediate Superior   101
Subordinates   103
Peer Managers   105
Ways of Knowing   106
Conclusion   109
Questions   109
Cases and Exercises   109
References   112

8 What Should a Manager Know About the Task to Be Done? 114
Purpose and Goals 115
Technology of the Task 116
Work Methods 118
Ways of Knowing 122
Conclusion 123
Questions 123
Cases and Exercises 124
References 126

Part III DEVELOPING MANAGEMENT SKILLS 129

9 How Should a Manager Set Goals? 131
Determining What Is Important 132
Tying In with Organizational Goals 134
Ways of Setting Goals 136
Conclusion 144
Questions 145
Cases and Exercises 145
References 150

10 How Should a Manager Lead? 151
Leadership Skills 152
Leadership Effectiveness 155
Ways of Leading 160
Conclusion 160
Questions 161
Cases and Exercises 161
References 166

11 How Should a Manager Make Decisions? 167
The Problem-Solving and Decision-Making Process 168
Maintaining Priorities 176
Implementation Issues 177
Ways to Make Decisions 177
Conclusion 179
Questions 180
Cases and Exercises 180
References 183

12 How Should a Manager Communicate? 185
The Communication Process 187
Communication Barriers 188
Ways of Communicating 193

Conclusion	196
Questions	196
Cases and Exercises	197
References	200

13 How Should a Manager Coach and Counsel? — 202

The Coaching and Counseling Process	202
Ways to Counsel	206
Conclusion	210
Questions	210
Cases and Exercises	211
References	214

14 How Should a Manager Manage Change and Conflict? — 216

What Is Change?	217
Ways of Managing Change	220
What Is Conflict?	223
Ways to Manage Conflict	227
Conclusion	229
Questions	229
Cases and Exercises	230
References	232

15 How Should a Manager Practice Political Skills? — 234

The Internal Political Environment	234
Types of Political Skills	236
Ways of Using Political Skills	242
Conclusion	242
Questions	243
Cases and Exercises	244
References	246

16 How Should a Manager Manage Time? — 248

Time as a Resource	249
Prioritizing Goals and Activities	250
Ways of Managing Time	251
Conclusion	258
Questions	259
Cases and Exercises	259
References	264

17 How Should a Manager Provide Incentives and Rewards? — 265

Purpose of Rewards and Incentives	266
Theory of Rewards and Incentives	267
Ways to Reward and Provide Incentives	270
Conclusion	275

Questions	276
Cases and Exercises	276
References	280

Part IV AVOIDING MANAGERIAL PITFALLS 281

18 What Are Some Common Managerial Mistakes? 283

The Activity Trap	284
Performing Nonmanagerial Work	288
Saying "Yes"	291
Ways to Recognize and Avoid Managerial Mistakes	292
Conclusion	292
Questions	293
Cases and Exercises	294
References	297

19 How Should a Manager Avoid the Bureaucratic Mind-Set? 299

Bureaucracy Defined	300
The Bureaucratic Shuffle	302
Humanizing Organizations	305
Ways to Avoid the Bureaucratic Mind-Set	309
Conclusion	311
Questions	312
Cases and Exercises	312
References	317

20 How Should a Manager Avoid Legal and Ethical Pitfalls? 319

Ethics, Morals, and Social Values	320
Legal Issues	322
Personal Responsibility	324
Ways to Avoid Legal and Ethical Dilemmas	328
Conclusion	329
Questions	330
Cases and Exercises	330
References	336

21 How Can a Manager Keep a Proper Career Perspective? 337

Career Planning and Life-Space Goals	338
Career Pathing and Personal Development	344
Balancing Life-Roles	348
Conclusion	349
Questions	349
Cases and Exercises	350
References	354

Index 357

To Roselyn

Part I
Introduction

The first part of this book looks at what effective managers do, know, and the skills they practice. Chapter 1 examines the resources used by managers to achieve organizational objectives efficiently and effectively. The types of decisions made in using these resources are highlighted in particular. The management process is viewed as making decisions about flows of resources through the organization.

Chapter 2 examines the knowledge a manager must have to be effective. What must a manager know about the environment, the organization, the people, and the task to be done? How can knowledge about these areas be obtained? These areas introduced in Chapter 2 are discussed in more depth in Part II of the book.

Chapter 3 examines the skills an effective manager should practice. These skills include goal setting, leadership, communication, problem solving and decision making, coaching and counseling, change and conflict management, political skills, time management, and evaluating and rewarding skills. Each of these skills are briefly introduced and then discussed in greater depth in Part III of the book.

Thus, the first part of this book serves as an introduction for the remainder of the book. Many concepts and ideas are raised briefly only to be addressed in greater depth later. It is important to have a broad overview of management effectiveness before examining each concept of effectiveness in greater depth. This way we will know how the entire puzzle fits together at the beginning before we break it up. By working from this common frame of reference, it will be easier to better understand the components of competent managerial behavior.

1
What Should a Manager Do?

    8:30 A.M. Meet with Jack to discuss production scheduling problem
10:00 A.M. Talk with Mary about absences
11:00 A.M. Review quarterly goals
12:00 noon Lunch with Professor Simmons at State University
  2:00 P.M. Read quarterly control report
  3:30 P.M. Attend staff meeting at Parkouski's
  4:30 P.M. Bring R&D report home to read and revise

Is this list management work? What makes management work unique? What is nonmanagement work? Exactly what should a manager do? In a word, a manager should *manage*—nothing more, nothing less. Managers are energizers, catalysts, organizers. They get things done by working through and with others. They set good goals and they obtain them. They can use resources effectively and efficiently. They know where they, their unit, and their organization are going, and they know how to keep action on track. In short, *managers help set organizational and unit goals and efficiently marshal human, financial, physical, and information resources to effectively achieve them.*

    Management consists of two very basic functions: *decision making* and *influence*. The essence of managerial work is to make decisions and see that they are carried out. If a manager is not involved in the decisional process, managerial work is not being performed. If a manager actually performs the operational work, nonmanagerial work is being carried out. While it is sometimes necessary to perform this work because of emergency conditions, it should be kept to an absolute minimum so that it does not take time away from managerial work.

Jane is a supervisor of eight social workers in a large human services agency of a state government. Because of a heavy case load and inadequate staffing, Jane often spends 50 percent of her time counseling clients. Hence, she tends to "manage by crisis" since she has little time to plan and prevent problems before they become crisis situations. Jane wonders what she can do to meet the case load demand and still perform managerial work.

All managers, regardless of level from supervisor to chief executive officer, should perform managerial work. If the manager doesn't manage, it will not get performed. This single fact has been the downfall of many managers and leads to much managerial ineffectiveness. It can occur at all levels, not just supervisory as we saw in Jane's case. For example, Ron was division vice president for a large utility. Between him and first-line supervision there were five levels of management. Believing he was solely responsible for the operation of the division, Ron frequently called supervisors to "check on things" and issue orders. With 122 supervisors to keep tabs on, he had no time to perform the managerial work a manager in his position should have been performing. In addition, he alienated his subordinate managers since he continually bypassed them in the chain of command.

Ron thought he was doing a good job. He prided himself on his sixty-hour work week. It made him feel important. In truth, while Ron was working hard, he wasn't working smart. He was afraid to delegate. After two years of the lowest profit margin of any of the firm's division, Ron was replaced by a more effective manager.

So we see that an effective manager must delegate authority and tasks to others. An effective manager doesn't necessarily work hard, but always works smart.

THE MANAGEMENT PROCESS

A manager makes decisions about resource use to achieve organizational objectives. All managers from top to bottom in any type of organization perform this function. Figure 1.1 shows how this process works using input-output analysis. Managers have four basic resources to use in managing: human, physical, financial, and informational. Decisions on how to best use resources include planning, organizing, staffing, directing, and controlling decisions. The whole point of this effort is to reach organizational objectives. These objectives include profitability (for a business enterprise), satisfied customers/clients and employees, a desired product/service mix, and efficiency. These outputs are used by people in the environment. Customers buy the product or service, employees spend their wages, government receives tax payments, and owners (in the case of business) receive dividends.

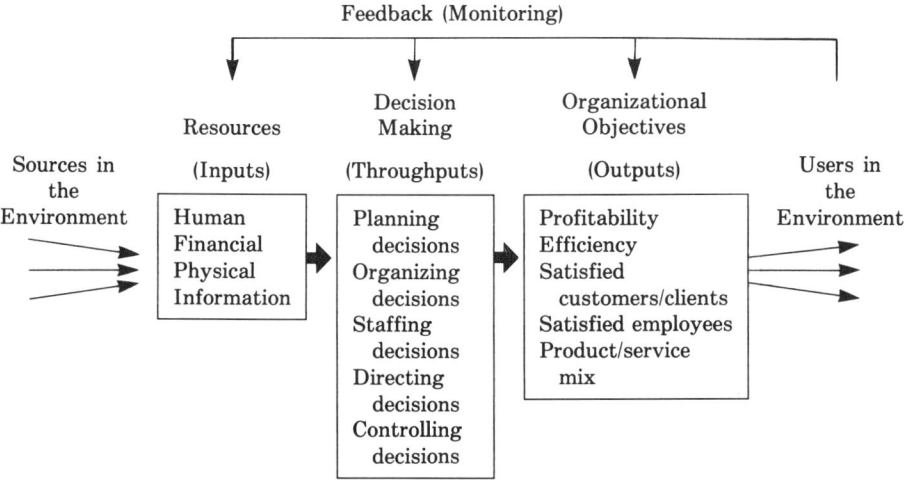

Figure 1.1 The management process

Effectiveness and efficiency

In using these resources to achieve organizational goals, managers attempt to achieve both efficiency and effectiveness. *Efficiency* is the achievement of some output with minimum resource use. *Effectiveness* is simply the achievement of a goal, which is appropriate, regardless of resource use. Efficiency is an input-output ratio, while effectiveness is a determination of whether the goal was achieved and whether the goal was appropriate. The final determination of the appropriateness of the goal rests with the customers/clients being served. Customers/clients, not the managers, determine whether the goal indeed helped satisfy their needs. Let's look at an example.

Suppose you are a planner working for a state department of transportation. You and your staff determine that a four-lane expressway is needed through the northern portion of your town in order to reduce traffic congestion in this section. Plans are drawn, approval is received from both the federal government and the state government, contracts are drawn, and construction is completed. The road is built on time, all budgets are met, there is little scrap or rework, and all safety and other specifications are met. (This is a rare case indeed!) We can conclude that you have been *efficient*. You achieved the desired output with minimum resource use.

Suppose, however, that during the construction of the highway, citizens chain themselves to large trees that have to be cut, lay in front of the bulldozers, write protest letters to state legislators and federal officials, and otherwise object to the building of the highway. They complain the highway is ruining the environment and destroying fine residential neighborhoods.

Furthermore, they insist that congestion with associated urban sprawl will result. Their protests indicate that the citizens of the community would much rather have had mass transit instead of another "large concrete parking lot."

In this case, we can conclude that while you and your staff have been *efficient,* you have *not been effective.* The goal was not appropriate as determined by the people being served. Because this situation is becoming all too frequent in highway construction, citizen panels are being incorporated into the planning process to ensure that citizen input is received and considered prior to building highways.

The efficiency-effectiveness issue is shown in Figure 1.2.

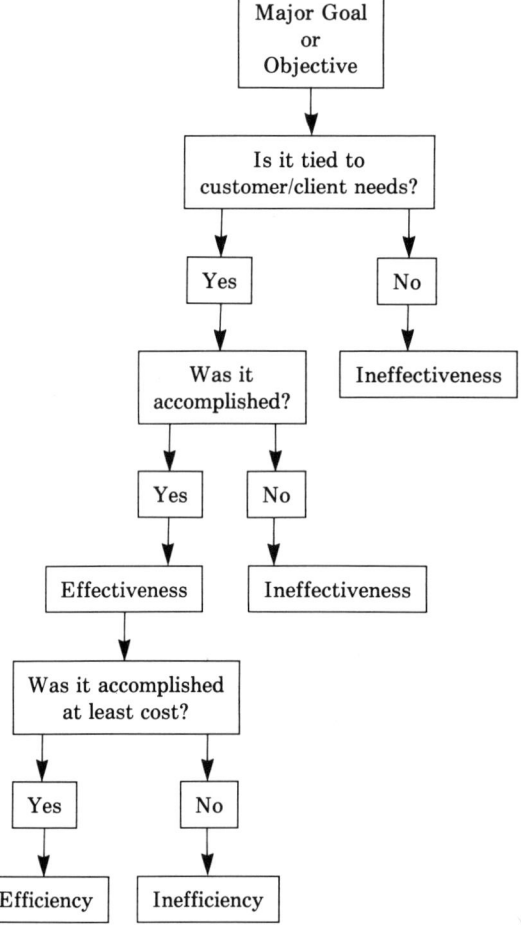

Figure 1.2 A definition of efficiency and effectiveness

Resources

Let's now turn our attention to the resources a manager has to use. The essential resources for management can be summarized in four major categories as seen in Figure 1.3. Note that under each major category there are specific resources. For example, people bring with them a set of skills and abilities, ideas, interests, aspiration levels, and certain physical characteristics such as strength.

Human resources. A manager must use human resources in the best interest of the organization, without creating dissatisfied employees. In fact, managers, have a dual goal with human resource management: (1) productive, efficient employees, and (2) satisfied employees. The achievement of this dual goal is difficult to obtain. One part of the goal does not always lead to the other. Satisfied employees are not always productive and productive employees are not always satisfied. It is possible to obtain short-run compliance and high productivity at the expense of long-term employee commitment. However, in the long term, most managers desire both high productivity and satisfied employees, believing that this satisfaction will lead to long-term commitment and productivity.

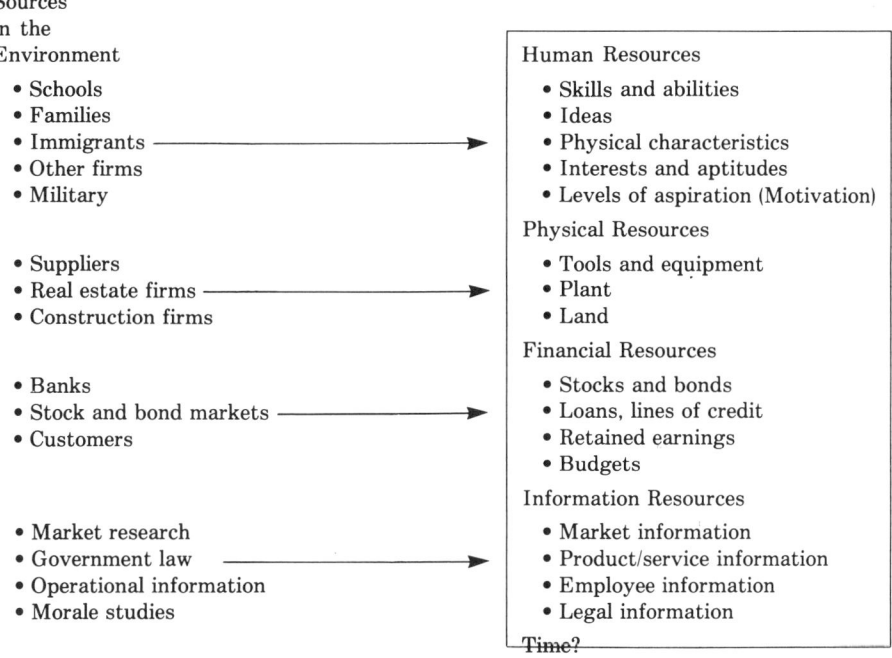

Figure 1.3 Essential resources for managing

Managers recruit employees from a variety of sources. Effective managers know the labor market for their employees, from floor sweeper to engineer, to sales person, to department head. They know how to obtain people who have the skills, abilities, and aspiration levels that match the available jobs. They can also influence the redesign of jobs so that people who are available, but who do not have all the necessary skills, can be employed.

Physical resources. A manager cannot operate effectively or efficiently without proper tools and equipment. Determining the configuration of equipment, plant layout, proper tools, and operations methods is an essential task of any manager. This does not apply to only production managers. Office managers, sales managers, and others must also be concerned with proper utilization of the physical resources necessary for effective job performance. Once again, just as a manager knows the labor market for human resources, so should an effective manager know the market and availability of physical resources.

Financial resources. All managers need a budget of some sort in order to manage effectively. Of course managers vary greatly in their extent of control and participation in the budget process. Some managers, even those at first-line supervisory levels, have considerable input in formulating budgets and in administrating them. Others have little to say in budget formulation and use. Yet, regardless of the level of this involvement or size of the budget, all managers must manage the budget entrusted to them effectively, meager as it may be.

Acquisition of funds in the money markets generally rests with the highest management levels in the organization. Most organizations attempt to diversify their funding sources so that they are not dependent on one or a few sources. This is even true of city and state agencies, for example. Many of these governmental organizations not only receive allocations from the respective legislative body, but also from federal sources and from investments of tax receipts.

Information resources. Managers need information to manage effectively. They need to know their markets, environment, product/service produced, operations, employees, and so on. They need to be able to gather, analyze, synthesize, and accurately interpret data. While they don't need to be computer whiz kids, they do need to know what a computer is and how it can be used. Information resources are so important that the entire next chapter is devoted to an examination of these resources.

Time. Is time a resource? Some managers view it as a resource and some view it simply as a constraint. All agree it should be used wisely. However, since there is a finite time available in one day, it cannot be expanded as can other resources. Consequently, time is placed half in and half out of the resource box. Chapter 16 examines the issue of time in greater detail.

Decision making

Five major types of decisions made by managers are shown in Figure 1.4. Once again, managers vary as to the authority they have regarding each decision. First-line supervisors tend to emphasize controlling types of decisions compared to higher level managers, but higher level managers tend to emphasize planning and organizing types of decisions. Directive and staffing decisions tend to be made at all levels. Let's look at each of these types of decisions.

Decision Making

Planning
- Setting goals
- Determining paths
- Scheduling

Organizing
- Determining structure
- Allocating resources

Staffing
- Recruiting
- Selecting
- Hiring
- Placing
- Equal employment opportunity
- Manpower planning
- Training and development
- Wage and salary
- Health and benefits
- Employee relations
  (or Collective bargaining)

Directing
- Leadership styles
- Task determination and assignment
- Communication
- Motivation and incentives
- Coaching and counseling

Controlling
- Monitoring and feedback
- Evaluation and adjustment
- Corrective discipline
- Performance appraisal

Figure 1.4 Types of management decisions

Planning. Planning is determining where you want to go and how and when you're going to get there. It involves specifying a target (goal or objective), a path or route to be followed, and a time schedule for achieving that target. Effective managers set clear-cut plans, realistic time schedules, and allow for contingencies. *Contingency planning* is "what if" planning. It is the alternative courses of action to be followed if things change or go wrong. It sets out a Plan A, Plan B, Plan C, etc.

Planning includes setting goals that are neither too hard nor too easy to achieve. Goals should be specific, measurable, and verifiable, not pie-in-the-sky generalities. The steps en route to achieving goals are assigned to people on a time frame. Thus, plans ought to be a way to achieve accountability for performance.

Organizing. Organizing decisions involve two types: (1) decisions made to set up the *structure* and *design* of the organization, and (2) decisions made to assign *resources* to the places where they are needed. Organizing decisions that affect the structure of the organization deal with such issues as determining the number and types of departments, the number and types of management levels, and the scope of managerial authority. They also address issues of accountability and reporting relationships. These types of decisions result in a *formal organization chart,* which is the officially sanctioned organization structure. These types of decisions tend to be made at the highest management levels in the organization.

Of course we know that a formal organizational chart does not tell everything about authority and accountability in the organization. Overlaid on the formal chart is the *informal organization structure.* These are the unofficial, nonsanctioned patterns of interaction among people in the organization. Sometimes these informal social relationships are more accurate and carry more weight in describing the organization than the formal ones depicted on the chart.

Managers usually do not make conscious decisions to design the informal organization. These decisions evolve from the people in the organization. Yet, effective managers know the informal organization at work in their unit and they understand how to use it for the good of the organization and its goals.

The second type of organizing decision involves assigning the proper amount of resources to people and places in the organization at the time they are needed. This means that the *work effort* is organized. Tools, equipment, space, and people are assigned to tasks. Usually these types of decisions involve the design of jobs and resource allocation decisions. Job design decisions result in job descriptions, which spell out the duties of people for various jobs. Budgets, in terms of money, people, space, facilities, etc., are also the result of organizing decisions, since allocations are made to organizational units in order that tasks may be carried out.

Staffing decisions. Staffing decisions involve personnel issues. They include making decisions on recruiting, selecting, hiring and placing employees, as well as decisions on manpower planning, training and development, wage and salary administration, employee health and benefits, employee relations, and equal employment opportunity. If a union is present, collective bargaining decisions are also made.

Personnel departments in organizations usually assist managers with their decisions. However, just because a personnel department exists does not mean managers can abrogate their responsibilities to make personnel decisions. They still must be concerned with staffing decisions and must view the personnel department as staff support which aids them in making these decisions.

Directing decisions. *Directing* is the leadership function. Decisions are made on leadership styles, task determination and assignment, communication, motivation and incentives, coaching and counseling, and other "people moving" issues. While management is more than leadership, good managers are also good leaders. Good leadership is often intangible and hard to describe. The many theories of leadership are explored in more depth in Chapter 10. These theories involve traits of effective leaders, appropriate leader styles, and the contingency theory of leadership. Fortunately, over the last twenty years there has probably been more research done on the leadership issue in organizations than on any other single people-oriented issue. Thus, while there are still many uncertainties, we know far more today than we did two decades ago.

Controlling decisions. *Controlling* means making sure what you want to have happen does indeed happen. It involves such concepts as monitoring and feedback, evaluation and adjustment, corrective discipline, and performance appraisal of employees. Effective managers control without being oppressive. They instill a spirit of self-control in subordinates so that the burden of preying managerial eyes doesn't rest heavily on the shoulders of subordinates. Obtaining the proper amount of control is a difficult managerial decision. Managers must frequently walk a tightrope between control that is so oppressive that subordinate creativity and problem solving is muted, and control that is so loose that subordinates are free to do their own thing without any guidance.

The quality of controlling decisions depends a great deal on the quality of previously made planning, organizing, staffing, and directing decisions. Control becomes much easier when clear-cut plans have been developed and when people have been assigned duties to carry out the plans. Effective organizing decisions help the control process in that appropriate structure has been established and appropriate levels of resources have been allocated to people when and where they are needed. Control becomes more difficult if

12 WHAT SHOULD A MANAGER DO?

the proper people with the proper skills, knowledge, and aspiration levels have not been hired. Thus, good staffing decisions help to insure good control decisions.

Effective leadership helps reduce the actual number of control decisions. Often, a manager who is not a good leader ends up being a full-time controller. A poor leader who cannot inspire performance in subordinates tries instead to mandate it.

Thus, we see that the better are planning, organizing, staffing, and directing, the better will be controlling. Effective managers spend time on the first four types of decisions and less time on the fifth. Ineffective managers obtain short-term compliance through control at the expense of long-term commitment, which can only be obtained by planning, organizing, staffing, and directing.

Organizational objectives

Managers make decisions on the use of resources in order to achieve organizational objectives. Accomplishment of appropriate objectives is the major hallmark of an effective manager. Figure 1.5 shows the categories of objectives that managers encounter. There are basically four ways to view objec-

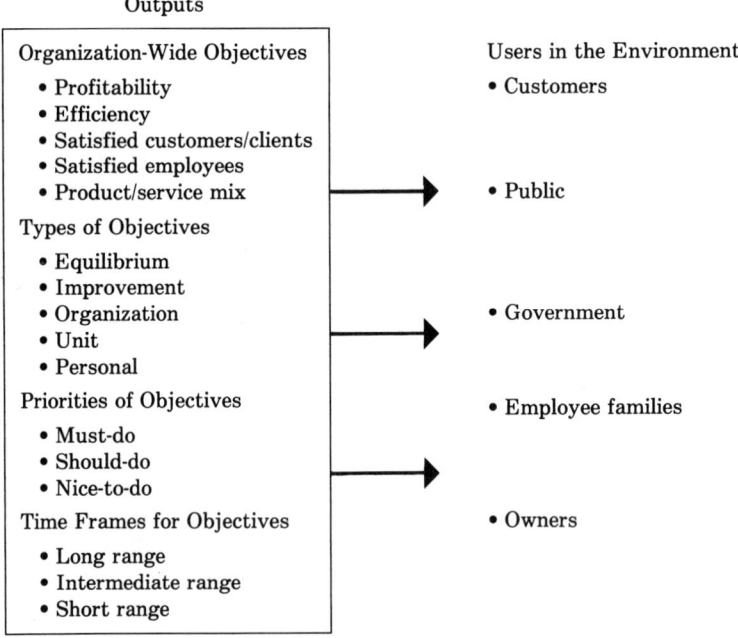

Figure 1.5 Categories of objectives for management action

tives. First, managers must be knowledgeable about the organization-wide objectives. Second, they must know various types of objectives, including their own and their unit's. Third, effective managers keep objectives in a proper priority perspective. And finally, time frames for various objective accomplishment are clearly specified.

These objectives are reached in order that users receive utility from the organization. The *ultimate* rationale for the existence of any organization is that it fulfills a need in society. Businesses provide a product or service for customers. Government satisfies (or should) needs of various citizens. Other users benefit. Employee families receive income. Even noncustomers of a firm can use the firm's output. For example, you may ride to work with your neighbor in his Chevrolet. Even though you don't own a car, you are a user of a GM product. Effective managers understand the receivers of their organization's output. They know how the accomplishment of objectives results in utility for the users of the organization's output.

Let's now briefly look at each category of objectives described in Figure 1.5.

Organization-wide objectives. Organizations need a sense of direction and unity. These are provided by organization-wide objectives which tie together the diverse efforts of various units within the organization. For these objectives to serve such a purpose, they obviously must be communicated to all members of the organization. They serve little purpose if they are known only by those at the highest level of the organization or if they are written up only to be filed away and seldom consulted. Furthermore, managers, even those low in the organization, should be given some opportunity to influence the setting of these objectives. This influence will likely be only minimal for those far down in a large organization, yet such input by all managerial levels should heighten managerial identification with the organization-wide objectives.

Organization-wide objectives should be concerned with profitability (rate of return on investment), efficiency (output relative to input), satisfying customers or clients, satisfying employees, and providing the proper product/service mix desired by customers. Even in a government organization, all but profitability ought to be achieved in organization-wide objectives. For government organizations, profitability is not an objective but avoiding or minimizing a budget deficit is.

Types of objectives. Not all objectives need be improvement oriented. Equilibrium objectives are objectives that attempt to insure that the organization continues something in the future that it is now doing. For example, "maintaining market share at 15 percent" is an example of an equilibrium objective. This may be entirely appropriate if 15 percent is deemed an effective level. However, most organizations are concerned with improving performance. They believe that you never stand still; you either get better or you get worse. Therefore, if no improvement is desired, the organization will be worse off relative to competitors who, it is assumed, will be trying to improve.

Managers must also have a clear idea as to their unit's objectives as they relate to organization-wide objectives. They need to insure that unit objectives are consistent with and help achieve organization-wide objectives. Furthermore, they must insure that their subordinates know how unit objectives meet with organization-wide objectives. This further helps to achieve the unity of purpose that organizations so desperately need.

Finally, managers should have personal objectives. Most of these should be improvement-oriented; that is, they should deal with career development. Often, they deal with increasing one's knowledge in one area. For example, "to become thoroughly familiar with current affirmative action law and policy" would be a good personal objective for a personnel manager in a firm doing business with the federal government. Effective managers do not lose sight of the fact that they need to grow and develop on the job, and they explicitly set out goals to help them do this.

Priorities of objectives. It is difficult to prioritize any list of objectives. Many managers find it easier to place objectives into one of three categories without worrying about their rank in each category. *"Must-do"* objectives are absolutely critical to the success of the organization and its units. They cannot be postponed. Their failure will likely result in the failure of the organization or a unit in the organization. For example, a plant experiencing high levels of customer returns of defective products might consider "to increase final inspection of products to be shipped to 75 percent of total shippage" as a must-do objective.

"Should-do" objectives are important, but they can be temporarily postponed for a short period of time. The failure to achieve these objectives will not seriously hurt the functioning of the organization, but may make it difficult to improve organization operations. For example "to institute a human resource information system of employee abilities and interests" could be considered a should-do objective. It is deemed to help organization operations, but it is not critical for ensuring the success of the organization and its units.

"Nice-to-do" objectives are also important, but they can be postponed for even a longer period of time than a should-do. It is not critical to the success of the organization or a unit, but its accomplishment will ultimately lead to more effective performance. For example, "to implement a market research department within the firm" might be viewed as a nice-to-do objective. The firm may now be contracting with consulting organizations to do market research. However, the volume of work is projected to grow and it is deemed desirable to begin in-house capability to perform this research. At

some point, however, this objective may become a should-do or a must-do, depending on the volume and costs of this research in the future.

Time frame for objectives. Effective managers don't lose sight of long-term objectives, nor do they maximize short-term goals at the expense of long-term ones. Long-term objectives specify targets to be accomplished five to twenty-five years from now. Some firms try to forecast for even a longer time period. Herman Kahn's group at the Hudson Institute is an example of a private think-tank specializing in helping organizations with studies of "futurism." Because of the rapid changes in today's society and markets, prudent managers try to forecast these trends so that their firm will be able to capitalize on them.

Intermediate term objectives specify targets generally for a two- to five-year period. They should dovetail with long-term objectives and tend to be more specific than long-term objectives. Short-run objectives are even more specific and usually deal with less than a two-year time frame. Of course, they too should dovetail with long and intermediate range objectives. As time passes, intermediate and long-term objectives should become short-term ones.

CONCLUSION

Effective managers can efficiently make decisions about resource use in order to achieve objectives. They are experts at decision making and influence. They expertly plan, organize, staff, direct, and control human, financial, physical, and informational resources. They focus on organizational, unit, and personal objectives in the appropriate priority and keep a proper focus on long-term, intermediate, and short-term objectives.

But what managers do is obviously only part of the story. We must also be concerned with what effective managers should know and also with the skills managers must practice. The next chapter examines the knowledge base that a manager needs for effective performance.

QUESTIONS

1. What is management?
2. What resources does a manager have to use?
3. What kinds of decisions does a manager make?
4. What kinds of objectives do managers try to accomplish?
5. What is the difference between managerial effectiveness and managerial efficiency?

6. In your opinion, which type of management resource is the most important? Why?

7. In your opinion, which type of objective is the most important? Why?

CASES AND EXERCISES

CASE 1: WHAT AM I DOING HERE?

Cliff Eubanks is a department head with Megatronics Corporation, a producer of computer peripheral equipment. Cliff has been a manager for twelve years and has been with Megatronics for three years. He currently manages twelve highly skilled subordinates who each supervise a group of first-line supervisors.

Jane Kuhling, one of Cliff's subordinates, was recently hired to fill a position that had been vacant for two months. Jane is a young, recent MBA graduate from a midwestern university. While going to school, she worked part-time in computer sales with a large manufacturer of peripheral computer equipment. The firm is a direct competitor of Megatronics. She was unsatisfied with her part-time job and vowed to go with another firm upon graduation.

Jane has been on the job for two weeks. She believed she was aware of the responsibilities of her job prior to taking it, based upon her previous work experience in the industry. Now she wasn't so sure. She felt that Cliff hadn't given her adequate guidance. For example, she had yet to have a conversation with Cliff which reviewed her job duties, responsibilities, and expectations. A week ago she asked Cliff about this and his reply was, "Not now, wait until you get your feet on the ground and then we'll talk."

Since another week had passed, she thought it was time to discuss her job responsibilities with Cliff. She cornered him in the hall after lunch one day and asked if they couldn't sit down and discuss her job duties. Cliff replied, "Look, the first thing you need to do is to find out what you should be doing. What are the other supervisors doing? What do you think your job demands? You've got a good group of capable employees, find out what they are doing and then you can help them. Don't come to me for answers. If I knew what you should be doing, I would do it myself. That's why I hired you."

Questions

1. Evaluate Cliff's style of management.
2. How would you react if you were Jane? Why?
3. Would you ever use the approach Cliff took? Why or why not?

CASE 2: WAIST DEEP

I always seem to be working on a problem. I know it's good to plan but who has time? I end up spending all of my time solving problems. This is really controlling, I guess. I know I should be planning to prevent these problems but who can remember to drain the swamp when you're waist-deep in alligators?

That's the whole problem with this management stuff anyway. It sounds good on paper, but it really doesn't work. Sometimes I think that professors and others who write books just do it to make money. No one has the answers to effective management. Either you're born a good manager or you're not. Most of management is common sense anyway. We can talk all we want about how good it is to plan, but the essence of management is solving problems. I really do wish it weren't so, but the mark of a good manager is one who can handle crises.

Questions

1. Do you agree with this individual's comments? Which ones do you agree with and which ones do you object to?
2. Do you find your job to be one of continually solving problems and handling crises? Can you do much to change this? If so, what?

EXERCISE: HOW DO YOU MANAGE?

During the next three days at work, keep track of the activities you perform. Try to put them into one of the five categories of decision making: planning, organizing, staffing, directing, and controlling. Monitor these activities in half-hour blocks. Try to identify the specific objectives each activity is directed toward, then try to identify the specific resources you need to carry out the decisions to meet specific objectives.

Be concerned with evaluating the results of your activity. Are you spending more time in controlling than you should? What kind of objectives are you working toward? Are you focusing on priority objectives? Are you getting the types and amount of resources you need?

You may want to use the chart in Figure 1.6 to help you analyze what you do. First, log your activities in half-hour blocks of time for three days. Then transfer these activities by total hours to the second column on the chart. Next, identify the major resources used for each function/activity and place these in column 3a. Then determine resources you still need to further carry out the task and list these in column 3b. In column 4, list those objectives that you tried to accomplish by carrying out each function or activity. Finally, in column 5, evaluate the appropriateness of the amount of time

(1) Function/Activity	(2) Total Hours Spent	(3) Major Resources		(4) Objective(s) To Be Reached	(5) Appropriateness of Activity
		(a) Used	(b) Needed		
Planning					
Organizing					
Staffing					
Directing					
Controlling					
Other (Nonmanagerial)					

Figure 1.6 Management function/activity analysis

spent in each function/activity relative to the resources you need in order to accomplish the desired objectives.

You may not be satisfied with your first effort in attempting to complete this chart, but don't be discouraged. Wait for a short period and then pick another three-day period to try it again. You'll soon see that it will help you to better understand and evaluate what you do as a manager.

REFERENCES

Drucker, Peter F. *Management: Tasks, Responsibilities, and Practices.* New York: Harper & Row, Publishing, 1974.
    A very comprehensive view of management from the professional practitioner's view. A shortened version published in 1977 by Harper and Row is titled *An Introductory View of Management.*

Glueck, William F. *Management.* Hendsdale, Ill.: Dryden Press, 1977.
    A comprehensive book that examines the management task, people at work, interpersonal skills, and the organization's resources.

Koontz, Harold, and O'Donnell Cyril. *Principles of Management: An Analysis of Managerial Functions.* 6th ed. New York: McGraw-Hill Book Co., 1976.
    This classic work describes in great depth the essential functions of a manager.

Mintzberg, Henry. "Managerial Work: Analysis from Observation." *Management Science* 18 (October 1971): B97–B110.
    An excellent discussion of characteristics of managerial work. The article is based on a good deal of research as to what managers actually do.

Richards, Max O. *Readings In Management.* Englewood Cliffs, N.J.: Prentice-Hall, 1978.
    An excellent current text that examines planning and decision making, organizing, leading, and controlling.

Weber, Ross A. *Management: Basic Elements of Managing Organizations.* Homewood, Ill.: Richard D. Irwin, 1975.
    A virtual encyclopedia of management knowledge. One of the most comprehensive texts ever written about the people aspects of management. Contains 773 pages.

2
What Must a Manager Know?

"RECENT QUOTA RESTRICTIONS CAUSE DECLINE IN OPEC OIL OUTPUT"

"INFLATION CONTINUES AT HIGH RATE"

"FCC RULES THAT AD CLAIMS MUST BE SUBSTANTIATED"

"MICRO CHIP REVOLUTIONIZES INFORMATION PROCESSING"

"CHINA OPENS TRADE DOORS WITH U.S."

"CONSUMER CLASS ACTION SUITS HIT NEW RECORD"

Are these headlines important? Would such headlines affect your organization's performance? Would they have any impact on the way you manage? Would such headlines ultimately have any bearing on your performance and success as a manager?

In this chapter, we are concerned with examining the basic information a manager must know to be competent. The chapter provides a broad review of these knowledge areas. Each area is addressed in more depth in Part II of the book. This review is important at this point, however, because a big ingredient for management competence is knowledge of very important areas that impact almost daily on management action.

We divide the knowledge a manager must have into four key areas, as shown in Figure 2.1. These major areas include: (1) the outside environment of the organization and the market for its products and services; (2) the in-

- Organization's outside environment and market
- Organization's internal workings
- People
- Task to be done

Figure 2.1 Key areas of managerial knowledge

ternal workings of the organization; (3) knowledge of people, including how and why they behave as they do; and (4) the task or job to be done.

ENVIRONMENT AND MARKET

Should a manager be concerned about actions of the OPEC nations? Is the rate of inflation important? What effect does a significant technological breakthrough have on a manager's performance? Of course, not all areas of the environment affect all managers. Sometimes, however, areas that are initially believed to be unimportant are later found out to be very important. This was the case with the OPEC oil embargo of 1973. Many managers not in the oil industry were unaware that the embargo and resulting price rise would so permeate an entire economic system that seemingly completely unrelated areas would be affected. Many products such as food, clothing, plastic pens, and so on, are so dependent on petroleum products and their derivatives that even a minor price rise in oil has a significant impact on the price of the product.

Yet, managers cannot know all there is to know about their organization's outside environment. There is simply too much to know. Nor do individual managers *need* to know all there is to know about the environment. What is critical is that managers know about parts of the environment that are important to the organization, as well as their individual role in the organization.

In this chapter, we will briefly outline the components of an organization's environment. In Chapter 4, we explore ways that managers can separate the important from the unimportant in the environment and how managers can learn the important.

Components of the outside environment

Every organization faces a different specific outside environment, but there is a common thread that runs through the entire outside environment for all organizations. These components that make up the common thread are depicted in Figure 2.2 and are discussed below.

22 WHAT MUST A MANAGER KNOW?

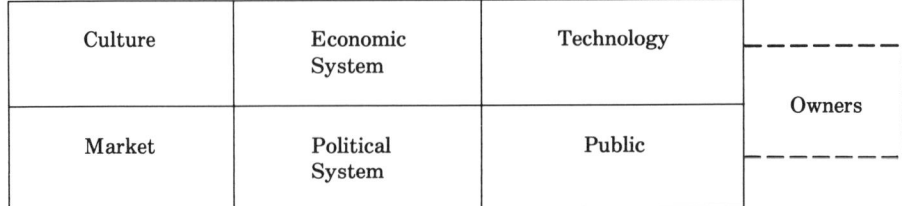

Figure 2.2 Components of an organization's outside environment

Culture. Culture consists of the social values, norms, mores, and institutions of a society. It is the fabric of society. Social values, the basic beliefs that hold a society together, serve as the basis for much of what goes on in the society. They tend to be abstract and vague, yet, because of their vagueness, social values provide a common rallying point that the vast majority of people can identify with. For example, in the United States, concepts such as freedom, brotherhood, peace, equal opportunity, and democracy come to mind as common cultural values.

Norms and mores are standards of behavior expected of those in society. They are based on cultural values. They specify what kinds of behavior are acceptable and unacceptable in a society. For example, the norm associated with the value of democracy is that everyone should register and vote on election day. The norm associated with brotherhood is that each of us should help our neighbor when in need.

Cultural institutions exist to interpret, redefine, and perpetuate our cultural values, norms, and mores. Common cultural institutions in the United States include the family, church, educational organizations, business organizations, unions, and civic associations. Each institution is usually concerned with interpreting and perpetuating a number of norms and values. The relationship between example cultural values, norms (mores), and cultural institutions in the United States is shown in Figure 2.3.

Example Value	Example Norm (Moré)	Example Institution
Peace	Don't fight	Church
Democracy	Vote on Election Day	School
Equal opportunity	Don't discriminate on basis of race or sex	Government
Hard work	Work for a living	Family

Figure 2.3 Example cultural values, norms (mores), and associated institutions for the United States

Economic system. The economic system consists of the way in which a society allocates resources, products, and services to buyers. For example, in the United States we use the mechanism of price operating within a market system known as "mixed free enterprise." Since the bulk of the factors of production are owned by private individuals, we have a capitalistic system, even though some factors of production are owned or very heavily regulated by government. (This case, however, usually exists only with monopolies such as utilities.)

In some countries, such as the Soviet Union, we find state ownership of the factors of production and the absence of a price mechanism operating in a market based on supply and demand. Rather, a central planning board is used to perform the functions of a free market.

Technology. The state of the art and science of the production and distribution of goods and services in a society is known as the technological level of that society. In the United States we have very sophisticated means of producing and distributing goods and services, which relies quite heavily on sophisticated machinery and a very complex network of transportation. In third world countries, the state of production and distribution is much more primitive.

Market. The market for an organization consists of the present and potential suppliers to and buyers of the organization. The market for an organization has a supply and a buyer side. The supply side consists of people and other organizations that supply raw materials, energy, labor, and other resources needed by the organization. The buyer side consists of customers (buyers) and consumers (users) of an organization's output of goods and services. Notice that a customer, the one who actually makes the purchase, may not be the same person who consumes the good or service. For example, mothers buy clothing for their small children but certainly do not wear it themselves. Knowledge of the market is so important for managers that we devote an entire chapter, Chapter 6, to examining it.

Political system. The political system consists of the laws of society and how they are developed and administered. In the United States, for example, we have a representative republican form of democracy which elects legislative bodies at the local, state, and federal level who, in turn, pass legislation. We use essentially a two-party system to nominate people for *both* executive and legislative offices. The executive branch administers laws passed by the legislative. Our court system interprets the laws and protects individual rights under the law. Police systems enforce the law and arrest violators.

We believe in a balance of power and a system of checks and balances among the legislative, judicial, and executive branches of government, and we also believe that the local, state, and federal levels of government should serve as a semi-check on each other.

The process of lobbying and private political action is an essential feature of our political system. Competing interest groups, as well as individuals, are expected to make their wishes known to legislative bodies. The rights of free speech, freedom of the press, and freedom of assembly are so essential to this process that they are guaranteed by our most basic document, the United States Constitution.

Public. The public consists of all those in the environment whom the organization affects but who are not suppliers, customers, clients, or consumers of the organization. These people are often affected by the organization, but usually the effect is indirect. For example, I may not own a motorcycle but I may be awakened by one every night when my neighbor comes "tooling" home on his big "hog."

Usually, the organization views the public as potential customers or consumers. If the organization is a publically-held corporation, it also may view the public as potential owners. In any event, most organizations wish to maintain a good image with the public, at least so that the public does not wish to have laws passed unfavorable to the organization or demonstrate in a picket line in front of the corporate office. To do this, most organizations are very media conscious, and often stage public relations episodes to garner favorable media attention.

Owners. Owners are sometimes considered part of the organization's outside environment even though, technically, they are members of the organization. If the organization is a large, widely-held public corporation, owners, especially those who own very small percentages of outstanding stock, have little if any impact on how the organization is run since they often give up their voting rights through proxy. They are, for all practical purposes, really members of the public.

However, in smaller organizations where ownership is not widely held this is not the case. Here owners are part of the organization and not part of the outside environment. The dashed line around the owner box in Figure 2.2 depicts this ambiguous relationship.

Multinational relations. One final note on the organization's outside environment must be made. Many organizations today deal in a multinational environment. Sources of supply, such as energy, may come from a foreign country. Buyers of products or services may reside in other countries. Manufacturing or sales facilities may be located in other countries. For these organizations the outside environment takes on an added dimension.

Each aspect of the environment may be completely different from country to country where the organization operates or sells. Laws, economic conditions, and technology common to one country could be completely foreign to another. Moreover, and perhaps more important, culture, which is so hard to measure and pinpoint, can be so different that proper ways of managing in the host foreign country might be entirely different from appropriate managerial techniques in the home base country. For example, American supervisors in offshoot plants in Central American countries often find that a participative management style is viewed as a sign of weakness on management's part. Apparently, a participative style violates a role expectation held by some employees which states that competent managers act autocratically.

Thus, it is important for managers to realize that the specific components that make up the outside environment for an organization in its overseas operations might be entirely different from the environment found in its home country.

ORGANIZATION

The second major knowledge area for managers is an understanding of the organization's internal operations. Managers must understand what makes organizations tick, particularly his or her organization. We briefly examine four key areas of knowledge here, as shown in Figure 2.4, and expand on them later in Chapter 6.

- Purpose and goals
- Products and services
- Structure, policy, procedure
- Key personnel

Figure 2.4 Key areas of organizational knowledge

Purpose and goals

All organizations have a purpose. It might not be written down, it might be vague, it might not be known by all, but it is there. Often, the collective personal purpose of a very small, powerful ruling management clique becomes the purpose of the organization. Other times, the purpose is clearly stated, communicated to all concerned, and continues into the future regardless of the ruling clique at any one time.

The purpose of the organization serves as its guiding light, its reason for being, its ultimate rational. It's the bottom line that answers the ultimate question "Why"? For a corporation such a purpose might exist in its corporate charter. For a government agency, it will appear in the law that established the agency. The purpose should be short, clear, and to the point. It should serve as a rallying point for organizational effort. For a business, it should be something more than to "make a profit." The purpose for all organizations should specify the following:

1. Customers/clients served
2. Product/service mix provided
3. Geographic region of operations
4. Commitment to productivity and economic efficiency

We look at some sample purpose statements in Chapter 6.

Organizational goals or objectives are specific targets of organizational action. They are the end-states, or results to be achieved in a given time frame. They flow from the purpose statement and their accomplishment helps fulfill the organization's purpose.

Prudent managers know the organization's purpose and its specific goals and objectives, and can relate these to the goals and objectives of their position. Sometimes this purpose and these goals and objectives are hard to discern but they must be determined. After all, "if you don't know where you're going, any road will take you there." More details will be covered in Chapter 6.

Products and services

Competent managers thoroughly know the products and services provided by their organization. Furthermore, effective managers can clearly specify the competitive advantage of these products and services in the marketplace. Most managers can easily see that the sales force needs this complete knowledge, but some have trouble understanding why production, financial, personnel, or other managers would need this knowledge. It is necessary for *all* managers to have this knowledge. We saw earlier that a key element of the purpose of the organization is to provide a product/service mix. It is very difficult to understand the purpose and have it serve as a guiding light unless all managers are thoroughly familiar with the product/service offering.

Of course, an understanding of the organization's product/service mix is essential to understanding the organization's market. The two are very clearly linked. The satisfaction of needs in the market occurs through the product/service mix. Managers who do not understand this mix will never know the market.

Structure, policy, procedure

All organizations have structure, policy, and procedures. Sometimes they are vague; in other organizations they are very detailed and highly codified. Competent managers thoroughly know these factors even if it requires a lot of digging.

Structure is the authority hierarchy in the organization. Structure shows reporting, accountability, and responsibility relationships. Its two elements include: (1) *formal structure,* which is officially developed and sanctioned by the organization and is usually shown in an organization chart, and (2) *informal structure,* which evolves from the people in the organization and is not officially developed or sanctioned by the organization. Both types of structure are important. Indeed, in some organizations the power, communication, and informal group relationships that evolve through informal structure are more important than the authority and accountability shown in formal structure. Effective managers use the informal structure to complement the formal structure in order to achieve purpose and goals.

Policies are guidelines to action. They specify the parameters within which managers can act in the organization. Once again, organizations have formal and informal policies. Effective managers know both and use them to advantage.

Procedures are methods. They specify how to carry out specific acts, usually involving a series of steps. Effective managers know the important procedures, be they formal or informal, but delegate the details of lesser procedures to trusted subordinates. Competent managers do not get bogged down in administrative trivia. There are more important things to do. Chapter 19 is devoted to this issue of bureaucracy.

Key personnel

Who makes the organization go? Where are the real power positions in the organization? How does one move into the power positions? What skills does the organization seem to truly value? Competent managers can readily answer these questions with regard to their organization. In every organization there are key individuals who have unique skills, high visibility, important information, and/or raw power. These individuals may or may not be people in high positions of formal authority. For example, a highly skilled, effective computer programmer may have power far beyond the formal authority of the position because of the expertise the programmer has.

Effective managers not only know who these key people are, but they also can work with them easily. They can cultivate the relationships needed with these individuals without compromising personal principles or turning into spineless "yes-people." Furthermore, effective managers are soon recognized for their competency and eventually become key people in the organization.

PEOPLE

Up to now we've seen that competent managers must know various aspects of two very important areas: the outside environment (including the market) and the organization itself. Now we move to the third area of knowledge: people. Good managers know people; they know what makes them tick; they know how to get along without alienating; and they know how to get people to perform at their highest possible level. We provide a brief overview here of this issue and address it in more detail in Chapter 7.

Superiors, subordinates, peer managers, customers or public

Managers react with at least three groups of people: superiors, subordinates, and peer managers. Some managers react with other groups existing on the outside of the organization—customers, the public, and/or the media. Some managers specialize in interacting with government bodies and purchasing agents; however, few managers interact with such a wide variety of groups at least on a regular basis. The exception to this is usually the chief executive officer of the organization who reacts with these groups as well as the owners.

Each group has needs and expectations and makes demands and requests on the manager's time and resources, as shown in Figure 2.5. Competent managers know how to balance these needs and requests of competing

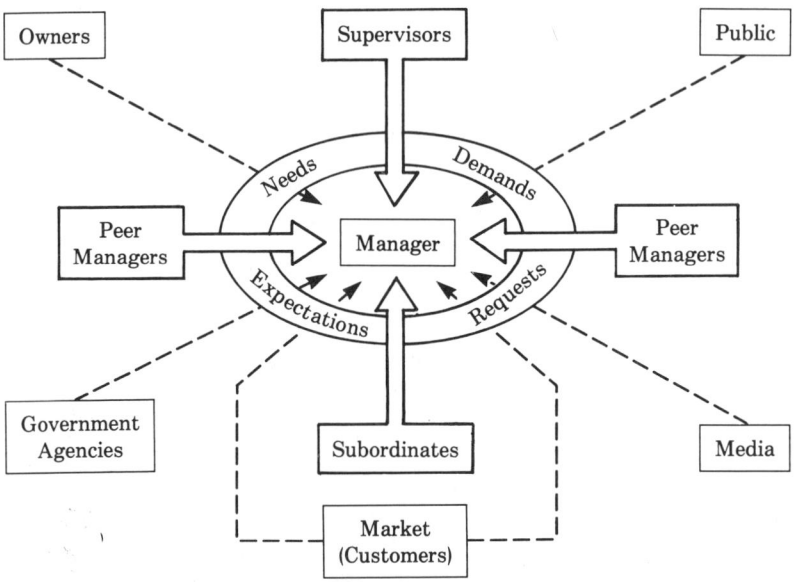

Figure 2.5 Balancing needs, demands, expectations, and requests of competing groups

groups without alienating any one group. This is extremely difficult, yet it can be done, as we see in Chapter 7.

TASK

Competent managers know what needs to be done and how to do it. They can see the goal at the end of the path and they can conceptualize the entire path before they take the first step. They know what is expected of them, and they know what tools, people, and other resources they'll need to move down the path to the goal.

Managers do not need to know the task in such detail that they are technical experts. In fact, unless managers are directly supervising a task, such as a foreman in an auto assembly line, it would be better if they were not familiar with the technical details of the task. Such familiarity leads to the "hands on" or "dirty hands" syndrome. We soon find our technical expert counseling the client, completing the books, or designing the part instead of managing those who do these tasks. If managers do not perform the function of management, no one will, and the planning, organizing, and controlling won't be done either or will be done haphazardly.

Of course there is a danger in having managers who never have performed the task. If this leads to a lack of appreciation for the task to be done, such managers develop an ivory-tower syndrome. This is almost as dangerous as managers with a dirty-hands syndrome. The key, then, is having enough technical knowledge to know the task without having so much that one cannot leave the job to others. Finding such a balance is the purpose of Chapter 8.

CONCLUSION

Managers need to have knowledge of the outside environment and market, the organization, people, and the task to be done. Competent managers know exactly what they need to know in these areas. Furthermore, they are able to synthesize and integrate information from one area with the next so that a system of knowledge of all four areas develop. Knowledge is power, and competent managers build their knowledge base to build their power basis.

Competent managers also avoid "unk-unk" situations. Unk-unks are unknown-unknowns. They differ from known unknowns. It's one thing to know that you do not know something and quite another to not know something and not even realize that you are supposed to know it. This is the worst of all worlds for managers.

This chapter has provided a brief review of the various areas of knowledge important for managers. Each of these areas is addressed in more depth in later chapters of the book.

QUESTIONS

1. Which part of your organization's outside environment, besides the market, do you believe is most important? Why?

2. Characterize the market of the organization you work for.

3. Do you consider yourself a key member of management in your organization? Why or why not?

4. How would you characterize the owners of your organization—as members of the organization or as part of the outside environment? Why?

5. Review Figure 2.5. Which group(s) do you deal with most often? Which group(s) are the most important? Reconcile any differences in the answers to these two questions.

6. Do the best sales personnel always make the best sales managers? Do the best production workers make the best supervisors? Explain your answers.

CASES AND EXERCISES

CASE 1: HORIZONS UNLIMITED

"John! Get in here! Did you see these monthly sales reports?"
"Yes, I did, B.J."
"Well, these are awful. Just awful. What in hell is going on anyway?"
"I don't know, B.J."
"This just shouldn't be. Look, most of the sales declines are in the mid-atlantic and mid-south regions. These are growing areas. Our sales should be soaring not stagnating or declining. What are Bud and Ellie doing anyway? I know they are fairly new regional sales managers but it shouldn't take them this long to get their feet on the ground. I just wonder if they're capable. They sure haven't shown me much yet. They're doing very little for the district sales managers in their respective regions."

"Well, B.J., I guess it takes a while to get things going. They've only been on the job about six months."

"That's long enough, John. We can't afford these sales declines anyway. I don't think Ellie and Bud are doing enough to get their people psyched-up. We've got a good product. We've got a good market. The demographics are with us. Economic conditions are good for us. We're selling in booming regions. They're dropping the ball. They've got to do more training for their sales managers. Broaden their horizons. Yeah, open their eyes. We need training and development in a whole host of areas so these sales managers better understand our product, market, and social and economic conditions which impact on us. Most of these district sales managers are new. Bud and Ellie appointed them. I want them trained. Look, John, get on it right away, will you? I want a first class management development program set up for these people as soon as possible."

Questions

1. What kind of training appears to be needed for these district sales managers?

2. Given the limited information in the case, do you think training will help? What other reasons could account for a decline in sales?

3. If lack of knowledge is the problem, how can this be rectified besides through training?

CASE 2: WHAT'S IN IT FOR ME?

I know what makes most people tick: *greed*. Everyone has their price. If you want to get someone to do something, pay them enough and they'll do it. We are all motivated by self-interest, especially on the job. We all want more. We're never satisfied with what we have. Good managers recognize this greed and capitalize on it.

People who are not motivated by greed are abnormal. Sure there are a few altruistic martyrs around but they are very rare and probably slightly mentally ill. Let's face it. The whole capitalistic system is set up on the idea of private ownership, private enterprise, private gain; in other words, greed. Adam Smith recognized this over 200 years ago when he said that capitalism depends upon self-interest and private gain.

So it all boils down to this in understanding people at work: everybody's out to get theirs. If you stand in their way, they'll step on you if it furthers their goals. Competent managers recognize this and get theirs before they get taken. You've got to be demanding and assertive and recognize people for what they are. That's how to understand people.

Questions

1. Do you agree that greed is the primary motivating force for most people? Why or why not?

2. Are people who are not motivated by greed abnormal as this person suggests? Why or why not?

3. Under what conditions are people likely to sacrifice their own self-interest for the good of others? Are these conditions common in business and government organizations? Explain your answers.

32 WHAT MUST A MANAGER KNOW?

Knowledge Area	Present Impact	Future Impact	Change + or −
Outside Environment			
• Culture			
• Economic system			
• Technology			
• Market			
• Political system			
• Public			
• Owners			
• Multinational relations			
Organizations			
• Purpose and goals			
• Products and services			
• Structure, policy			
• Procedure			
• Key personnel			
People			
• Supervisors			
• Subordinates			
• Peer managers			
• Customers			
• Public			
• Media			
• Government agencies			
• Owners			
Task			

Figure 2.6 Impact of knowledge areas

EXERCISE: WHAT IS IMPORTANT TO KNOW?

We know that not all areas of the outside environment, organization, people, or task impact equally on us in terms of intensity or importance. Figure 2.6 lists the knowledge areas we have discussed. Evaluate these in terms of *present* impact on your job and in terms of their *future* impact. Use a 1-5 scale with 5 meaning greatest impact and 1 meaning least. What are you doing to prepare for these changes?

REFERENCES

Beardsley, Monroe C. *Thinking Straight.* New York: Prentice-Hall, 1950.
  A classic work on human thought processes and logic.
Black, Max. *Critical Thinking.* New York: Prentice-Hall, 1946.
  One of the best discussions of developing ways to critically analyze ideas and concepts.
Brownstone, David, and Carruth, Gorton. *Where to Find Business Information: A Guide for Everyone Who Needs the Answers to Business Questions.* New York: John Wiley & Sons, 1979.
  A list of 5,100 entries of business sources, primarily books and articles, on a wide variety of business subjects.
Management Information Exchange, Inc. *Business Services and Information.* New York: John Wiley & Sons, 1979.
  This guide details government resources available to businesses in the form of bulletins, newsletters, special programs, information centers, counseling services, and computerized data bases.
Mintzberg, Henry. "The Manager's Job: Folklore and Fact." *Harvard Business Review* (July-August 1975): 49-61.
  An excellent treatment of the informational roles of managers as they relate to other roles managers have.
Mintzberg, Henry. *The Natural of Managerial Work.* New York: Harper & Row, 1973.
  The nature of managerial work is explored with particular emphasis placed on the skills and knowledge a manager needs to be effective.
Nordland, Rod. *Names and Numbers: A Journalist's Guide to the Most Needed Information Sources and Contacts.* New York: John Wiley & Sons, 1978.
  A single comprehensive national directory of names and numbers of people and places in government, media, business, and over 100 other categories. Over 20,000 listings.
Rosenberg, Jerry M. *Dictionary of Business and Management.* New York: John Wiley & Sons, 1978.

An extensive reference of business terms which contains over 8,000 entries covering more than forty major areas with thirteen appendices.

Rothman, Stanley, and Mosmann, Charles. *Computers and Society.* 2nd ed. Chicago: Science Research Associates, 1976.

The role of computer information storage and retrieval and its impact on knowledge use in organizations and society as a whole is examined.

Schnachel, Harry S. *The Art of Business Reasoning.* New York: John Wiley and Sons, 1930.

A dated yet excellent treatment of the reasoning and thinking process in business organizations. Most concepts still apply today.

Shannon, Claude E., and Weaver, Warren. *The Mathematical Theory of Communication.* Urbana: University of Illinois Press, 1949.

An excellent early work on the applications of mathematical study to the information transmission process.

Voich, Dan, Jr.; Mottice, Homer J.; and Shrode, William A. *Information Systems for Operations and Management.* Cincinnati: South-Western Publishing Company, 1975.

Comprehensive coverage of information and knowledge transfer within organizations. A managerial, not technical, approach is taken.

3
What Skills Must a Manager Practice?

"Good managers, first and foremost, must have the ability to get along with people."

"Competent managers are tough-minded; they drive their people to the point of rebellion."

"An effective manager knows where to go and how to get there."

"Effective managers let their group evolve their own work goals."

"The essence of managerial skill is communications."

"Competent managers give their subordinates just enough information, and no more, to get the job done."

These quotes reflect commonly held perceptions as to what really are the most important skills a manager must practice. Notice how some of the quotes conflict with one another. Do competent managers have the ability to get along with others or do they drive their subordinates as hard as they can? Do they clearly set job goals or do they let the group evolve goals? Do they communicate freely or do they keep some information secret?

This chapter addresses these and other issues related to the essential skills that competent managers must practice. We see that the practice of these skills is not always clear-cut or reflected in the above quotes. In this chapter we provide an overview of these skills and then look at them in more detail in Part III of the book.

WHAT ARE MANAGERIAL SKILLS?

Suppose you manage six clerical workers in an office. Jane, a typist, has come in twenty minutes late for work for the third day in a row. You've warned her about her lateness several times in the past six months, but you have tolerated it. She is by far the most effective and efficient typist you have. Do you continue to tolerate her lateness or do you take more drastic action?

Or suppose you find yourself in the following situation. Sally, your boss, has announced a significant increase in your group's sales quota for the coming year. In your opinion, there is absolutely no way your group will even come close to meeting this new target. Do you ignore the new quota, work with Sally to change it, or simply pass it on to your employees? Sally has criticized you in the past for not being a team player and for your apparent inability (in her mind) to set meaningful goals for your employees.

These are but two examples of problem areas where the right management skills must be practiced. What are these skills? We identify and briefly explain nine essential skills managers must practice in order to be competent. These are summarized in Figure 3.1.

- Goal setting

- Leadership

- Problem solving and decision making

- Communications

- Coaching and counseling

- Managing change and conflict

- Political skills

- Managing time

- Evaluating and rewarding

Figure 3.1 Nine essential skills for competent management

Goal setting

Competent managers work with superiors *and* subordinates in setting meaningful job goals. They are able to serve as mediators and compromisers in setting goals that satisfy both superiors and subordinates. This is not to say that there are not some goals which are mandated by higher-level management. These should be few, however, and should be taken as "givens" by the individual manager. Yet, even here, managers usually will have the option in setting subgoals that will lead to the accomplishment of the main goal. There may even be occasions where subordinate managers can influence the setting of these mandated goals.

For example, suppose you are told that the sales of your group during the coming year are expected to increase by 15 percent. It should be up to you to set sales goals by territory and by month in order that the overall increase of 15 percent be reached at the end of the year. In fact, you might be able to demonstrate through study and supporting figures that a 15-percent increase is not as realistic as a 12-percent one.

Goals should be working guides to behavior. They must be communicated to all concerned with their accomplishment, not just written up and then filed away. Goals should inspire performance. They must be viewed as realistic, achievable, measurable, and specific. People must feel that goals give them a stake in the organization. As shown in Figure 3.2, goals bridge the gap between individual and desired organizational output.

All of this does not happen automatically. It's up to managers to make it happen. A top priority for competent managers is to first work with various groups to define the goals before any other effort is undertaken.

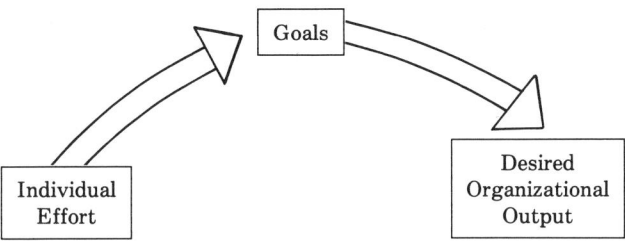

Figure 3.2 Bridging gaps with goals

Leadership

Closely tied to the goal-setting process is leadership. Leadership is getting people to do what they're supposed to do. As Figure 3.3 shows, leadership inspires performance toward goal achievement.

There is no one best leadership style. Competent managers vary from a tough, hard-line, autocratic approach to a participative, democratic approach. The proper style depends on the task to be done, the competencies of the manager, the competencies of the subordinates, and the time allowed for completion of the task. Effective managers are those who can properly perceive these variables and then adopt the appropriate leadership style. They also know when they might be the wrong person for the job in the sense that they are unable to modify their leadership style to fit the situation. They'll admit this mismatch and ask for a transfer or reassignment rather than continue to be the wrong person at the wrong time and place.

38 WHAT SKILLS MUST A MANAGER PRACTICE?

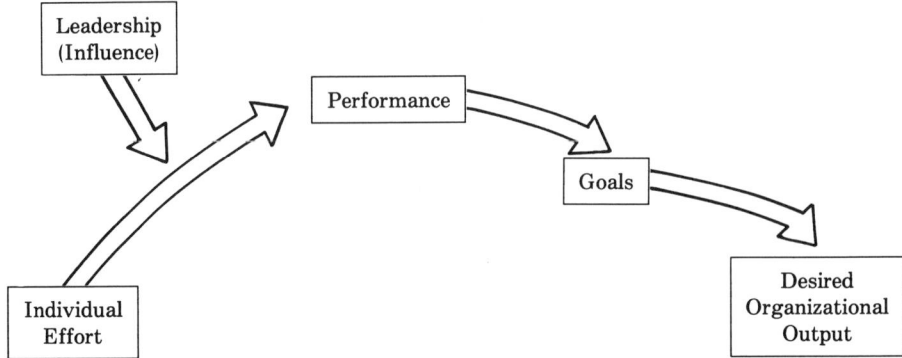

Figure 3.3 Leadership as an influence process

Problem solving and decision making

We saw in Chapter 1 that the two essential elements of management are decision making and influence. In this section we briefly review the decision process, then address it in more detail in Chapter 11.

Skilled managers know what decisions need to be made and how to make them. They can quickly cut through a problem to its core and then develop an appropriate decision. They do not waste time on trivial problems and decisions but instead focus on the important issues. Effective managers also can assess problem importance by relating them to the goals that need to be achieved.

Analytical ability is also important for managers' problem-solving powers. They're not content with superficial answers. They keep asking "why?" until they get to the cause of a problem. By doing this, they gather enough information to adequately define the problem, thus avoiding the tendency of going off half-cocked with decision solutions for ill-defined problems.

Competent managers do not postpone problems and decisions hoping they'll eventually go away, nor do they use the excuse of the need for more information as a delaying tactic. Further, they do not assign all decisional needs to a committee. *Competent managers make decisions.*

Communications

Passing information and understanding from one person to another is the essence of communication. Even the best managers will have difficulties unless good communication skills are practiced.

There are three primary aspects to good communication skills, as shown in Figure 3.4. First, managers must practice *empathy,* the ability to see

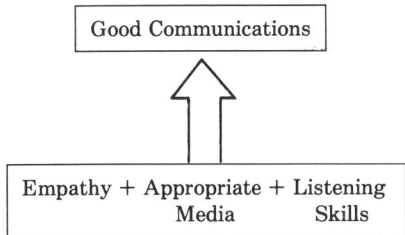

Figure 3.4 Primary aspects to good communications

things from another person's viewpoint. Before any communication is begun, effective managers ask, "How will the person with whom I intend to communicate likely view and receive this information?" Too often communication is from our personal viewpoint, not from the receiver's viewpoint. For example, if you were a botonist you would not explain what a tree is to a six-year-old child the same way you would to a college freshman class in biology. Nor would you explain aspects of a tree to a freshman biology class as you would to a professional meeting of fellow botonists.

The second key to good communications is using the appropriate *media*. When should a letter or memorandum be used? When is a telephone call better? What about personal face-to-face communication? What kinds of information are best communicated through staff and other types of group meetings? These are important questions that must be answered *before* communication takes place. We address these in Chapter 12.

The third essential skill for good communications is being a *good listener*. One cannot be a good communicator unless one attempts to listen to what the other person has to say. We often screen or block out certain messages we receive because we don't really wish to understand them. Or we interpret a communication message entirely from our own experience and background rather than from the communicator's background. Here again, the key to good listening is empathy. Good listeners also have a responsibility to provide feedback to the communicator. This feedback can take the form of a nod, question, comment, or simply a blank stare. Whatever means we use to provide feedback, we should try to be sure that we convey to the communicator how the message is being received.

One final note on listening: we should not confuse understanding with agreement. We should not be unwilling to understand a message simply because we are afraid our understanding will be misinterpreted as agreement. It is important to try to understand a message sent to us whether we disagree with it or not. If we disagree, we can always voice our disagreement in order to insure our understanding is not misinterpreted.

Thus, the foundation of good communication skills rests on practicing empathy, choosing the appropriate media for the message and circumstances, and being a good listener.

Coaching and counseling

Managers are coaches and counselors with members of their organization. Interpersonal and performance problems are bound to arise in the daily task of managing; dealing with these effectively is one mark of a good manager.

Generally, counseling skills should be limited to job-oriented problems. Occasionally, however, it might be necessary for managers to provide some counseling on personal problems of subordinates. This should be done sparingly. Most people do not want other people's advice on personal problems unless they ask for it. Even here, the problem might be so significant and complex that the proper response for the manager is to refer the person for professional counseling advice from a psychologist, psychiatrist, or other person professionally trained in counseling skills.

Good managers are also concerned with coaching their subordinates, providing guidance and encouragement. They offer praise and other incentives to good performance, as well as assist subordinates in their performance of functions and duties when problems arise. Much like the coach of an athletic team, managers act like sparks or catalysts to bring out the best performance in subordinates.

The delicate process of coaching and counseling is examined in more depth in Chapter 13.

Managing change and conflict

There are few things we can be absolutely certain of today except that things are bound to change. Change is a fact of life in almost every managerial role. Competent managers recognize this and consciously work to manage change as opposed to being swept along with it. They start change when appropriate, guide and direct it, reduce it when necessary, sometimes stop it, and sometimes amplify it. Change is bound to happen: the questions are who is going to make it happen and what type of change is it going to be? Good managers address these questions and then do what they can to manage the change process so that their goals, as well as the goals of their subordinates and organization, can be reached.

With most change comes conflict. Effective managers realize that a certain amount of conflict is good for an organization. Conflict, in the form of healthy competition for resources or ideas, often inspires people to higher levels of performance. This is certainly not to say that conflict cannot become destructive in an organization. But, if managed properly, the benefits of conflict can far outweigh the costs. It is up to competent managers to manage conflict in this way rather than to simply ignore it or sweep it under the rug. We'll examine some ways of managing change and conflict in Chapter 14.

Political skills

Most books on management usually ignore the essential political skills required of managers. This is unfortunate because the managerial role has a political element. These political skills provide managers the room to maneuver. They can be used to cut red tape in order to get things done more quickly. They are required in most any type of organization, not just in political organizations such as government agencies.

By political skills, we are not referring to simply being an apple-polisher. We are referring to a wide range of activities that are legitimate and should be recognized and practiced by competent managers. Some of the political skills we look at in Chapter 15 include such activities as forming coalitions, bargaining, compromise, trade-offs (you scratch my back and I'll scratch yours), direct and indirect influence mechanisms (like lobbying), the use of the media, the timing of actions, bluffing, and gaining personal visibility. Each of these actions can undoubtedly be misused, but we will discuss them from a constructive standpoint while pointing out the ethical (and possible legal) dilemmas that managers must watch out for in practicing these political skills. While it is true that these skills can be misused, it is also true that most any other managerial skill or tool can be misused. Most of us seem to feel that inherently there is something slightly dirty or unfair in practicing political skills; and, of course, most of us would agree that managers should not exclusively rely on these skills at the expense of other managerial skills. We all know managers who are masters of political skills and seem to be all form and no substance. I am not advocating this; rather, managers should use appropriate political skills in the appropriate manner as part of their total range of skills.

Managing time

Time can be viewed as an essential resource or as a terribly limiting handicap to managerial action. Competent managers can manage their time efficiently and effectively. They recognize that time is a limiting factor in that there is only so much available; yet they treat the time available as a very valuable resource. They are seriously concerned about wasting time in the sense of carrying out actions or duties that do not contribute to desired performance and goal accomplishment.

It is not necessary to make every second or even every minute count of every workday. This is probably beyond human ability and, even if it weren't, it probably would not be desirable. A short chat in the hallway on the weather may not have much to do with goal accomplishment, yet it is certainly a normal part of organizational life. Should these chats become longer and more frequent, however, then organizational performance would become seriously impaired.

Time management involves planning, organizing, and controlling one's time. It means using schedules and other mechanisms to keep performance and activities flowing smoothly along some desired time line. It also means the ability to help others, such as subordinates, manage their time effectively. Time management means being able to practice participative management so that effective delegation to subordinates occurs. (Effective managers do not have the time to do the work of their subordinates.) Effective time management means managing interruptions so that work can be carried out efficiently in appropriate blocks of time.

Finally, time management involves the fine art of saying "no." This may even mean saying no to a superior. Of course, the consequences of saying no must be carefully weighed before such action is taken, and it should be done tactfully, but there are occasions when such action should be taken.

Managers are responsible for personal work performance. If such performance is seriously threatened by emergency requests and demands from a superior, these should be resisted. If their requests are all too frequent, then it's up to the managers to confront their superiors with the issue and attempt to redefine goals and performance expectations in view of the continuing "emergency" demands. Not doing this implies to the superior that you aquiesce to the situation. The superior may very well think that you don't have enough to do to keep yourself busy after all! We'll explore ways to manage time in more depth in Chapter 16.

Evaluating and rewarding

People work in order to get something in return for effort and performance on the job. Good managers recognize this and are involved in the evaluation and reward process. These rewards involve such actions as promotion, merit salary increases, new job assignments, praise, providing additional resources such as budget or personnel, providing extra time off, or providing perquisites such as country club memberships, special parking spaces, or executive dining room privileges. Some managers may not have the authority to directly provide these things for subordinates, but may only be able to recommend individuals for various rewards. Yet all managers can provide praise and can vigorously lobby with the powers-that-be to obtain these rewards for subordinates.

It is the responsibility of every manager to evaluate subordinate performance. This feedback and the resultant dialogue and problem diagnosis is essential for top-level performance of subordinates. Most people really do not want to know how they are doing in their job. What they want to hear is that they're doing a good job. However, managers must make subordinates aware of poor job performance and the fact that they *know* the subordinate's job performance is inadequate. Of course using coaching and counseling skills, it's up to managers to work with subordinates to improve job performance.

It's not necessary to make a subordinate aware of poor performance in a threatening, punitive, or vindictive manner. It should be done in a positive and tactful manner, using appropriate communication skills. *But it should be done!* Furthermore, it should be done directly with a subordinate. He or she should not hear of the boss' displeasure with performance through hallway or office gossip.

Finally, such evaluation and feedback should occur as needed. Most organizations require formal annual or semi-annual performance appraisals. However, this should not prevent managers from evaluating subordinate performance and communicating this on a more frequent basis if needed.

We'll review some methods of evaluating and rewarding in Chapter 18.

CONCLUSION

Effective managers practice nine essential skills: goal setting, leadership, problem solving and decision making, communication, coaching and counseling, managing change and conflict, political skills, managing time, and evaluating and rewarding. These skills are practiced within a framework of essential management knowledge which we examined in Chapter 2. They are practiced in such a way so that the essential management functions of planning, organizing, staffing, directing, and controlling are carried out. These skills can be learned by managers who are seriously concerned about improving their managerial performance.

In the next part of the book we take a more detailed look at the important knowledge needed by managers. We revisit the issue of managerial skills in Part III.

QUESTIONS

1. Of the nine skills examined, which one do you believe to be most important in your present job? Why?

2. Are planning, organizing, staffing, directing, and controlling skills or functions of management? Explain your answer.

3. In your experience, the absence of which specific skills seems to lead most often to management failure or incompetence of those around you?

4. What seems to be the best way for managers to learn the skills discussed in the chapter? Do you agree that any conscientious manager can eventually learn the skills through experience and serious study? Why or why not?

5. Do you believe incompetent managers are aware they lack certain of these skills and could articulate which skills they lack? Explain your answer.

6. Do you believe that competent managers are aware that they practice these skills and could articulate this fact? Explain your answer.

CASES AND EXERCISES

CASE 1: YOU'RE MAD AS HELL AND I'M NOT GOING TO TAKE IT ANYMORE!

Don did it again. He lost his temper in a violent outburst with Betty, one of his best subordinate managers. Betty had failed to turn in a client services report on time. She explained that Operations was late in getting important data to her thus causing her report to be two days late.

Don exploded in anger twice; first when Betty told him the report would be a few days late and then again when Betty finally turned in the report. It really upset Betty but she held her temper. She did threaten to quit if it happened again, saying she would not continue to take Don's abuse any longer.

Don was ashamed of himself, but it wasn't the first time he had lost his temper, although the outbursts seemed to be occurring more frequently. He knew he couldn't afford to lose Betty. He also knew he would probably have trouble replacing her with someone as competent since his reputation for a violent temper was well known.

"Where have they ever taught me how to control my temper?" he thought to himself. "I've had six years of college and numerous management development seminars and not once has even tactfulness been discussed—let alone the issue of temper control."

The longer Don thought about it, the more he became convinced that temper control was an essential management skill. Furthermore, he saw an apparent dilemma: how to forcefully push people to carry out work and meet deadlines and yet not alienate them. "How can I be demanding and forceful and yet not obnoxious? I sure don't want to have the reputation of a weak, spineless manager," he thought. "Yep, they sure don't deal with this problem in management courses," he concluded.

Questions

1. Is temper control an essential management skill? Is it a part of one or more of the nine skills we discussed in the chapter? Explain your answers.

2. How can one be taught to control one's temper?

3. Critique Don's thoughts in the last paragraph of the case.

CASE 2: THE BOSS' SON

Barry faced a very ticklish situation. One of his new subordinates, Jack, just happened to be the son of the Chief Executive Officer. Jack had worked for Barry for six months, and it was time for Barry to conduct Jack's first semi-annual performance report. The trouble was that Barry had done a very poor job during the period.

Barry had talked with Susan, his boss, about this dilemma, and she informed him to treat Jack just like any other employee and to give him an honest rating. She told him to ignore the fact he had a Stanford MBA, had only been with the company for six months, and was the President's son. Furthermore, she said it was essential that Jack know how he had been doing in the job and that it would be best for him in the long run.

"That's easy for her to say," thought Barry, "she isn't the one who signs the performance report. My name is on the line and I have a feeling my job will be too if I give him an honest evaluation."

Barry didn't know what to do. On the one hand, he could see Susan's viewpoint and, in fact, agreed with it. But he didn't think he could follow through with it. He knew Jack and his father were very close and he was sure that Jack would be upset with his evaluation. Barry wondered what options were open to him.

Questions

1. What alternative courses of action could Barry take? Which one should he choose and why?

2. What skills would need to be practiced for Barry to carry out this course of action?

3. Would this case be different if Jack were simply a close friend of the President? Would it be different if Jack were merely an acquaintance of the President? Would it matter if Barry was a close friend of the President? Should friendship have anything at all to do with the situation? If it should, then isn't making personal friendships an essential managerial skill? Explain your answers.

EXERCISE: WHAT MANAGERIAL SKILLS DO YOU PRACTICE?

We often practice managerial skills without realizing it. Sometimes we practice two, three, or even four skills at once. For the next two days keep track of the various managerial skills you practice for the various incidents, experiences, and issues you face in your daily job. Use the form below (Figure 3.5) and complete the number of times you use each skill (column a). Indicate how important this skill is to you in your present job using a 1–5 scale with 5 being very important and 1 being unimportant (column b). Then project how important each skill will be to you in the future, say two to three years from now (column c). In the last column (d), calculate the amount each skill will increase or decrease in the future. Do you see any discrepancies between the number of times you practice each skill and the present importance of each skill? Will you be prepared to practice the important skills required of you in the future?

Managerial Skill	a Number of Incidents Where Skill Used During Past 2 Days	b Skill Importance On Present Job (1–5)	c Skill Importance In Future (1–5)	d Number Changes (+ or −) In Future (c minus b)
Goal setting				
Leadership				
Problem solving and decision making				
Communications				
Coaching and counseling				
Managing change and conflict				
Political skills				
Managing time				
Evaluating and rewarding				

Figure 3.5 Managerial skills you practice

REFERENCES

Hill, Norman C. *Increasing Managerial Effectiveness: Keys to Management and Motivation.* Reading, Mass.: Addison-Wesley Publ. Co., 1979.
  An excellent, practical, handbook for managers which focuses on ways to improve interpersonal effectiveness on the job.

Huse, Edgar F. *The Modern Manager.* St. Paul, Minn.: West Publ. Co., 1979.
  A well written book which blends theory with practice by integrating actual cases into relevant textual material dealing with managerial skills and work.

Knudsen, Harry R.; Woodworth, Robert T.; and Bell, Cecil H. *Management: An Experiential Approach.* New York: McGraw-Hill Book Co., 1973.
  A series of twenty-three comprehensive exercises dealing with such managerial skills as leadership, conflict management, managing change, and communications.

Lau, James B. *Behavior in Organizations: An Experiential Approach.* Homewood: Richard D. Irwin, Inc., 1975.
  An excellent list of articles, cases, and exercises dealing with coaching and goal setting, leadership, communicating, team action, and other managerial skills with a behavior orientation.

Maier, Norman R. F.; Salem, Allen R.; and Maier, Ayesha A. *The Role-Play Technique: A Handbook for Management and Leadership Practice.* La Jolla, Calif.: University Associates, Inc., 1975.
  Twenty cases and exercises use the role-playing technique to apply essential leadership skills.

Schuler, Randall S., and Huse, Edgar F. *Case Problems In Management.* St. Paul, Minn.: West Publ. Co., 1979.
  Thirty-nine cases provide an opportunity to practice management analytical skills.

Part II
Developing Managerial Knowledge

We are now ready to take a fairly detailed look at the areas of managerial knowledge required for competent management. In this part, there are five chapters that focus on specific knowledge areas. Chapter 4 examines the aspects of the outside environment. Particular focus is placed on zeroing in on the important aspects of the environment from a management perspective. We examine ways in which managers can separate the important from the unimportant.

In Chapter 5, we take a more detailed look at the supply and the demand sides of the market. We'll look at products, services, and information that come into the organization from the resource market and are disbursed by the organization to the buying market. In the buying market, we'll take a particular look at customer/consumer behavior.

From here, we move to an examination of the organization itself. The purpose, goals, products, services, structure, policy, and key personnel of organizations are examined in Chapter 6. In Chapter 7, we examine what competent managers must know about people. The means of reconciling conflicting demands made by people with whom managers must act are of particular interest.

Finally, we end this part by examining what competent managers must know about the task to be done. Here we are interested in the activities and duties that constitute the work that managers direct.

From Part II, we move to a discussion of essential managerial skills in Part III, and to a discussion of certain pitfalls that managers must avoid in Part IV.

4
What Should a Manager Know About the Environment?

We saw in Chapter 2 that there are seven basic areas of knowledge in the outside environment that concern managers: culture, the economic system, technology, the market, the political system, the public, and owners. In this chapter, we address each of these areas, except the market, which we address in Chapter 5. Our focus is on ways of pinpointing areas in the environment which are of critical concern to effective management.

EFFECTS OF COMPONENTS OF THE ENVIRONMENT

The seven major components of the environment impact on the organization in different ways. Consider this situation. Apex Latex moved its production operations to a small town in Alabama one year ago. This was done in the hope of paying a lower wage rate, because of tax relocation allowances, and for the warmer climate. Apex is the largest employer in this town, employing 600 people on the assembly lines, three shifts a day, five days a week. The vast majority of employees are from surrounding farms and small retail, wholesale, and service industries. Apex continually has a problem with tardiness, absences, and over-extensions of break and lunch periods which the company finds quite costly. Top management complains that the people in the plant don't seem to have "the industrial work ethic like the people up North."

In this situation, a subcultural difference seems to be having an effect on the punctuality of the work force. Since most of the employees had never held a factory job, it is quite possible that the strong demand for punctuality required on continual process assembly lines is very new to them. Adjusting work habits to this requirement will take time. Here, a very real subcultural difference is having a direct impact on the productivity of the company.

Or consider this situation. Johnson Materials, Inc., is a producer of several components and parts used in various production processes. A year after the 1973 OPEC oil embargo, they experienced a strong surge in product demand at a time when the economy was facing a serious recession. At first, the company was at a loss to explain this strong demand until they realized that many of the component parts they made were being purchased by firms that installed scrubbers in smokestacks. Since many utilities and other firms began to convert to coal as an energy source, they began installing scrubbers so as to be able to burn coal and meet environmental pollution standards. Johnson Materials initially had no idea many products it manufactured would be useful in the cleansing process for coal-burning firms. Now that they knew this, however, they were out to exploit this demand as best they could.

These two incidents are examples of three key concepts related to the organization's outside environment. First, the environment serves as a source of both *opportunities* and *constraints* for an organization. What might be a constraint or limiting factor for one organization can be a very real opportunity for another. Second, the effect of the environment can be direct and immediate or it can be indirect and delayed. Often it is difficult to tell in advance what kind of affect an environmental component or change will have on an organization. Third, the environmental impact affects both the resource supply side and the demand for product/service side of the organization. Using our input-output analysis, the environment can affect the inputs supplied to an organization and the demand for products and services produced by the organization. These three concepts are summarized in Figure 4.1.

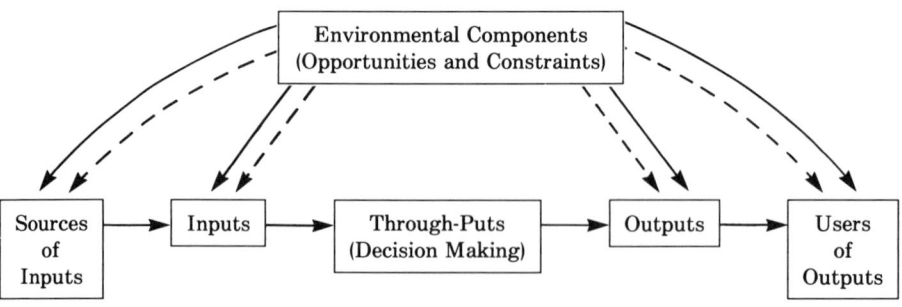

Key: Solid arrow is direct affect.
     Dashed arrow is indirect affect.

Figure 4.1 Effects of environment

RELEVANCY OF THE ENVIRONMENT

Given that there is such a large, unstructured outside environment, how do managers get a handle on what should be known? How is the important information separated from the unimportant? Of course, the answers to these questions depend on the industry of the organization and the type of position held by each manager. For example, the president of an oil company needs to know different things about the environment compared to a manager of counselors in a state welfare agency.

Regardless of the type of organization or position held, all managers need a mechanism or tool for distinguishing important from unimportant factors in the environment. In this section we briefly review three key concepts to help make this distinction: *task environment, organizational domain,* and *domain consensus.*

Task environment

Does the plant manager of a General Motors plant need to know the fluctuations of the price of cattle? Perhaps, if some of the cars produced have leather upholstery. Does the branch manager of a savings and loan institution need to be concerned with the rising oil costs? Yes, if they impact on the costs of construction for which loans are being made. Does a Dean of a College of Business need to be concerned about new developments in chemical fertilizers? Probably not. So what factors do matter? What matters are things that exist in the organization's *task environment.* The task environment are those components of the environment that are relevant or potentially relevant for organizational goal setting and attainment. What is the organization trying to do? Whom is the organization serving? What resources are needed to produce products and services? These questions are addressed in the development of an organization's purpose statement as we saw in Chapter 2. Thus, defining the organization's purpose vis-à-vis the opportunities and constraints in the environment is the first step to determining what is important in the environment.

An organization cannot be all things to all people. Resources cannot be spread so thin that nothing is done well. An organization must split up the environment into three categories as shown in Figure 4.2: that which is relevant for goal setting, that which is potentially relevant, and that which is irrelevant. That which is relevant is the task environment and that which is potentially relevant is the potential task environment. Once these distinctions have been made, then the managers in the organization should monitor and know the relevant and potentially relevant environments and should spend substantially less effort in monitoring the nonrelevant environment. *But they should not ignore it!* What is nonrelevant today may be potentially relevant two years from now and very relevant four years from now. In other words, these three environments are fluid and shift.

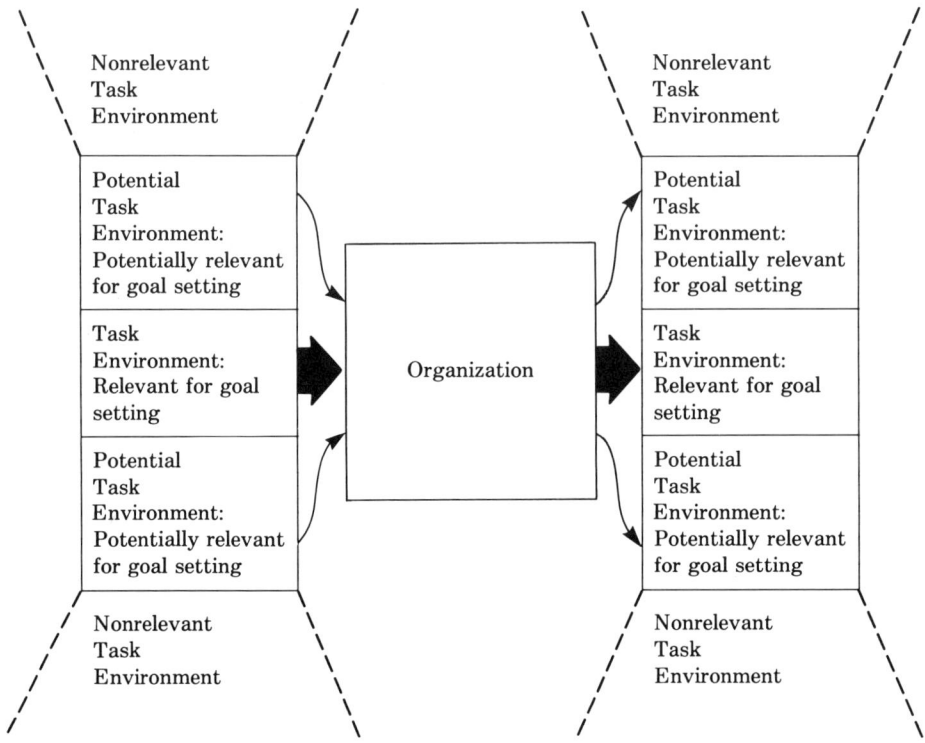

Figure 4.2 The organization's task environment

One of the best examples of this is the railroad industry. A particular railroad company, such as the Pennsylvania Railroad, viewed themselves as being in the railroad business, not the transportation business. They ignored developments in other areas of transportation such as automobiles and airlines. Had they not ignored these factors, perhaps today we would have a Pennsylvania Airlines as a subsidiary of the Pennsylvania Transportation Company.

Yet steam engines don't fly. They require different resources and expertise to manufacture, market, and operate. Would the Pennsylvania Railroad Company had spread itself too thin if they tried to get into the airline business? Perhaps. But they didn't and they died. Can an organization really ignore significant changes in environmental opportunities and constraints and expect to survive? No, not if these occur in the task or potential task environment, or if they occur in the irrelevant environment in such a way that that environment now becomes part of the potential or task environment.

Domain and domain consensus

An organization defines its task environment by determining its *domain* and achieving *domain consensus*. The organization's domain is that area of the environment that an organization stakes out for itself. They are the claims made by the organization in terms of products offered, services rendered, and population served. It's what the organization says it will do in providing products and services to people (customers/clients) that exist in the environment.

Second, the organization tries to achieve *domain consensus*. This is defining the expectations of members of the organization and those with whom they interact concerning the activities of the organization. In other words, it's a "contract" that the organization develops with its environment. Parts of the contract may be written, such as contracts with suppliers, banks or distributors, or parts may be unwritten, such as implied warranties with customers. Through domain consensus, the organization attempts to specify what it will and will not do in the environment and what it expects in return.

By determining domain and domain consensus, the organization specifies its task and potential task environments and distinguishes parts of the environment that are important from parts that are of little or no concern to the organization.

The organization or managers?

We have been using the word *organization* as if the organization takes action to do or not to do something. This is not technically correct. *Managers* on behalf of the organization act. Thus, the definition of task environment, domain, and domain consensus is done by managers, usually top managers in the organization, on behalf of the entire organization.

When managers make these decisions they are expressing their management philosophy. They also interpret and express the organization's heritage and tradition. These two key elements are important to ascertain if we are to understand how a particular organization goes about determining its task environment, domain, and domain concensus. This process is shown in Figure 4.3.

Management philosophy. We see in Figure 4.3 that the management philosophy is a very important factor in determining the kinds of decisions managers make in reaching domain, domain consensus, the definition of the task environment, and, ultimately, goal setting. A managerial philosophy is simply the underlying values managers observe in decision making. Managers have a philosophy of management whether they can articulate it or not.

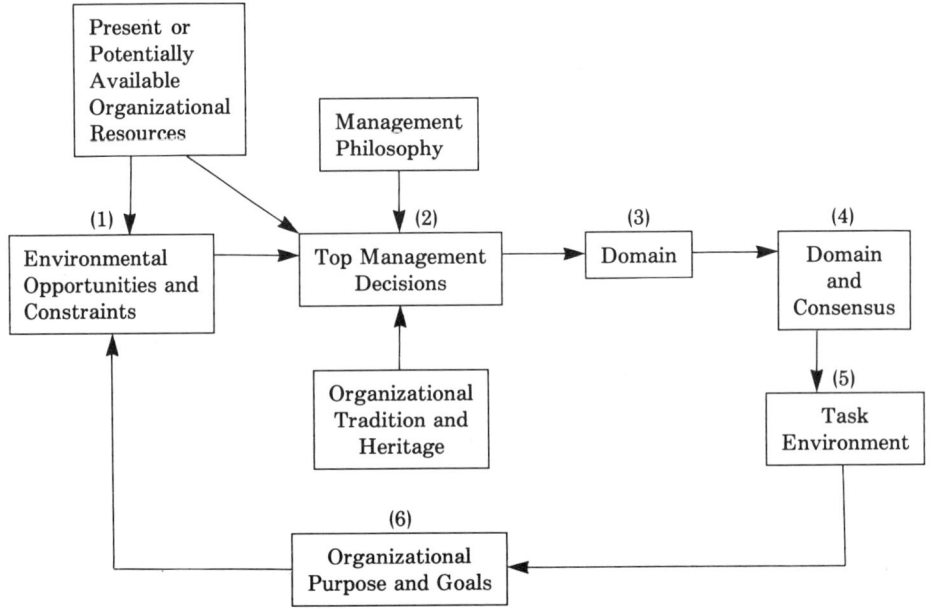

Figure 4.3 Interpreting environmental opportunities and constraints to set goals

In other words, the philosophy of a particular manager might be implicit rather than explicit. We can often infer a philosophy based on the things a manager says or on the things a manager does. For example, such statements as, "It's a dog-eat-dog world," "Get all you can when you can," and "Sometimes you have to step on people to get ahead," reflect a certain management philosophy. "Always be kind to subordinates, no matter what," "An ounce of prevention is worth more than a pound of cure," and "Managers are helpers," reflect a very different philosophy. Whatever the philosophy held by managers in the top management group, the consensus of this philosophy will affect the decisions made in determining domain and domain consensus.

Organizational tradition and heritage. Top managers also interpret and make manifest the organization's tradition and heritage. All organizations have a tradition, even rather new ones. The first of several factors is precedence—the way things have been done in the past. Second, the image the organization tries to portray to its employees, customers, and general public is an important part of the tradition and heritage. Third, the experience and educational backgrounds of individual managers, particularly those near the top that have been with the organization a number of years, reflect tradition and heritage.

This tradition and heritage, along with the management philosophy, has a significant impact on the decisions made regarding domain and domain consensus.

WAYS OF KNOWING

Given all of this, how can managers in the organization best learn about the organization's outside environment? First, managers must *scope* the environment. Second, information about the area scoped must be located and studied. Let's look at each of these processes.

Scoping the environment

Using concepts from the previous section, managers seek answers to questions which narrow and define the part of the outside environment of importance to the individual manager. These key questions are shown in Figure 4.4.

---

1. What are the environmental opportunities for our organization?
2. What are the environmental constraints for our organization?
3. What is the top management philosophy?
4. What is the heritage and tradition of our organization?
5. What is our organization's domain?
6. Have we reached domain consensus? If so, what is this consensus?
7. What is our organization's task environment?
8. What are our organization's purpose and goals?
9. How does my job and my unit tie into this purpose and goals?
10. If my unit and I perform effectively, will the organization meet its environmental opportunities and constraints?

Figure 4.4 Key questions for scoping the environment

You may not be able to clearly see how your job ties into the organization's purpose and goals (question 9), nor may you easily see how the performance of your job will help meet environmental opportunities and constraints (question 10). It depends on your level of management and your functional or divisional specialty. It might be easier for a vice president of sales to answer these questions than a production line supervisor or the head of the bookkeeping section. Yet all managerial jobs—indeed, *all* jobs—should be ultimately tied to organization purpose and goals and meeting environmental opportunities and constraints. Such a tie gives the organization a sense of direction and unity of action. It helps achieve coordination and control. It helps people feel that they have a sense of worth and meaning in their job. But how can a manager get answers to these questions?

Knowledge sources on the environment

The identification of information to answer the twelve key questions in Figure 4.4 requires a conscientious effort by managers. This information usually doesn't just pop up, nor can it simply be absorbed by osmosis in carrying out daily job functions. But the information is there. "Seek and ye shall find" applies in this case as in many other situations in life. Figure 4.5 presents some major sources that should be examined by managers in order to answer these questions.

CONCLUSION

Knowledge about the environment is an absolute requirement for competency in management. Even though the type and amount of environmental information needed by a particular manager will vary by type of organization and level of management, *all* managers need to know these aspects of the environment that impact on their specific organization and industry and their particular job.

Information about important parts of the environment is usually available to managers, but it does require some effort to obtain, review, and study it. Well-rounded educated managers make this effort. They do not operate with blinders which limit their field of vision. They are "up on what's happening" in the world and can translate these events to present and potential impacts on their organization and their job.

There is still one part of the environment which we need to address: the market. The market consists of customers, consumers, and clients who purchase and/or use a product/service mix. This issue is addressed in the next chapter.

QUESTIONS

1. What are some factors that could cause the irrelevant environment to become part of the task environment for an organization?

2. In your opinion, which of the sources listed in Figure 4.5 are the best for finding out about the environment? Why?

- Environmental Opportunities and Constraints
    - Professional general business periodicals
        (e.g. *Wall Street Journal, Business Week*)
    - Trade magazines specific to industry
    - Books
    - Professional and trade association meetings
    - Updating series or series on legal developments
    - Management update educational seminars
- Top Management Philosophy and Organization History and Tradition
    - Organizational charter
    - Annual reports
    - Employee manuals
    - Code of ethics
    - Public relations documents
    - "Image" advertising
    - Orientation programs
- Organizational Domain, Domain Consensus, and Task Environment
    - Suppliers
    - Product/service line
    - Distribution network
    - New product R&I
    - Customers/consumers
    - Key government regulatory groups
- Organization's Purpose and Goals
    - Annual reports
    - "Management by objective" statements
    - Employee manuals
    - Sales, production, and service quotas
    - Management and organizational audits or assessments
- Own Job and Unit Tie in to Organization's Purpose and Goals
    - Job descriptions
    - MBO statements
    - Organization charts
    - Work flow process
    - Planning and policy documents
- Own Job and Unit Performance Tied to Meeting Environmental Opportunities and Constraints
    - Personal performance reviews
    - Unit performance reviews
    - Management audits
    - Merit or other incentive-based remuneration
    - Own and unit's visibility
    - Awards or citations to unit
    - Cost/benefit analysis

Figure 4.5 Sources of information for scoping questions

3. Given that so few managers are at the top of the organization, why should *every* manager try to know the outside environment?

4. Given that the environment is changing so rapidly, what helpful hints can a manager follow to keep current?

5. In your opinion, what part of the outside environment has the most dramatic impact on your organization? Why?

CASES AND EXERCISES

CASE 1: THE SAME OLD BUNK

"So what, Professor Williams, so what?" Jim asked. Then he added, "It seems to me that you are just spouting off academic mumbo-jumbo. Of what possible relevance are terms like *domain, domain consensus,* and *task environment* to me? I'm a manager of a fairly good sized warehouse and I have twelve supervisors reporting to me. I know what I need to do to get my job done. I keep my costs down and get my orders shipped in time."

"I guess I told him," Jim thought as he left the seminar. "Nothing more than the same old bunk. Sometimes I think professors make up these fancy terms and write books and lecture on them just to make money. I've got better things to do."

(Later . . .)

"Well, Jim, how'd the seminar go yesterday?" asked Carol.

"O.K., I guess, Carol. Same old stuff though. Anything happen while I was gone?"

"Yeah, plenty, Jim. We heard from Matco. Their shipment will be delayed three days. Apparently there is a temporary diesel fuel shortage in the Northeast. And, oh yes, R&I called about those parts. They're under the gun to get that water treatment plant completed. Anyway, they want a rush delivery by the fifteenth."

"The fifteenth!" interrupted Jim. "Man, I don't know about that, I . . . "

"Oh yes, then there was the guy from Electrosol with the electric fork lift trucks. He'll call back Tuesday. And Elliott was back again about their overseas shipments. He needs them desperately."

"Overseas shipments hell," said Jim. "He knows we don't ship overseas."

"Well, that's about it," concluded Carol. "Now, tell me some more about the seminar, Jim."

Questions

1. Is there evidence here that the task environment and domain for Jim's warehouse operation might be shifting? If so, in what way?

2. Do you agree with Jim's assessment of the need to know about the environment? Why or why not?

3. What advice would you provide Jim to learn about his environment?

CASE 2: PROFIT IS NOT A DIRTY WORD

I've been with the company now three years. You'd think by now I'd know what was going on. But I think in the last six months I've lost ground. I'm really not sure what we're trying to do. We're in so many different product lines—soaps and detergents, meats, athletic equipment, restaurants, and entertainment. I even hear we're about to enter the energy business through purchase of a coal mining operation. Where will it end? How can this company keep a sense of direction? We are going in twenty different directions.

I liked the CEO's (Chief Executive Officer) speech at the annual stockholder meeting. When questioned about exactly what business this company was in he answered plain and simple: the profit-making business! Not the meat business or soap business or entertainment business—no—just the profit business. I love it! What does that tell us? Nothing, that's what, nothing. The whole world's our market. Anything that has a potential profit is our business.

Well, it just ain't gonna' work. Yeah, I know, profit is the name of the game. But there is just no way we can be all things to all people. We're spread too thin. We're in lines of business we have no business being in. What do beef and movie theaters have in common anyway, for heaven's sake? We keep expanding, expanding, expanding. Buying smaller companies right and left. The whole world's our stage. But I think we're about ready to fall off.

Questions

1. Do the concepts discussed in the chapter apply equally well to a multinational, diversified conglomerate business corporation as to a single product domestic operation? Explain your answer.

2. Is it wrong for a company to be in the "profit-making business" as opposed to being identified with a specific product or industry such as entertainment, foods, transportation, or energy? Explain your answer.

3. What advice would you give to this individual?

EXCERCISE: SCOPING YOUR ENVIRONMENT

Briefly carry-out each of the following steps for your present organization and job. You should be able to complete the entire exercise on three sheets of 8½" x 11" paper.

1. List the three most important environmental opportunities faced by your organization.

2. List the three most important environmental constraints faced by your organization.

3. In a paragraph, summarize the top management philosophy in your organization.

4. Briefly list key points that make up your organization's tradition and heritage.

5. Summarize the domain of your organization. Has consensus been reached?

6. List the key parts of your organization's task environment.

7. Summarize your organization's overriding purpose and three or four of its key goals.

8. Indicate how your job and unit tie into these goals.

9. Indicate how your unit helps the organization to meet environmental opportunities and constraints.

REFERENCES

DeGreene, Kenyon B. "Organizational Best Fit: Survival, Change, and Adaption." *Organization and Administrative Sciences* 8 (Spring 1977): 117-133.
The need for knowing the environment so as to be able to properly structure the organization is explained.

Dill, William R. "Environment as an Influence on Managerial Autonomy." *Administrative Science Quarterly* 2 (March 1958): 409-443.
An excellent discussion of the task environment is presented.

Emery, F. E., and Trist, E. L. "The Causal Texture of Organizational Environments." *Human Relations* 8 (February 1965): 21-31.
A classic article that discusses environmental contexts in which organizations exist. In particular, the idea of a "turbulent" environment gained widespread use after this article appeared.

Hodge, B. J., and Anthony, William P. *Organization Theory: An Environmental Approach.* Boston: Allyn and Bacon, Inc., 1979.
See in particular Chapters 4 and 5 for a discussion of the outside environment and relevancy of this environment to an organization.

Lawrence, Paul R., and Lorsch, Jay W. *Organization and Environment.* Homewood, Ill.: Richard D. Irwin, Inc. 1969.
An excellent and well-known work that examines organizations and environmental change. Particularly useful chapters are on environmental demands, organizational states, and practical application.

Thompson, James D. *Organizations in Action*. New York: McGraw-Hill, Inc., 1967.
See in particular Chapters 1 and 2 for discussions of domain and domain consensus.

Toffler, Alvin. *Future Shock*. New York: Random House, 1970.
A somewhat dated yet still popular look at the enormous changes in our environment.

Turkovich, R. "A Core Typology of Organizational Environments." *Administrative Science Quarterly* 18 (September 1974): 380–394.
Develops a system for naming and classifying various environments faced by organizations.

5
What Should a Manager Know About the Market?

In the last chapter, we reviewed ways of knowing the organization's outside environment. We examined all of the various components of the environment except one: the market. Since the market is such a key part of the environment, this entire chapter is devoted to examining it.

The reason for an organization's existence is to satisfy some need or desire in society. If a potential business firm believes it can marshal the necessary human, financial, and physical resources to satisfy the need at a profit, it will come into being. If a legislative body sees an unmet societal need that it deems appropriate for government to satisfy, it will create an agency. If a group of people see the need to act together to satisfy each other's interests, a mutual benefit-type organization will result. Organizations develop and continue to serve some need of some group in society.

This group is the customers or clients of the organization. They receive the outputs of the organization's effort. They may buy this output directly, such as purchasing a television set; or they may buy it indirectly, such as paying taxes to a government unit. In either case, something of value (money) is being exchanged for something else of value (the output or service produced).

Consider this example. Suppose you believe that there is a need for low-cost trans-Atlantic air service. No organization now provides such service but you believe such service is highly desirable by a significantly large group of customers. Believing that satisfying this need can be profitable, you form your organization, get your resources, and start your service. Viola! Laker Airlines.

Of course, not all business ventures will succeed this dramatically. It may not be legal to go into the business; the extent of the need may be misread; necessary resources may be unattainable; or perhaps the competitor beats you to the market or soon takes over the market. Success of the business venture will depend on general entrepreneural and management expertise.

CUSTOMERS VERSUS CONSUMERS

Customers are the people who *buy* a product or service. Consumers are the people who *use* a product or service. Often they are one in the same. You buy a tuna sandwich, then eat it. You buy a pair of shoes, then wear them home. You receive income tax preparation service and pay for it. However, often they are *not* one in the same. An adult buys clothes for young children. A parent pays college tuition for a child. A businessperson treats a group of business associates to lunch. I pay city taxes but have never used the city's fire service. The person who pays for a product or service may not also consume it.

In understanding the market, managers in organizations must not only know who buys the product or service and why, but also who uses or consumes it and why. This is important because the reasons for buying and for using the product or service may be quite different. When I buy a product or service but don't use it myself, I am acting as a *purchasing agent* for someone else. I should be acting in the best interests of this other person, not necessarily in my own best interests. For example, my son might wish to attend Pine Tree State University. I might hope that he attends Sand Hill State where I received my degree. Yet, if he really wants to go to Pine Tree State, I will pay his tuition there and not require him to attend Sand Hill State. Should I require him to attend Sand Hill State, I am now acting in *my* own best interests, even though I tell him it's in *his* own best interests to go to Sand Hill. I am interpreting his interests for him. (Of course, I could always tell him he's old enough to pay his own tuition any place he wants to go and can afford.)

This distinction between buyers and users of a product or service is also very important when we look at the supply side of the market. Organizations obtain their resources through purchasing agents who act, not in their own personal best interests, but in the interests of the organization. Purchasing agents do not use the products they buy; others in the organization do. So we see that this customer/consumer distinction is important at both the supply and demand sides of organizational activity, as shown in Figure 5.1. Notice in this figure that the organization purchases all resources in the market through agents. That is, purchasing managers buy materials and equipment; plant location directors buy land and plant; financial directors buy money; personnel directors buy labor. Each of these people must act in the best interests of the organization.

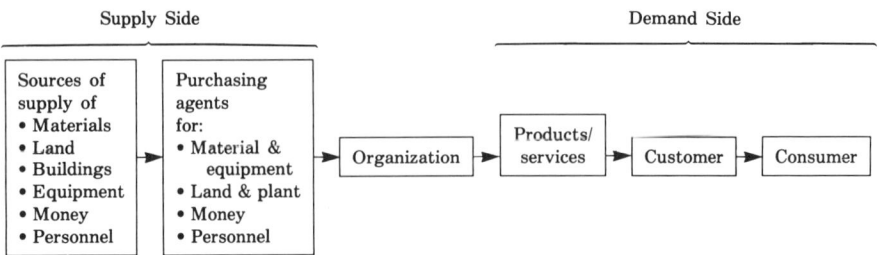

Figure 5.1 Customer/consumer distinction at the supply and demand sides of organizational activity

Buying behavior

When a person buys a product or service, something of value is exchanged for something else of value. The medium of exchange is usually money. The actual purchase decision involves the issue of *choice*. A person makes two separate decisions: first, to buy or not to buy, and second, which particular product or service to buy. For example, I decide I want a new car, then I decide what model and make. Often these two decisions blend. I really didn't know I wanted a new car until I saw the new Belchfire 500; now I think I want a new car.

When making the purchase, the customer is obtaining *utility;* it is useful. It can perform some function or satisfy some need. There are five separate types of utility a customer must balance with every product or service purchased, as shown in Figure 5.2. Let's look at each of these.

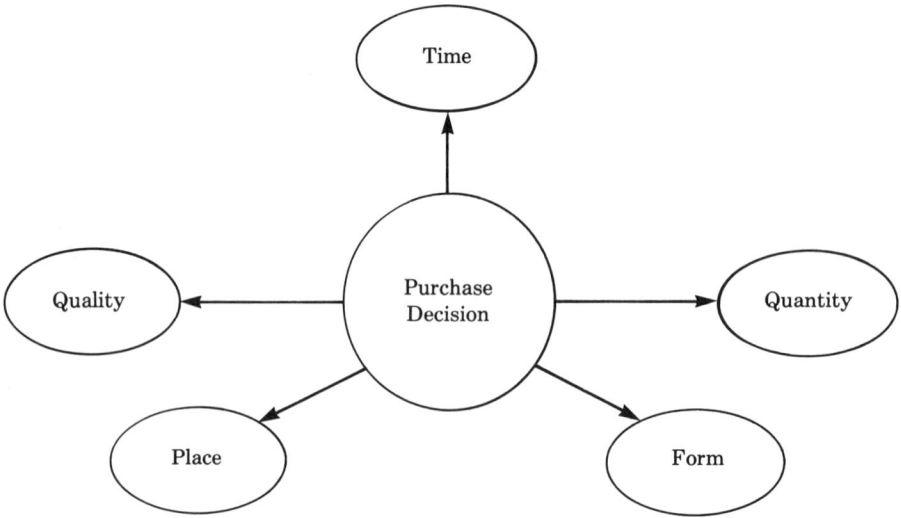

Figure 5.2 Five types of utility involved in a purchase decision

Form utility. Will the product or service do what it is intended to do? Will a car give good transportation? Will the purchase of legal service to draw up a will result in a good will that protects your assets for your family? We usually rely on claims made by the producer of the product to ascertain form utility, but we also inspect the product or service, rely on our past experience with it, talk to others who have used it, and, perhaps, consult independent product rating services such as Consumers' Union.

Quality utility. Closely related to form utility is quality utility. How well will the product do what it's supposed to? How long will the product last? Is the product simply adequate to do the job (form utility) or is it the best on the market (quality utility)? Once again we rely on producer claims, past experiences, and rating services for quality determination.

Quantity utility. We want the proper quantity of the product or service. I wish to purchase one car and I don't want to be forced to buy two or three at a time. On the other hand, a leasing service may want to buy in quantities of one hundred and not one or two cars at a time. I want one hour of legal service not ten minutes or a full day. I may want just a few nails for a repair job and not be forced to buy them in prepackaged five-pound bags. Much merchandising for mass produced-mass consumed products requires purchase in quantities not desired by individual customers.

Place utility. Is the product or service available *where* it is desired? I don't want to drive to Detroit to buy my car. I want it here in town or a town close to where I live. I want clothing at a nearby store; I don't want to drive to a factory outlet hundreds of miles away even if I can save a few dollars.

Time utility. Is the product or service available *when* it is desired? I want that new car now; I don't want to wait six or eight weeks for delivery. I want to fly during the day and not on the "red-eye" night-coach special. Or I may wish to purchase that new suit now but not pick it up for two months, so I'll use the store's lay-a-way plan.

Balancing of utilities. Each of these five utilities is balanced with each other. I may defer my purchase to get the quality I want so I order my new car and wait six weeks to obtain a car with the exact quality features I want. I will sacrifice one type of utility for another depending on what I deem desirable. The determining factor that helps the balance is *price*. Product or service price is the moderating variable. Let's look at this further.

Role of price in buying

The price of the product represents its value to the customer. In a competitive market, it is determined by supply and demand factors. Products in short supply relative to demand will have a higher price than products in great supply relative to demand. Diamonds cost more than rhinestones.

In balancing the five utilities, price plays a very important role. I may fly on that night-coach red-eye special if I can save a lot of money. I'll give up time utility if it's worth it to me. On the other hand, I may fly first-class day-service no matter what. I want the time and quality utility and am willing to pay for it. I'll drive to Detroit for my car if I can save hundreds of dollars and get what I want. Or, even if I can save hundreds of dollars, I may not be willing to do so if I need and want my car today. We give up something in one area relative to other areas depending on price considerations.

At some point, price becomes so important that people refuse to buy the product. When coffee goes to $5.00 a pound, I drink tea even though I dearly love coffee. For others, coffee may have to reach $10.00 a pound for this switch to occur. For still others, it may have to reach $100.00 a pound.

Price is only important relative to purchasing power or income. If we are at a high income level, a few cents more for a pound of coffee is meaningless to us. If we are at a low income level, price is so important that we may not even see a dentist or doctor for services even though we need such services badly. (This assumes, of course, that we don't have insurance or that such services are not provided free by the doctor or dentist or are not provided under government subsidy.)

If prices go up dramatically as they have in the last decade or so, we become concerned. But this concern is not as serious if our income has increased proportionately. Inflation is a serious problem, but it is less serious in a society if income increases at least as fast as prices. For some individuals and groups of people in our society, this has not happened, and the effects of inflation weigh as a very heavy burden on their shoulders.

If prices of particular products or services increase much faster than the general rise in prices in our economy, this becomes a concern to everyone whether incomes have increased or not. The tremendous increase in gasoline prices over the last decade is an example. At some point, fuel-efficient autos take precedent over quality, luxury, and other factors. At some point, bus and train transportation becomes more attractive and people may sacrifice the "luxury" of a personal form of transportation (the automobile) simply because gasoline has become so expensive.

Price plays another role in our buying behavior. It often represents quality when quality features are difficult for the buyer to determine. Most of us would not buy a diamond at $50 a carat because we reason something must be wrong with it. We believe that the more expensive a diamond is the better quality it must be. Consultants who charge $100 a day have more trouble getting work than those who charge $300 a day. A lawyer who is willing to represent you in court for $5 an hour will probably not be hired over the one who charges $50 an hour. What quality of legal service can you get for $5 an hour?

Implications for management

What does all this mean for management? It means that management must adopt a pricing strategy that reflects the selling goals the organization is trying to achieve. It means that price should be used as the tool to convey the quality, quantity, form, place, and time utility the organization wishes to convey to the marketplace. Competent managers know this strategy and know how the organization's product/service meets these five utilities in the marketplace.

There is a second implication for management. Management must use the *market segmentation* concept when pricing a product. That is, management must appeal to particular market segments which are carved out for particular organizational products or services. Not all people want the same quality, quantity, place, time, and form utility at a particular price; therefore, a range of products or services are offered by the organization. This range is well illustrated by individual auto companies, such as General Motors, which not only offer various brand names (such as Chevrolet, Pontiac, etc.), but many models within each brand name (such as Chevrolet's Monza, Chevette, Monte Carlo, etc.). This is done in recognition of the existence of market segments each with a varying utility mix and price preference.

The same segmentation occurs with service offerings. Uncontested divorces cost less than contested. Government services are also segmented, but perhaps not as much as they should be. Usually there is only one level of police, fire, or welfare service provided by an individual town. Of course, there is less differentiation of services offered by government because there are few competitive pressures to do so. Also, competitive pressures that do exist are often not recognized by government planners. We'll look at the role of competition in more depth later in the chapter.

CONSUMER BEHAVIOR

The previous section has focused on buyer behavior; we now need to address the issue of consumer behavior. As we pointed out earlier, the purchaser and consumer of a product may be one and the same, but they could be two different people. Since the consumer is the one who actually consumes or uses the product or service, there are certain things unique to the consumer.

Consumer needs and wants

A product or service reflects a want that satisfies some *need*. *Wants* are culturally conditioned ways to satisfy a need. *Needs* are basic requirements for life and living that people try to satisfy. Needs and wants serve as *motivators* for action. We undertake activity to satisfy some need.

When we say wants are culturally conditioned ways to satisfy needs, we mean that these wants are learned in our culture. For example, if you are hungry (need for food), you may want a hamburger since you grew up in a culture where hamburgers are advocated as a desirable food. In another culture, snake or dog might be viewed as a way to satisfy hunger even though most of us raised in the United States would not find these foods desirable.

As managers in organizations, we try to convince consumers that they should want our products or services over others. We use promotion and advertising to convince consumers that they can receive the best utility for the price with our product or service. These relationships are shown in Figure 5.3. The promotion and advertising effort serves as the link between our products, consumer wants, and consumer need satisfaction. If the product is purchased by someone else other than the consumer, we must convince this person that our product or service will satisfy the consumer's need.

Of course this promotional and advertising effort is not as strong where there are low levels of competition. For this reason we often see low levels of promotion and advertising in government agencies. Yet, even here some promotion and advertising is needed so citizens know what services are offered or not offered by government. For example, a person's home might burn to the ground if it is incorrectly assumed fire service was provided by the county. (Such a case received wide publicity in 1979 when a home lo-

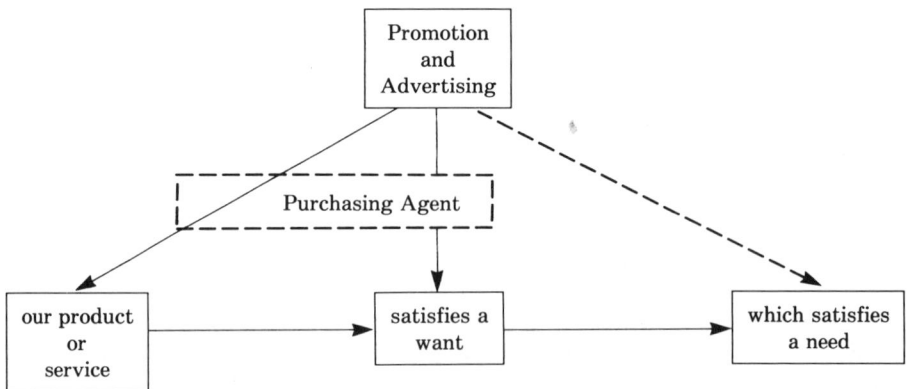

Figure 5.3 Promotion and advertising linking need satisfaction with wants and product/service offerings

cated in a western state in the United States burned because the homeowner had not joined the local Voluntary Firefighter Association. He claimed he was unaware of the requirement to join the Association and assumed the county provided fire service.)

Others may not know of the tax-supported job placement service provided at no cost to users in each state. State employment offices should advertise and promote their services to employees and job seekers alike, and many have begun to do so. The same is true with many other government provided services. For example, those eligible for food stamps are entitled to know of the program's existence and the services offered. Such advertising and promotion could very well increase the efficiency of government services since much of the information communication can be done through mass media, thus placing less reliance on personal "selling." This is what has happened in the private sector. Mass merchandising and communication has substantially reduced the role of personal selling with many products and services, thus helping to control the costs and prices of these products and services.

Consumer needs. Using Maslow's need hierarchy, we can describe five need levels that all people have, as shown in Figure 5.4. The most basic level is *physiological* needs. These include such things as shelter, food, water, and

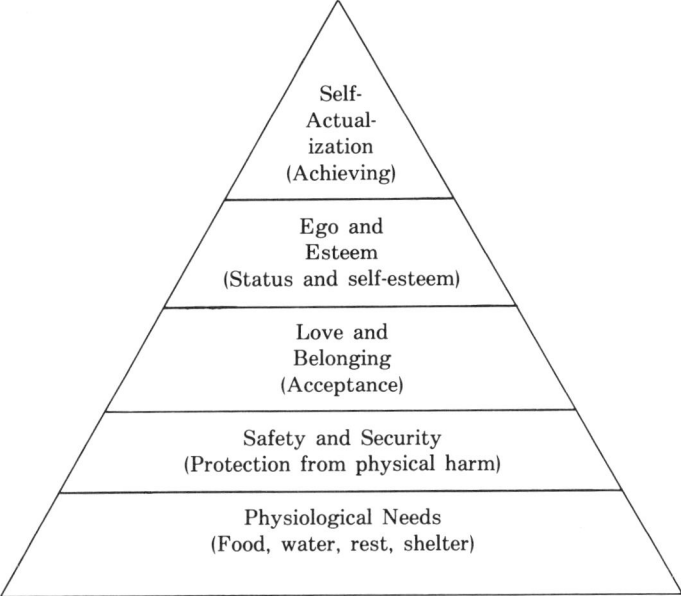

Figure 5.4 Maslow's hierarchy of needs

rest. Once these needs are substantially satisfied, people become concerned about satisfying the next need level, *safety and security* (or protection from physical harm). The third level of need satisfaction is *love and belonging*. People want to be accepted and loved by others. The fourth need level is *ego and esteem*. People want to be respected and want to have self-respect. Finally, the fifth need level is *self-actualization*. This is the need to become all that you can become; to achieve or to excel in something; to be self-fulfilled.

Maslow maintains that these needs exist in a priority. That is, we are concerned with *substantially* satisfying our lower order needs before we begin satisfying our higher order needs. If we are *truly* hungry, we are willing to satisfy our need for safety and other needs in order to get food. The lower order needs are finite in their capacity. At some point we become full and stop eating, even though we'll get hungry again soon. The higher order needs are not finite. We can never get enough esteem or self-actualization. Most of us want more.

Furthermore, Maslow maintains that these need levels exist in this hierarchy for all *normal* people. Those who forego a lower order need—such as a starving artist or a martyr burned at the stake—are abnormal. They represent a very small percentage of people. Maslow also maintains that we vary individually as to how much satisfaction we need at each level. I may need a 60-percent satisfaction of love and belonging before I become seriously concerned with achieving status and esteem. You may need only a 50-percent satisfaction, and still another individual may require an 80-percent level of satisfaction before higher order needs become important.

While these needs are common to all people, the ways that they go about satisfying these needs differ substantially. In other words, the wants of people vary greatly. For example, I need status so I buy a Cadillac, but you join the local country club. Our wants differ because we perceive the ability of the wants to satisfy needs differently. We perceive them differently because each of us has been culturally conditioned somewhat differently and have had different experiences that have shaped our individual perceptions and expectations.

A particular want may satisfy more than one need. For example, I need food, so I serve prime sirloin steaks at a dinner party not only to satisfy the need for food but also in hopes of achieving love and acceptance (need level three) and status (need level four) among my friends. I may not simply purchase a car to satisfy a need for transportation and security, but also because of the status a new car might bring me. In fact, I may be able to reach some level of self-actualization through buying a car since "owning a Cadillac" may have been my life's ambition and I've "now arrived."

One final point on need satisfaction: in affluent societies, such as the United States, most people have been able to satisfy lower order needs fairly easily. Therefore they are striving to satisfy the higher level needs.

We should be aware of this in structuring promotional and advertising efforts. If possible or appropriate, our product or service should be shown as a way to satisfy these higher order needs.

COMPETITION

Let's now turn our attention to the final consideration in understanding the market. Who are our competitors? And, more important, why would someone buy or use our product or service instead of someone elses? This issue deals with our competitive advantage in the marketplace. We ought to be able to do something better or differently than others so that people will want our product or service instead of our competitor's.

This implies that we know who our competitors are, what products and services they offer, how our offering is different from theirs, and why ours is better than theirs. Unless we can answer these questions we don't have a good knowledge of the market.

In very competitive markets this information is absolutely essential for competent management, regardless of an individual manager's position in the organization. We would expect salespeople and salesmanagers to know this information. But *all* managers, including production, personnel, financial, and others, also need to know market information. How else can a manager guide and direct production, personnel, or financial resources unless a clear conception of the market and competitors exists? How can the organization's purpose and goals be articulated and followed unless we know our role vis-à-vis our competitors in the marketplace? How can we take advantage of environmental opportunities and avoid or reduce constraints unless we fully understand our market niche? We can't. Therefore, it is incumbent on all managers who wish to be competent to understand competition in the market place.

Competition in government services

Most business managers have little trouble grasping the need for knowledge of the marketplace and competition. Even those business managers in monopolistic situations, such as a telephone utility, understand the need for marketplace and competitive information. (After all, Ma Bell understands that there *are* communication alternatives besides the telephone and Western Electric equipment.) But many managers of government agencies do not fully realize the need for market and competitive information. This is because the whole development of marketing science in government lags far behind its development in business. Yet, government agencies often exist in a competitive situation. There are alternatives to the government's public employment service (private employment agencies, direct application, etc.).

There are alternatives to the state universities (private universities). In fact, within a state, there usually are *several* state universities. There are also alternatives to the state mental health hospital (private mental health care, private association mental health clinics). Furthermore, agencies at one level of government can compete with those at another level. For example, by law, if a state does not effectively operate a vocational rehabilitation program, the federal government will step in and operate it, although as of this writing it has not yet done so.

The point is that there are alternatives to many but not all government services. These alternatives act somewhat like competition acts in the private marketplace. What is usually missing, however, is a profit incentive. Without an incentive, a government agency may be reluctant to respond to competitive pressures. One reason why the U.S. government established the U.S. Postal Service as a private corporation was to make it more responsive to marketplace and competitive pressures. By making the organization respond to profit incentives, it is hoped that better mail service will result as the post office competes with United Parcel Service, other private delivery services, telephone, and teletype services.

Thus, prudent managers, even in government agencies, see the need to know about the market and the organization's particular competitive advantage.

WAYS OF KNOWING

To learn about the market, competent managers must first thoroughly understand economics and marketing. This information can be obtained through credit or noncredit university courses and workshops, or through a diligent program of reading and self-study.

Second, competent managers must understand their organization's marketing and promotion strategy. A thorough knowledge of product and service offerings and the competitive niche each product or service is meeting in the market vis-à-vis competitors is important. This requires knowledge of the organization's advertising messages. It also requires knowing competitor products and services and their respective advertising messages and promotional strategies.

Third, competent managers must know how their job and unit's performance ultimately ties in to customer and consumer need satisfaction. This knowledge is critical for unity of action and a sense of common purpose in the organization. Without this knowledge, we lack a sense of meaning in our work. We are not sure how our individual efforts act collectively to satisfy customer or consumer needs. Job descriptions, performance statements, MBO-type statements, and unit authority statements should provide this information to the manager. Figure 5.5 summarizes these key questions and information sources for learning about the market and job relationship.

1. What is economics and marketing?
   Sources: Credit and noncredit university courses
   Reading and self-study
2. What is the organization's market?
   Sources: Market research reports
3. What is the organization's marketing and promotional strategy?
   Sources: Product/service offerings
   Advertising and promotion messages
4. What is competitor marketing and promotion strategy?
   Sources: Competitor product/service offerings
   Competitor advertising and promotion messages
5. How is my job and unit's efforts tied to customer/consumer need satisfaction?
   Sources: Job descriptions
   Performance statements
   MBO-type statements
   Unit authority statements

Figure 5.5 Key questions and sources to understand the market and competition

CONCLUSION

A key aspect of the organization's outside environment that must be thoroughly understood by competent managers is the organization's market and competitive advantage. All managers regardless of level or type of organization—including government—must have this knowledge to perform effectively. Such knowledge gives a sense of purpose and unity of effort to managerial action. While such information is not always easy to come by, it is available through study of marketing and economics, organizational and competitor product/service offerings, and promotion and advertising messages. Furthermore, knowledge as to how individual management jobs and unit performance tie in to customer and consumer satisfaction is essential.

There are many other areas in understanding the market that were not addressed in this chapter. Only the key concepts have been highlighted. Conscientious managers will want to further study economics and marketing. Some important books in each of these areas are listed in the references at the end of this chapter.

In the next chapter we move to an examination of what managers should know about their organization.

QUESTIONS

1. What is the difference between a customer and a consumer?

2. Of the five factors involved in weighing the utility of a service or product, which ones do you believe to be most important for the services or products your organization provides?

3. Why should managers in government agencies be concerned about the market and competition for their agency services?

4. As part of understanding the market, should not demographic characteristics of customers (age, income, geographic location, etc.) also be studied? Why or why not? How are demographic variables related to why people buy and consume products or services?

5. What role does price play in buying behavior?

CASES AND EXERCISES

CASE 1: THE CUSTOMER IS ALWAYS RIGHT?

For several years automatic inflating air bags have been available as an option on many automobiles. Yet very few automobiles have been sold with this option. Not only do auto companies not advertise this option, but auto salespeople actually discourage customers from requesting it. The dealers carry very few, if any, cars in stock with the option. Should a customer ask if it is available, the salesperson often says it is but that it is expensive, unreliable, and will delay delivery of the auto for several months. Most customers, therefore, do not purchase this option.

Research to date, however, indicates that the air bag system is reliable and, if used widely, would greatly reduce death and injury in accidents. Furthermore, data show that the systems are not that expensive to install since the technology exists for mass production and installation.

Auto salespersons maintain that customers really do not want the option. Since so very few do request it, the actual expense of installing them in a few cars is extremely high. Consumer advocate groups argue, on the other hand, that customers do want the option since it would save many lives. The only reasons the system is not requested are because customers do not know about it since it is not advertised, and salespersons discourage buyers. Furthermore, these consumer groups believe the government should make these air bags a mandatory option since it is in the best interest of the country to reduce injury and death on the highway.

Questions

1. In a situation such as this, are customers knowledgeable enough to make a solid judgment as to the worth of the air bag? Why or why not?

2. What responsibility does the federal government have to speak on behalf of the consumer?

3. What responsibilities do auto makers and dealers have with regard to air bags? Should they simply give people what they want or should they educate them so that they want something different?

CASE 2: GOVERNMENT DOES NOT SELL ANYTHING

The idea that government actually sells a service is absurd. People do not voluntarily buy a government service. We collect taxes and provide services people want as a legislative body mandates. In other words, people elect representatives to speak for them when passing laws. Taxes are raised to pay for the services. People do not elect to pay or not to pay taxes. Everyone *has* to pay taxes. Thus, they do not voluntarily exchange something of value for something else of value. There is no selling and hence no buying.

Since there is no selling or buying, there are no markets or competitors. Sure there are consumers of government services, but there are no *customers*. A welfare client does not pay for the services provided. A user of the state job placement service uses it at no cost. It's free.

I believe I can speak with authority on this matter since I've been a manager in both business and government organizations. I worked with a large business firm for ten years and have been with a state agency for six years since then. We were concerned with markets and competition in business because we had to be. We were out to make a profit. In government, we're not here to make a profit so why should we care about markets and competition? Besides that, there is such little competition for government services, it's hardly worth getting stirred up about.

Questions

1. Do you agree that there is no selling or buying of government services?

2. Do you agree that people *have* to pay taxes? (Consider here tax revolts such as Proposition 13-type actions or the Boston Tea Party.)

3. Are government services free to the user as this person maintains? Explain.

Major Types of Customers	Major Types of Consumers (if different from customers)	Major Product/ Service Offered to Each Type	Key Utility	Consumer Needs Met	Consumer Needs Not Met	Your Job and Unit Tie-In

Figure 5.6 Market matrix

EXPERIENCE: WHAT IS YOUR ORGANIZATION'S MARKET?

This exercise requires you to complete a matrix (Figure 5.6) that ties in your organization's major product/service offerings with customer/consumer needs. It also asks you to tie in your particular job with these offerings.

If your organization provides a wide range of products or services, pick those which are key to your organization's success. If a wide variety of customers/consumers are served, pick those who are most critical to the organization's services.

You might think about your organization's market and general marketing strategy prior to completing Figure 5.6. You might also review the questions and sources listed in Figure 5.5. After completing the matrix, you might wish to compare your responses with others in the organization.

REFERENCES

Engle, James F.; Kollat, David T.; and Blackwell, Roger D. *Consumer Behavior.* New York: Holt, Rinehart and Winston, Inc., 1973.
   A well-accepted, comprehensive analysis of buyer and consumer behavior. Well written but requires some previous study of consumer behavior to understand thoroughly.

Kotler, Philip. *Marketing Management.* Englewood Cliffs, N.J.: Prentice-Hall, Inc., 1976.
   An advanced and comprehensive treatment of marketing management. Requires some previous study of marketing to grasp fully.

Maslow, Abraham H. "A Theory of Human Motivation." *Psychological Review* 50 (1943): 370–396.
   The classic where Maslow sets out his theory of human motivation and the hierarchy of needs.

McCarthy, E. Jerome. *Basic Marketing: A Managerial Approach.* 6th ed. Homewood, Ill.: Richard D. Irwin, Inc., 1979.
   The most widely used college text in basic marketing, the book takes a managerial approach. Quite comprehensive.

Rosenberg, Larry J. *Marketing.* Englewood Cliffs, N.J.: Prentice-Hall, Inc., 1977.
   Integrates management, consumers, and society under an economic umbrella. Includes cases for analysis.

Samuelson, Paul A. *Economics.* 19th ed. New York: McGraw-Hill Book Co., 1976.
   The classic introductory work on economics, which is also quite comprehensive. Well written and easily understood even by those with no previous economic training and education.

Schoner, Bertram, and Uhl, Kenneth P. *Marketing Research.* New York: John Wiley & Sons, Inc. 1976.
   A set of thirteen booklets in a slipcase, this resource sets out the various steps involved in conducting marketing research.

Stanton, William J. *Fundamentals of Marketing.* New York: McGraw-Hill, 1978.
   A comprehensive introductory look on marketing which takes a total business systems approach.

6
What Should a Manager Know About the Organization?

To efficiently and effectively manufacture and sell a lightweight high quality surfboard along the East and Gulf Coasts of the United States at a price lower than competitors' products.

We believe that each child should have the opportunity to grow intellectually, emotionally, and culturally to the fullest extent of his or her potential and, we intend to offer an innovative elementary academic curricula which best fosters this growth in each child.

To be a profit and product leader in our industry, we intend to grow rapidly, diversifying our product and service line to such an extent that we are internationally recognized as the leader in the recreational industry.

To provide efficient and effective client counseling services to the greatest number of clients throughout the state with the fewest number of employees at the least possible cost consistent with federal and state laws and regulations.

By reading these statements do you get a sense of purpose for each of the organizations the statements represent? Could you speculate what some goals are for each of the organizations? Does your organization have a purpose statement?

Competent managers must know the organization where they work. This means that not only must the organization's purpose be known, but also its goals, products and services, structure, policy, procedures, and key personnel. One must know one's home.

In this chapter we look at each of these important areas of organizational knowledge. We begin by focusing on organizational purpose and how goals evolve from this purpose. Next we look at the development of structure, policy, and procedure as ways to achieve goals. We then examine the role of key personnel in the organization.

PURPOSE AND GOALS

The old saying, "If you don't know where you're going, any road will take you there" has much meaning in organizational life. Purpose and goals provide a sense of direction which guide organizational and individual effort. Every organization has a purpose. It may not be clearly written down anyplace, and it may only exist in the minds of a few top key managers, but it is there. Prudent managers know what this purpose is. Not only is the organizational purpose known, but so is the purpose of the particular unit where the manager works.

Characteristics of purpose statements

Purpose statements should provide broad general guidance for organizational effort, reflecting the organization's explicit recognition of its environmental opportunities and constraints. They should recognize the market and indicate, in a broad sense, the product or service being delivered to the market. They should make a commitment to profitability (if a business) and to economic efficiency and effectiveness.

Purpose statements should be developed through broad consensus of the top managers and major owners of the organization. They should be made explicit and written copies sent to all employees as well as owners. For example, they should be a key part of the annual report. Included in these purpose statements should be a *differentiation* of the organization from other organizations in the industry. The statements should say what is unique about the particular organization vis-à-vis competitors.

The statements should be continuing, yet they should be reviewed periodically. That is, they should provide general, overall guidance for at least three to five years, but they should be reviewed annually and modified if necessary. They should serve as a broad or overall goal for action. As a broad goal, they should act as a foundation for specific organization goals and objectives. Specific goals and objectives should *evolve* from the organization and unit purpose statements.

Method of setting purpose statements

It is not always easy to develop a purpose statement if none exists. The first step is to go to the organization's charter or, if a governmental agency, the law which established it. This will provide initial guidance, but it is usually too vague to tell us much. We must realize that the statement represents owner and top management's perception of environmental and market opportunities and constraints, as shown in Figure 6.1. If we know these perceptions and constraints, we're well on our way to understanding the organization's purpose.

We also must understand that there is some bargaining and negotiating in setting purpose statements. Owners negotiate with key managers who in turn negotiate with other managers. Government and consumer groups have their input. Unions and employees impact on the statement. What evolves, therefore, is usually a consensus statement.

Key managers and owners interpret environmental opportunities and constraints in terms of the managerial philosophy and present and potential resources of the organization. What results, then, is the organization's purpose. Once this is known, then the purpose of each unit in the organization can be developed. Each unit's purpose should tie in to and be consistent with the organization's purpose.

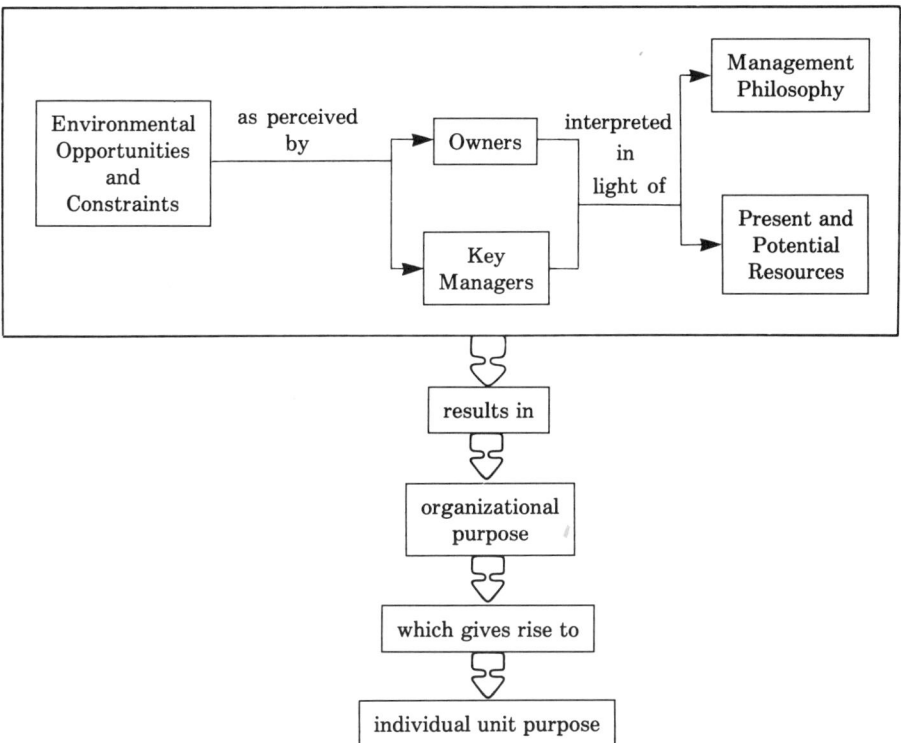

Figure 6.1 Interpretation of opportunities and constraints for organizational purpose

Organizational goals

Goals evolve from purpose. They are specific, measurable, result-oriented targets. They state what is to be achieved, not how it is to be achieved. They answer the question, "What do we intend to accomplish?"

All organizations have goals whether they be written down or not. Some organizations, in fact, many organizations, use a very explicit method of goal setting known as Management by Objectives (MBO). Sometimes this is called Program Planning Budgeting Systems (PPBS), Zero-Base Budgeting (ZBB), Plan of Service, IMPACT, or a hundred other variations. Whatever it is called, it is still Management by Objectives. (A rose by any other name is still a rose.)

MBO-type programs are generally good for an organization, provided they are implemented properly and don't result in a blizzard of paperwork or a narrow-minded devotion to accomplishment of written objectives "come hell or high water." Too often, organizations treat written objectives as if they were cast in concrete instead of the somewhat flexible goals they should be. Also, organizations sometimes achieve short-range objectives at the expense of long-term ones. MBO can place too much emphasis on immediate payout.

But, given these limitations, MBO-type exercises or programs are relatively good ways to identify organization and unit goals or objectives. MBO is addressed in more depth in Chapter 9. However, since this is not a book on MBO, you are referred to one of the many excellent texts and handbooks on the subject listed at the end of this chapter and at the end of Chapter 9.

The need for goals. People do better if they're working toward some target rather than just putting eight hours in every day on a job. It is not always easy to develop goals for each job, but it should be easy to develop goals for every unit in every organization—be it a business, government, church, or charitable organization. Naturally, it is sometimes difficult to quantify intangible service delivery, but there are ways. For example, see the list of objectives for an elementary school in Figure 6.2. Education is very hard to quantify, yet this school has done a reasonably good job of coming up with some specific, measurable objectives.

The objectives in Figure 6.2 should result in accomplishing the school's purpose which should, in turn, result in accomplishing organization goals and purpose. In other words, unit goals and objectives tie in with unit purpose which tie in with organizational goals/objectives and purpose. This relationship is shown in Figure 6.3.

Types of goals/objectives. There are long-term (more than five years), intermediate term (two to five years), and short-term (one year or less) objectives. Some objectives are improvement-oriented (to increase sales 10 per-

PURPOSE AND GOALS   85

**Indian Hills Elementary School
School-Wide Objectives
1981-82**

1. To ensure that the median reading level of each grade is at least 10 percent above the statewide norm for that grade.
2. To ensure that the median mathematic level of each grade is at least equal to the statewide norm for that grade.
3. To ensure that at least 80 percent of the fifth graders who take the statewide functional literacy assessment test pass the test.
4. To increase the percent of parents participating in the PTO to 15 percent of all parents.
5. To install a central air conditioning system by June 1982.
6. To develop and implement a program in music appreciation.
7. To begin participating with other schools in the district in the intramural basketball and softball program.
8. To hire six new, highly qualified teachers.
9. To operate within all budget projections.
10. To offer at least 144 hours of inservice training suitable for teachers at all grade levels and special disciplines.
11. To secure at least $75,000 from the School Board in federal teacher-aid money.

Figure 6.2 Example of objectives for an elementary school

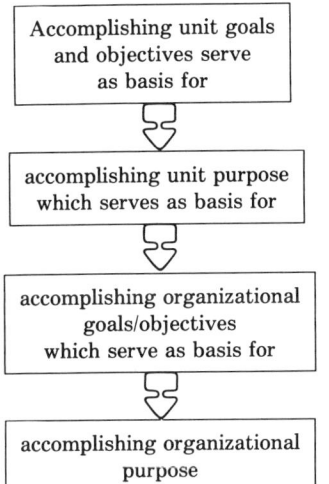

Figure 6.3 Relationship of unit goals and purpose to organizational goals and purpose

cent, to reduce turnover 30 percent, etc.), and some are equilibriums in nature (to maintain present market share, to continue 0.1 quality control reject rate on Milax component, etc.). Some objectives are organizationally oriented (expand marketing effort into the upper midwest, etc.), and some are personal (to improve my knowledge of EEO by completing company-sponsored course, etc.).

Some objectives satisfy customers (to offer three major price reduction sales this year); some satisfy government regulations (to reduce effluent from Plain City Plant by 50 percent); some satisfy employees (to increase wages 7.5 percent); some satisfy owners (to improve price-earnings ratio by 50 percent); and still others are addressed to other groups such as suppliers (to develop at least three viable sources of supply on each major product component by 1981).

Every organization should develop each type of objective, and every competent manager will know these for the organization and will develop them for his or her individual unit. Writing and knowing objectives is no simple matter, but the alternative is aimless wandering or managing by reaction or crisis.

STRUCTURE, POLICY, PROCEDURE

Structure, policy, and procedure should exist to facilitate accomplishment of purpose and goals. It is sometimes the reverse in organizations, especially heavily bureaucratic ones, where the sheer weight of the organization rests heavily on managerial shoulders, thus inhibiting action. All skilled managers know how the organization is structured, know its *key* policies, and know *important* procedures, which prevents them from getting bogged down in trivia.

Structure

Organizations have two structures. First there is the *formal* structure—the organization chart written on paper. This shows the organization's *officially sanctioned* reporting and authority relationships as well as its official communication channels. It may look like an elongated pyramid and thus be called a *tall* structure, or it might be a wide pyramid and be called a *flat* structure. One's position in the organization is shown in the formal organization chart. The job title, one's superior, subordinates, and area of job responsibility are all specified in the chart.

At most, this tells only half the story; for superimposed on this formal structure is an *informal* structure which is not officially sanctioned by the organization but rather *evolves* from the people in the organization. This structure consists of informal reporting relationships, the grapevine (informal communication channels), informal power networks, informal leaders, and informal work groups. This structure is harder to know than the formal structure, but competent managers know it because, in many organizations, this informal structure is more important than the formal! After showing someone the formal organization chart, people in these organizations say, "Now let me tell you how it *really* operates."

While it is difficult to chart the informal organization, there are a few tools. Moreno's sociometry is one method, grapevine charting another, and the Least Preferred Co-Worker (LPC) still another. More detail on each of these methods is provided in the reference list at the end of the chapter. Using these methods could result in the hypothetical example shown in Figure 6.4.

Sometimes even the best manager is hobbled by an ineffective structure. A rigid, mechanistic bureaucracy inhibits forward motion in an organization just as a square bow would on a ship. Yet those managers who know how to use the informal structure quickly slice through the bureaucratic maze and redtape. It is easy to hide behind mother bureaucracy in claiming why something can *not* be done. It takes foresight, courage, and perception to climb out of the protective bureaucratic cacoon. We'll look more at this issue later in Chapter 19.

Policy and procedure

Just as structure exists to facilitate the accomplishment of purpose and goals, so should policy and procedure. We often view policies and procedures as straightjackets to action instead of helpful guides. In some organizations policy and procedures are so specific, so inflexible, so rigidly enforced, and so unchanging that they actually *prevent* goal accomplishment. People in these organizations exist to meet policy and procedure, not to meet goals and objectives. Instead of being a means to an end, policy and procedure become an end in themselves.

Managers fool themselves if they believe they can write a policy or procedure that could cover every conceivable situation that might arise. Impossible as it is, some managers in some organizations actually try to do this. Their efforts result in policy manuals several inches, if not feet, thick. And once it gets in the manual—watch out—it will never change. It's been etched in granite. The result is that subordinates never exercise any initiative, innovation, or problem-solving behavior. If a problem comes up, they simply look up the answer in the policy manual and rigidly apply it regardless of the particularly unique circumstances.

Competent managers do not write action-shackling policy and procedure. They view policies as guides to behavior, not detailed restrictive rules inhibiting flexibility and initiative. Competent managers also know impor-

88 WHAT SHOULD A MANAGER KNOW ABOUT THE ORGANIZATION?

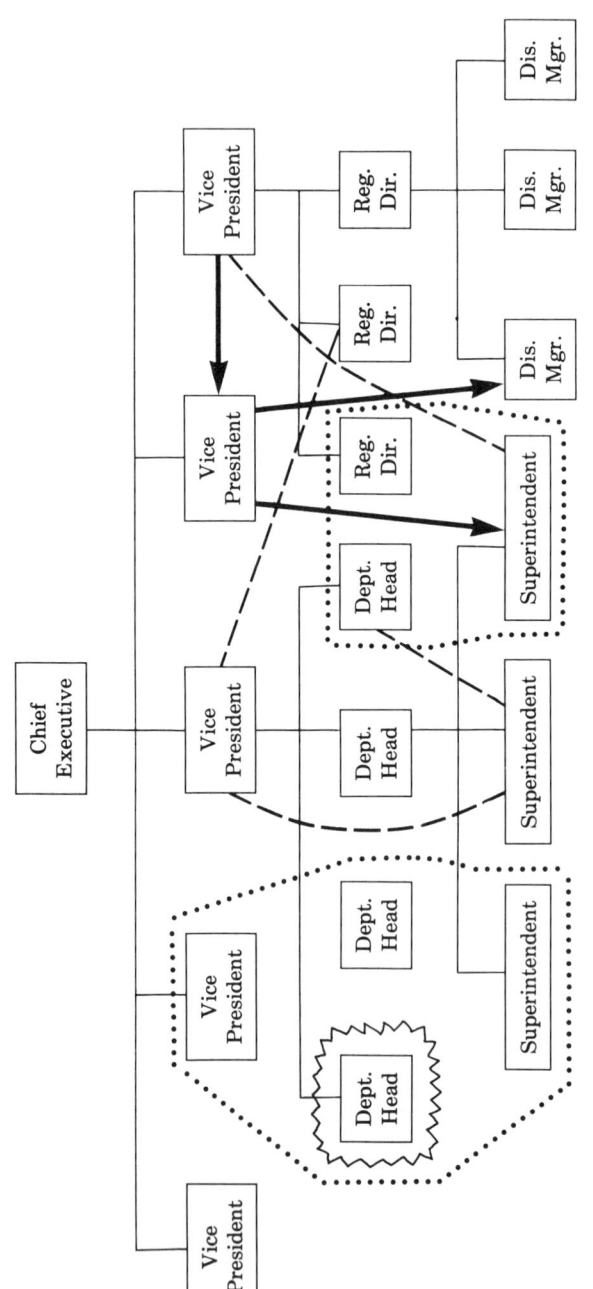

Figure 6.4 An example of a formal and informal structure

tant organization policy and procedure and don't bother with the trivia. Further, they work to reduce the trivia, to simplify policy statements, and to update and keep important policies and procedures flexible. When faced with excessively confining policies or procedures, they find a way around them so that performance does not suffer. Finally, competent managers make sure that subordinates are fully aware of and understand *important* organizational policy and procedure.

KEY PERSONNEL

We now move to the next important area of organizational knowledge—the key personnel in the organization. These are the people with the power, authority, and skills that are highly valued by the organization. They are on the move—upwardly mobile.

Effective managers know these people, not in a self-serving or subservient way, but rather in a collegial way. This professional relationship is nurtured and built on trust and mutual respect. Competent managers know they are good and do not need to brag about it. Actions speak louder than words. Nor do competent managers need to make excuses or rationalizations for mistakes. Sure, mistakes will be made, but they will be infrequent, relatively minor, and rapidly corrected.

Furthermore, competent managers can learn a great deal from associating with key managers. They ask to serve on committees and task forces with them and they do a superior job. They ask to be transferred to key manager units. They avoid working for a manager who is not going any place and who is viewed by the organization as mediocre deadwood floating in circles. There is some truth to the old saying, "You are judged by the company you keep." Working for a bright and aggressive manager gives one visibility in the organization.

Finally, competent managers are concerned with developing a mentor in the organization and as acting as mentors for others in the organization. An organizational mentor is someone high up in the organization who takes a personal interest in someone else down in the organization. The mentor coaches, guides, and makes sure that the person being watched is not overlooked by the organization for promotion or merit salary increases. The use of mentors is becoming increasingly more common in organizations.

PRODUCTS AND SERVICES

The final area of knowledge important in the organization is the organization's product and service line. Many concepts in this area were reviewed in the last chapter, so we will highlight only a few important additional areas here.

New products and services

Progressive organizations have strong new product and service development operations. They are innovators in the market. They have strong market research units that assess changing consumer interests and wants. Furthermore, these organizations actively acquire other organizations with strong product/service lines.

Competent managers associate themselves with new product/service development. Not only are they aware of these developments, but they assist with them as appropriate. These managers believe in the old saying, "Either you get better or you get worse; you never stay the same." The rationale for this is that if your organization is not developing new products and improving existing ones, another organization will. Thus, relative to the market, your organization does not stay the same; instead it declines.

Key products and services

Competent managers are associated with the key product/service divisions of the organization. They know the firm's bread and butter product offerings and are not stuck in Siberia working on products or services that are of only tangential interest to the organization (unless, of course, these tangential products or services are new ones that will soon be the mainstay of the organization's activity).

Every organization has key products and services that provide the bulk of the revenues for the organization or commands the firm's share of the budget. One estimate is that 20 or 30 percent of the product/service offerings provide 70 or 80 percent of the revenues for many organizations. These bread and butter lines of the organization give high visibility to associated managers.

WAYS OF KNOWING

How do managers learn about organizations? How do we find out about purpose, goals, structure, policy, procedure, key personnel, products, and services? We learn by observing, reading, experiencing, and talking with key people.

Most organizations have MBO-type statements that provide information on purpose and objectives. Often such statements appear in the annual report, orientation pamphlets, or public relations documents. Of course, just because these items are printed and bound in fancy books and brochures does *not* mean they are actually followed or used. Prudent managers can distinguish pretty paper statements from the actual operational purpose and objectives of the organization.

Formal structure is shown through a formal organization chart which often appears in the annual report or orientation package. Informal structure is more difficult to determine. Perhaps one of the more systematic methods mentioned earlier in the chapter could be used. However, more often, direct observation and talking with key people gives one the rudiments of the informal structure.

Policy and procedure is almost always written out someplace in the organization. Some organizations have quite comprehensive policy, procedure, and practice manuals. The trick is, of course, to determine which policies, procedures, and practices are really important. Experience, observation, and talking with key personnel will usually answer this question.

Key personnel usually stand out in the organization. They may have positions of authority and, therefore, can be identified from the organization chart. Or they may be associated with key product/service lines. However, it usually is also necessary to talk with others and to observe who really makes things happen to know who are key personnel. Also, people who have been promoted very rapidly over the past few years are usually key personnel.

Key products/services are usually featured in accounting reports and the annual report. Careful study of these will indicate which products and services make the greatest contribution to sales, profit, or budget. New products/services being developed are often kept secret until they appear on the market. However, some product development or market research reports may be available for study. Also, by talking with key people in the organization, it is sometimes possible to learn about new product/service development. Being aware of new product introductions of competitors might also give an indication of what your organization might be coming up with soon.

CONCLUSION

Competent managers know their organization. They actively search and question until they learn as much as they can about how their organization operates. Not only do they know the developing trends in organization action, they also learn as much as they can about present and potential product/service offerings. They understand organizational purpose and objectives and see how their unit's purpose and objectives tie into them. They know their organization's structure, important policy, procedure, and key personnel. They also make a conscientious effort to ensure that their subordinates know these aspects of organizational life.

In the next chapter we examine the importance of knowing and understanding the people at work in the organization. This examination builds on our understanding of key people and expands it to a general understanding of human behavior in the organization.

QUESTIONS

1. Do all organizations have a purpose even if it may not be written down? Explain your answer.

2. Do organizations have goals? Have you had experience with an organization that did not seem to have any goals?

3. Why do you think informal structure always develops in an organization? Is this because of some inherent weakness in the formal structure?

4. How can a manager get to know key managers without appearing to be an apple-polisher or name dropper?

5. Do you have any influence in setting the goals of your organization? Of your unit? Why or why not?

CASES AND EXERCISES

CASE 1: BUT EVERYBODY DOES IT

"Are you sure I can claim these charges on my travel expense account, Fred?"

"Sure, Jan, everyone does it."

"But the travel policy says that first class air travel and Expenso Rent-A-Car is only to be used in an emergency situation."

"Yeah, I know it says that, but this company can't expect us to ride with the peasants and to rent our cars from El Cheapo. Come on, we are a prestigious outfit and we've got to make a good impression. Anyway, the company can afford it. You're just still too new, Jan."

"I know, but I sure don't want to get off on the wrong foot, Fred. Maybe I better call Brad on this."

"Why? You don't need to bother him. He'll just tell you the same thing I did."

"Another thing, Fred. It says that the procedure for expense reimbursement requires receipts and that only if receipts are provided should the reimbursement form be sent through. But I notice you sent yours through without any receipts."

"Yeah, I know I did. No one saves their receipts. It's just too much trouble. I'm on the road eight or nine days at a time, two or three times a month. I'll be damned if I'm going to save all those receipts. We all feel the same way about it, Jan. No one has said anything about it yet."

"Then why does this company have this travel policy and travel procedure in the first place if no one follows it? Look, there must be a reason for the policy and procedure. I'm not going to stick my neck out. I'm still new here. You guys have been around a while. They're not about to fire you. I'm not taking any chances."

"Well, I wouldn't follow the policy or procedure if I were you. You follow it, and they'll soon expect the rest of us to follow it. Just go along with us on this. As far as a reason for the policy goes, there probably was one once, but it's been forgotten. Some ole' green eyeshade accountant probably wrote it up long ago. If it were really important the company would be enforcing it."

Questions

1. Is unenforced policy and procedure still policy and procedure? Explain.

2. Should Jan follow the travel policy and receipt procedure or ignore it as Fred wants her to? What are the consequences of each action?

3. What action should the company take in view of the present situation?

CASE 2: WHAT GOALS?

It sounds nice that every organization should have a purpose and a list of goals/objectives. It makes sense and it's logical; but why doesn't it work that way? Oh sure, I know lots of organizations have well written purpose statements and fancy, impressive lists of objectives, but why don't they follow them? We talk about laying all these things out in a nice planning document but they're just PR exercises. They are used more to impress outside groups than as guides to managerial action. Often the real purpose and goals of the organization are implicit. They aren't the ones that are written down and shown to everyone. This is what a manager should know, yet these are so hard to find out. They are often just the personal goals of a few managers.

Even though these personal goals may not reflect the written organizational goals, they become in effect *the* organizational goals by default. No one pays attention to the fancy goals all neatly typed up and bound in folders.

Of course, some organizations don't have any goals at all. They just drift along, bumping from one crisis to another. One sees this most often in government where everyone is playing CYA (cover your ass).

So it sounds nice that it's important to learn about an organization's purpose and goals, but let's face it, it's damn near impossible to do.

Questions

1. In your opinion, do organizations have a purpose and goals? If they do, can one learn what they are? Explain your answers.

2. Do you agree with this individual that more often than not the written purpose and goals are virtually meaningless? Why or why not?

EXERCISE: WHAT IS YOUR ORGANIZATION'S PURPOSE AND MAJOR GOALS?

1. In fifty words or less write what you believe to be your organization's purpose.

2. How do you know that this is its purpose?

3. List five to eight key objectives for your organization.

4. How do you know that these are key objectives?

5. Ask your superior to write the organization's purpose and five to eight key objectives. Are they similar to what you came up with?

6. What are the implications if your perception of the organization's purpose and goals differ from your superior's? What specific effects, if any, would this difference have on your job?

7. You might wish to repeat questions 5 and 6 with some of your key subordinates.

REFERENCES

Davis, Keith. *Human Behavior at Work.* 5th ed. New York: McGraw-Hill, 1977.
   Chapter 16 has an excellent, easy to understand discussion of the informal organization. Moreno's sociometry is also discussed.

Fiedler, Fred E. *A Theory of Leadership Effectiveness.* New York: McGraw-Hill, 1967.
   Presents a discussion of and the form for the Least Preferred Co-worker (LPC) scale.

Knippen, Jay T. "Grapevine Communication: Management and Employees." *Journal of Business Research* (January 1974): 47–58.
   Managers were found to be more knowledgable of informal information than nonmanagers in a study of 170 managers. The higher the level in the organization, the greater the amount of knowledge.

McConkey, Dale D. *Management by Objectives for Staff Managers.* Chicago: Vantage Press, 1972.
Staff managers have a particularly difficult time in writing quantifiable objectives. This book provides guidance for staff managers to help them become part of the MBO process.

Morrisey, George L. *Management by Objectives and Results for Business and Industry.* 2nd ed. Reading, Mass: Addison-Wesley Publishing Co., 1977.
An excellent handbook which discusses the complete Management by Objectives process. Good emphasis on mission (purpose), determination, and writing goals and objectives.

Morrisey, George L. *Management by Objectives and Results in the Public Sector.* Reading, Mass: Addison-Wesley Publishing Co., 1976.
Good handbook which applies the MBO process to governmental organizations.

Raia, Anthony P. *Managing By Objectives.* Glenview, Ill.: Scott, Foresman and Co., 1974.
A comprehensive, yet concise view of MBO which deals with the actual implementation of the process.

Reif, William E.; Manczka, Robert M.; and Newstrom, John W. "Perceptions of the Formal and Informal Organizations: Objective Measurement through the Semantic Differential Technique." *Academy of Management Journal* (September 1973): 389–403.
A good example of the semantic differential technique to chart both formal and informal structure.

7
What Should a Manager Know About People?

"Janet, what's the matter with you? This is the third time you've typed this letter and it's still full of errors."

"But, I did what you told me to Ms. Pitts. Why didn't I get a raise? I followed all of your orders."

"Bill, I need some help on that quality control report. Are you free next Wednesday?"

"Get in here, Leitz! I want to see you immediately!"

"Nancy, your trouble is that you are too quiet and withdrawn. You've got to be more demanding around here. The squeaky wheel gets the grease."

Sound familiar? Everyday we interact with our boss, subordinates, and peer managers in a complicated way. Each of these groups make demands and requests on our time and expect something from us. We know we cannot be all things to all people, but on the other hand, we want to be cooperative and helpful. How to balance these conflicting demands placed on our time by others with whom we interact is a very real challenge to effective management.

In this chapter we discuss this balancing act by examining some basic concepts about people in organizations. Of course, no book of this length can comprehensively examine all facets of human behavior at work. Yet, there are some key concepts that we should look at that help us to understand this complex role we all play as managers in dealing with others.

NEEDS, DEMAND, EXPECTATIONS, AND REQUESTS

A common definition of management is "getting things done through others." Inherent in the managerial role is being able to work effectively with others. This effective working relationship one builds with others can take many forms. The proper way depends on the situation faced. This is known as the *contingency theory of management*. The proper management style in dealing with others is contingent on the particular circumstances faced.

For example, a military combat team under fire would call for a much different management style than a supervisor of a group of Ph.D. research chemists at a pharmaceutical house. The time, personal background, and task factors all vary. A strong, quick-acting, autocratic style appropriate for the military situation would contrast sharply with the facilitative, deliberative, democratic style appropriate for the chemists.

But how do we know these contingencies? How do we know which style is right under certain circumstances? To understand these questions we need to understand the nature of the needs, demands, expectations, and requests made on our time by top management, superiors, subordinates, and peer managers. We need to understand these in light of the task to be done and in light of our needs, demands, requests, and expectations we make on others.

The ledger sheet

People act to satisfy needs. As we saw in our examination of consumer behavior, Maslow's need hierarchy is one convenient and accurate way to explain need satisfaction. The same explanation applies in understanding need satisfaction by managers and employees. When we work with others, constant exchange is occurring. We give something in order to get something in return either immediately or at some future date. By the same token, when people interact with us they have the same expectations—they do in order to receive.

We keep track of these exchanges in a ledger which we keep tucked in our head. For some actions, we do not record much on the ledger if we view them as appropriate actions to be performed in the normal course of our work. After all, that is what we are being paid for, and we may view pay and continued employment from the organization as an approximately equal exchange for our normal job efforts. But when we go above and beyond the call of duty for someone—either a supervisor, peer manager, or even a subordinate—we expect something extra in return in the not too distant future. Perhaps that something will be a strong recommendation for a desired promotion, or perhaps an extra year-end bonus. Whatever it may be, we expect at some point to collect on that exchange.

While doing this, most of us try to keep our credits and debits in approximate balance. We do not want to be beholding to too many people, nor do we necessarily want a lot of people to be beholding to us at any one time. In other words, we don't necessarily want to be labeled solely as a "taker" or a "giver." Such an exclusive label could type us as greedy or as a patsy in the organization.

Some managers do not ever want to be beholding to anybody. They want to be free and independent; thus, they may be quick to do favors but seldom, if ever, rely on others for favors. While these managers are relatively rare in today's complex interdependent organizations, there is much to be said about getting too far in debt to others.

Analysis of these issues has become fairly sophisticated. A whole area of organizational science has developed known as *exchange theory* which is the study of these givers and takers. Such factors as the importance and timing of the exchanges as well as the status among people making the exchange are subjects of study. However, our purpose in examining this area is not to delve deeply into the various complexities but, rather, to see it as one major underlying basis to understand people in organizations.

Demands versus requests versus expectations

"Will you please complete this report by February 12, Gloria? I need it for my 8:00 A.M. meeting on the 13th."

Is this statement, even though in question form, a demand or a request? So often we receive and make demands on others which we tactfully couch in language to make them appear as requests. A request can voluntarily be carried out or refused. There is always some cost in refusing a request, but that cost will be less than the cost for refusing to carry out a demand. Demands are job requirements that technically cannot be refused without jeopardizing one's job. They are duties, functions, and responsibilities that must be carried out in the job.

Both demands and requests are related to the fulfillment of expectations—both ours and others. We may be expected to carry out all requests made of us by our boss because that is the tradition in our organization. We may expect to receive refusals on requests made to peer managers from time to time since people in our organization may be more concerned with satisfying their own immediate supervisor rather than with cooperating with others. Furthermore, these expectations are influenced by the balance on our ledger. We may expect action on a request made to a superior because we've built up a good size credit balance on which we wish to collect. On the other hand, we may not expect action even on a demand made to a subordinate to whom we owe much.

In determining whether a demand or request made on us should be fulfilled, the following questions should be answered:

1. Is the action required under my present job duties and responsibilities?
2. What are the expectations of the person making the demand or request?
3. What is the balance on my ledger sheet with this individual?
4. What are the costs of refusal?
5. Will I be in a position to expect reciprocity in the near future?

A model showing how these issues are related is shown in Figure 7.1. The model implicitly assumes that demands will be carried out and that the only real choice exists with requests. Of course, we could refuse a job demand, but this is usually only at great cost and could result in termination. Since demands are sometimes disguised as requests, the second block in the model is critical. The request could be, in reality, a tactfully stated demand.

By following the model with each demand or request we receive, we will weigh or balance one demand or request against others. Implicitly we begin to determine how important demands and requests are relative to other demands and requests. This then becomes a major factor in our deliberations and serves as the basis for us to manage our time as we will see in Chapter 16.

Also, by following the model prior to dealing with a subordinate or peer manager on a given issue, we can try to predict the response prior to our initiating the demand or request. By determining how our request or demand is likely to be received, we should be better able to word and time our request or demand to obtain the kind of response we want.

TOP MANAGEMENT

Top management speaks for the whole organization. They also sometimes speak for groups outside the organization, especially governmental regulators, suppliers, or powerful public interest or consumer groups. Demands and requests made by the top management group are usually ignored at great peril to the individual manager. Even when the chain of command is broken and the request or demand comes not through the immediate superior, but directly from the top, the individual manager usually should comply and inform his or her immediate superior later. However, there are times when the action will be very disruptive to normal expected work output. At these times, the manager should first clear actions with the immediate superior prior to carrying out top management requests.

Top management requests that break the chain of command should be few and far between. They should occur only under emergency situations. Competent top managers should not be concerned with managing subordi-

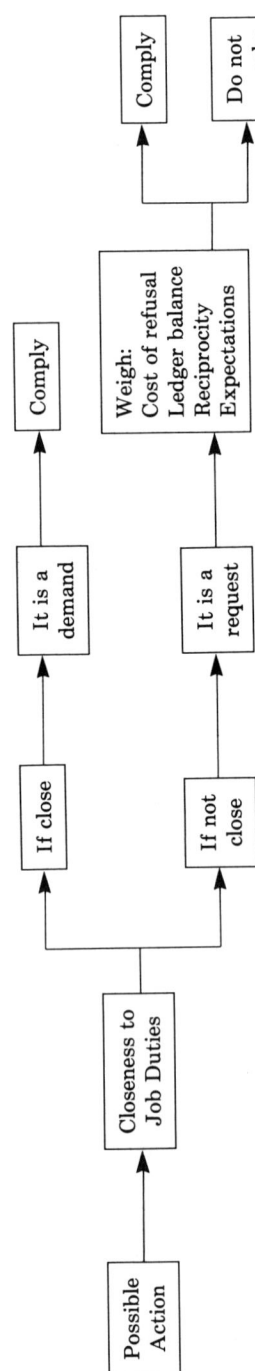

Figure 7.1 Responding to demands and requests

nates three or four levels below them. There are other managers appointed for this purpose. Yet, some top managers want to have their hands in every pie and so will create a psuedo-crisis in order to have excuses for breaking the chain of command. This makes these top managers feel important and powerful, and they can point with pride to their seventy- and eighty-hour work weeks they put in in order to manage people three or four levels below them. If there is a situation where top management continually breaks the chain of command, there is little delegation occurring, and the organization has serious problems.

IMMEDIATE SUPERIOR

Demands and requests from one's immediate superior are more likely to happen than top management demands. These can be top management or peer manager requests transmitted by the immediate superior, or they can be initiated by the immediate superior.

In general, these should fall within the negotiated scope of action—the job description—of the subordinate. If there is consensus between the superior and subordinate as to one's job duties, functions, authority, responsibility, and objectives to be reached, there should be little disagreement as to whether a superior's demands or requests should be followed. In other words, consensus on these issues goes a long way toward resolving superior-subordinate conflict on expectations as to what should and should not be done. Refer to Figure 7.2.

Too often, superiors do not spend enough time or effort spelling out these expectations with subordinates and achieving consensus. Simply relying on a vague or outdated job description is not enough. More time spent in achieving this consensus will result in the less time spent in obtaining subordinate compliance with superior demands and requests.

Competent managers work with superiors in helping them to shape their expectations of subordinate performance. If the superior does not initiate this action, then the subordinate should initiate it. The attempt should not be to come up with a list of detailed functions, duties, and so on, so as to straightjacket action. Rather, the attempt should be to come up with a reasonable consensus on action—one that is neither too broad nor too specific. Then, if a request or demand arises on which the subordinate is not clear, it should take little effort to see where that fits in the consensus mold.

Of course, precedent has an effect on determining what is legitimate and what is not. Sometimes this precedent has developed under a previous jobholder: "Jane always made the coffee in the office so you will too, even though it is not part of your job description." The new job holder should attempt to redefine these expectations based on precedent if he or she does not know them or agree with them. Immediate adherence with past prece-

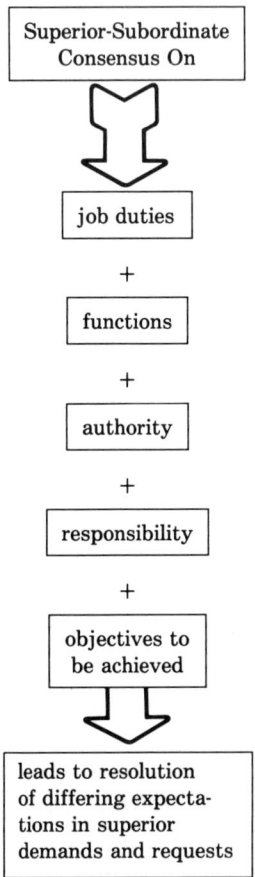

Figure 7.2 Superior-subordinate consensus

dent will be viewed as an implicit okay on the subordinate's part and the superior will expect continued action in the future.

Of course, other precedents will develop as the new employee continues in the job. Thus, if a subordinate is asked to do something considered outside the job scope, and yet decides to do it anyway, it is up to the subordinate to ensure that the superior understands that carrying out this action is not to be interpreted as a precedent.

Action by default

There are occasions when a subordinate must act for a superior because the superior neglects to act. In effect, the subordinate covers for the superior. This action may be necessary to protect the operations of the organization or unit. It usually occurs in an area that the superior does not consider to be an area of job responsibility. For example, I am familiar with a public utility where several subordinates spent time in the evenings speaking to civic clubs because the chief executive officer (CEO) did not do this. Many key managers believed this was a duty of the CEO, but the CEO did not perceive it as such. Since a strong liaison with community groups was essential to the health of the organization, managers subordinate to the CEO informally took on these speaking chores even though they were never asked to by the CEO.

On other occasions, subordinates will cover or hide mistakes made by superiors without being asked to do so. They do this because if the errors were to become known, it would damage not only the career of the superior but also that of the subordinates and the health of the unit or the entire organization.

Of course, subordinates must be careful covering or acting in default for superiors, or they soon may find they are doing their superior's job for them. This will cause poor performance on the subordinate's job and might even result in some formal sanction by others in the organization for sticking one's nose where it doesn't belong, exceeding one's job authority, or covering up important facts. Much of the behavior of Watergate actors, for example, can be explained by understanding that many subordinates were trying to cover for superiors when they should have let the facts see the light of day.

SUBORDINATES

Much of what we have examined between superior and subordinate in the previous section also applies in this section. Superiors are in a powerful position; to a great extent they control their subordinates' fate in the organization. (It can also be argued that subordinates together can control the fate of their supervisor.)

As we saw in the last section, we most often think of superiors making demands and requests from subordinates, but subordinates also have needs and expectations and make demands and requests on superiors. An example is presented in Figure 7.3, which is from a hand-lettered sign I came across several years ago in the restroom of a factory in Ohio. It expresses well the essence of the expectations of at least one worker in the factory, and it probably represents the sentiments of many subordinates throughout the world.

Subordinates generally are not in the position of making demands on the superior since they are not in a position of authority over the superior. Therefore, they usually request certain actions, and may even expect that certain things be done for them without even asking for them; they may be viewed as implicit in the job relationship. These might include such things as steady employment, safe and healthful working conditions, and a decent wage. On the other hand, subordinates may become quite vocal in asking for

> What I Want From My Boss:
>
> - Fair treatment
> - Fair play
> - Security
> - Understanding
> - Guidance
> - Tolerance
> - Patience
> - Acceptance
> - Recognition for a job well done
>
> But Most Of All:
>
> - Individuality—I want to be treated as an individual human being worthy of respect.

Figure 7.3 Hand-lettered sign found on restroom wall of Ohio factory

these things even to the extent of working through a collective bargaining agent (a union) to, in effect, make *demands* on the employer. Or, they may lobby a legislative body to make demands on their behalf (the passage of OSHA and EEO legislation, for example). Of course, such actions are not limited to factory workers, as we have seen with the growth of unions and lobbying efforts among teachers, nurses, social workers, counselors, and other professional groups.

Skills, abilities, interests, aspiration (motivation) level

Competent managers know their subordinates thoroughly. They know not only their needs, expectations, demands, and requests, but they also know their skills, abilities, interests, and aspiration levels. Such knowledge enables managers to know what and how much they can do through their subordinates.

Skilled managers are energizers or catalysts to action. Their goal is to satisfy and help subordinates meet their needs and their aspirations so that the work groups and the organization reaches their goals. In effect, competent managers believe that if you take care of your subordinates, they will take care of you.

Space does not permit us to examine in more detail the complexities of such group behavior. We will revisit some of these issues in the chapter on leadership. Also, the references at the end of the chapter contain additional material in the area of work groups and superior-subordinate relationships.

PEER MANAGERS

Peer managers are managers who are all at approximately the same level in an organization. They are managers who do not exist in a superior-subordinate relationship. Peer managers have line authority (direct, command authority) and staff authority (indirect or advisory authority).

For many competent professional managers, peer managers also include managers in other organizations. In other words, they include fellow members of the management profession. While this feeling is as not as widespread among managers as it is among lawyers, medical doctors, professors, or other groups, there is an increasing movement toward managerial professionalism spearheaded by such groups as the American Management Associations, American Society of Training and Development, American Society of Public Administration, and the American Society of Personnel Administration. These and other professional groups are sponsoring professional management training, certification, and codes of ethics which will lead to an increasing feeling of professionalism among managers.

Peer managers, be they inside or outside of the organization, have needs, expectations, demands, and requests that they make on an individual manager. While individual managers are accountable to an immediate superior and have several immediate subordinates, they are also expected to cooperate with other managers in the organization. In this sense, they are expected to be a team player. By the same token, the individual manager will make demands and requests on peer managers in order to get a job done. This exchange of demands and requests is a natural and essential part of organizational life. After all, an organization is supposed to be greater than the sum of its parts because of the fact people working together can accomplish more than people working separately.

Peer manager working relationships

Peer manager working relationships can be formalized and structured, or informal. Formal working relationships include such mechanisms as ad hoc and standing committees, task forces, staff groups, liaison teams, and the use of compulsory staff advice. All of these methods force peer managers to work together. Compulsory staff advice is a technique that requires line managers to listen to the advice of staff managers prior to making a decision. For example, in deciding to close a plant, the V.P. of Production should be required to weigh and consider advice from people in personnel, purchasing, accounting, and other key staff areas before making the decision whether or not to close the plant.

Of course, there are also informal ways peer managers work together. They meet and discuss problems at lunch, at a party, or at a company-sponsored social event. They may be neighbors or see each other at the local country club. Or, they simply may have their offices located near one another. Whatever the means, many informal ways exist to get peer managers to cooperate with one another.

Some organizations require all demands and requests made by peer managers to be funneled through one's immediate superior. This technique helps keep the manager from becoming overloaded or overcommitted and keeps these demands and requests in perspective with those made by the superior. The only disadvantage with this approach is that it can delay the response to a demand or request while the peer manager hunts down or waits for a reply from the superior of the manager.

WAYS OF KNOWING

How do managers learn about the people in the organization with whom they must deal? What ways can be used to determine these needs, expectations, demands, and requests from top management, superiors, subordinates, and peer managers? We examine seven methods that can be used.

Job description

The first place to look for an explanation of these demands and requests is the job description, which should outline the duties, functions, and responsibilities of each job. However, since these are often vague, general, out of date, or sometimes nonexistent for a manager's job, the search should not end here.

Consensus conferences

Managers will probably have to hold conferences with superiors and subordinates to achieve consensus about role expectations on the job. Each person (the superior and the subordinate) will try to shape each other's expectations, which will result in some negotiation and bargaining. The final result should be some agreement as to what is expected of each other—what each party will or will not do.

MBO-type statements

If the organization is on some formalized system of Management by Objectives, the unit's purpose statement and list of key objectives should exist in writing for a superior and each of the subordinates. These should also be carefully reviewed and understood by each party. Furthermore, any setting of these purpose statements and objectives should be done on a mutual basis with each party having meaningful input.

Precedent

Managers must also review precedent to determine what has and has not been done in the job by the previous jobholder. These should be carefully reviewed with superior and subordinates in classifying the role.

Management audits

If a management or organizational audit has been recently performed, these should be reviewed to determine if the recommendations from the study impact on the job. Management and organizational audits are becoming increasingly more common in organizations. They are assessments of the strengths and weaknesses of the organization and its units, not just mere financial data. For example, these assessments or audits usually try to answer such questions as the following:

1. What are the strengths of this organization?
2. What are the problems of this organization?
3. Which problems are more important than others?
4. What is the quality of training and development of people in the organization?
5. How well does this organization satisfy customers/clients?
6. How well does this organization meet stockholder, employee, and governmental expectations?

An examination of the answers to these questions can provide insight for managers as to what extent and how their particular role in the organization should be redefined in order to effect solutions to any problems identified.

Survey feedback

A technique related to assessment that is becoming increasingly more common to define roles is a process called survey feedback. Using this approach, data are systematically gathered from members in the organization and fed back to various managers in the organization. There are two basic survey feedback approaches: top-down and bottom-up. Using the top-down approach, the subordinates of each superior are surveyed starting at the top management echelon and the data are fed back to each superior for response. This continues to each level down through the organization. Using the bottom-up approach, the subordinates of first-line managers are surveyed first. The survey of each manager's subordinates then occurs all the way up the organization. The data are fed back to each manager as the survey progresses up the organization.

This technique helps managers to understand what subordinates perceive as problems and issues. It enables managers to ascertain subordinate needs, expectations, demands, and requests. Often an outside consultant is used to conduct the process and to analyze and feed back the information. This helps to ensure anonymity of responses and helps managers to better understand the data.

Human resources information system

One way organizations use to better know their employees is by implementing a human resource information system. This system, usually but not always computerized, gives the organization current accurate data on all employees. The components of these data are shown in Figure 7.4. Information on each of these components is kept on each employee and is updated at least annually, if not quarterly. Such information is provided to employee superiors for decision-making purposes such as job assignment, promotion, merit raises, and so on.

By installing and using a human resource information system, superiors are better able to know the capabilities of present and potential subordinates. In most large organizations, such a system is almost a must since there are so many employees who are frequently being moved about because of transfers and promotions.

There are other methods to learn about people in the organization, such as organization development and training workshops, but the methods discussed here should get conscientious managers started in the right direction.

• Skill level	• Interests
• Key abilities	• Salary history
• Significant test scores	• Performance evaluation history
• Formal educational background	• Promotional history
• Noncredit management development background	• Aspiration level (e.g., jobs desired)

Figure 7.4 Major components of a human resource information system

CONCLUSION

In this chapter we have examined what competent managers should know about people in an organization. We have not probed deeply into the various psychological or social-psychological theories of human behavior. Rather, we have taken a more pragmatic approach and have, instead, focused on understanding the needs, expectations, demands, and requests of the people with whom managers must deal.

We have looked in particular at top management, the superior, subordinates, and peer managers, and their affect on the individual manager. Skilled managers can balance their response to each of these groups in order to meet their expectations without necessarily alienating any one group. Competent managers can do this while achieving high levels of productivity in their job performance.

In the next chapter we will look at the last area of job knowledge needed by managers. This is an understanding of the task or job to be done. This area of technical competence is also necessary for competent managerial performance.

QUESTIONS

1. Should a manager be more concerned with meeting the expectations of a superior or of subordinates? Why do you feel this way?

2. Does your superior provide you with the types of things listed in Figure 7.3? Do you provide your subordinates with these things? Explain.

3. How often do you hold conferences with superiors or subordinates to achieve consensus on role expectations? Is this often enough? Are you successful?

4. Do you have a job description which is accurate, current, and meaningful? Why or why not? If you don't, would it help you if you did?

5. It has been said, "A manager is only as good as his or her subordinates." Do you agree with this statement? Why or why not?

CASES AND EXERCISES

CASE 1: HELP!

Susie Bernstein has been a vice president for CMW, Inc., for about six months and she believes it is time to act. Since joining CMW she has never had a conference with Steve Heshizer, the president and chief executive officer, about what her duties and responsibilities are to be.

Susie is head of the forest products group and has worked for CMW in a variety of positions over the last twelve years. She has been rapidly promoted during this time.

Steve has been President of the organization for three years and has been with the company for a total of six years. He is known throughout the company for his free and easy style of management, often referred to in CMW office gossip as a "lay-back" style of management.

Susie feels uncomfortable with this style. She believes she needs more direction and some role clarification with Steve about exactly what she should or should not do. Therefore, she decides to have a meeting with Steve in order to achieve consensus. Following is the dialogue from that meeting.

Steve: Come in Susie. Have a seat. What's on your mind?

Susie: Well, we have had so few chances to talk since I was promoted to vice president, I'd like to talk with you briefly about the duties and responsibilities of my job.

Steve: Yes, I know I've been busy. Go ahead.

Susie: Well, I'm not sure I'm doing what I'm supposed to in this job. I think I need a little more direction from your office.

Steve: I see. Like what, for instance?

Susie: In several areas. Take the Pointex contract, for example. Are you satisfied with the way it is being handled?

Steve: Yes. You are doing fine. Look Susie, you go ahead and do your job as you see fit. That's why I promoted you. The first thing you have got to do is to figure out what needs to be done, then do it. If I knew what needed to be done and how it should be done, I'd do it myself. But I hired you to do this. You just go ahead and do your job and I'll let you know if you mess up. If you don't hear from me, just assume you are doing okay. Any questions?

Susie: No, I guess not. I guess I wish you could be a little more definite.

Steve: Well, surely you don't want me to write a job description for you, do you? Not for a vice president!

Questions

1. Does a vice president need a job description? Why or why not?

2. What are the advantages and disadvantages of the style of management practiced by Steve?

3. What would you do now if you were Susie?

CASE 2: KNOW PEOPLE, BUT DO YOUR OWN THING

I believe really competent managers know people inside and out. I also believe they need to know the needs, demands, requests, and expectations of all those with whom they work. But, in the final analysis when you come right down to it, effective managers do what needs to be done on the job. In other words, they do what is right within legal and ethical boundaries, regardless of what others say to do or not to do.

Each manager brings a personal style to the job. Each manager molds the job to suit him or her. Oh sure, there are job descriptions for many managerial jobs, but these should provide only broad general guidance. A manager has to be free to exercise judgment and initiative, and not be straightjacketed by some worn-out job description.

Competent managers may not be popular with superiors, subordinates, or peers. Many things they have to do are not popular, but they must be done for the good of the organization. They cannot be concerned with always satisfying needs and expectations. Frequently these should *not* be satisfied because they are not in the best interest of the organization.

For example, a significant shift in job reassignment of subordinates will likely make them angry and unhappy. Yet, if such a shift is necessary for organizational health it should be done. By the same token, if some poorly organized superior constantly plays havoc with a manager's time, the manager must say no and stick by it even if it upsets the superior. In the long run, the organization will be better off.

So, in the final analysis, when you get right down to it, managers must first satisfy themselves that a good job is being done and that the organization is being served best. If this is done, everything else will take care of itself.

Questions

1. Do you agree with the last paragraph of this individual's statement? Why or why not?

2. Does the necessity of making tough decisions mean that other people will be upset? Should this be of concern to competent managers?

3. Do you agree that managers mold their jobs to fit their own interests? If this is so, of what value are job descriptions?

EXERCISE: DO YOU KNOW YOUR SUPERIORS, SUBORDINATES, PEERS, AND TOP MANAGEMENT?

1. Know Your Superior
   a. The three most important things my superior expects of me are:
      1.
      2.
      3.
2. Know Your Subordinates
   a. The three most important things I expect of my subordinates are:
      1.
      2.
      3.
   b. The three most important things my subordinates expect of me are:
      1.
      2.
      3.
3. Know Your Peer Managers
   a. I expect to help my fellow managers in this organization by doing the following:
      1.
      2.
      3.
   b. I expect my fellow managers to help me in this organization by doing the following:
      1.
      2.
      3.
4. Know Top Management
   a. The three most important things really valued by top management in this organization are:
      1.
      2.
      3.

REFERENCES

Anthony, William P. "Get To Know Your Employees: The Human Resource Information System." *Personnel Journal* 56 (April 1977): 179–183, 202. A complete overview of the purpose, design, and components of a human resource information system in nontechnical language.

Blau, Peter M. *Exchange and Power in Social Life.* New York: Wiley, 1964.
   A comprehensive explanation of social exchange theory. The classic in the field.
Davis, Keith. *Human Behavior At Work.* 5th ed. New York: McGraw-Hill, 1977.
   A well-written comprehensive look at why people act as they do in organizations.
Gouldner, Alvin. "The Norm of Reciprocity." *American Sociological Review* 25 (1960): 161–178.
   Explains the norm of reciprocity as an underlying principle which explains exchange in all cultures.
Hamner, W. Clay, and Organ, Dennis W. *Organizational Behavior: An Applied Psychological Approach.* Dallas: Business Publications, Inc., 1978.
   A very good summary of social-psychological principles applied to human behavior in organizations.
Homans, George C. *Social Behavior: Its Elementary Forms.* New York: Harcourt, Brace and World, 1961.
   This books explains the concepts of distributive justice, personal profits, and personal investments as the roots of the social exchange process.
Huseman, Richard C., and Carroll, Archie B. *Readings in Organizational Behavior: Dimensions of Management Actions.* Boston: Mass: Allyn and Bacon, 1979.
   An excellent collection of articles indicating management actions in response to understanding human behavior in organizations.
Vroom, Victor H. *Work and Motivation.* New York: Wiley, 1964.
   The classic work on human motivation in work settings.

8

What Should a Manager Know About the Task to Be Done?

Had it happened to Burt? Had he been promoted to his highest level of incompetency? He was a damn good design engineer—one of the best in the company, if not the industry. He was a good first-line supervisor. Even his promotion to department head was well received and he believed he did a good job. He never thought, however, he'd become division vice president of engineering.

He felt helpless. The job was much broader in scope than he initially believed. Burt had trouble juggling so many balls at one time, and he felt as if things were slipping away from him. His seventy- to eighty-hour work weeks were ruining his family life. Worse yet, he didn't think spending even one hundred hours a week on the job would help matters.

What was Burt to do? He did not want to request a demotion—he liked the pay and prestige of the new job. He was afraid to tell his boss that he could not handle the job. He kept thinking things would improve but he'd been on the job for three months and they hadn't. He knew that it would soon become apparent to others in the organization that he was out of his element. What was he to do?

If you were Burt, what would you do? Can people be promoted to their highest level of incompetency? Does skill in a technical area or even skill in lower level management positions necessarily qualify one for effective job performance at higher level management positions?

We address these and other questions in this chapter. We are concerned with managerial knowledge of the task or job to be done as a key ingredient to management competence. What do managers need to know about the work to be done in order to be effective? We address three issues to answer this question as follows: (1) the purpose or goals of the work, (2) the technology of the work, and (3) the methods needed to successfully complete the work.

PURPOSE AND GOALS

Every manager should know the reason why a task or job must be done: the purpose of the task and the goals of the work effort. The purpose serves as the rationale for the work; the goals or objectives are the end results to be achieved by the work. Unless managers know these two key factors about the job or task, there will not only be difficulty in directing work effort of others, but also in achieving a sense of meaning in their own job.

Multipurpose, multigoal effort

Most tasks managers are responsible for achieving more than one purpose in the organization and with achieving multiple goals. This is as it should be. We ought to be concerned about getting the biggest bang for our buck. For example, a sales manager should ensure that calls made by sales personnel achieve several goals. Not only should the sales personnel be concerned with selling the product or service, but they also should be concerned with the following activities:

1. Ascertaining customer/client satisfaction with existing products or services.

2. Determining any unmet needs that could be met by other products or services of the company.

3. Determining any unmet needs that could result in new product/service development by the company.

4. Informing the customer/client of new products that will be out soon.

5. Resolving any servicing complaints the customer/client has with the product/service.

6. Helping to resolve any billing complaints the customer/client has.

Covering all of this information with one sales call is much more efficient than having to make three or four calls. Perhaps the salesperson cannot resolve each of these immediately for the customer or client, but could begin initiation with others in the company to resolve these issues. In this example, if the present sales job is structured narrowly so that the only concern is to make a sale, then consideration should be given to restructuring it so that other purposes are also served.

Thus, a consideration of purpose and goals of work in a job could very well lead to restructuring of jobs in the organization. When this restructuring occurs in order to make jobs more challenging and interesting to jobholders, this is called *job enrichment*. Job enrichment is an effort to build higher levels of responsibility and increased task challenge into jobs. Many organizations are concerned with job enrichment as a way to increase the motivational level of jobs, but they also ought to be concerned with enriching jobs in order to make work more effective and efficient. That is, job restructuring ought to explicitly recognize the need for achieving multiple purposes and goals through the work effort.

Managerial versus nonmanagerial work

We saw in Chapter 1 that managers manage other people to carry out work in order to achieve unit and organizational goals. Much of the management task at lower levels in the organization is actually concerned with making sure that nonmanagement work gets done by the operatives (nonmanagers) performing the work. But, as one moves up the organization, there is less and less concern with the operative work and more and more concern with purely managerial work.

This is as it should be, but there is an inherent danger. Upper level managers may get completely divorced from the operative work of the organization. Examples of this abound: a university vice president loses appreciation for what goes in the classroom; a divisional manager in an auto company has little idea of what it's like to work on the assembly line; the head of the state welfare agency never has counseled food stamp applicants. To the extent that these and other similar examples exist, there is low appreciation of top managers for the real work, and hence the purpose, of the organization.

Yet, as we saw in the first chapter, higher level managers should avoid trying to supervise the work of operatives; they should not jump the chain of command. Avoiding the tendency to get into the details of operative work without becoming aloof is a real challenge for contemporary managers. Yet it must be done. If managers become too divorced from the operative work, there will be a tendency to lose sight of the purpose of organizational effort. Pretty soon they will feel like they exist solely to meet deadlines, read reports, dictate letters, go to meetings, and so on. These activities become the goal of organization effort in and of themselves instead of being the means to the goal of providing a better product or service to customers or clients.

TECHNOLOGY OF THE TASK

Managers must know the technology of the task they are managing. Technology is the art and science of the production and distribution of goods and services. The technology of a particular task is the art and science involved in carrying out that task. It implies a configuration of machinery, equipment, processes, and methods used in production or distribution.

Technology itself can be quite sophisticated, such as in electronic data processing (EDP) operations, or fairly simple, such as in an office janitorial service. Machinery is usually, but not always, present in technology. For example, counseling an unemployed worker for job placement is a sophisticated process even though no actual machinery is used in the face-to-face counseling process. Of course, much machinery *supports* this process, such as computer banks of job placement information and job openings.

The need for technical knowledge

We saw in the previous section that managers must strike a happy balance between becoming too involved in the technical aspects of the task and becoming too aloof from the task. We also saw how this varies by management level with lower level managers needing to know more about the task than higher level managers.

This idea, summarized in Figure 8.1, is related to two other types of knowledge needed to be a competent manager. Notice that some amount of technical knowledge is required even by the very top management group. Notice also that knowledge about people is equally important at all management levels. Furthermore, note that conceptual knowledge becomes increasingly more important the higher one goes in the management hierarchy.

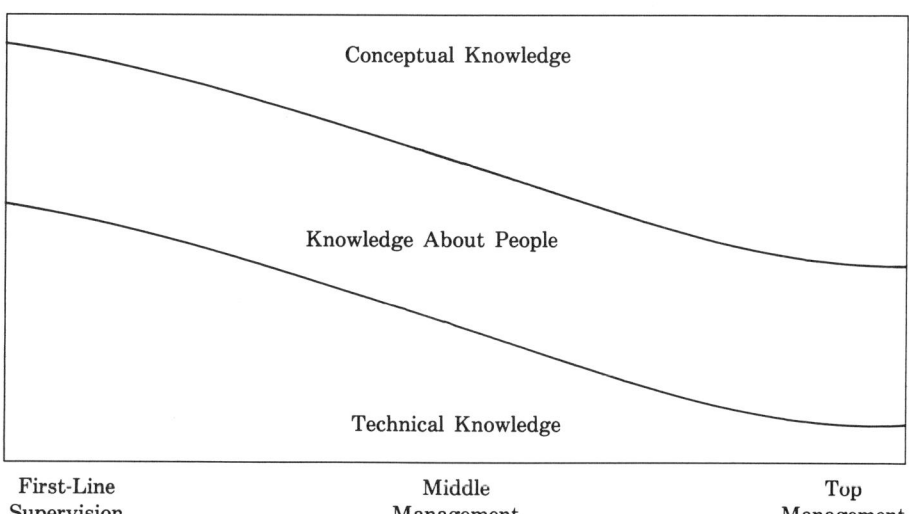

Figure 8.1 The need for technical knowledge declines as one progresses up the managerial ladder

Types of technology

Borrowing from the works of James Thompson, we can identify three basic types of technology with which managers could be involved. *Long-linked* technologies are technologies that depend on one another in a serial way. They are common in assembly-line operations such as in the automobile industry. In this industry subcomponents are manufactured and assembled. These then feed into the assembly of other subcomponents and finally into the assembly of the car. For example, there might be departments for engine assembly, transmission assembly, interior assembly, body assembly, and so on. Understanding this technology requires managers to visualize a series of technological subsystems and their relationships. These interactions are often called *interfaces* in the language of systems theory.

The second type of technology identified by Thompson is *mediating technology*. This type of technology ties numerous customer groups together. For example, banks and other financial institutions bring lenders and borrowers together. Ad agencies tie customers to producers by providing information about products to consumers. Employment agencies bring employers and job seekers together. Managers who are involved with mediating technology must be flexible and responsive so as to give consideration to all parties' interests. Furthermore, they must understand how the technology affects the customers or client group and how the technology links the organization to the customers or clients.

The final type of technology, *intensive technology*, involves the application of a variety of technologies to the solutions of problems of organizing. Intensive technologies focus on innovative ways of combining various technologies to solve complex problems. For example, in the space program the building of the space shuttle requires numerous firms to apply sophisticated technologies in a new way to solve a complex problem. The actual development and application of the technology requires the organization to organize itself around it. Intensive technologies, therefore, usually require the organization to adopt a *matrix* or *project* form of organization so as to be flexible in using resources on projects when and where they are needed. We are seeing more and more use of intensive technologies with today's problems, especially in the field of energy.

We summarize Thompson's three types of technology in Figure 8.2. It is important for managers to determine the type of technology at use in the organization and to act accordingly. The actual technology used has a significant impact on the way the organization structures itself and, consequently, the way managers in the organization should act.

WORK METHODS

The early industrialists in the United States were methods' engineers. They were constantly finding a better way to make a product. Henry Ford exem-

Type	Definition	Example	Type of Managerial Knowledge
Long-linked	Technologies that are serially linked	Automobile assembly line	Interface of production systems
Mediating	Technologies that tie customer groups together	Advertising agency	Effect technology has on customer or client
Intensive	Technologies that apply a variety of technologies to complex problems	Shuttle program	Sophisticated technologies used in complex problem solving

Figure 8.2 Types of technology

plifies this group. Also, the early writers in Management were industrialists who sought to improve work methods on the shop floor. Frederick Taylor is the best example of these pioneers in management.

Today we are still concerned with methods improvement, and we study these in the disciplines of operations management, industrial engineering, and human engineering. However, we have expanded our consideration of these notions. No longer are we simply interested in improving work methods in production operations on the shop floor. Rather, today we are interested in studying work methods in all phases of organization activity—from the shop floor to executive action, from production management to promotional management, and from manufacturing to hospital administration.

All managers must have some minimum understanding of the methods involved in the production or distribution of products or services as they affect their job. In this section we briefly review some of the key concepts involved in understanding work methods.

Operations analysis and management

Managers must understand the operations of their organization. This understanding will rest in their particular functional area of expertise. For example, the traditional area of operations management applies to production operations. Supervisors, superintendents, division chiefs, department heads, and so on, in production must understand such production concepts as inventory control, queuing theory, quality control, scheduling, and waste control. But today, managers in other areas of the organization must understand and be able to manage operations in their respective operations. For example, personnel managers must understand and manage personnel operations. Sales managers must manage sales operation. EDP managers must manage EDP operation. Financial managers manage financial operations.

Knowledge of functional operations is essential. There are very few general managers who manage the entire organization. The vast majority have responsibility for a particular functional area.

In examining these functional operations, we can break down activities into tasks, positions, and jobs. *Tasks* are specific activities required to be performed over a specified time period. They are units of work. They might include placing a phone call, typing a letter, filing a report, painting a car, mowing a lawn, or filling an auto gasoline tank. A group of tasks make up a *position*. A position is a collection of tasks that are assigned to an individual for work, commonly called a job. However, a *job* is a collection of similar positions. For example, in an organization the job of assembler may contain thirty positions, or the job of assistant professor in a particular university may consist of 300 assistant professors.

Understanding how tasks are grouped into positions and positions into jobs will help managers to understand the work that goes on in their unit.

Time and motion study

One area of operations management that has had a significant impact on understanding work methods is time and motion study. This area is concerned with examining tasks in minute detail in order to establish standard methods and times to complete the tasks. Also, by studying the tasks minutely, they could be simplified and regrouped so as to increase efficiency.

Early applications of time and motion study centered around repetitive jobs on the shop floor. These jobs were fairly standardized and usually dealt with the production of a physical product. This made the output easy to measure. The highly specialized, repetitive nature of the work made it easy to develop standard times and output.

Lately, however, principles of time and motion study have been applied to other jobs including secretaries, salespersons, billing clerks, and even teachers and counselors. While this application is not yet widespread, there has been some effort to simplify and set standard times for typing a letter, billing a customer, counseling a client, making a sales call, or placing a person in a job. Because of the varying circumstances under which these tasks are done in different organizations, and because these tasks often involve the provision of an intangible service instead of a product, much more research is needed before time and motion study principles will apply here as well as they do in production operations. Yet, there is much to be learned from studying work operations of nonproduction operations. Much secretarial work has been streamlined and made more efficient by closely examining the work of a secretary for several days and recommending changes. The same is true for nurses, teachers, counselors, filing clerks, and supervisors.

Improving operational effectiveness and efficiency ought to be the goal of every manager.

Scheduling

In addition to time and motion study, studies in the field of scheduling have had a significant impact on improving the understanding of work methods. One mark of effective managers is the ability to efficiently schedule work.

There are some sophisticated methods of scheduling including PERT methods, Markov chains, probability analysis, and so on. While these methods certainly are helpful, most managers can make do with a simple Gantt chart (see Figure 8.3 for an example) or a calendar of events. The key idea is to be able to visualize the activities that must be completed from the beginning to end of a project, the sequencing and concurrency of these activities, and the time required for completing each activity. The issue of scheduling will be revisited in more depth in Chapter 9.

Activity	Month				
	January 1 15 30	February 1 15 28	March 1 15 30	April 1 15 30	May 1 15 30
Conduct training needs assessment	───────				
Develop topics and instructors		───			
Order materials and resources		──────			
Identify and invite participants			──────		
Schedule training (reserve room, etc.)			────		
Conduct training				──────	
Monitor and evaluate training				───────	
Design follow-up program					────

Figure 8.3 Gantt chart for developing and conducting a management training program

Knowledge of one's industry

The final area of knowledge on work methods involves an understanding of one's industry. For example, if a manager is employed in the footwear industry, then the processes of making and distributing shoes should be known. If a manager is in the air travel industry, then facets of this industry must be known. While it is true that higher level managers need to have less detailed knowledge about the work methods of the industry than lower level managers, *all* managers need to know about the industry where they are housed. Knowledge about the specific industry where one is working is not a prerequisite for obtaining a managerial job in the industry, but it is necessary for ultimate success or competency as a manager in that industry.

This knowledge can be learned on the job. Some examples exist where a manager in the food industry becomes a successful manager of a telephone utility, or a manager in the steel industry becomes a successful manager in the auto industry. In other words, people with good managerial skills can practice them anywhere if they are willing to learn something about the industry.

WAYS OF KNOWING

How do managers learn about the task to be done? How are technology and work methods studied? How does one learn about an industry? Most of us learn these things through ever-expanding job experience as we mature in the organization or industry. Even though there are a few celebrated examples of managers who successfully move from industry to industry, in reality very few managers actually move to a different industry during their work life. While they do change organizations, they seldom leave the industry.

There are other ways of learning. First, if a person has a pretty good idea of what he or she wants to do in a job, then that field should be studied in college. For example, to be a sales manager a person should study this field in college of business. The same is true of personnel management, financial management, production management, advertising management, and so on. Formal study in a field of interest early in one's career can enhance managerial competency.

Technology and work methods can also be studied in courses on operations management. This can include credit as well as noncredit courses offered by colleges, universities, consulting, or trade organizations. On-the-job experience is also a good teacher, as well as reading in professional journals or technical books.

Knowledge of the industry can often be gained during the job search effort. Resource material on various industries are usually available in libraries. Talking with friends or relatives in the industry is usually helpful.

On-the-job experience, of course, is the way most of us learn about the industry where we are employed, but this knowledge tends to be rather narrow and heavily biased since we see the industry through the glasses of our own organization. Joining trade organizations, reading trade journals, and attending trade conventions also will teach us much about an industry.

Working with an expert is an excellent way to learn about work methods. We briefly reviewed this earlier in the book. A person who thoroughly knows the job, is well organized, efficient, and effective is invaluable as a work partner, particularly for a new manager just starting out. There is much to be said for the apprenticeship style of training, and this method ought to be used more in management training and education.

CONCLUSION

Understanding efficiency and effectiveness in work methods and understanding the technology of the task are key competencies for effective management. All managers do not need to be technical experts in the details of particular processes. First-line managers must be more familiar with the details of the task being managed than top level managers. All managers should have an appreciation of work processes and know when and how to rely on the technical expertise of others for more detailed knowledge.

In the next section we look at the skills required for management effectiveness. The first skill we examine is goal setting. Managers use the knowledge we've reviewed in this section as the basis for the application of certain skills. The skill of goal setting, in particular, relies heavily on knowledge of the market, organization, and task to be completed.

QUESTIONS

1. Does an engineer necessarily make a good engineering manager? Why or why not?

2. Why do you think so many of the early industrialists were so skilled in methods engineering as opposed to other areas of management, such as personnel, marketing, or accounting? In today's environment would these early industrialists likely be successful? Why or why not?

3. Do you believe the president of a steel company would make a good president of a rubber company? Of a textile company? Of a food company? Of a large bank? What criteria would you use in making this judgment?

4. Should every manager have one or two college courses in operations analysis and management? Why or why not?

5. Suppose you were responsible for planning and giving a dinner party for sixty guests. In a step-by-step process, list the activities and their sequence that would need to be carried out for the party which would result in the *most efficient* way of proceeding. What technology would you employ in carrying out the dinner party? (Consider the configuration of machines, processes, and methods.)

CASES AND EXERCISES

CASE 1: THE WAY TO THE TOP

Blacklick Steel Rod Company believed the cream always rose to the top. The company prided itself on its strict adherence to a merit system based on demonstrated performance as the basis for promotion. Consequently, the company always promoted the best engineer, accountant, production worker, or salesperson to the managerial ranks.

Fred Solomon, the company president, was a firm believer in the merit principle as the basis for promotion, but he saw two problems with it. First, the promotion would remove one of the best workers from the operative ranks. In other words, the operative work turned out by that top-flight accountant or engineer would be lost once the person was promoted to the management position. Second, the best salesperson did not always make the best manager. Solomon believed that because a person was highly skilled and competent in a technical or operative field did not necessarily qualify the person for competency in management. He'd seen plenty of top-flight engineers, accountants, salespeople, etc., fail as managers. They were good in their technical field of expertise, but terrible as managers.

Mr. Solomon was at a loss for a solution to the problem. On the one hand, if he no longer promoted the best operatives to management he believed he would be giving up merit and demonstrated performance as the basis for promotion. He wondered if camaraderie or guesswork would replace it. On the other hand, if he stuck to the present system for promotion to management he foresaw plenty of mistakes on the horizon and lost output from some of the firm's best operative workers.

Questions

1. What would you suggest as a solution to Mr. Solomon's dilemma? Why?

2. In your opinion do most organizations that use merit as the basis of promotion face the same problem as Blacklick Steel?

3. Does the organization for which you work face a problem similar to Blacklick's? Has your organization tried to solve it? If so, how?

CASE 2: SMART MANAGERS ARE TECHNICALLY DUMB

A manager is only as smart as those around him or her. No manager can possibly know all the intricacies of the hundreds of technical processes and machines that affect most management jobs in today's complex organizations. Therefore, smart managers surround themselves with a covy of sharp technical assistants in a variety of specialty fields. These people serve as staff resources on whom managers can call for technical advice when it is needed.

Therefore, managers don't need any technical knowledge themselves; they just need to know where to go to get technical advice. In fact, the less managers know about the technical operations, the better. This will make it less likely that managers will be continually meddling in day-to-day operations. People will be left alone to do the work without being constantly bothered by some nosy overseer. Managers will then be free to plan, organize, and control total operations and to assist in problem solving when needed. Monitoring scheduling and evaluation activities also can be carried out. The often popular notion that one has to get one's hands dirty to be doing work is an anachronism that has no relevance in today's management world.

Give me half a dozen or so sharp technical assistants I can draw on in the organization, and I'll give you top-flight management performance in any area in the organization—or in any industry!

Questions

1. Do you agree with this individual that managers need only know where to look for technical advice and don't themselves need any technical knowledge? Why or why not?

2. To what extent should managers be involved with the day-to-day operational details of the tasks of their unit? What criteria do you use in making this judgment?

EXERCISE: YOUR TECHNICAL EXPERTISE

1. List the three most important areas of technical knowledge required of you in your present job.

2. List the three most important areas of technical knowledge which will be required of you five years from now either in your present job or in a new job that you hope to obtain.

3. How do you plan to ensure that you have the technical knowledge required in five years?

4. Pick one work process that you currently manage and streamline it to make it more efficient. In carrying out this activity, be aware of any finan-

cial and psychological costs as well as benefits that will likely result in simplifying this process. Address the following questions:
   a. What procedure will you use to streamline the process?
   b. Will you ask your superior for assistance?
   c. Will you ask any of your subordinates for assistance?
   d. Will you seek specialized staff advice?
   e. Will you study any articles or journals?
   f. Will you call other organizations with similar processes to see what they are doing?
   g. How do you plan to implement the streamlined change in the process?
   h. Who will do what, when?
   i. How will you monitor and evaluate the change in the process?

REFERENCES

Aldag, Ramon J., and Brief, Arthur P. *Task Design and Employee Motivation.* Glenview, Ill.: Scott Foresman and Co., 1979.
   An excellent, short, well-documented book that covers the essentials of task design and redesign so as to increase and improve employee motivation.

McCormick, E. J. "Job and Task Analysis." In *Handbook of Industrial and Organizational Psychology,* edited by M. D. Dunnette. Chicago: Rand McNally, 1976.
   A brief but comprehensive look at the key factors involved in job and task analysis.

Nadler, G. *Work Design.* Homewood, Ill.: Richard D. Irwin, 1963.
   A good look at work design issues; helpful for managers considering improvements in work efficiency.

Pierce, J. L., and Dunham, R. B. "Task Design: A Literature Review." *The Academy of Management Review* 1 (1976): 83–97.
   A complete review of all major writings and studies on the issues involved in designing tasks or jobs.

Sims, H. P.; Szilagyi, A. D.; and Keller, R. T. "The Measurement of Job Characteristics." *Academy of Management Journal* 19 (1976): 195–202.
   A discussion of a method for analyzing a job and its tasks in order to relate them to key job characteristics.

Taylor, F. W. *The Principles of Scientific Management.* New York: Harper, 1911.
   The classic work by Taylor develops time and motion study and other principles as a means for improving factory jobs.

Thompson, James D., *Organizations In Action.* New York: McGraw-Hill Book Co., 1967.
   Provides a detailed discussion of organizations, especially the types of technology discussed in this chapter.
Walker, C. R., and Guest, R. H. *The Man on the Assembly Line.* Cambridge: Harvard University Press, 1952.
   The classic study of employee attitudes and reactions to repetitive assembly line jobs.

Part III
Developing Management Skills

We are now ready to examine the essential skills competent managers must have. We have looked at the important knowledge required of managers, and in this section we see how certain managerial skills are carried out based on this knowledge.

We examine nine essential managerial skills. First, in Chapter 9 we take a fairly detailed look at the skill of goal-setting. We pay particular attention to Management by Objectives (MBO) as a popular and effective goal-setting method. Then, in Chapter 10 we move to an examination of the leadership process. This process of influence is a requirement for effective management.

Decision making is the focus of Chapter 11. All managers make decisions; competent managers make the right decisions in an effective and efficient manner. Issues involved with effective communication skills are reviewed in Chapter 12. Competent managers coach and counsel subordinates in order to obtain maximum performance and output. These processes are reviewed in Chapter 13.

Managing change and conflict is a fact of life for every manager. In Chapter 14 we examine some ways to manage change and conflict so as to achieve competency in management. Competent managers also know how to use political skills to their best advantage. These skills are reviewed in Chapter 15.

There never seems to be enough time in a workday to do all we should do and do it well. Chapter 16 addresses the issue of time management and places this skill in perspective with other management skills. Finally, in Chapter 17 we examine the managerial skills involved in providing incentives and rewards for employees so as to maximize their performance and at the same time treat them fairly and equitably.

The practice of these managerial skills are required for competency in management. While these skills are not necessarily easy to learn, they can be learned through conscientious effort. Some of the ways of learning these skills are examined in each chapter.

9
How Should a Manager Set Goals?

The Warriors Athletic Boosters, Inc., Board of Directors set the following goals for the coming year:

1. Increase stadium capacity from present level to 55,000.
2. Improve concession and bathroom facilities at stadium.
3. Improve facilities for baseball and track.
4. Refurbish athletes' dormitory.
5. Raise $1,000,000 in contributions.
6. Establish a 10 percent reserve fund.

The production department of Rightex Chemicals will focus on the following for the coming year:

1. Increasing all chemicals produced by 10 percent.
2. Reducing the cost of waste in production by 6 percent.
3. Reducing the employee absence rate to 2.5 percent (daily average).
4. Replacing all equipment used on HTH line.
5. Meeting all safety objectives.
6. Meeting all EEO objectives.
7. Completing switch over to alternative emergency fuel system.

St. Mary's Parish will accomplish the following this year:

1. Increase donations to a level at least equal to the expected rise in inflation.
2. Increase parish congregation membership by 12 percent.
3. Increase average Sunday attendance at mass by 15 percent.

4. Develop and implement a pre-school program.
5. Develop and implement a teen-club program.
6. Reduce energy expenditures by 8 percent.

The claims processing unit of Safe-Hands Insurance Company desires to accomplish the following objectives for next year:

1. Reduce annual turnover from 35 percent to 20 percent by year end.
2. Reduce average time for processing claims from nine working days to seven (beginning to end).
3. Meet all EEO objectives.
4. Reduce errors in reporting to no more than 5.3 per 1,000 claims.
5. Open six new branch offices in southern region.

These examples are actual objectives of four vastly different organizations. *All* organizations should have clear-cut goals and objectives regardless of the type of organization or industry. *All* units in every organization and *all* managers in each unit also should have objectives.

In this chapter we carefully examine the process of setting objectives. (The terms *objectives* and *goals* will be used interchangeably.) We look at the entire process: the requirements for good objectives, and the steps involved in implementing and achieving objectives.

Competent managers work to achieve objectives as if it were second nature to them. They do not use it as something to be done "if there is time." They do not write nice objectives and then file them away never to look at them again. They realize that the alternative to managing by and for objective accomplishment is "management by crisis."

DETERMINING WHAT IS IMPORTANT

The first thing managers must do in setting objectives is to determine what is important. The process of determining what is important is relatively simple—*provided* that the manager understands the material in Chapters 1 to 8 of this book. In other words, careful preparation based on sound knowledge about the organization's environment, market, key resources, competitors, etc., is required *prior* to writing up a list of objectives, as we see in Figure 9.1. A conscientious effort here will pay off in handsome dividends later.

Second, managers must carefully examine any "home office, governmental, or superior mandates." These *mandates* are nonnegotiable requirements that must be met. They could include a government law in safety and health, EEO, etc., or they could include an overriding organizational goal deemed extremely important by the organization. The point is, these man-

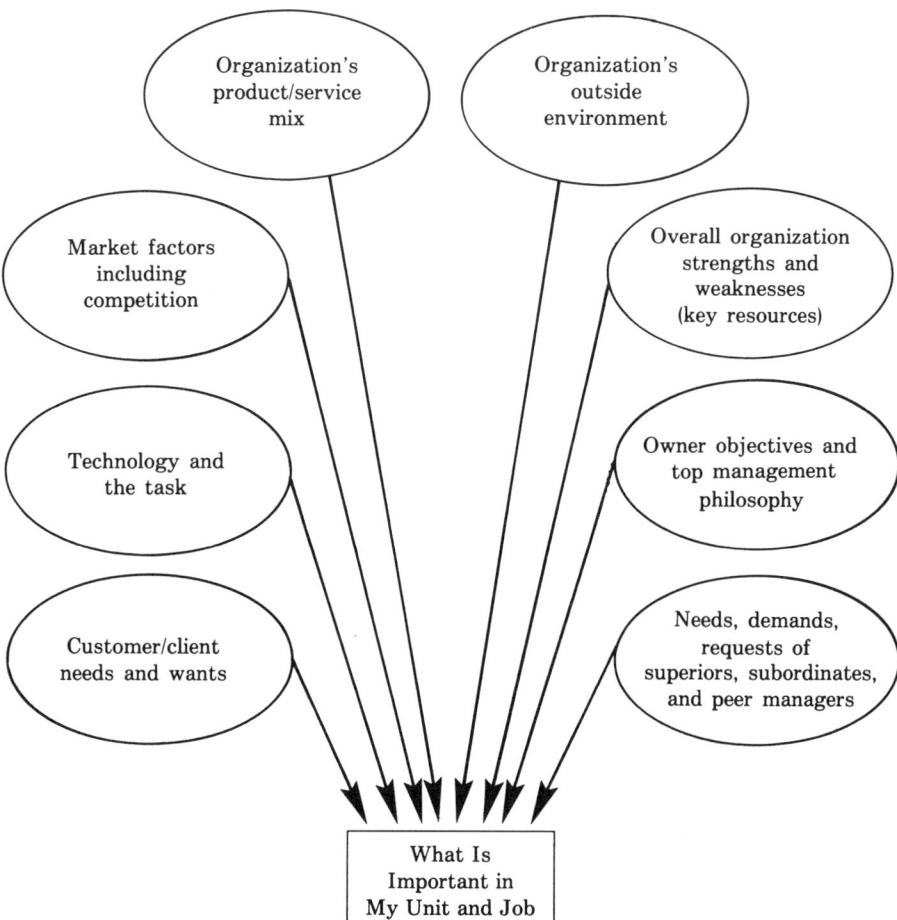

Figure 9.1 Areas to be examined to determine what is important

dates must be known prior to setting any objectives since specific objectives will have to be developed to carry out the mandates.

Third, managers must have thorough knowledge of the resources available for their use prior to setting objectives. If resources are not presently available, some estimation must be made as to how easy it will be to obtain them within a time frame. These resources include people, financial (budget), material, equipment, and information. The availability of these resources for the *planning horizon* (the period for which we are setting the objectives) is needed so that we can write objectives that are realistic and sufficient—neither too easy nor too difficult to achieve.

TYING IN WITH ORGANIZATIONAL GOALS

Objectives within an organization must be tied in with one another in a comprehensive and consistent manner. Managers working in units within the organization must not work at cross purposes with one another. The achievement of lower unit objectives must result in the achievement of higher unit and organizational objectives, as shown in Figure 9.2. This is important for three main reasons: (1) to achieve integration and coordination (unity of effort), (2) to avoid goal displacement, and (3) to avoid organizational gaps or overlaps. Let's look at each of these in more detail.

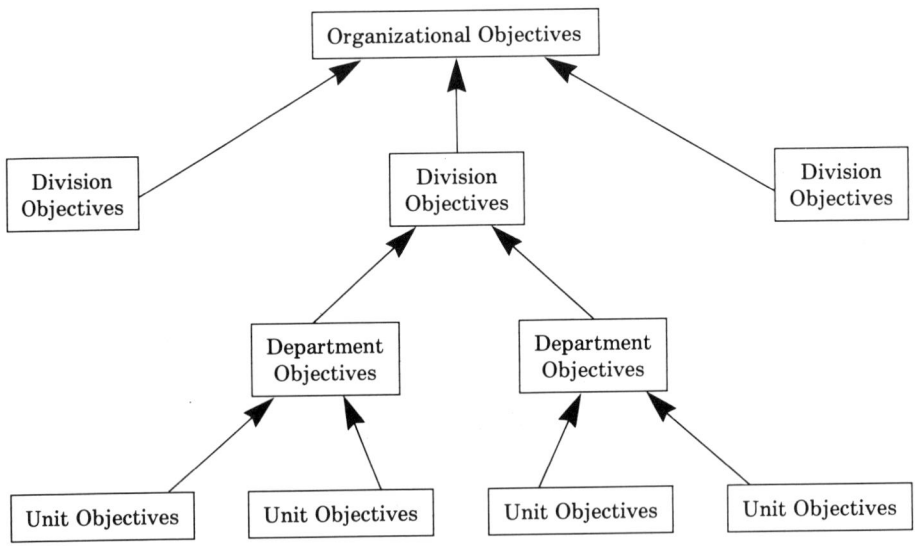

Figure 9.2 Accomplishing overall organizational objectives

Achieving integration and coordination (unity of purpose)

If organizations have good statements of purpose and if each unit within the organization also has a good statement of purpose that ties to organization purpose, then chances are unit and organization objectives will also be tied together and integrated. This integration is necessary so that organizational units cooperate and coordinate with one another and not be in conflict. There are two ways to get this integration in setting objectives—by using the top-down approach or by using the bottom-up approach.

Top-down approach. Using the top-down approach, the objectives of the chief executive officer are set in conjunction with the immediate subordinates. They meet as a group to negotiate and write the CEO's objectives. Then they write the objectives for each of the subordinate units as a group. This *mutual goal setting* assures the consistency of objectives at the top.

Following this, each subordinate manager then meets with his or her subordinates and repeats the process. While doing this, the previously set objectives with the superior are used as guidance. This continues at each level down through the organization. Once the bottom management rung is reached, the lists of objectives are forwarded up the line for review and final approval. Finally, all objectives for each unit should be placed in a notebook and given to each manager—in the vertical or horizontal (lateral) chain concerned with their accomplishment.

Bottom-up approach. This approach starts with the superiors of the lowest management rung and their subordinates. They meet as a group and negotiate superior and subordinate objectives. These are then used for guidance for the superior of each unit when meeting with the next higher level superior. This continues on up the organization until the final meeting occurs with the CEO and the immediate subordinates. Finally, objectives are then passed down the organization for final approval. Once again, they are then placed in a notebook for use by all those concerned with their accomplishment.

The bottom-up approach shifts much of the authority for writing objectives to those lower in the organization who, in fact, will be responsible for their achievement. However, this approach requires a decentralized management structure and great skills on the part of higher level managers to integrate desired objectives as they come up from the bottom.

I've used both approaches in consulting, and I prefer the top-down approach since it usually results in greater unity of effort and consistency among objectives. Of course in using this, it is important that *mutual* objective setting occur between superiors and subordinates at *each* level.

The bottom-up approach can raise expectations of lower level managers and cause much wheel-spinning. People at the lower levels spend a great deal of time writing objectives only to find out later that the objectives don't integrate well with higher level objectives throughout the organization.

Avoiding goal displacement

Organizational and unit goals can become displaced without management initially realizing it. Goal displacement occurs when objectives of lesser or no importance are achieved over those of greater importance, or when means to an objective become the objective themselves. For example, if we are concerned with implementing a reporting-in and -out procedure for subordinates in our office in order to reduce tardiness, we may require that everyone sign in and out when they enter or leave the office and to indicate the time. Suppose that one of our best employees, who is never tardy, simply fails to sign in and out as we request. It would not be wise to take strong action against this individual since the objective of not being tardy is being met even though the means of monitoring is not. (This assumes of course that we are able to visually monitor this person's comings and goings.)

Or suppose that we believe it is necessary to set an objective to reduce the employee *turnover* rate by 10 percent this year. It would not be appropriate for a supervisor to focus attentions on reducing the *absence* rate if this rate is at a satisfactory level. If turnover is the issue, then this is what we want supervisors to focus on—not absences.

Avoiding organizational gaps and overlaps

The third reason unit and organizational goals should be consistent with one another is to avoid organizational gaps and overlaps. An *organizational gap* occurs when an important goal needs to be accomplished, but no one is assigned the authority to accomplish it and so it does not get done. For example, if we believe that reduction of scrap is an important goal, then it must be assigned to production supervisors, quality control, training, or someone else. Unless it is, scrap will not be reduced. It just doesn't happen automatically. In fact, all three areas might be assigned some responsibility for scrap reduction, but each area must know the *specific duties* expected of it so as to avoid organizational overlap.

Organizational overlap occurs when two or more units are assigned the same objective at the *detriment of objective accomplishment.* For example, suppose busboys and waiters are both assigned to clear tables in a restaurant. When they both do, however, they interfere with each other. Their duties overlap and when each carries out the duty, it becomes *dysfunctional*—they actually work *against* each other. In fact, a few times of bumping in to one another will lead to an organizational gap. No one will clear the table since each group will think it's the other party's responsibility!

WAYS OF SETTING GOALS

The goal-setting process goes by many names, such as management by objectives (MBO), zero-base budgeting (ZBB), comprehensive planning, plan of service, or program planning budgeting systems (PPBS). Whatever it's called, it is a system of management based on setting goals and determining how they are to be accomplished. Since MBO was the first term used for this effort in the early 1950s by Peter Drucker, and is the most popular term used in business, we will use it to represent all other terms.

Management by objectives (MBO)

Let's first set out a few key ideas before we get into the details of MBO:

1. MBO is not a panacea. It will not cure all managerial or organizational problems. It is a tool. If used properly it can reduce problems and crises and make it easier to solve those that do crop up.

2. MBO should be implemented in a participative manner, either using a top-down or a bottom-up approach. Autocratic implementation will cause it to be viewed simply as another management control measure rather than as a planning tool which it really is.

3. MBO takes time, effort, and education to implement properly. In an organization of any size it will take anywhere from two to five years for full implementation in all units. People need to be trained and educated in the principles of MBO *before* they are expected to use it.

4. MBO *can* be implemented by an individual manager in individual units even though the rest of the organization is not on the system. It helps to have top and peer management support, but this should not deter or detract from MBO implementation at the unit level.

5. There are many side benefits of MBO, such as communication, understanding, and consensus, which are an added bonus to the process.

6. Finally, managers should avoid two very common mistakes in using MBO. First, it's common to maximize short-term objectives at the expense of long-term ones. This occurs because most managers down in the organization tend to be too concerned about the immediate future and not concerned enough about long-term developments. Second, managers must watch out for creating a blizzard of paperwork when implementing an MBO program. It's easy to get lost in the technique of completing the forms and forget the whole purpose behind the system.

Having laid out these essential points, let's look at a comprehensive MBO system that works.

Steps in the MBO process

There are several MBO systems, but they all must be comprehensive if they are to work properly. The system presented in Figure 9.3 is comprehensive. It takes MBO through the preliminary planning stages all the way through monitoring and corrective action. Notice also that each step is connected to a review and reconcile box. This indicates the flexible and dynamic nature of MBO. Just because an objective is written down, it is not set in concrete. I've used this system both in training and as a consultant with several organizations, and have found that it works. The model itself is a modification of the one developed by George Morrisey. Let's look at each step in the model.

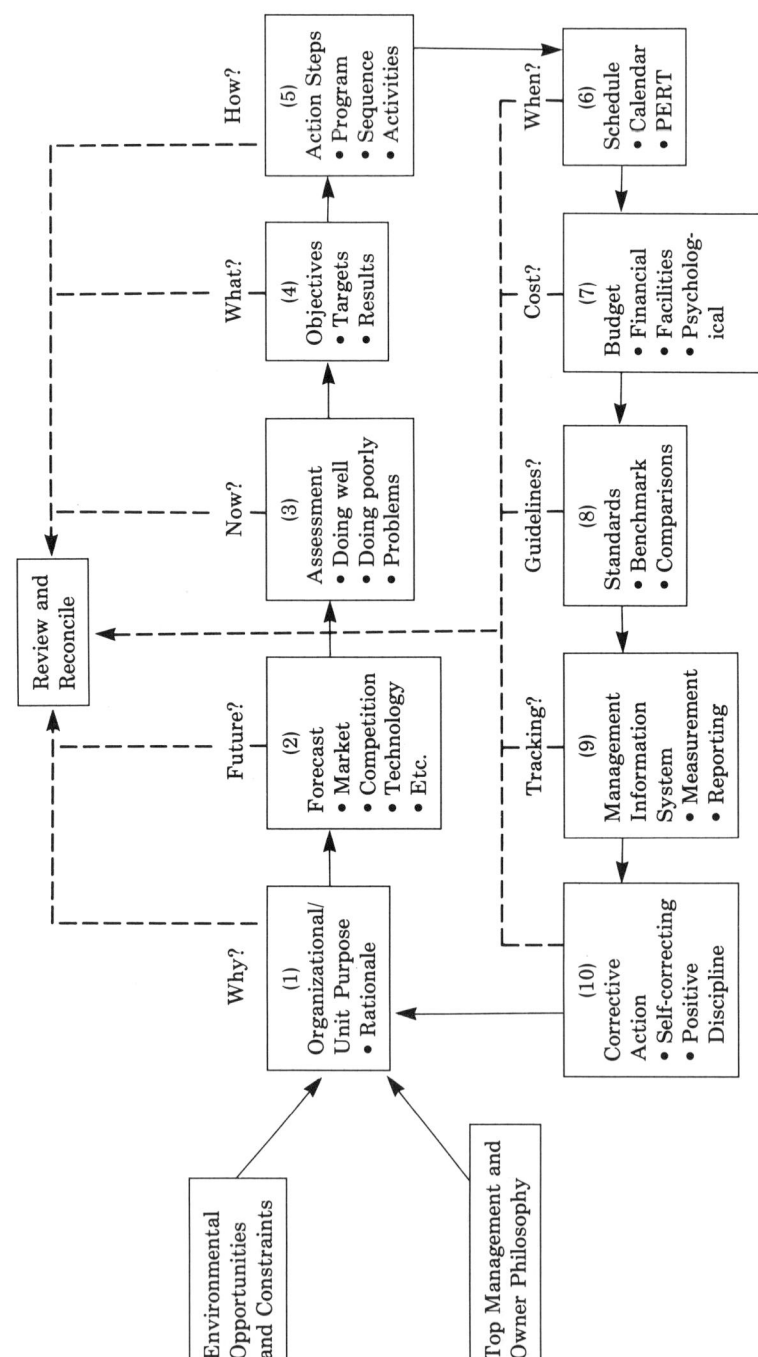

Figure 9.3 A comprehensive management by objectives system (Adapted from George Morrisey, *Management by Objectives and Results* (Reading, Mass.: Addison-Wesley, 1970).)

Organization and unit purpose. This is the rationale for existence of the organization and each of its subunits. It answers the question,"Why?" It is determined by an examination of environmental opportunities and constraints, and is a reflection of top management and owner philosophy. It should stake out the organization's customer/client group(s), geographic region served, and products/services offered, and it should make a commitment to profitability (if a business) or to economic efficiency. The following is an example purpose statement for an independent telephone company:

> To provide efficient and effective telecommunications service and products to business and residential customers throughout Central Florida within applicable federal law and State Public Service Commission regulations so as to earn the maximum allowable return on stockholder investment consistent with pricing structure and service provided.

This pretty well sums up the reason why this telephone company exists, and it provides an umbrella statement for organizational objectives and unit purpose and objectives. Every manager of every unit in an organization should have a purpose statement that sets out the reason for existence of the unit and ties into organizational purpose.

Forecast. Managers should not plan in a vacuum. They need to forecast relevant market, environmental, technological, and social forces likely to impact on their jobs during the period for which objectives will be set. They also need to forecast the needs, wants, demands, and expectations of superiors, subordinates, and peer managers. In most large organizations, specialized planning and forecasting staff units will assist managers with this forecast.

Assessment. We must know our organizational and unit strengths and weaknesses prior to setting objectives since we want some objectives that capitalize on strengths and others that overcome problem areas. This assessment can be done through an organizational or managerial audit, or can be a continuous type of monitoring activity.

Objectives. Now we come to the heart of MBO. Objectives deal with *what* is to be accomplished. They should be specific, measurable (trackable), quantified if possible, realistic and sufficient (neither too hard nor too easy), time-bounded (have a specific date), and able to tie in with purpose statement and higher and lower unit objectives.

Objectives can be improvement-oriented or equilibrium, as explained in a previous chapter. They also can be long range (more than five years), intermediate range (one to five years), and short range (one year or less). Personal improvement, as well as unit objectives, should be written for each manager.

Objectives should be placed into one of three categories for priority purposes. *Must do* are critical for mission attainment. *Ought to do* are important, but can be temporarily postponed for a longer time period. *Nice to do* are also important, but can be postponed for a longer period.

Objectives should be short, clear, and to the point. Obscure phrasing and big words should be avoided. Only one object should appear in each objective. The objective should begin with the word *to* and be followed by an action verb. Listed in Figure 9.4 are objectives compiled from a variety of organizations. Each one meets the requirements for a good objective.

- To reduce waste and scrap costs in all production units by 15 percent by June 1, 1981.
- To increase market share to 19 percent by January 1, 1980.
- To develop, test, and market three new products by July 1, 1984.
- To reduce annual turnover among factory employees from 35 percent to 22 percent by September 30, 1981.
- To meet all applicable OSHA standards by January 1, 1980.
- To continue implementation of the affirmative action program so that all phases are implemented by July 1, 1981.
- To increase return on investment to 18 percent by December 31, 1982.
- To improve my knowledge of coaching and counseling techniques by January 1, 1980.
- To increase annual earnings per share to $2.25 by June 30, 1982.
- To improve public image by instituting an institutional advertising program of $1,000,000 by August 1, 1980.
- To complete reconversion to coal-fired electrical generation by January 1, 1983.
- To plan, develop, construct, and open three new Class A stores in the Southeast by October 1, 1984.

Figure 9.4 Examples of objectives for a variety of organizations

Action steps. Each objective should have a list of action steps that detail the program to be followed to accomplish the objective. The action steps answer the question, "How?" Taken together, they should result in objective accomplishment. If they do not, then a step or two was omitted or the objective was poorly written. When writing action steps, it is important to keep in mind six essential points:

1. Do not go into too much detail. Avoid setting out long lists of substeps.
2. Assign each step to someone for performance and accountability.
3. Be concerned about sequencing and concurrency of the steps.
4. Keep each step short and simple.
5. Be sure accomplishment of the steps will result in objective accomplishment.
6. Be sure you have a way to track each step.

Figure 9.5 shows the action steps for the first objective in Figure 9.4. Notice that these steps are major chunks of activity and that each step will have its own action steps. In fact, some of these action steps will become objectives for others in the organization. Notice also that some steps can be done concurrently while some must be done in sequence.

Objective

To reduce waste and scrap costs in all production units by 15 percent by June 1, 1981.

Action Steps

1. To improve inspection of component parts prior to assembly.
2. To more closely control and monitor raw materials inventory spoilage and deterioration.
3. To implement an earlier QC check at the first stage of fabrication.
4. To increase training of roto assembly personnel to sixteen hours from four hours of classroom training.
5. To add one inspector-expediter to each line for each shift.
6. To improve personnel testing and selection procedures to screen out less agile employees for micrometer assembly.

Figure 9.5 Action steps for an objective

Schedule. Scheduling requires that dates be placed on each action step for each objective so that when all steps are completed the objective will be accomplished. Not only must each action step be scheduled, but managers must also schedule their daily work and that of the unit. Some techniques of scheduling include the following:

1. Start at the end point and work backwards to the present.

2. Decide on an *optimistic* (if everything went right) and *pessimistic* (if everything went wrong) time for each step. Then pick a *realistic* time between the two parameters.

3. Use a PERT diagram (Figure 9.6) or Gantt (bar) chart (Figure 9.7) to schedule. A simple desk calendar also will help. Identify the critical path (longest series of events) and focus on this since a delay in this path will cause a delay in the entire project.

4. Make sure all concerned know the schedule and follow it.

Budgets. The budget is built around the action steps for each objective. Besides budgeting money, human effort, space, facilities, and equipment,

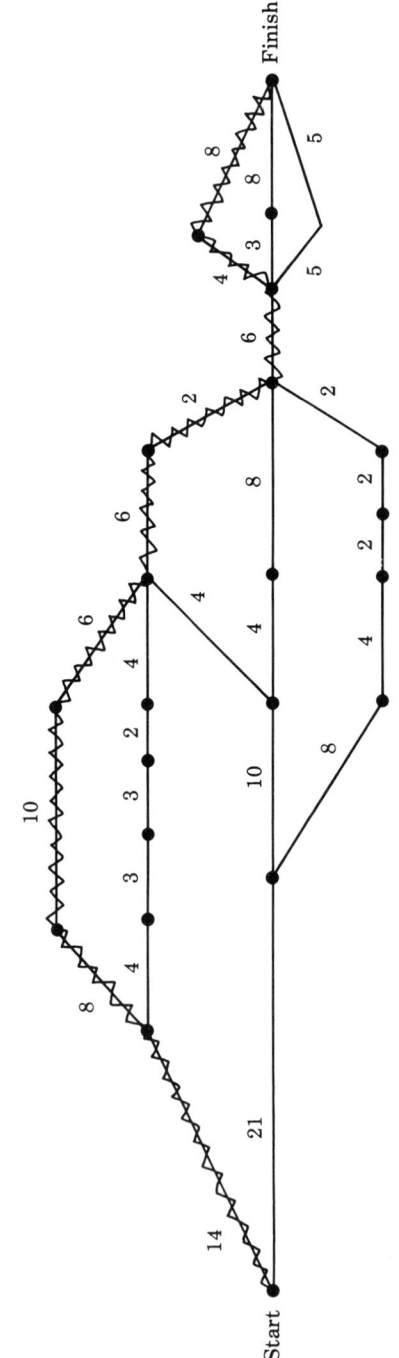

KEY: Dots are events or steps in the schedule.
Numbers are realistic time estimates in days between events.
∧∧ critical path (longest series of events)

Figure 9.6 Simplified program evaluation and review technique (PERT) chart

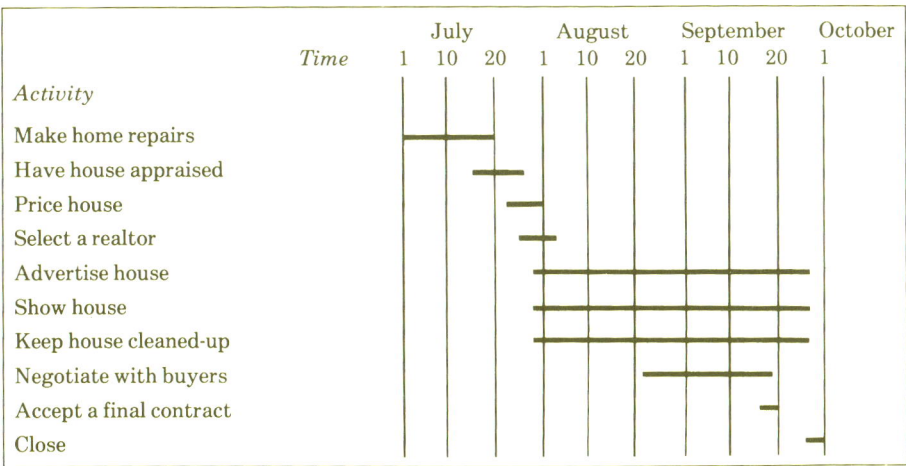

Figure 9.7 Sample Gantt (bar) chart for use in selling a house

also try to assess psychological costs. (Zero-base budgeting focuses on the financial aspects of budgeting for objectives.)

Notice that the budget is built around objectives, not vice-versa. Managers decide what it will cost to reach what they have set out. This enables them to show clearly what will have to go if the budget is cut. Of course, it is usually at this step in the process where much review and reconciliation occurs as it is seen that certain objectives cannot be reached with the money that is available. It is also here that good managers can develop integrity in budgeting by reducing the vicious cycle of asking for more than needed because they know their request will be cut—and it *is* cut because it is known that they asked for more than needed!

Also at this stage money can be moved from objectives of lower priority to ones of higher priority.

Standards. Standards are benchmarks for comparison. They compare desired performance against some basis. For example, monthly standards help management to stay on target to meet year-end objectives. Other standards may compare performance against some industrial standard. Still other standards are historical in that they compare present performance to performance during some previous time period. Standards help keep managers on track, and give managers some idea how they are doing compared to some important reference point or group. They also help carry out the next step in the objective-setting process.

Management information system (MIS). The MIS is how to track objective accomplishment without creating a blizzard of paperwork. It is a computer-based system of information for management decison making. Information is provided to managers in the form and style they want it, and at the time they need it.

This information system is critical for a good MBO system to work. A lack of a good MIS will sink an MBO program faster than anything else. Without it, managers spend so many hours and hours writing, tracking, and measuring objectives, that they don't have time to get any other work done! Only in smaller organizations and units will hand-tracking work.

Corrective action. The last phase of goal setting is designing a system for corrective action to bring deviant performance back on line. This corrective action usually includes positive and progressive discipline, performance appraisal, career counseling and development, and training. These actions will help managers and employees to better carry out work to meet objectives, and they will improve action where needed.

The best system of corrective action is one that is self-correcting. The work is monitored and feedback is provided quickly and efficiently to managers and employees in the organization so that they can take action to correct behavior without having to be told to do so by a superior.

CONCLUSION

Setting effective objectives is a required competency for good management. In this chapter we have reviewed a comprehensive process of goal setting that will help managers determine where they want to go and how they will get there.

The alternative to managing by objectives is either managing by crises or simply aimless wandering. While goal-setting actions do not solve all managerial problems, they do help substantially in reducing them. Furthermore, people work better when they have identifiable, meaningful goals they are trying to reach.

Goal setting is not an easy task. Managers should read and study information on management by objectives before using it. Also, the goal-setting process itself requires thorough knowledge of important areas affecting the organization and its units, as we saw in this chapter. It also requires managerial skill and ability to communicate, bargain, and negotiate with superiors, subordinates, and peer managers when setting objectives.

Finally, the process requires some degree of tenacity. It's easy to give up on MBO after one or two discouraging failures. But if implemented properly and carefully, and if given a fair chance, it *will* work. Competent managers realize this and work to make the goal-setting process almost a habit in managing.

QUESTIONS

1. Should the bottom-up approach to MBO be used over the top-down approach?

2. How can managers avoid the tendency to force objectives on subordinates?

3. How can goal displacement be prevented or avoided?

4. If your organization is on a formal system of goal setting, how well is it working? How can it be improved? If it is not on such a system, should it be?

5. Critique the following objective: "To improve our company's public image." Is this objective written in appropriate form? Does it deal with an area which should be of concern to a company? Does your organization have a similar objective?

CASES AND EXERCISES

CASE 1: YOU CAN'T QUANTIFY EDUCATION!

Fairfield County Public Schools recently was required to develop a method of comprehensive planning for school-based management by the state legislature. This mandate applies to all school systems in the state. The law requires that each school system, as well as each school within the system, develop a statement of purpose and short- and intermediate-range key objectives.

Fairfield is in the process of designing these objectives. They have designed a statement of purpose and were now debating the development of objectives for the elementary schools. Following is a dialogue between the Superintendent of Fairfield and the Planning Committee, which consists of the associate superintendent for instruction, the associate superintendent for administration, three principals (high school, middle school, and elementary school), one teacher (middle school), and one parent of a high-school student. The planning committee has consulted with several groups over the past six months at all three school levels to assess needs and problems.

Carol Henderson (superintendent): Well let's see, we seem to be making good progress. Dick, please read that purpose statement again for our elementary schools which we agreed on last time.

Dick Heinz (elementary school principal): Elementary school education should provide an opportunity for the child to develop intellectually, physically, culturally, and emotionally, and to aid him or her to reach a level of academic functioning commensurate with his or her capability and interests. We believe that the education process is on-going and should foster the ideals of a free society in which liberty, justice, and equality prevail.

Carol: That sounds pretty good. The rest of you agree? (All nod in agreement.)

Carol: Good, now let's get on with the elementary school objectives. Dick, I believe you were going to work up a draft list for us to discuss. Do you have copies for everyone?

Dick: Yes I do. (Distributes list.) Let's go over them. (Listed below are the objectives Dick distributed for elementary school education in the district.)

Elementary School Objectives for 1981–82 School Year

1. *Reading:* At least 75 percent of the students tested on the 1981–82 state assessment will answer correctly 75 percent of the items included in the communications skills section.

2. *Mathematics:* At least 75 percent of the students tested on the 1981–82 state assessment will answer correctly 75 percent of the items included in the arithmetic skills section.

3. *Writing:* At least 75 percent of the students tested on the 1981–82 state assessment will answer correctly 75 percent of the items included in the writing skills section.

4. *Spelling:* Sixty percent of the students tested during the 1981–82 school year will perform at or above their anticipated achievement level in spelling as determined by scores on the Test of Basic Skills.

5. *Career Education/Guidance:* All K–5 students will be involved in a sequentially planned program in Career Education and Guidance designed to increase self and career awareness.

6. *Personnel:* The ratio of adult personnel to students, as evidenced by instructional personnel and/or teacher aides, will be increased.

7. *Art:* (a) To insure each student the opportunity to develop a higher value for art within everyday life. (b) To provide each student the opportu-

nity to reinforce and gain insight into basic reading and math skills through correlation with art skills and concepts. (c) To provide each student the opportunity to explore various media and materials at an individual ability level to insure increasing involvement and personal satisfaction. (d) To increase each student's ability to apply personal artistic judgement and visual discrimination to everyday life.

8. *Physical Education:* To provide each student with a program adapted to his or her capacity and geared to his or her developmental needs.

9. *Pupil Personnel Services:* To request additional psychological services so that all referrals made to the Student Services Team will be processed within a four- to six-week period of time.

10. *Facilities:* To request that all elementary school kitchen facilities be enlarged and renovated to provide a self-contained kitchen.

Carol: How did you develop these, Dick?

Dick: I talked with teachers in a variety of subjects at our elementary schools and asked them to come up with some objectives. Then I distilled them into the list that we each have.

Carol: OK. Who would like to start out with some comments? Yes, Lance.

Lance Sheffler (associate superintendent for instruction): Dick, I think this is a fair start. I especially like your first four objectives, even though I might quarrel with the 75 percent figure. But objectives 5 through 10 are in great need of improvement. They're too vague and general. They would be hard to measure. They're motherhood, apple pie, and ice cream. Number 7 is particularly bad.

Dick: Yes, I know what you mean, but it sure is hard to get these teachers to quantify learning. I don't think we would have done so well with the first four had it not been for the state assessment test requirement passed two years ago by the legislature. But honestly, I'm not sure what we can do with objectives 5 through 10.

Carol: Well, does anybody else have any suggestions?

Questions

1. How can objectives 5 through 10 be improved? Rewrite each objective to make it conform to requirements for good objectives.

2. What factors must be considered when writing objectives in hard-to-quantify areas such as learning or service delivery? Do these same factors

have to be considered when writing objectives for manufacturing or sales of a physical product?

3. Critique the method used in this case for coming up with the objectives. (That is, critique the committee structure and process and the method Dick used. How would you improve it?)

CASE 2: LOOK BUSY

I'm all in favor of planning and goal setting, but my boss isn't. He just doesn't think in those terms. He confuses activity with output. I'll never forget the time he told me he denied me a merit raise because I seldom looked busy and that I should try to look busy to set a good example. I told him to look at my unit's output and to match it with any other unit in the organization. We do the best job of placing clients in jobs compared to any other office. Not only do we place the most people consistently each month, but we also have higher skilled placements. Hell, anyone can look busy. The key isn't to work hard but to work smart. That's what matters.

So what can I do? I try to operate this office efficiently on an MBO basis, but I sure don't get any encouragement from him. Why, I think I even intimidate him. He just does not understand the terminology used in MBO. Furthermore, with an objective basis for measuring output, he can't use his old-boy network when handing out raises and promotions. He actually resents it when I present him with my annual list of objectives for the office. He has few comments and what he does say is mostly negative.

My subordinates like MBO and so do a number of other office managers. Of course they work for more progressive regional managers. My regional manager is the pits. He's a prime example of a person who has risen to his highest level of incompetency. It's a good thing for him there are so many sharp office managers who consistently make him look good. Otherwise, he'd soon be fired, I'm sure. Oh well, I guess I'll just keep on using MBO. At least he hasn't told me I can't, even though I know he wishes I wouldn't.

Questions

1. Can a subordinate manager use MBO even when his or her superior is neutral on it at best? What are the risks for the subordinate?

2. Can a superior manager use MBO if it is resisted by subordinates? What are the risks?

3. Does the fact that this deals with providing a service (job placement) have anything to do with the situation? Would it matter whether this was a private or public employment agency? Why or why not?

EXERCISE: WRITING YOUR PURPOSE, OBJECTIVES, AND ACTION PLANS

This exercise is to develop the purpose, objectives, and action plans for your unit. First, write the purpose statement for your organization on a sheet of paper. Then below it, write the purpose for your unit. (Try the best you can to write the organizational purpose even if one is not formally written by the organization.)

Then list eight to ten key objectives for your unit. Make sure that they meet the requirements for a good objective and that they are consistent with your organization's and unit's purpose statements.

Next, make copies of Figure 9.8 and use it to list the action steps for each objective, the date for each step, the person accountable for carrying it out, and how it will be tracked or measured. (What report or system will be used?) You might ask each of your subordinates to do the same in their respective areas of job responsibility. Are their objectives and action plans consistent with yours? Are yours consistent with your superior's?

Objective:	Date for Completion	Person Accountable for Performance	Tracking or Measuring System to Be Used
Action Steps:			
1.			
2.			
3.			
4.			
5.			
6.			
7.			
8.			
9.			
10.			

Figure 9.8 Form for objective action planning and scheduling

REFERENCES

Anthony, William P. *Participative Management.* Reading, Mass: Addison-Wesley, 1978.
  Handbook which offers many traditional and new ways to achieve participation. Can be used to make MBO the participative process which it should be.

Carroll, Stephen J., and Tosi, Henry L., Jr. *Management by Objectives: Applications and Research.* New York: MacMillan Co., 1973.
  One of the few works which has actually tried to assess the effectiveness of MBO programs.

Hodge, B. J., and Anthony, William P. *Organization Theory: An Environmental Approach.* Boston, Mass: Allyn and Bacon, Inc., 1979.
  Chapter 7 gives a comprehensive summary of goals, the goal-setting process, and work.

Hodge, B. J., and Anthony, William P. "MBO: Clear Channel Communication." *Supervision* (December 1975): 26–28.
  An examination of the improved communication that usually comes about through an MBO program.

Humble, John W., ed. *Management by Objectives in Action.* London: McGraw-Hill, 1970.
  A good collection of articles dealing with the issues of MBO. In particular the section on "Training MBO Advisers" is helpful for firms beginning an MBO program.

Morrisey, George. *Management by Objectives and Results.* Reading, Mass: Addison-Wesley, 1970.
  An excellent, short, yet comprehensive handbook for use in implementing MBO systems. Has since been revised into two new editions published by same publisher: *Management by Objectives and Results for Business and Industry* (1977), and *Management by Objectives and Results in the Public Sector* (1976).

Odiorne, George S. "Management by Objectives and the Phenomenon of Goal Displacement." *Human Resources Management* 13 (Spring 1974): 2–7.
  A good look at this all too common nemesis to MBO programs.

Odiorne, George S. *Management Decisions by Objectives.* Englewood Cliffs, N.J.: Prentice-Hall, 1969.
  Odiorne's earlier work, *Management by Objectives,* is more widely known, but this book ties in MBO with decision-making and problem-solving processes.

Raia, Anthony P. *Management by Objectives.* Glenview, Ill.: Scott Foresman and Co., 1974.
  An excellent comprehensive, yet short, handbook on implementing MBO programs. Well grounded in the academic literature.

10
How Should a Manager Lead?

"Boy, these sales figures are awful, aren't they Paul?"

"They sure are, Diane. Really bad. If our monthly reports continue much longer like this, we'll have one of our worst years ever."

"This just confirms what we said earlier, Paul. Ever since Chet has become Regional Manager, we've had a complete lack of leadership. He's a 'do-nothing' manager. You can't get him to act at all."

"You're right Diane. He's afraid to make decisions. Just a nice guy—a back slapper who's afraid to make anyone angry."

"He just typifies the style that's becoming common at the top of this company. Paul, if this continues much longer, you and I will need to look for another job. This company will be eaten alive by our competitors."

Many people believe that the lack of effective leadership is the number one problem facing our organizations today. No doubt that there are many managers who cannot lead. Leadership is not a *sufficient* condition for competent management, but it is a *necessary* condition. Leadership inspires performance. It makes the difference between merely meeting a standard and achieving excellence. It is a catalyst to action.

Achieving effective leadership has been a goal of human beings throughout history. We desire leadership in all types of our organizations—business, government, church, military, schools, hospitals, and so on. It is certainly a key ingredient for effective organizational performance.

If leadership is so important, then why is it in such short supply? Why are there so many cases as that shown in the dialogue at the beginning of this chapter? A shortage exists because leadership is extremely complex to understand, hard to learn, and difficult to practice. Let's look at the skills required of a good leader.

LEADERSHIP SKILLS

What skills are required of a good leader? First, it must be realized that leadership is an *influence process*. This means that leaders influence members of groups to work together to seek some goal or set of goals. Second, leadership is only one part of management. It concerns the *directing* function. Management also includes planning, organizing, controlling, and staffing functions. However, many of the same skills required of managers are also required of leaders. These include perceptual ability, the ability to crystallize and communicate a goal, the ability to define a good path to the goal, the ability to understand people, and the ability to offer rewards and incentives that motivate people.

Leadership also requires other skills. Two of the most important are *consideration* and *initiation*. Consideration skills refer to the extent to which a leader considers the feelings, attitudes, and beliefs of the group when leading. Initiation skills refer to the extent to which the leader initiates or starts action in the group as opposed to the group initiating or starting action. Both of these skills are required by good leaders, as are the other skills also required for good management, but there is no set amount of these skills to be practiced in every situation. Rather, the skills must be practiced within a *contingency* or *situational* framework. What this means is that the contingencies of a given leadership situation will determine what is good leadership.

Contingency leadership

A leader of a military combat team under fire may not make the best leader for a group of Ph.D. research chemists at a chemical corporation. The people, task, and situation are all different. Recognition of these differences has led to the development of the contingency theory of leadership. What this theory says is that a leader must understand the particular circumstances under which the leadership is to occur *prior* to practicing leadership. Unless this is done, it is quite possible that the wrong leadership style will occur in the wrong situation. To understand this better, let's take a look at a continuum of leadership styles.

Leadership style continuum. Leadership style varies from autocratic to laissez-faire (democratic) with several points in between, as shown in Figure 10.1. At the left of the diagram is the autocratic leader who alone makes all decisions. At the right is the situation where the group makes the decisions and the leader simply does what the group wants. Along the continuum there are three other major styles indicated. Points between each style on the continuum are combinations of style.

Notice that the key element that distinguishes styles along the continuum is the *amount of decision-making power* of the leader vis-à-vis the

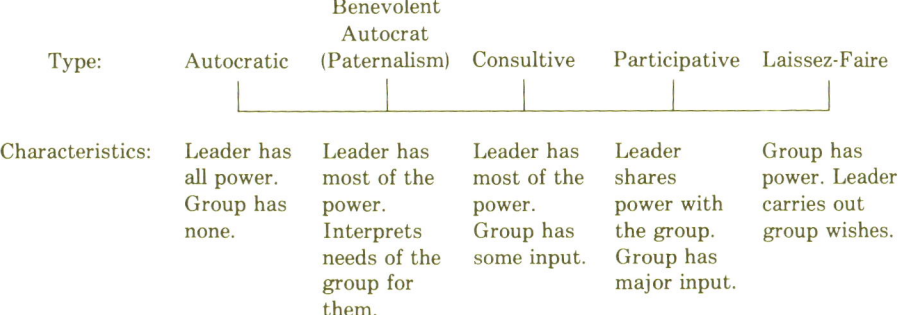

Figure 10.1 Varying leadership styles (Adapted from Robert Tannenbaum and Warren H. Schmidt, "How to Choose a Leadership Pattern," *Harvard Business Review* (March–April 1958): 95–101.)

group. The amount of power displayed by the leader is the key element in determining style because it defines the relationship the leader has with the group. Thus, it influences all that the leader does in controlling or guiding the group.

When applying this continuum to contingency leadership, each of the styles along the continuum may be appropriate under a certain set of specific circumstances. In other words, leaders who are autocratic are appropriate under certain conditions, as are benevolent autocrats (paternalistic father figures), consultive, participative and laissez-faire leaders. *There is no one leadership style appropriate in all situations.*

Fiedler's contingency factors. What factors determine which leadership style is appropriate? How do leaders know which style will work? Fiedler provides us with some guidance here. He indicates that there are three important influences that determine appropriate leader style. However, he addresses the style issue a bit differently. He says that style can take only *two forms:* a *task* orientation or an *employee* orientation. (This is a development from Blake and Mouton's Managerial Grid concept.) A task-oriented leader is concerned with achieving the task or goal of the group and places primary emphasis here. On the other hand, the employee-oriented leader is concerned with achieving good employee relations and places primary emphasis here instead of accomplishing the task.

Fiedler indicates that there are three factors that directly influence whether the manager's leadership style should be task- or employee-oriented: (1) Leader-member relations, (2) Structuredness of task, and (3) Leader-position power. *Leader-member relations* refer to how well the leader gets along with members of the group being led. The *structuredness of the task* refers to how well defined the task is. Is the task to be done by the group concise and routine, such as cleaning a room, or is it unstructured and complex, such as redesigning an organization? *Leader position power* refers to the amount of power and authority the leader has in the organization. If these three variables are either very good or very bad, then a task-oriented leader is appropriate for the situation. If, on the other hand, these three variables are somewhere between very good or very bad, an employee-oriented leader is appropriate. These relationships are shown in Figure 10.2.

Since many people equate an autocratic style with a task orientation, when leaders take a task orientation, they tend to be toward the *left* side of the leadership continuum (Figure 10.1). On the other hand, employee-oriented leaders tend to be more participative and operate toward the *right* end of the leadership continuum. Also, since most leaders face intermediate favorableness on each of these variables, then an employee-oriented leadership style is called for more often than not.

Finally, note in Figure 10.2 that the three factors vary in importance. The most important factor influencing this relationship is the quality of leader-member relations. The second most important is the structuredness of the task, and the third is leader position power.

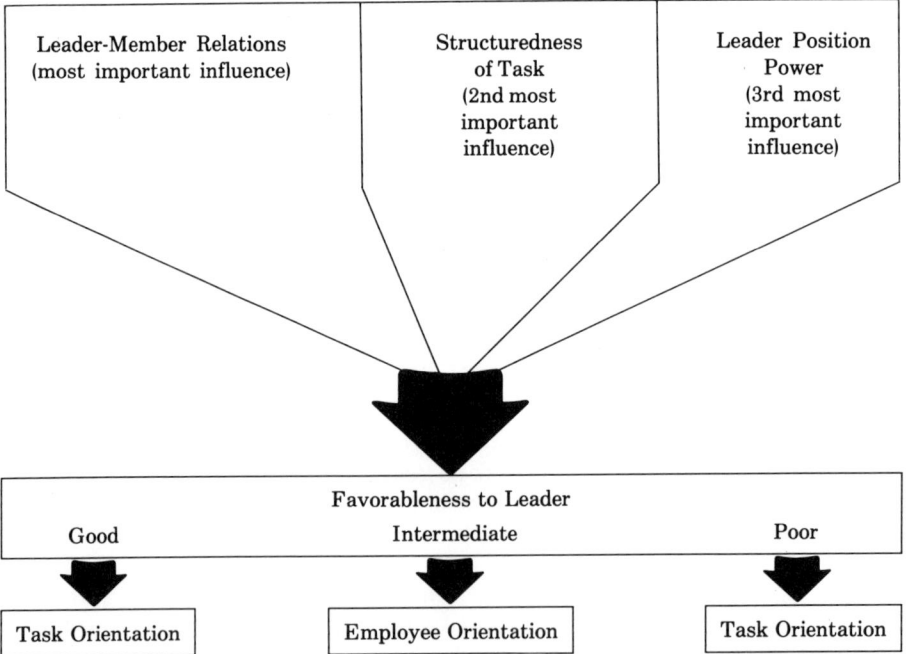

Figure 10.2 The contingency theory of leadership (William P. Anthony and Edward Nicholson, *The Management of Human Resources* (Columbus, Ohio: Grid, Inc.), and Fred Fiedler, *Theory of Leadership Effectiveness* (New York: McGraw-Hill, 1967).)

What does all of this mean? First, leaders must understand the quality of leader-member relations, task structure, and their own organizational power in a given situation. Knowing these will indicate which style is appropriate; that is, whether to be employee or task oriented. Second, it means that some leadership style flexibility is necessary. It might be, however, as Fiedler maintains, that an individual leader cannot change style significantly from one situation to another. That is, leadership style for an *individual* leader is not flexible. A task-oriented autocratic leader does not become participative/employee oriented and then switch back as situations change. There is some evidence that leadership style for a *particular* person is set and doesn't change much. If this is so, then it is up to management to put leaders in situations that require a style consistent with the leaders' style. This would imply that much shifting around of leaders is required as job situations change. Management must make sure that the right leaders are in the right place at the right time. The combat sergeant would *not* be the right person to direct Ph.D. research chemists.

Third, Fiedler's theory states that there may be *other* variables that could be important in determining leadership style. That is, since the theory is still developing and conclusive research has not been completed, it opens the door for the examination of other variables that could influence appropriate leadership style within a contingency model. Therefore, building upon the contingency work done by Fiedler and others, we can expand the contingency model. Other variables effect leadership effectiveness besides those already discussed. We examine these other factors in the next section.

LEADERSHIP EFFECTIVENESS

We saw in the previous section that leader style can vary all the way from a task-oriented autocratic one to an employee-oriented laissez-faire style. We also saw that each style is appropriate in a certain situation. Leader-member relations, structuredness of task, and leader position power were identified as appropriate situational factors to be examined by leaders. There are other factors that also should be examined. In this section we discuss four additional categories of factors that must be examined by a leader to determine the leadership style: leader variables, member variables, situational variables, and time considerations.

Leader variables

To what extent does the leader identify with the task to be done? What are the leader's skills, abilities, and interests as they relate to the task? These two key questions are critical for examining the appropriateness of a leader for a given situation. For example, a supervisor of a construction team may be very successful in getting others to put in a sewer, but would likely have difficulty directing a team of brain surgeons. By the same token, the chief brain surgeon would likely do horribly directing the group putting in a sewer. *Task identity* is critical! If leaders cannot identify with the task at hand they will fail.

Leader skills, abilities, and interests must also coincide with those required by the task. Leaders must be placed in a situation where task requirements for performance match the skills, abilities, and interests of the leader.

Member variables

Just as with the leaders, members must be able to identify with the task. They also must have skills, abilities, and interests required in the task. A group of plumbers would probably do poorly in laying a brick wall. Business professors would likely not do well teaching pre-school children. Matching member characteristics with those required by the task is essential.

Task and goal variables

How complex is the task? Is it routine? Is it dynamic or static in nature? How familiar are leaders and group members with the task? How clear is the goal to the group? The more routine and structured the task and the more familiar the group is with the task and goal, the *less* is the need for any leadership at all. There's one best way to do the job and the people know this way, so why have strong leadership? The people can lead themselves by just following a prescribed work routine with which they are familiar.

However, if the task is unstructured and complex, and the people are not familiar with it, then there is a strong need for leadership to guide, solve problems, and point the direction for the group. Directing a group of programmers to design a new training system for billing clerks would call for this type of leadership. The computer programmers know how to work with the computer, but they do not know how to design training. Someone with training design expertise would need to provide leadership in this environment.

Time variable

If there is a short time frame to perform the task, then a somewhat autocratic leader is needed in order to get quick group action. A participative employee orientation takes time and is not appropriate in a crisis situation. However, beware of those managers who manufacture crises so that they can continue to manage autocratically. Management by crises is a situation often invented by managers to justify their own ineptness.

We can summarize these four critical variables for leadership effectiveness in Figure 10.3. Notice that this model reinforces the contingency theory, but extends it to include consideration of other factors. The model is

LEADERSHIP EFFECTIVENESS 157

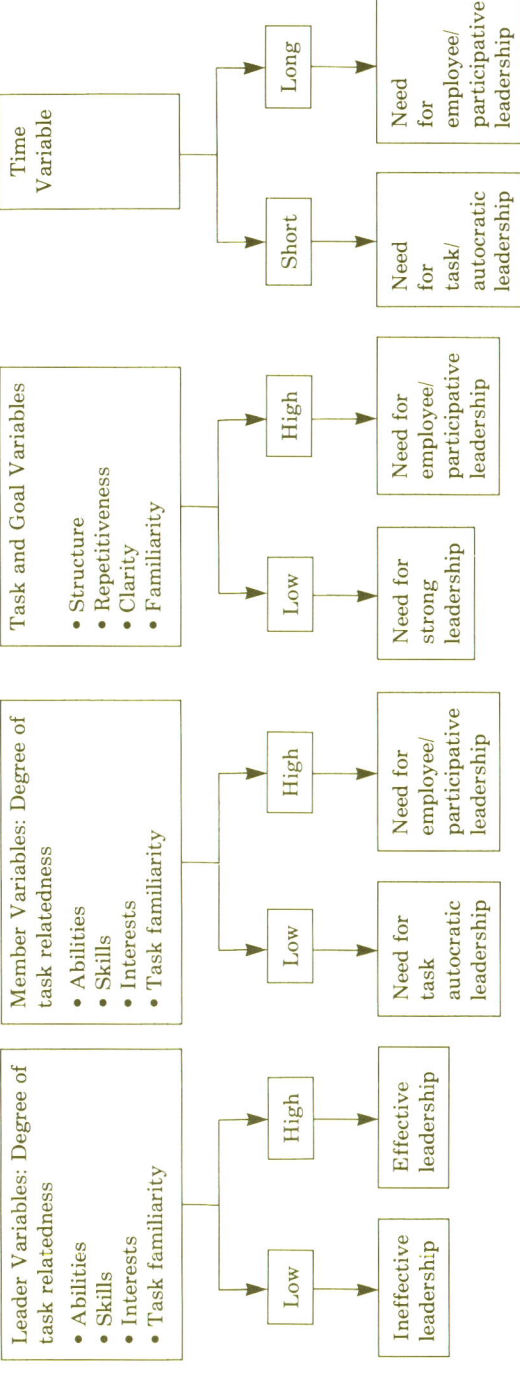

Figure 10.3 Variables for effective leadership

mostly speculative at this point and is not supported by a perponderance of evidence in leadership research. Yet, intuitively the model makes sense and provides us with some guidance when examining the appropriateness of different leadership styles in various leadership situations. It's important for each manager to assess the specific situation faced to determine the appropriate leadership style that will lead to maximum effectiveness.

Measures of leadership effectiveness

How do we know when a leader is effective? There are two broad measures of effectiveness for leadership. First, an *appropriate goal* or set of goals will be achieved at least cost. Second, members of the group will be *satisfied* with their own and their leader's performance.

The effective leader has the group work toward a goal or set of goals with which they can *identify*. The goal is not imposed on the group against their will. Rather, the group, under the direction of the leader, *evolves* the set of goals they wish to accomplish. This does not mean the group is free to do its own thing regardless of the desires of the organization or higher management. Even in a laissez-faire leadership situation, the development of goals by the group are constrained or modified by goals developed by other groups in the organization.

What it does mean, however, is that effective leaders are able to help and guide the group to develop goals consistent with goals required by the organization. They work with the group to achieve consensus and unity of action by mediating, compromising, and bargaining. Also, the leaders ensure that the group is made up of people who have interests in the area required by the general goal of the organization so that the specific goals of the group will be consistent with those of the organization.

Of course this assumes that the leaders have some authority to constitute the group which is being led. If they do not have such authority, then they should influence the person with the authority to include people in the group with the skills, abilities, interests, and task familiarity required in the situation. Leadership effectiveness is very difficult to achieve unless the leaders have some say as to the people who will constitute the group they will lead.

Another alternative to leaders or someone else higher up selecting group members is to have the members self-select themselves. This ensures that people with interests required by the task will make up the group, but it does *not* ensure that group members will have the skills and abilities necessary to carry out the task. Perhaps a description of skills and abilities necessary could be stated and then people with these skills and abilities invited to volunteer for the group. Voluntary self-selection of group members also ensures members of the group have some level of *motivation* to complete the task at hand. This makes the leader's job easier and helps ensure leadership and group effectiveness.

In addition to efficiently achieving an appropriate goal, the second measure of leadership effectiveness is member satisfaction with their own and their leader's performance. Goals can be achieved through compulsion. In an autocratic situation, appropriate goals will be achieved, but the research shows that they are achieved at the expense of member satisfaction. Most people do not like to work for autocratic leaders. It makes them unhappy. Furthermore, even though short-term goals can be achieved through autocratic leaders, its difficult to achieve long-term ones. That is, it is possible *to buy short-term compliance at the expense of long-term commitment*. People will not go beyond the bear minimum required working for autocratic leaders.

Since the desirable state of affairs is where people will go beyond the mere minimum required, group members should be satisfied with their own and their leader's performance. This satisfaction will lead to commitment. This commitment should lead to performance in the future, which goes beyond the mere minimum required. We can summarize these relationships in Figure 10.4.

Thus, we aren't interested in having a satisfied group just for the sake of satisfaction. Rather, we see this as a way to get even better group performance in the future. But to get a true measure of leadership effectiveness, we need to be concerned about both goal achievement *and* satisfaction. The two are intertwined and influence each other.

What happens when the group members are satisfied with the group's performance but the leader isn't? Suppose I am a member of a group which has just designed a training program for our company. We are very satisfied with it and show it to our firm's Organizational Development Director. She indicates it is not appropriate and needs much rework. Here is a case where the group is satisfied with the effort but the leader is not.

First of all, the leader should have clearly stated what was required at the outset so that there was consistency in expectations between her and the group. Second, the leader has a responsibility to monitor and provide

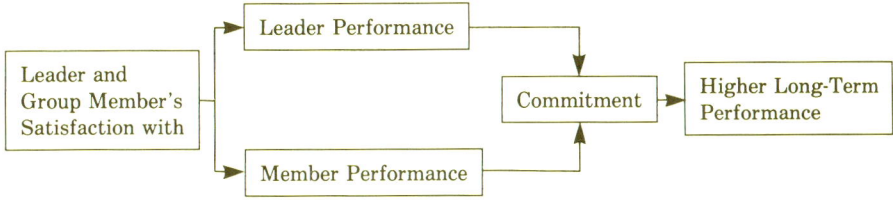

Figure 10.4 Satisfaction with performance

constructive feedback and guidance to the group as it completes the task. If the group is turned loose, then why have a leader at all? Third, the leader needs to provide the resources (secretarial help, equipment, books, materials, etc.) required by the group to get the job done. And fourth, the leader needs to be sure that the people in the group have the skills, abilities, interests, and knowledge needed to complete the task properly. If these conditions are met, then chances are that the level of leader and member satisfaction with group performance will not differ.

WAYS OF LEADING

People must choose the leadership style appropriate for them in a particular situation. While it is true that most of us cannot jump around from one extreme to the other on the leadership style continuum, we can vary within a specific range on the continuum. Autocratic leaders, for example, can be benevolent autocrats or even consultive on occasion, even though it is doubtful they would ever be participative or laissez-faire.

Managers should recognize that if their particular leadership style is not appropriate for a specific situation with a certain group of employees, then they should remove themselves from the situation and have someone else lead the group. Perhaps another manager could be brought in or perhaps an *informal* leader could emerge from the group. Smart managers use informal leaders regularly. These individuals emerge from the group and are usually trusted by the group. When managers find that they themselves have the wrong style for the situation, helping the group identify an informal leader to work through might be entirely appropriate.

All managers need leadership training at some point in their career. Good leadership skills result because of innate skills people have that are developed, refined, and sharpened in leadership training. Leaders are like athletes. Some basic level of interpersonal skill is required, but this skill can be coached and developed through training just as an athlete's inherent ability can be developed through practice and coaching.

People do not learn to be leaders automatically. It takes practice. Leadership can be learned on the job, but it is best learned through on-the-job training and classroom learning experiences in leadership. Effective leaders do not cease to learn.

CONCLUSION

Leadership is a complex influence process that all competent managers practice effectively. It is a necessary condition for competent management, but not a sufficient condition. Other skills are also required for competency in management.

A short supply of effective leadership has plagued nations throughout history. All organizations in all societies need good leaders—business, government, educational, political, religious, and so on. Effective leaders are not necessarily strong leaders. The autocratic style is appropriate in certain situations; the laissez-faire style appropriate in others. Effective leaders are those who practice the leadership style appropriate for the situation, task, and followers.

Leaders are made, not born. Effective leadership can be learned if individuals initially have some minimal level of leadership ability.

Leadership is determined by two key measures: (1) Was an appropriate goal or set of goals achieved efficiently? (2) How satisfied are the leader and members with their own and the leader's performance? These two key measures are closely related and, in the final result, determine leadership effectiveness.

QUESTIONS

1. What is leadership? How does it differ from the concept of management?

2. What is meant by the statement, "Good leadership is a necessary condition, but not a sufficient condition for competency in management"?

3. Identify someone in your organization who is generally recognized as an effective leader. What makes this person effective?

4. Do you believe leaders can change their personal style of leadership to fit the specific requirements of a situation or group? Why or why not?

5. Can a person learn how to be a good leader? If not, why not? If so, how?

CASES AND EXERCISES

CASE 1: MEDIOCRE MILDEW U.

Organizations today face a complex web of rules that affect their operations. These rules are fostered on them by the government (federal, state, and local laws) by unions, and by top level management. Today's organizations are also quite large and complex. They typify many characteristics of a bureaucracy—inflexible policies and procedures, rigid reporting relationships, poor communication, static structure—in short, hardening of the organizational arteries.

Some people maintain that such a situation prohibits effective leadership. They say that managers are not even *permitted* to become good leaders let alone *encouraged* to become good leaders. Chelsea King, President of a large state university in southeastern United States recently reflected on these developments in a meeting with the University's Board of Governors. Following is a partial dialogue from their meeting.

Ms. King: Ladies and gentlemen, you have been criticizing my administration for a lack of leadership. We have received the same criticism from some of our faculty members. I'll tell you the same thing I told them. Bureaucracy doesn't inspire good leadership. The legislature, you, and the faculty union tie my hands with your complex rules, regulations, and procedures. It simply reduces my job to one of following and enforcing rules made by others.

Mr. Vanelli (board member): I think we can appreciate that Ms. King, but you're going too far. We don't mean to tie your hands, but all organizations must have rules, or else we couldn't operate.

Ms. King: But your rules take away any incentives. They lead to mediocrity. As far as I am concerned, we have a mediocre university not an outstanding one. An outstanding university requires effective leadership to bring in outstanding faculty and students. What faculty members would come here to teach and do research? What really bright students would attend? All of your rules and the union push everyone down to the same level of mediocrity.

Ms. Shalenz (board member): But as Mr. Vanelli said, all organizations need rules. Even business organizations have rules and have unions, but yet you still see good leadership in business.

Ms. King: As you know Ms. Shalenz, I worked in a major corporation before becoming university president. To some extent you are right, but I really see more *similarities* between the constraints on good leadership in business and the university than I see dissimilarities. In both cases it's difficult to be a good leader. This is really a sad state of affairs because we could be a really great university. But my hands are tied. This university will mildew on the vine and I wish I had the freedom to do something about it.

Questions

1. Do you agree that the flexibility and freedom of action allowed top leaders in an organization has become increasingly constrained and narrowed? Why or why not? Does it matter whether the person is in a business or governmental organization?

2. What action would you suggest for Ms. King? Why?

3. Are there convenient excuses and rationalizations available to a leader *not* to practice good leadership? Are they valid? Explain your answer.

CASE 2: THE NORM OF INCOMPETENCY

When you have incompetent leaders around you the norm is incompetence, but is viewed as the proper everyday state of affairs by the people involved. Any deviation from this norm is viewed as incompetency by those around you, not as competency. You might institute great improvements, but they'll be viewed as incompetent behavior simply because they do not reinforce the present way of operating—the improvements violate the expectations of the people around you. You'll be accused of rocking the boat, stirring things up, causing chaos.

Well, let me tell you, sometimes things *do* need to be stirred up. Sometimes leaders do have to create chaos to get some people off of their fat cans. Most people can't recognize good leadership anyway. They don't know what a good leader is. To many people, a good leader is someone who does what you want them to do, not what *needs* to be done.

So, we have a dilemma. One criterion for effective leadership is satisfaction of the group, yet if the leader tries to be nice to satisfy the group and make them happy, the job won't get done.

I believe I know what I'm talking about. I've had twenty-five years of management experience—all the way from being a supervisor of a construction crew to a director of maintenance for a large company. Your good workers know what needs to be done and really require very little leadership. Your poor workers need lots of leadership, but the kind you have to give them sure won't make them happy.

Questions

1. How does this person seem to be defining the term *leadership?* Do you agree with the definition?

2. Can a leader be effective in satisfying the group and still get the job done? If so, how? If not, why not?

3. Do you believe people in a group can recognize a good leader from a poor one? Why or why not?

4. Do you agree with the person's views as outlined in the first paragraph? Why or why not?

EXERCISE: DO YOU HAVE AN APPROPRIATE LEADERSHIP STYLE?

This exercise asks you to assess your present leadership style and to determine if it is appropriate for the leadership situations you generally face in your present job. Since we all face various leadership situations to some extent in our job, approach this from the aspect of identifying those situations that seem to occur *most often* in your job.

The first part of the exercise asks you to rate the leadership situations you face on the job along three key dimensions. The second part of the exercise asks you to evaluate your style of leadership. Finally, the third part asks you to determine if your style is appropriate for the situations you face and, if not, what style would be appropriate. Please rate each item *honestly*.

Part I: Determining the Characteristics of Leadership Situations on Your Job (Circle the appropriate number.)

	Agree Disagree
Leader Variables	
1. I have a fairly good relationship with my subordinates.	1 2 3 4 5
2. My position gives me some but not a lot of power in this organization.	1 2 3 4 5
3. I am very knowledgeable about and interested in the tasks my subordinates and I do.	1 2 3 4 5
4. I have skills and abilities that are relevant to the jobs my subordinates and I have to do.	1 2 3 4 5
Subordinate Variables	
1. My subordinates have the skills and abilities needed to get the job done.	1 2 3 4 5
2. My subordinates are very interested in the job they do.	1 2 3 4 5
3. My subordinates are very familiar with the job they must do.	1 2 3 4 5
Task Variables	
1. The goal of the task or job to be done is very clear to my subordinates.	1 2 3 4 5
2. My subordinates and I have some leeway in deciding on how to do the task or job; that is, the task is not highly structured for us.	1 2 3 4 5

3. We have enough time to properly carry out the task; we are not under continual crises.   1 2 3 4 5

Part II: Determining Your Leadership Style (Circle appropriate number.)

	Agree Disagree
1. More often than not, my subordinates and I decide things as a group rather than me telling them what to do.	1 2 3 4 5
2. My subordinates have skills and abilities appropriate for the job we must do that are at least equal to or better than my skills and abilities.	1 2 3 4 5
3. I value my subordinates' suggestions and ideas on complex issues which we face.	1 2 3 4 5
4. I regularly set aside time to get meaningful input from my subordinates.	1 2 3 4 5
5. I almost always accept most of the suggestions my subordinates give me.	1 2 3 4 5
6. My subordinates view me as a team leader rather than the "boss."	1 2 3 4 5
7. I have a very good relationship with all of my subordinates.	1 2 3 4 5
8. My subordinates and I communicate with each other openly and honestly.	1 2 3 4 5
9. My subordinates do not hesitate to tell me if I'm doing a lousy job.	1 2 3 4 5
10. If I ask for extra effort from my subordinates they readily carry it out voluntarily.	1 2 3 4 5

Part III: Matching Situation With Style

1. Total your scores for each Part separately by adding the numbers you circled for all ten items in each Part.
2. Divide each total by 10.
3. If the total for Part I is 2.5 or less, then the total for Part II should be 2.5 or less. If the total for Part I is 2.6 or more, then the total for Part II should be 2.6 or more.
4. If the above is not the case then you are practicing leadership inappropriately for most of the situations you face on your job. A score of 2.5 or

less in Part I calls for a participative/employee style which is indicated by a score of 2.5 or less in Part II. A score of 2.6 or more in Part I calls for a task/autocratic style which is indicated by a score of 2.6 or more in Part II. The more your score in Part II varies from your score in Part I, the more inconsistent is your leadership style with the situations you face on your job.

5. If your scores are substantially inconsistent, what can you do about it?

REFERENCES

Fiedler, Fred E., and Chemers, Martin M. *Leadership and Effective Management.* Glenview, Ill.: Scott, Foresman and Co., 1974.
    Further develops Fiedler's original contingency theory of leadership and provides some practical applications.

Fiedler, Fred E. *A Theory of Leadership Effectiveness.* New York: McGraw-Hill Book Co., 1967.
    Sets forth Fiedler's contingency theory of leadership and some of the research findings which led to this theory.

Fiedler, Fred E. "Style or Circumstance: The Leadership Enigma." *Psychology Today* (March 1969): 38-43.
    A popularized discussion of Fiedler's theory in layman's terms.

Kerr, Steve, et. al. "Toward A Contingency Theory of Leadership Based on Consideration and Initiation Structure Literature." *Organizational Behavior and Human Performance* (August 1974): 62-82.
    A well documented article tying the literature dealing with consideration and initiation variables in with the contingency theory writings.

Sayles, Leonard. *Leadership: What Effective Managers Really Do and How They Do It.* New York: McGraw-Hill Book Co., 1979.
    A very readable, comprehensive book on leadership that tells it "like it is." Ties leadership in with the management process and with motivation. Based on the author's many years of formal and informal research in organizations.

Shaw, Marion F., and Costanzo, Philip R. *Theories of Social Psychology.* New York: McGraw-Hill Book Co., 1970.
    A serious attack and criticism of Fiedler's theory is presented on p. 320, which led to the development of some of my ideas in this chapter.

Tannenbaum, Robert, and Schmidt, Warren H. "How to Choose a Leadership Pattern." *Harvard Business Review* (March-April 1958): 95-101.
    The classic article on leadership style. So popular it was represented in its entirety in a later issue of the *Harvard Business Review.*

11
How Should a Manager Make Decisions?

Let me tell you my philosophy on decision making: I don't like to make them. If I make a good decision, someone else gets credit for it. If I make a bad decision, I get all the blame. Therefore, I believe in postponing hard decisions. There are several ways I do this, including appointing a committee to study it to death.

I don't believe that postponing a decision is all that bad. If the problem gets bad enough, someone else higher up will solve it for me. If the problem doesn't get bad enough, it will go away and a decision really wasn't called for. Either case I win.

This candid reflection by a middle level manager in a large organization unfortunately is representative of the attitude held by many managers today. One factor, above all else, that characterizes competent managers from incompetent ones is that *competent managers can make good decisions*.

The essence of management is decision making and influence, as we've pointed out several times. Take away decision making and you do not have management. The manager's job becomes an empty shell—consisting of pushing paper, attending meetings, writing reports, and little else. The job becomes a shallow bell with a hollow ring to it.

Therefore, all competent managers make good decisions without shying away from them, and they are willing to live with the results of their decisions. They have a high analytical ability that enables them to get to the core of any problem, and they have creative ability to come up with new alternatives. Effective managers are risk takers, willing to try something different that might work better than the tried-and-true. They can implement their decisions and monitor the results, and they can take corrective action to bring desired decision results on line.

In this chapter we examine the decision-making process and look at some important points which must be considered in order to maximize decision effectiveness.

THE PROBLEM-SOLVING AND DECISION-MAKING PROCESS

One of the things that troubles many managers is their uncertainty as to whether they are spending their time on *important* compared to unimportant decisions. The model of the decision-making process we discuss in this chapter recognizes this concern. The model we review is comprehensive. It recognizes that all decisions stem from the people we are trying to serve—our customers or clients. From this basic point, we examine several additional factors in the decision-making process. A summary of the model is presented in Figure 11.1. Let's look at each step in this process.

Customers/clients to be served

We've discussed elsewhere in this book how important it is for the organization to focus on the reason for its existence in all matters that concern it. Businesses exist to provide a service or product to customers at a profit. Government exists to provide a service or a product to clients (citizens) at the least cost consistent with desired service levels. These simple facts serve as the basis for good decision making whether in business or nonbusiness organizations.

If we have a clear idea of the market for our products and services, we are well on our way to determining what and how decisions should be made. We need to know what customer/client needs we are trying to serve and which ones we are trying to meet. We need a market research staff and other means to tell us this.

In some cases, such as a government agency, a *legislative body* will interpret these needs and wants for us by passing pieces of legislation at the federal, state, and local level. This legislation in a democracy should reflect the will of the people governed.

Also, certain "home office" mandates are developed which supposedly reflect the way certain needs and wants are to be met. In the public sector these can be in the form of executive orders, proclamations, or court rulings. In business the mandates can be in the form of broad statements of policy from headquarters. We must know these mandates if we are to understand how customer/client needs are being interpreted by those at the very top in our organization.

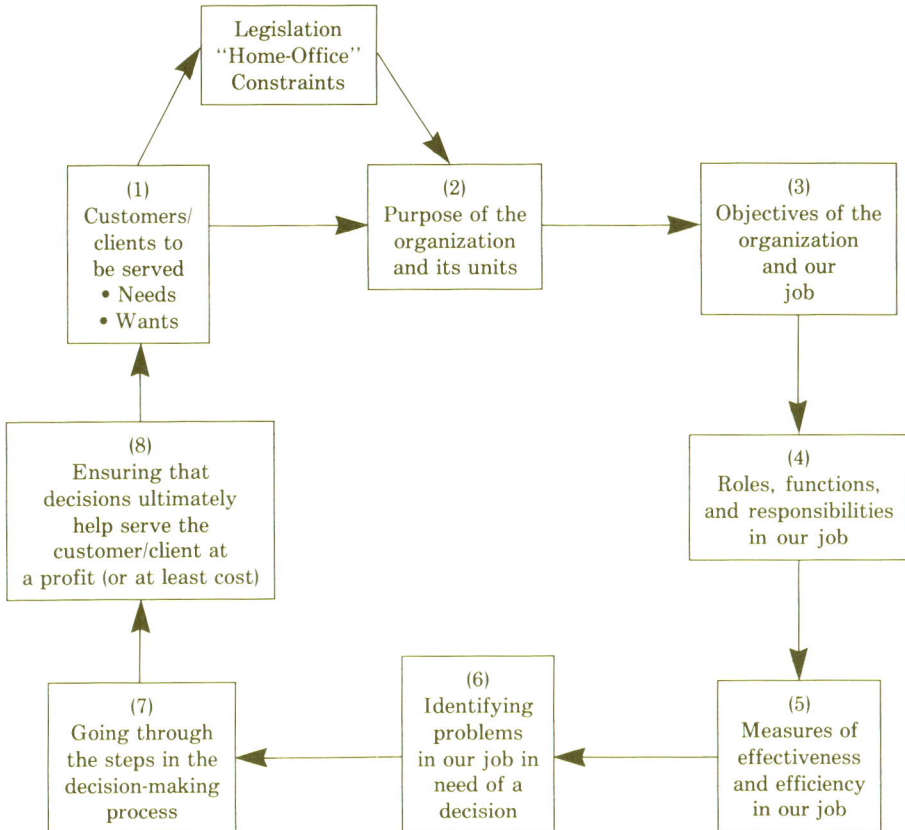

Figure 11.1 A model of decision making

Knowing legislation and "home office" mandates is not the only way to understand customer/client needs. Managers in the organization also must be concerned with directly examining these needs. Not all needs and wants are necessarily addressed in legislation or mandates, and those addressed might only be addressed in a general sort of way. We need to fill in the gaps. We need to be concerned about achieving the intent of the legislation or mandates, not with just following the *letter* of the law or mandate.

This requires some judgment on our part. It also involves some degree of risk-taking since we may err and be called to task for it. But this judgment is what distinguishes a true manager from just a bureaucrat. Bureaucrats exist in both government *and* business. They get hung up on procedure and process and forget about content. They are the paper pushers and strict rule followers we all dislike.

Purpose of the organization and units

Once we have a good idea of whom we are trying to serve and why, we are ready to examine the purpose of our organization and its major units. In particular, we need to know the purpose of our unit and how it relates to the organization's purpose and the people being served. This has been discussed elsewhere in the book, especially in the chapter on understanding the customer and setting objectives, so it might be beneficial to review these sections of the book at this time. The point is, we cannot make good decisions unless we first understand our unit's and our organization's purposes.

Objectives of the organization and our job

We cannot make good decisions unless we first know what we are trying to accomplish. Thus, we must know the objectives of our job and our organization. We must see how these are tied to purposes and, ultimately, how they are tied to providing products and services that satisfy customer/client needs and wants. The role of objectives is discussed in the chapter on setting objectives. You may wish to review this if you are unfamiliar with the details.

Roles, functions, and responsibilities of our job

How can we make good decisions if we do not know what the duties and responsibilities are in our job? We can't. We must know our authority and the areas for which we are responsible so we know what decisions we are expected to make.

If we do not know our authority, functions, and responsibilities, organizational gaps or overlaps will result. Either some decisions will not get made because no one sees it as their responsibility, or three or four people or groups will be working on the same decision and trying to implement different solutions. Either case results in ineffectiveness and inefficiency.

This is not to say that managers cannot use a staff group to provide advice for use in making decisions. However, managers should make clear to the staff group that it is acting in an *advisory capacity* only and that the final decision authority rests with the individual manager.

Managers may also be asked to act in a staff capacity for others in the organization making decisions. In other words, they may be asked to provide advice on a decision over which they have no authority. This is fine as long as both managers recognize that one of them is acting in a staff-advisory capacity for the other and that the other has the responsibility to make and implement the final decision.

A good job description and job consensus with superiors, subordinates, and peer managers should give managers a good idea as to just what the roles, functions, duties, and responsibilities are in a particular job.

Measures of effectiveness and efficiency

We need to be able to tell when we are doing a good job and when we are not. Unless we can tell this, it's difficult to determine if a decision needs to be made, and if it does, what it should be. We need criteria for performance. These include such things as standards of performance, cost-benefit measures, budgets, performance reviews, and so on. All of these things can help us determine what we are doing well and what we are doing poorly, which in turn will help us make the right kind of decisions to improve performance.

Identifying problems in need of decision

If we have some measures of effectiveness and efficiency in our job as they relate to our duties, functions, objectives, and purpose, then we are able to clearly pinpoint problems. Problems come up when we are not reaching a desired state of affairs or if the desired state of affairs is unclear or inappropriate.

Notice that if an organization is under some system of management by objectives, information in boxes 1 through 5 of Figure 11.1 will be readily available to managers. Thus, the actual act of identifying problems should be easier than if a system of MBO is not being used. Also notice that we do not become concerned with identifying a problem until we first understand the information in boxes 1 through 5. This helps us to focus on *important* problems and to put various issues we face in proper perspective. It helps us to place a priority on decisions we must make so we aren't "stamping on ants in the basement while elephants run wild on the first floor."

Steps in the decision-making process

Now we are ready to actually make the decision. The decision-making process can be summarized in eight steps, as shown in Figure 11.2. Let's look at each of these.

Define the problem. If we have done a good job in boxes 1 through 6 of our model it should not be difficult to define the problem. Box 6 tells us if we have a problem and now we are interested in defining it.

We must be sure we focus on the problem, *not* its symptoms. Symptoms are manifestations of the problem; they are not the problem itself. If we

1. Define the Problem. Distinguish it from its symptoms.
2. Gather all pertinent data including people's emotional states, facts, and precedent.
3. Make necessary, reasonable assumptions about unknown information.
4. Generate a list of alternative solutions—be creative.
5. Evaluate each alternative. Determine its costs and benefits.
6. Select and justify appropriate alternative.
7. Implement alternative.
8. Monitor, evaluate, and take any necessary corrective action.

Figure 11.2 Steps in the decision-making process

treat the symptoms we may never solve the problem. We will be swatting flies when we should be cleaning up the manure pile where they are breeding. Dealing with symptoms is a very common action of those who manage by crises. They are too busy putting out fires to ever clear the forest of underbrush so fires won't start or spread.

This brings up a key point. We essentially make two types of decisions—*currative* and *preventive*. We should try to maximize the number of preventive decisions we make and minimize the number of currative. A currative decision simply treats the problem we have but does nothing to prevent it from happening again. It's the fire-fighting type of solution. A preventive decision may treat a present problem, but more important, it prevents similar problems from occurring again. It is the brush-clearing type of decision.

If we focus on symptoms we will be making curative decisions at best, not preventive ones. Furthermore, we probably won't even cure the problem. It's like taking aspirin for a headache. The headache is the symptom so we treat it with aspirin. In most situations this is okay because a minor ailment has caused the headache and we want only temporary relief while it cures itself. But if a brain tumor or job stress is causing our headache, we better not rely on aspirin. We need to remove the cause itself to get rid of the headaches.

Therefore, to really define the problem we need to ask the question, "Why"? We need to keep asking until we get to the root cause of the problem. Once we've done this we've defined the problem. The ability to keep asking why and not be satisfied with simply answers is a key mark of managerial analytical ability.

Focusing on the cause of the problem is also why low morale or high absenteeism are *never* problems. These are symptoms of problems. In fact, what may appear to be four or five different problems may actually be traced to one problem, such as poor supervisory skills. Tackle this problem and the four or five symptoms will disappear. This also helps managers to focus on one key problem rather than going in six different directions trying to tackle six different symptoms.

Gather information. In defining the problem and structuring its parameter, we need to gather all relevant information that affects the problem. This information includes facts, relevant opinions, people's emotional states, and precedent (how we or others have handled similar problems). We do not want to go off half-cocked in dealing with the problem, so we must know this pertinent information. On the other hand, we do not want to use this step as an excuse *not* to make a decision. We don't want to study problems to death, never coming up with a solution. Sometimes committees are used in this way and the problem never is solved.

What we do want to avoid are *unk-unks*. These are *unknown-unknowns*. We described these in an earlier chapter. They involve not knowing things we should know, and not even knowing that we should know them.

We'll never have perfect information when defining a problem. But we want to insure two things: (1) that we have not overlooked an *important* piece of information, and (2) that we have made all unk-unks into known-unknowns. If we can do this then we're ready for the next step in the process.

Make all reasonable assumptions. Since we will never have all of the information we would like to have in defining a problem, we need to make reasonable assumptions about information we do not have. We need to make assumptions about our known-unknowns. We recognize we do not know something and we realize that it is important that we know it. We, therefore, make an assumption about it.

For example, the price and availability of unleaded gasoline two years from now are key elements in a decision to buy a car today. We know we need to know this information, but we do not know what it will be. It's a known-unknown. (If we completely ignored the future price and availability of unleaded gasoline in making an auto purchase today we would have an unk-unk—we don't know this information and we don't know we need to know it.) So we make a reasonable assumption about the price and availability of unleaded gas. We may use a quite sophisticated method to make the assumption, such as probability, trend, or expert analysis, or we may simply use a hunch, seat-of-the-pants type guess. Whatever method we use, this assumption becomes a key factor for us to consider in making our decision.

Generate a list of alternatives. Now we're ready to develop a list of alternative solutions to the problem. We've defined it and made key assumptions. At this point we should realize that all decisions have at least two alternatives. We can do something or we can do nothing. Not taking action is a decision. We've decided not to act. So, even managers who hate decisions and continually postpone them have made a decision: they have decided not to make the decision!

But most decisions have more than two alternative solutions. It's at this point that managerial creativity comes to bear. List a lot of alternatives. Be creative. Talk with others and see what else might work. Don't always stay with the tried and true. Use *brainstorming*. Have a group of people meet and toss out ideas no matter how crazy they may seem. Don't worry about evaluating each idea at the time they are offered. *Unless you consider an alternative at this point, it will never be the one you choose.* So, don't make decisions with blinders on that narrow your field of vision— be willing to expand your horizons and explore new vistas.

Evaluate each alternative. Now we are ready to pare down our list of alternatives. When evaluating each alternative, we must realize that each alternative costs us something. There is no free lunch. These costs can be economic, financial, psychological, political, social, time, or effort costs. What we want to do is to pick that alternative which gives us our biggest bank for our buck—the alternative which maximizes benefits relative to costs.

Again, there are quite sophisticated means for assessing the costs and benefits of each alternative. We can use probability analysis, sophisticated computer programs, or complicated statistical and forecasting techniques. We can develop *scenarios,* series of events which follow an if-then format, to forecast results of alternatives we might choose. Or we can use our own judgmental intuition, which for some types of decisions is fine.

What we want to avoid, however, is overlooking some cost or benefit that is related to a particular alternative. This is why group decision making is often used. (Two heads are better than one.) Not only does this help us generate a good list of alternatives, it also helps assure us that we have not overlooked an important political, economic, psychological, social, time, or effort cost associated with a particular alternative.

Select and justify the alternative. Now we are ready to actually make the decision—to choose the alternative we want to implement. If we've done a good job in steps 1 through 5, this step will be a cake walk. The appropriate choice should fall right out. The alternative will actually select itself.

Often the alternative we choose will be a combination of several we considered in the previous step. We may take the good points from several options and combine them into one alternative. This is another reason why considering a varied list of alternatives is so important.

We need to be sure that the alternative or combination of alternatives we select will actually solve the problem as we defined it previously. If we cannot answer in the affirmative, we need to select one that will. We also need to be able to clearly justify the alternative we choose so we can explain why we chose it over the others. We need to know why its advantages and disadvantages outweigh other alternatives.

Implement alternative. The best alternative is worthless unless it is implemented. This is the influence process we discussed previously. When choosing an alternative we need to give explicit consideration to the implementation issue. How easy will the alternative be to implement? What barriers are likely to exist to hinder full implementation? How can we remove these barriers? What key people and processes must we depend on to get full implementation? Will they cooperate? Who has the authority to see that full implementation is achieved?

Answers to all of these questions are important, but the last one in particular is very important. Unless someone or some group is given the explicit authority to implement a decision it likely will not be implemented. A person or group has to have *ownership* of the decision solution. They have got to identify with it and see it as their specific responsibility. Otherwise there will be much buck-passing and the decision will float.

When identifying someone or some group responsible for implementing a decision, be sure it is within their job role, functions, duties, and responsibilities, and that it is consistent with their unit's purpose and objectives. Otherwise, they will not accept ownership. They might comply with, but not be committed to, decision implementation.

Monitor, evaluate and take corrective action. Every decision solution will have its problems in implementation. Things will not go perfectly. Thus the decision solution chosen must be carefully and systematically monitored and evaluated so any necessary corrective action or adjustment can be taken promptly. Decision solutions do not monitor themselves. It takes conscious management attention and effort.

The monitoring should be more systematic than a casual hallway, "How's everything going?" type of approach. Periodic times for gathering appropriate monitoring data should be set up, such as weekly or monthly intervals for example. Evaluation meetings or conferences should be held to fully explore ramifications of major decisions. Periodic corrective action conferences should be held. Often these can be tied to the quarterly, semi-annual, or annual performance appraisal conference. This is not to say that informal office visits or luncheon discussions should not be used as a means to monitor and follow-up, but these means *alone* are not enough. They result in biased and incomplete information that can pull the wool over a manager's eyes.

Ensuring that decision results reach customer/clients

The final step in our decision model builds right on the last step in the decision process. We need to be sure that the decisions we make ultimately result in providing a better product or service which better meets customer/client needs at a profit or at least cost. This ought to be either the direct or indirect effect of all major decisions we make in the organization. In the final analysis, it is the overriding criteria that tells us if we've made the right decision.

It isn't always easy to see how a particular decision result links to satisfaction of customer/client wants and needs. Some decisions seem to be far removed from serving customers/clients. But if we cannot ultimately trace all major decision results to this point, then we have either made an inappropriate decision or focused on the wrong problem.

This is a particularly difficult undertaking for people in staff support groups, such as accounting or planning groups. Often it is difficult for them to see how their jobs ultimately affect better serving the customer/client at a profit or at least cost. Line management must assist these people in clearly defining their role so that they more easily see this tie-in to the customer/client.

MAINTAINING PRIORITIES

It's easy for managers to lose sight of job priorities even if a conscientious effort is made to follow the decision-making model and process. Usually managers face several decisions at one time, each at various stages in the decision process.

Competent managers place their time on those decisions that have the greatest payout for their unit and the organization. These decisions may *not* be the ones that best satisfy the customer or client in the *short run*. Hence, the dilemma. What managers have to realize, however, is that a particular short-run decision might have the greatest payout in the long run, even though it's not necessarily tied to meeting customer needs in the short run. The decision to build a larger more efficient plant, for example, ultimately should lead to better customer service at a profit. Yet the payout from this decision will not be realized for several years.

Competent managers don't lose this sense of perspective. They resist the temptation to always make decisions that maximize short-run gains at the expense of long-term ones. They always keep in mind the following questions when facing decisions:

1. How will the decision help us to better serve the customer/client at a profit (or at least cost) in both the short and long terms?
2. How is the decision tied to our purpose?
3. How is the decision tied to our key objectives?

Maintaining priorities in making decisions is not easy. It requires careful, systematic analysis.

IMPLEMENTATION ISSUES

Getting people to accept and follow a decision can be extremely difficult. This acceptance does not always exist in a top-down way. Managers often have to convince superiors or peer managers to make and accept decisions as well.

As reflected in the quote at the beginning of this chapter, many managers do not like to make decisions. A manager working for a superior with this type of attitude faces a very challenging and frustrating situation. Since a key element for management is influence, it's up to the subordinate to try to influence the superior to make good decisions. This influence can include setting a good example in one's own decision-making behavior, encouraging the superior to get more training and education in management, or even going over the superior's head to the next management level. (This last step is a serious one and is not without some potential adverse consequences, but is a necessary last resort in some cases.)

Blockages to effective decision making can come at all three levels —superior, subordinate, and peer managers. Effective managers recognize this and take steps to remove these blockages prior to implementing decisions. Wheels are greased and the runway is cleared *prior to* implementing the decision so that it isn't forced down people's throats. This is what is meant by the often used phrase, "he's got all his ducks in a row" when referring to people who are particularly adept at implementing decisions. (The second case at the end of this chapter examines this issue further.)

WAYS TO MAKE DECISIONS

In this section we briefly look at two concerns in making decisions: individual versus group decisions, and some tools for decision making.

Individual versus group decisions

There are essentially two ways to make decisions: individually or in groups. There are advantages and disadvantages with each approach, as we see in Figure 11.3. Competent managers must weigh these advantages and disadvantages with regard to each decision and then choose the best method.

Whichever method is used on a decision, beware of always having to reach a consensus on a decision. Sometimes it's not good to reach a consensus. Sometimes unpopular decisions must be made for the good of the organization. Sometimes a consensus decision is the one least offensive to all concerned. It doesn't make anyone unhappy, but it doesn't make anyone particularly happy either. It's a mediocre decision that only minimally gets the job done or doesn't accomplish it at all.

There are times when individual decision making is clearly the better option. Managers should not be afraid to make the decision alone when the situation clearly warrants it.

Tools for decision making

In this section we briefly touch on some of the tools that can be used for decision making. A complete discussion of these is beyond the scope of this book. Suffice it to say that there are some very sophisticated decision tools that make extensive use of mathematics and statistics that can aid man-

Individual		Group	
Advantages	*Disadvantages*	*Advantages*	*Disadvantages*
1. Fast 2. One person accountable 3. Make unpopular yet necessary decisions	1. Can miss key information 2. Ignore monitor and follow-up issues 3. Reaches no consensus or ownership on acceptance of decision	1. Two heads better than one; pooling of expertise 2. Covers basis; develops ownership 3. Can be creative	1. Time consuming 2. Can raise expectations that "my solution" will be accepted 3. Can lead to mediocrity; "groupthink" 4. No one person willing to take responsibility for decision

Figure 11.3 Advantages and disadvantages to individual and group decision-making methods

agers in making decisions. These tools are particularly useful in making scheduling, quality control, inventory control, capital budgeting, manpower planning, or transportation planning decisions. Some of the references listed at the end of the chapter deal in depth with these tools.

One word of caution is in order, however. Even though these highly sophisticated quantitative tools are available, and should be used as appropriate, they are *not a substitute* for managerial judgment. They are simply tools that aid managers in making decisions. They do *not replace* managerial decision making. Maybe at some point in our evolution we will create artificial intelligence that enables us to quantify everything we consider in making a decision, but we are far from that point now. While there are aids to judgment, there are no substitutes for it.

This does not mean that such tools should be ignored, however. Hip-pocket managers who make decisions based on seat-of-the-pants gut feelings are, happily, a dying breed. Judgment in decision making is careful analysis of important issues, not following one's gut reaction. Hip-pocket managers will occasionally be successful even in today's complex world, but for every one that makes it, at least twenty try and fail.

CONCLUSION

Making effective decisions is the hallmark of prudent managers. Being able to exercise sound managerial judgment to make appropriate decisions that meet customer/client needs at a profit or at least cost is no easy task. The day of the seat-of-the-pants managerial decision maker is at an end. Good decisions require careful and thorough analysis of problems and issues. The use of analytical techniques is often required for optimum decision making.

Good decision making does not occur in a vacuum. Competent decision makers must relate their decisions to customer/client needs, organizational purpose and objectives, their job's purpose and objectives, and their job duties and responsibilities. Being able to place the decision-making process into its proper perspective helps managers maintain a sense of priority when addressing decisions. This enables them to focus on the important decisions that must be made instead of wasting time on the unimportant.

Using the eight steps of the problem-solving decision-making process becomes second nature to competent managers. Not only do they use this on the job, they also apply the process to off the job types of decisions. It's not necessary to write out all steps of the process, although on certain complicated decisions it will help. Rather, going through the process in one's mind every time an important decision must be made should become a habit. This will ensure that important problems are not only solved but prevented from reoccurring.

QUESTIONS

1. Do you spend most of the time on your job making currative or preventive decisions? What can you do to maximize the preventive decisions you make?

2. On which decisions do you use group decision processes and on which ones do you use individual decision making? Why?

3. Why do so many managers seem to have trouble defining problems to be addressed? That is, why do we so often deal with symptoms and not problems?

4. Would you characterize the decision making done in your organization as one of management by crises or as one based on planning and objectives? Why?

5. What would you do if you had a subordinate who believed as the individual does quoted at the beginning of the chapter? What would you do if your superior felt this way?

6. In your opinion, is the decision-making process any different in government than it is in business? Explain.

CASES AND EXERCISES

CASE 1: LOW PROFILE

It was finally beginning to make sense to George. The way you get ahead in this organization is to do your job quietly and efficiently and to keep a low profile. As his boss said, "Keep your nose clean and don't attract too much attention."

George had been with Walker-Rondo for two years now. He was a department head in one of the firm's pet food processing plants. George had an MBA from a southwestern school and had worked for six years with a beverage bottling company before joining Walker-Rondo.

George felt that to get ahead, a manager had to perform. A key to this performance was making the right decisions at the right time. George believed he had been successful. He had quickly moved up in the beverage firm and the position with Walker was viewed as a significant step up by him in his career ladder. But he hadn't been promoted since joining Walker two years ago. His boss had told him that his ideas were "too far out, too radical" for Walker-Rondo. He had told George that they were too risky and that George had attracted too much attention with his radical ideas.

George did not believe they were radical at all. The beverage company was already doing many of the things George was recommending. He also knew that some of Walker-Rondo's competitors in the food business were already practicing some of the things George was suggesting.

Yet he seemed to have trouble in getting his ideas accepted. He believed the company was too conservative in its approach to decision making. They seldom would consider anything new. Often when he made a suggestion, he received a response such as, "What other firms are doing this?" "That may work elsewhere but not here," "We tried it before and it did not work," or "Sounds good, let's appoint a committee to study it further."

George did not want to become just another "ho-hum" mediocre manager like so many around him in the firm had become. He wanted to make a mark for himself and he also wanted the firm to become more profitable. (Company profits were average in the industry.) Yet he did not want to jeopardize his job or his salary. He was satisfied with both, and he saw a great future for himself with Walker-Rondo if only he could shake the blinders off of those around him.

Questions

1. What techniques could George or any manager use to open the horizons of the managers about them so that they would be more receptive to new ideas?

2. Do you think the situation George faces is common today in industry? In government? Explain your answers.

3. What role does risk-taking play in the decision-making process?

CASE 2: DUCKS IN A ROW

Around here it seems like you have to touch base with everyone before you go ahead with something. Everybody and their brother wants to be in on it and tell you how to do your job. Sure, I know on certain key or sensitive decisions it's a good idea to check alternatives with certain key people, but is this necessary on every decision? Everyone is concerned about being left in the dark or surprised. They are all concerned about covering their ass.

This organization is just too political and not rational. Things are done for political reasons, such as pleasing the boss or a key subordinate, not because it's the right and efficient thing to do. People are too concerned with greasing the wheels and clearing the runway before making a decision Hell, you've just got to go ahead with some decisions no matter what people tell you. All decisions aren't popular, but they still must be made. Around here, people are afraid to make these unpopular decisions.

Well, I don't think we should be running a popularity contest. I don't think we should tolerate namby-pamby, buck-passer types. We need people with guts in management positions. We need people who don't study decisions to death. If I am asked one more time whether I "have my ducks in a row" before I go ahead with something, I think I'll explode.

Questions

1. There is a fine line between keeping people properly informed on a decision and the situation described by this individual. What factors should a manager consider in making this judgment?

2. Why is it that other people in an organization so often believe that they can tell you how to do your job?

3. When, to what extent, and how should staff groups be used to assist a manager with a decision?

EXERCISE: APPLY THE DECISION-MAKING PROCESS

The purpose of this exercise is to give you an opportunity to apply the decision-making process to a decision you have previously made in your job. This will give you a chance to see how the process worked for you from beginning to end.

Pick a decision you've made during the last month or so. The decision could be one dealing with a personnel, financial, operations, or marketing problem. The decision should have been made long enough ago so that you can determine its effect to some extent.

1. Identify the problem you addressed. What symptoms manifested the problem?

2. List the key information elements you examined related to the problem.

3. List any key assumptions you made about information you needed but did not have.

4. List the alternative choices you considered to solve the problem.

5. What were the key advantages and disadvantages for each alternative?

6. Which alternative did you choose and why?

7. What action did you take to implement the solution you chose?

8. Is the solution working? Is it solving the problem? Have you had to take corrective action or make any adjustments? How are you monitoring and evaluating the decision?

REFERENCES

Ackoff, Russell L. *The Art of Problem Solving: Accompanied by Ackoff's Fables.* New York: John Wiley, 1978.
Provocative and witty treatment of problem-solving techniques which offer a practical guide to tapping creative sources.

Alexis, Marcus, and Wilson, Charles Z. *Organizational Decision Making.* Englewood Cliffs, N.J.: Prentice-Hall, 1967.
A comprehensive review of the decision-making process in organizations. Has a more complex model of decision making on p. 160 than the one in this chapter.

Delbecq, André L.; Von de Ven, Andrew H.; and Gustafson, David H. *Group Techniques for Program Planning: A Guide to Nominal Group and Delphi Processes.* Glenview, Ill.: Scott Foresman, 1975.
A very good discussion on how to use two key group problem-solving techniques known as NGT and Delphi.

Guth, William T., and Taguiri, Renato. "Personal Values and Corporate Strategies." *Harvard Business Review* (Sept.–Oct. 1965): 123-132.
An excellent discussion of how individual values affect organization decision making.

Janis, Irving L. "Groupthink." *Psychology Today* (November 1971): 42-46.
Examines how the groupthink syndrome pervaded decisions made on Pearl Harbor, Vietnam, and the Bay of Pigs.

Maier, Normal R. F. "Assets and Liabilities in Group Problem Solving: The Need for an Integrative Function." *Psychological Review* (July 1967): 239-249.
A good review of the advantages and disadvantages of group decision-making processes.

Mentzberg, Henry; Raisinghani, Duru; and Théorêt, André. "The Structure of 'Unstructured' Decision Processes." *Administrative Science Quarterly* (June 1976): 246-275.
Presents empirical evidence for patterns of decision making followed by management in ambiguous situations.

Moore, P. G. "Techniques vs. Judgment In Decision Making." *Organizational Dynamics* (Autumn 1973): 68-80.
An excellent discussion of the debate on decision tools versus judgment in decision making.

Nystrom, Harry. *Creativity and Innovation.* New York: John Wiley & Sons, 1979.
Considers the differences in how companies and individuals react to environmental conditions and design, and implements strategies for change. Focus is on company creativity to make successful innovation possible.

Rokeach, Milton. *The Open and Closed Mind.* New York: Basic Books, Inc., 1960.

A good look at the phenomenon of closed mindedness often held by decision makers when approaching an issue.

12
How Should a Manager Communicate?

Subject: Further Clarification of "Part-Time" and "Short-Term" Training

We are issuing further policy interpretation of "Part-Time" and "Short-Term" training (see PS–78–31, 78–10, and 78–2) based on an additional inquiry relative to P.L. 93–647, Part A, Title XX, Section 2002(a)(1), 45 CFR 74, Appendix C, Subpart Q, Part II (B26) and 45 CFR 228.84(a)(2) and (3).

Inquirer's Discussion: Part II (B26), Appendix C, Subpart Q, of 45 CFR 74 provides for training and education as an allowable cost.

Question: Is PS–78–2 and subsequent memorandum inconsistent with 45 CFR 74, Appendix C, Subpart 2, Part II (B26)?

Answer: No. It is not.

Under B26 "in-service training" corresponds to the definitions of part-time and short-term full-time training in 228.84 (a)(2) and (a)(3).

"Out-of-service training" under B26 corresponds to the definition of long-term full-time training in 228.84(a)(1) and the interpretation given 78–2. It is from that regulation that APS derives authority and responsibility for in-service training expenditures in grant-in-aid programs under Title XX.

Sec. 228.34(a) is really an amplification or clarification of the language in Part II (B26) in that it specifies what particular in-service and out-of-service training costs are eligible for FFP.

There is no legal requirement that 228.84(a) be consistent with Part II (B26) because an agency's own regulation as to what costs are eligible for FFP, if inconsistent with the general cost principles set forth in Subpart Q of 45 CFR Part 74, supersedes those cost principles. 45 CFR

74.4(a) (revised as of August 2, 1978. 43 Federal Register 34082) expressly provides that the provisions of Part 74 are applicable to all HEW grants, except where inconsistent with Federal statutes, regulations, or other terms of a grant. In other words, PS-78-2 and 228.84(a) are viewed as inconsistent with Part II (B26), but they need not be so. Also, the statute specifically authorizes out-of-service training in Section 2002(a)(1).

Disposition: Retain until superseded.

Whaaaat?!! (Try reading it aloud; it's even funnier.) This is communication? Would you believe that this is an *actual* memorandum from a government agency reproduced verbatim? But you say you expect this from government. Well, check out this paragraph from an actual letter written by a manager in a medium-sized manufacturing firm.

It has come to my attention that your interfacing activities with RATCL has not resulted in a viable prioritization of goals which meets the requirements of the MODPLAN as indicated on page 23 of MODPLAN manual (Section 21.2). Henceforth, please send all second draft goal lists (those which have been reviewed by task force 3, subgroup a) to me for review, unless, of course, you have completed form 21.6 prior to completing the draft, and have reviewed such form with me at least two weeks prior to our consensus meetings. (Disregard this if goals from previous year were discussed at the winter quarter retreat with Mr. Jenkins present. We have minutes of that discussion on file.) Please copy the following offices: personnel, task force 3, task force 5, interunit planning team, and my office on any correspondence.

Notice the long sentences and multiple references made in each sentence. Of course if we were in the organization we would know what RATCL and other references mean. Or would we? If we had recently joined the organization or had just recently been placed in a position to work with these projects, the letters would be Greek to us. Also notice the qualifying statements in each piece—do this or that unless you've done this or that. Who can remember exactly? Straightforward statements should be made as often as possible.

This leads us to a primary principle in communication: KISS—Keep It Short and Simple. There's no need to write long complicated sentences to impress the reader. Instead, they will confuse. There is no need to cover up what you don't know by cloaking it in gobbledy-gook. If you are not sure about something, you should find out the answer before writing about it. Big words and complicated sentences don't impress, they repress. They repress reader thought, interest, and understanding. There are two very important thoughts always to keep in mind when communicating. First, remember that the essence of communication is the passing of *information and understanding* from one person to another. This is why we communicate anything. We want to achieve understanding, not an information dump. Second, always practice *empathy*. Ask yourself, "How would I react if I received the information I am about to communicate?" Put yourself in the other person's shoes *before* you communicate and communicate from *that* perspective, not your perspective.

THE COMMUNICATION PROCESS

Communication is the passage of information and understanding from one person to another. It involves seven steps, as shown in Figure 12.1. Let's look at each of these.

Ideation

Know what you want to communicate *before* you attempt any communication. For communication to be effective, the sender has to have a pretty clear idea of what he or she wants to say or write. If the sender does not have a clear idea to begin with, how can we expect the receiver to have a clear idea when it's received? We must not forget to engage our mind before we engage our mouth or pen.

Encoding

Put your idea in the proper message form. Choose the proper words to convey the idea you have in mind. We all know people who stutter and stammer about and then end up saying, "Well, you know what I mean." One fault of adolescents is their constant use of the phrase "you know," probably caused by their lack of experience in putting complex thoughts in proper terminology. Choose your words carefully and practice empathy. Use the language of the receiver. After all, to pass information and understanding to this person is your whole reason for communicating. And remember to practice KISS.

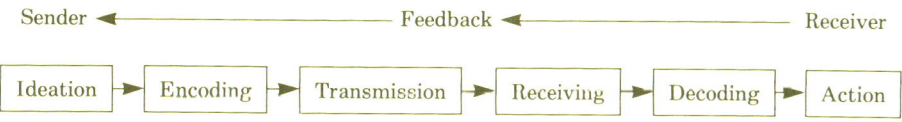

Figure 12.1 The steps in the communication process

Transmission

Choose the proper media for communication. Do you want to use oral methods? If so, should you give a speech, have a meeting, or use the phone? Each has its advantages and disadvantages, which we explore further later in the chapter. If you use the written word, do you want to use a letter, memorandum, or report? Will you send your words via teletype, computer, or some other means? What role does electronic transmission have in your communication?

Receiving

The receiver has the responsibility to practice good listening. The sender has the responsibility to ensure the message is being received. Is the message getting to the receiver?

Decoding

This refers to the listener's interpretation of the message. Is the listener decoding the message properly so that the meaning the sender intended to convey is, indeed, being conveyed?

Action

What is the listener doing with the information? Is a specific course of action required or is the receiver simply expected to store the information for future use later? One course of action is immediate forgetting of the information. Of course we hope the receiver does not do this, for why did we communicate in the first place?

Feedback

The receiver has a responsibility to provide the sender with feedback on the communication, and the sender has the responsibility to elicit and observe feedback. Communication is a *two-way* street. The sender must practice listening skills also.

At each step in this process, communication barriers can crop up. Let's look at these.

COMMUNICATION BARRIERS

The barriers to the communication process are shown in Figure 12.2. They are real and must be dealt with by sender and receiver alike. They do not disappear automatically.

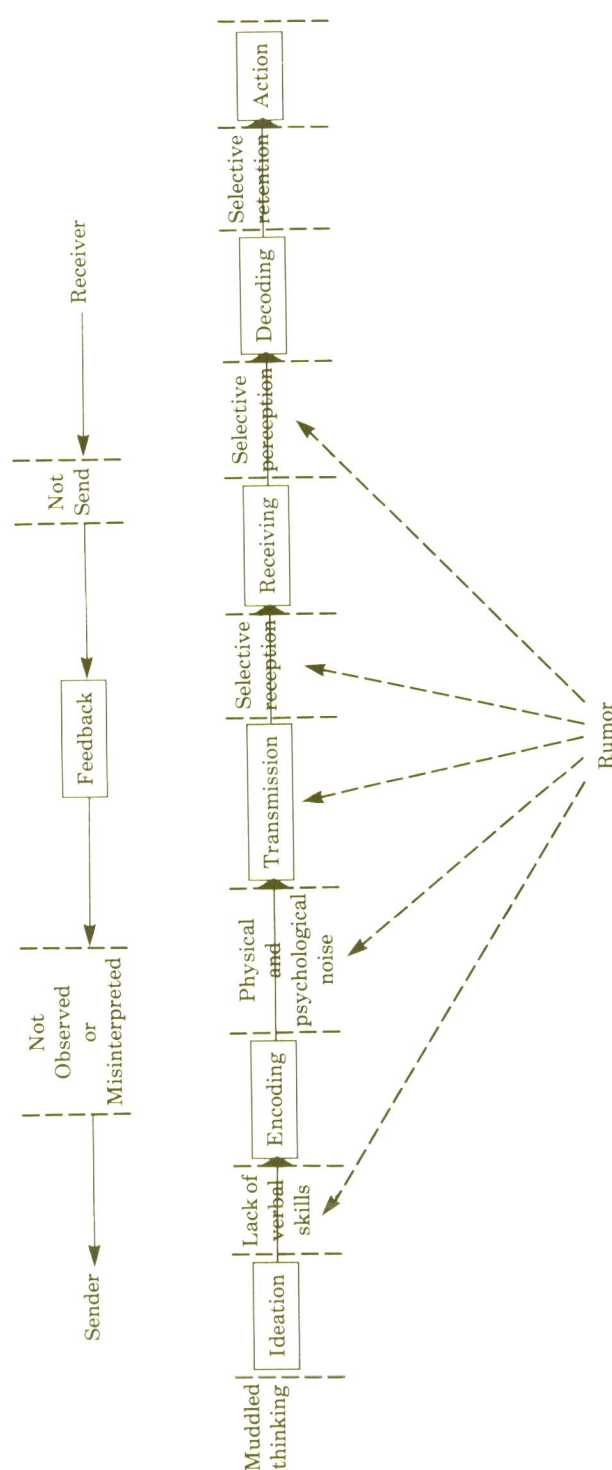

Figure 12.2 Barriers to effective communication

Muddled thinking

A major barrier to ideation is the inability to clearly think of what you want to communicate. Some people just cannot come up with a complete thought before jumping to something else. Unless clearly thought out ideas are first achieved, effective communication will be very difficult, if not impossible.

Lack of verbal skills

Some people have good ideas but seldom seem to find the proper words. Either they can never encode or they encode improperly. They cannot practice empathy and seem to write or talk as if they were communicating with themselves and no one else. Of course, with people like this it's very difficult to determine if they had a good idea to begin with.

Physical and psychological noise

Transmission can be blocked by noise. This noise can be actual physical noise, such as static on a phone line or TV picture tube or the noise of an air hammer outside, or it can be psychological noise. Physical noise is relatively easy to recognize and remove compared to psychological noise. Psychological noise consists of the biases, attitudes, and beliefs people hold that block the transmission of ideas.

Selective reception

Sometimes we only expose ourselves to information we want to hear or read. This is called *selective reception*. According to psychologist Leon Festinger, we do this to avoid *cognitive dissonance* or having nonfitting attitudes or beliefs. We find this dissonance uncomfortable to us. For example, if I am politically conservative, I may only read conservative publications and ignore liberal ones, thinking they are rubbish because they don't fit with my beliefs. The reverse would be true of a liberal. All of us practice closed-mindedness to some extent because we don't like cognitive dissonance.

The danger here is that we cease to learn because we cease to be exposed to new ideas. What if we are wrong? There is nothing worse than the Jonestown-type true believer. Their course is the *only* course. None others count.

Selective perception

Once information is received we often distort it to make it fit with our existing beliefs, again in order to avoid cognitive dissonance. Each of us sees the world through our own set of glasses. Some are rose-colored and reflect personal optimism, others are gray and reflect pessimistic gloom. Each of us have values, attitudes, and beliefs which have been shaped through our rearing and experiences. These reflect how we interpret information sent to us. A good sender recognizes these perceptual biases by practicing empathy and tries to overcome them during encoding.

We must all try to remember an important point made in an earlier chapter. *We should not confuse understanding with agreement.* We should not be afraid to understand an idea simply because we might agree with it or because the sender might misinterpret our understanding as agreement. People ought to have enough confidence in their ideas that they can refute information received if they do not agree with it. However, one must first understand the information *before* one can refute it. One mark of an educated person is the ability to see a complex issue from many sides and, indeed, to be able to argue each side convincingly whether the side is agreed with or not. For example, I may be against the death penalty but I ought to be able to eloquently argue in favor of it, even though I may never do so. In other words, I ought to be able to recognize and understand viewpoints different from my own. If I can't, how do I ever know that my viewpoint is "better" than the other person's? I cannot since I do not have a basis for comparison.

Selective retention

We tend to remember things we want to remember and forget things we want to forget. We likewise tend to remember things that fit our existing attitudes and beliefs because we want to avoid cognitive dissonance. We often place such low credibility on something we disagree with that we don't act on the information and soon forget it. For example, a firm might communicate a new travel policy requiring employees to file all receipts for any expenditure for reimbursement. If employees disagree with this, they will conveniently "forget" to do this, especially if they know the big wigs get away with it. If nothing is said to them after they don't file the receipts, they will continue not filing them because they figure the policy will not be enforced. Soon everyone forgets such a policy was ever adopted.

Reinforcement and repetition of the message by the sender in alternative ways help to overcome all selective barriers caused by cognitive dissonance. Selective exposure, selective perception, and selective retention can all be reduced by a well planned multimedia program with proper reinforcement and follow-up. However, it is doubtful that the selective barriers will ever be completely eliminated.

Feedback barriers

Two types of barriers block effective feedback from the receiver to the sender. First, the receiver may simply not convey any feedback at all. He or she sits there stone-faced. This, in a sense, is feedback but it's difficult to determine what it means. Second, the feedback may not be observed or, if observed, may be misinterpreted by the sender. In either case, the feedback the receiver wishes to communicate doesn't reach the sender.

It's very difficult for the sender to know if communication is taking place unless feedback is received and properly interpreted. It's also difficult for the sender to adjust or change the message or media unless feedback is sent, received, and properly interpreted.

We need to look at one other serious barrier that pervades the *entire* communication process: rumor.

Rumor

Rumor is false information that is transmitted in the organization. By definition, all rumor is false. Rumor can be transmitted through official communication channels (letter and memoranda do sometimes err), but we normally associate rumor with the *grapevine*. The grapevine is the informal communication network found in every organization. It is *not* officially sanctioned by the organization, but it is a *necessary* part of communication. Smart managers use the grapevine for their own and the organization's advantage by feeding it accurate information.

Rumor should be stamped out immediately. There is no such thing as a verified rumor. "Rumor" that is later found out to be true is simply a piece of information on the grapevine which is true. It is not rumor; it is true grapevine information. All rumor is false information by definition.

Rumor arises when people are kept in the dark about important matters. It arises when there are significant gaps in important information. People manufacture information to fill in the gaps, and the rumors soon spread like wildfire. Therefore, it's up to management to ensure that employees are provided with accurate up-to-date information, particularly on sensitive or emotional issues, in order to keep rumor from occurring.

In order for management to keep rumor down to a minimum and to maximize effective communications, an atmosphere of open, candid, honest and trustful communication must be created. This is no easy thing to achieve. It starts by having people willing to lay all their cards down on the table. It also involves severely cracking down on back-biting—talking about others behind their back. Vicious office gossip about an individual's character or personal behavior has no place in the organization trying to achieve honest, open, and candid communication. Rumor, lies, and innuendo will kill effective communications in any organization. People become afraid to speak what's on their mind. People begin worrying what others are saying about them. Their job output and effectiveness decrease as they begin playing CYA and other little games. The morale in the organization goes down. The political game becomes the only game in town. People find the situation intolerable and leave.

Management must continually try to achieve honest, open, and candid communication within a trusting and supportive organizational environment. It's not something to be done only when there is time.

WAYS OF COMMUNICATING

There are many ways to communicate. We will look at five major methods: oral, written, meetings, nonverbal, and electronic. We will also explore the role of a Management Information System (MIS) in this process. Competent managers use all forms of communication in appropriate ways.

Oral

Communication through the spoken word, either on a face-to-face basis, over the phone, or in a small group, has the advantage of being personal. It also provides the opportunity for the sender to observe feedback, answer questions, and provide additional information for clarification. Often, it is faster than other forms of communication.

Its greatest disadvantage lies in the lack of a written record as to what transpired. This can lead to all sorts of disagreements. Some managers tape conversations or immediately reduce conversations to typed notes in order to overcome this disadvantage.

Written

Using a letter, memorandum, or report to communicate allows you to more carefully organize your thoughts, and provides a written record for future reference. It's also possible to provide more material to the receiver than through oral communication methods. However, it's impersonal, somewhat more time consuming than oral communication, and provides little opportunity for the sender to observe feedback and offer clarification. Written communication is essentially one-way communication with a delayed response.

Meetings

Meetings usually involve both oral and written communication methods. They usually include a written agenda, advanced study of written material, and the reduction of proceedings to written minutes. The actual meeting itself, however, relies heavily on oral communication.

Meetings can be small or large, from a staff group of employees who regularly work together to a large convention-type of meeting involving several thousand. Of course the larger the meeting the more the communication resembles speech-making.

Effective oral communication principles should be practiced at meetings. Parliamentary procedures are often followed to help ensure order. The primary advantage to a meeting is the opportunity for many people with common interests to share ideas. The primary disadvantages are their length and uneven interest in the participants regarding various speakers and ideas. This often requires that various attention-getters and attention-maintainers be used, such as films, slides, transparencies, videotape, chalkboards, and flipcharts.

Nonverbal communication

People also communicate through body language. Facial expressions, posture, and hand and eye movements all communicate. Often this is used as a way to provide feedback by the receiver, but the sender also uses nonverbal communication. Looking someone in the eye when speaking to them conveys directness, personal concern, and full attention. Crossing one's arms or speaking behind a desk or lectern can be viewed as creating a barrier between sender and receiver. The way one dresses or where one sits also conveys messages. The position at the head of the table usually conveys authority to those present in the room. Meeting in one's office gives the office-holder power, as opposed to meeting at some neutral site.

All of these nonverbal communication methods have meaning. They are usually sent simultaneously with verbal communication, so it's difficult for most receivers to separate meaning between the two.

Electronic

Radio, TV, telegraph, or electronic data systems are various nonverbal ways to transmit information. The media used is electronic, even though words or numbers are being transmitted. The advantage of eletronic transmission is its ability to reach relatively large numbers of people quickly and at a fairly low cost per person.

Management information systems

This leads us to an important consideration in communication. Every organization must manage its information flows. Information must be managed as a resource just as other resources in the organization are managed. The concept which encompasses this idea is the Management Information System (MIS).

The MIS is the system of information in the organization designed to provide decision makers with information when, where, and in the form they need it. Figure 12.3 lists the characteristics of a good information system. Let's briefly examine each of these.

> An Effective MIS Is:
>
> 1. A system of information systems.
> 2. Managed as a resource.
> 3. Designed around user needs and user language.
> 4. Timely, accurate, and reliable.
> 5. Usually EDP based.
> 6. Cost-benefit effective.

Figure 12.3 Characteristics of an effective management information system

A system of systems. An MIS is a system of information systems. It ties together the various information systems in the organization and treats these as subsystems of the larger system. The accounting system, marketing information system, human resource information system, inventory control system, and other systems are integrated so as to minimize overlaps and duplication and increase efficiency. Duplicate forms, reports, memos, etc., are reduced or eliminated. The information system is a system of integrated information subsystems.

Managed as a resource. A person or office is given primary responsibility to manage the system. This gives the function visability, credibility, and viability.

Designed around user needs. The system is designed for the people who will use the information. It's designed around user needs for management decision making. It's *not* designed for the computer jocks who use the system, but for the managers who use system results. This is perhaps the most important point for an effective MIS. The output of the system should be written in user language and geared to user needs, not in computer language for programmer needs. This is one reason why you should never have a computer technician or programmer direct the MIS office in the organization. Naturally, the organization needs someone with some basic understanding of computers and what they can and cannot do, but more important, a director with knowledge of management and decision making is needed. Programmers with technical knowledge can be hired to work for this director.

Timely, accurate, and reliable. The system should provide information to managers that is timely, accurate, and reliable. That is, the information should be accurate and be provided to managers early enough so that appropriate action can be taken if need be. There's little use in learning about something two months *after* action should have been taken (unless it's to prevent its reoccurrence).

Usually EDP based. In order to achieve ease of access and update, and to handle large volumes of information, most MIS's are computer based. However, this is not an absolute requirement, especially in smaller organizations.

Cost-benefit effective. The entire system and each information piece in the system should be more than worth the cost of obtaining and providing it. Obtaining and providing data "just in case" is not a good idea. There should be a clear reason for every piece of data, memorandum, letter, or report generated. Rooms full of boxes of computer print-outs gathering dust in many organizations indicate this principle often is not followed.

Cost-benefit justification for information is also important to prevent information overload. Too much data can be generated and provided in the system. Managers soon drown in a sea of paperwork and print-outs. Be sure each and every manager who gets information needs to have it and wants it. Overcommunication is never a problem, but information overload often is. Be sure the information provided is information that will help managers in decision making.

CONCLUSION

Communication is the passage of information and understanding from one person to the next. Competent managers are articulate communicators. Their organizations have a well designed management information system so that the entire organizational communication process is properly managed.

Competent managers appropriately use various forms of communication so as to maximize the advantages and minimize the disadvantages of each. They communicate to inform, not to impress. They practice empathy and good listening skills. They follow the KISS principle religiously. They ensure that others receive accurate information in a timely manner for effective decision making.

The grapevine is used to supplement the formal communication channels. Managers work toward an open, honest, candid, and supportive climate for communications in order to minimize rumor and gossip. They also hone and sharpen their communication skills through practice, always looking for ways to improve understanding.

QUESTIONS

1. Can you rewrite the two example passages quoted at the beginning of the chapter to make them understandable?

2. Why do so many people write like those authors?

3. In your opinion, which is the most important step in the communication process? Why?

4. In your opinion, which barriers to effective communication seem to most often occur in your organization? Why? Can they be reduced? If so, how?

5. Which form of communication do you use most often? Why? Do you use each form appropriately?

6. In which area of communication do you feel you personally need to improve most?

CASES AND EXERCISES

CASE 1: KNOWLEDGE IS POWER

Linda: Why didn't you copy me on this letter, Harry?

Harry: I didn't think you'd be interested in it.

Linda: Well I need to know about things like this. You guys in accounting seldom copy me on important memoranda and letters. I've asked you before for copies.

Harry: I guess we believe it's not relevant to your job.

Linda: But it is. It's very important that I know information like this. How do you know whether it's important or not for my job? You really don't know all that I do here.

Harry: Maybe that's part of the problem. Maybe we don't know the role and functions of various people around here. We're such a big organization.

Linda: Yes we are, but your group in accounting should be providing us with information that we need. You better find out who needs what when and be sure that we receive it.

Harry: Okay. I'll take it up with Ray. I've got to see him this afternoon anyway.

Later that afternoon . . .

Harry: Ray, Linda says she needs copies of those cost letters and memos we send out weekly.

Ray (accounting supervisor): I know. She's mentioned it to me before. I don't think she needs them. She won't understand the stuff anyway.

Harry: I agree, but she says she wants them; maybe we should start copying her.

Ray: That's our information. Some of it is sensitive. Some is preliminary. I don't want the stuff blabbed all over the place.

Harry: Well, some of the material is confidential. You don't suppose we are just sensitive to criticism which some of the material in the letters and memos might create?

Ray: No, I don't. We can take criticism. Look, just tell her we'll try to do a better job in getting her some copies of our correspondence, but don't promise her anything.

The next day . . .

Harry: Hi, Linda. Talked with Ray yesterday. We'll try to start copying you on some of the material.

Linda: Good. How about all of it?

Harry: Well . . .

Linda: Look, I know your game over there. You want to keep secrets. Knowledge is power. You guys figure that if you're the only ones who know key financial information you'll have the rest of us at a disadvantage. Isn't that right, Harry?

Questions

1. Do you agree that knowledge is power? Why? Could this be a reason why accounting is not sharing information with Linda's group?

2. It's difficult to determine what type and how much information should be shared with others in the organization. What criteria should be used in making this decision?

3. If you were Harry, how would you respond to Linda's last comment? If you were Linda what would you do now?

CASE 2: COMMUNICATION OPPOSITES

Mary really is a super boss. She keeps me informed about important matters relating to my job. She really is concerned about communicating with me. I can get in to see her just about any time I need to and she frequently stops by my office with important information. She's easy to talk with and speaks very clearly. She also runs an excellent staff meeting. We get things accomplished and seldom meet more than an hour. I like the fact that she has uncomfortable chairs in our meeting room so that people don't get too settled in.

She keeps me informed on important correspondence via copies. Frequently, she sends me copies of parts of various reports pertaining to my job. I like the fact she sends me the excerpts of the reports relevant to me so I don't have to wade through reams of material.

Overall she really tries to build an honest, open, candid, and supportive communications environment which minimizes rumor. I wish Bob would communicate like Mary. It's funny how two managers who work side by side take such different approaches to communication. I have trouble communicating with Bob. I'm sure glad I don't have to work for him and I pity those that do. He's so clandestine. He keeps everyone in the dark. When he does talk, he talks out of both sides of his mouth. He'll tell you one thing and someone else the opposite. You never know where he stands on an issue. And his letters! Wow! Are they bad. Pure gobbledy-gook. The worst thing is he isn't getting any better.

Questions

1. Why is it that an organization can have two people in close proximity with such different communication styles?

2. List the specific good points this person likes about Mary's communication and the bad points about Bob's.

3. If you were the supervisor of both Bob and Mary what would you do and why?

EXERCISE: HOW WOULD YOU COMMUNICATE?

Suppose you found yourself in the following situation. Assume you are a forty-five-year-old white, middle-aged, male office supervisor. Patty, a twenty-six-year-old black female typist who has worked for you for three months, consistently is late in meeting typing deadlines. Yet her work is excellent. She also is never late for work and has not missed a day since she started to work for you.

On at least three occasions you've mentioned to her about missing deadlines. She appears to have heard you, but she has not changed her behavior. Lately, you've given her work to do that has a long lead time. However, your office was recently just given an assignment that will require all typists to meet a series of very tight deadlines over the next six weeks. You must now confront Patty with this information. The office employees are not unionized and there is no written organizational policy on missing deadlines. However, there is a clear policy on tardiness, absences, and quality of work.

Using the communication model (steps 1 through 7 below), indicate how you would communicate on this issue with Patty.

1. What *idea* would you attempt to convey?
2. How would you *encode* this idea? (What words would you use?)
3. How would you *transmit* this idea? (What media would you use, e.g., oral, memo, letter, nonverbal, etc.?) Why?
4. How do you anticipate that the message would be *received?*
5. How would Patty likely *decode* (interpret) the message?
6. What *action* do you want Patty to take? What action do you think she'll take?
7. What *feedback* will you look for from Patty?

Now, anticipate the various communication barriers that might come about in the communication process. How will you deal with each of these?

REFERENCES

Anthony, William P. "Get to Know Your Employees—The Human Resource Information System." *Personnel Journal* (April 1977): 179–183, 202.
An overview of the purpose and design of the human resource information system.

Anthony, William P. "Managing Effective Staff Meetings." *Personnel Journal* (August 1979): 547–550.
Provides some helpful guidelines to make staff meetings an effective and efficient communication experience.

Anthony, William P., and Anthony, Philip. "Now Hear This—Some Techniques for Listening." *Supervisory Management* (March 1972): 19–24.
A short article which explains the importance of the role of listening and empathy in the communication process.

Davis, Keith. *Human Behavior at Work.* 5th ed. New York: McGraw-Hill, 1977.
Chapters 21–26 have an excellent treatment of all facets of communication.

Festinger, Leon A. *A Theory of Cognitive Dissonance.* New York: Harper & Row, 1957.
Sets out Festinger's now famous theory on nonfitting attitudes and beliefs.

Gerbner, George, ed. *Mass Media Policies In Changing Cultures.* New York: John Wiley and Sons, 1977.
   A collection of articles which examine the evolving American role in worldwide communication.
Green, Thad B., and Pietri, Paul H. "Using Nominal Grouping to Improve Upward Communication." *MSU Business Topics* (Autumn 1974): 37–43.
   Excellent discussion on the use of NGT as a technique to improve upward communication in the organization.
Hatch, Richard. *Communicating in Business.* Chicago: SRA, 1977.
   An excellent handbook on written communication principles in business and governmental organizations.
Hodge, B. J., and Anthony, William P. "MBO: Clear Channel Communication." *Supervision* (December 1975): 26–28.
   Shows how MBO can improve the communication process in an organization.
Schmid, Calvin F., and Schmid, Stanton E. *Handbook of Graphic Presentation.* 2nd ed. New York: John Wiley and Sons, 1979.
   Shows how to use graphs and charts to translate statistical data into attractive, succinct, readily understandable diagrams.
Voich, Dan; Shrode, William; and Mottice, Homer J. *Information Systems for Operations and Management.* Cincinnati: Southwestern Publishing Co., 1975.
   An excellent comprehensive text on the design of management information systems. A nontechnical discussion is provided.

13

How Should a Manager Coach and Counsel?

Look again at the exercise in Chapter 12. This is a situation that would require counseling action on your part if you were Mary's manager. It's difficult to separate the counseling process from the communication process. Good coaching and counseling depend upon good communication.

Coaching and counseling also involve problem solving, guidance, and leadership skills to some extent. Competent managers bring all of these skills to bear in the coaching and counseling process.

Most coaching and counseling activities are directed toward problem employees or to employees who have problems. There is a difference. A problem employee is one who *continually* has a problem that hampers job performance. This could be a personal or job-related problem. An employee with a problem is one that *occasionally* needs assistance in solving a *job-related* problem. Obviously, the employee who has an occasional job problem is much easier to work with than one who has a personal or job-related problem that regularly interferes with job performance.

All of us as managers must practice coaching and counseling skills from time to time on our job. The way we practice these skills will determine to a great extent how we can build and maintain the human assets in our organization. Coaching and counseling are asset building and maintenance skills dealing with our most important asset—people.

THE COACHING AND COUNSELING PROCESS

What is the objective of the coaching and counseling process? What does it try to do? Are coaching and counseling the same process? The end result of the coaching and counseling process is to *help employees to better solve problems themselves.* Just as coaches work with teams, so should managers work with subordinates. Managers should view themselves as team leaders—whose responsibility it is to help the team do a better job. In this role, managers become leaders, catalysts, exciters. People are encouraged to excel on the job, not merely to meet minimum standards or to try to get by with the least they can. Managers who can make this difference are those who exercise leadership and practice coaching and counseling skills.

Figure 13.1 outlines the steps in the coaching and counseling process. Let's look at each of these steps individually.

Encouragement and guidance

First of all, employees need to be provided with encouragement and guidance as to what they are supposed to accomplish. This is the exciter or catalyst function in the process, resembling more coaching activity than counseling activity. It's this kind of activity that gets people excited to try to do a good job. This activity can be provided through pep talks to sales personnel, training sessions, or consensus clarification meetings.

Examine performance

Part of the coaching and counseling process is to monitor employee performance toward goal achievement. Managers must receive feedback on employee performance. Measures must exist to determine how well the employee is doing. The employee should also know these measures and be able to use them to self-monitor performance.

Evaluate performance

Is the performance inadequate or is it good? If the performance is inadequate, then the counseling process kicks into gear. On the other hand, if it is good, coaching may be all that is necessary.

Identify problems

If the performance is inadequate, then it is necessary to determine why. The problem identification process is applied here. Since this has already been reviewed in the chapter on decision making, we do not examine it again here. However, we should realize that the problem involved might be very personal to the employee. It might be an off-the-job situation, such as a divorce, excessive drinking, drugs, or a death in the family, that is affecting job performance. Or it might be an on-the-job situation such as inadequate training, lack of staff or equipment, or lack of job interest, that is leading to poor performance.

204 HOW SHOULD A MANAGER COACH AND COUNSEL?

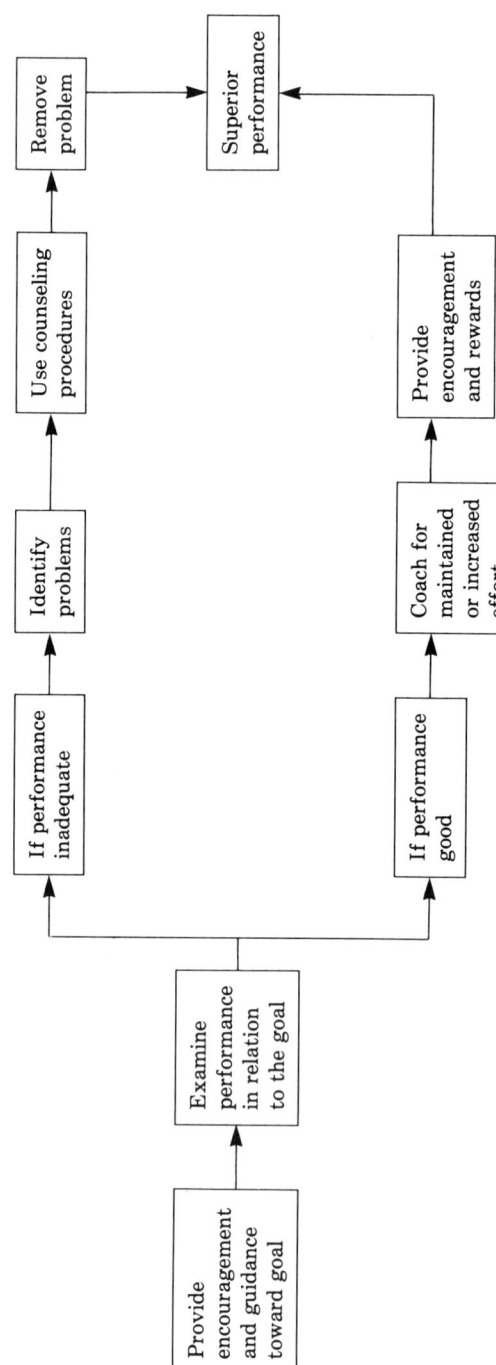

Figure 13.1 The coaching and counseling process

Use counseling process

Once the problem is identified, then the manager should counsel the employee to help remove it. Several methods of counseling can be used which we examine later in the chapter. Managers must always be careful, however, that the bounds of expertise and propriety are not overstepped. Often, professional counseling is needed, so managers must simply refer the employee to a professional in the field.

Remove problem

The goal of the counseling technique used is to remove the problem in order to improve job performance. If this cannot be done, then the employee may need to be transferred to another job more suitable to his or her capabilities, or be terminated. Dismissal is the ultimate corrective action, but it sometimes must be used for the good of the organization.

Coach for maintained or increased effort

If the monitoring process shows the employee is doing a good job (the bottom sequence of boxes in Figure 13.1), we do not ignore the employee. We must be concerned with maintaining or even increasing the effort. Coaches do not stop coaching the team after they win their first game. So should managers be concerned with coaching to maintain and even improve performance.

Encouragement and rewards

Essential to proper coaching is providing encouragement and rewards for continued and improved effort. Rewards tell employees "well done" and serve to reinforce appropriate job effort. Of course, the primary reward for most employees is pay, but rewards are also provided in the form of job security, fringe benefits, promotion, status symbols, praise, and even job or task assignment. (Remember how KP duty was used to punish soldiers?)

The key to making rewards effective motivators for increased effort is to tie them with job performance. Wage incentive systems work best, for example, when they are tied directly to increased output.

A particular manager often does not have control over the pay and fringe benefits package for employees, so there is not much flexibility here as far as the individual manager's discretion in applying these rewards. However, the individual manager can affect promotion possibilities for subordinates. Also, praise and encouragement are within the province of the individual manager. This includes oral praise as well as letters and memos citing outstanding performance.

The individual manager can also offer praise and encouragement during the formal performance appraisal. Finally, and perhaps most importantly, the individual manager can use job assignment as a form of reward to some extent. Not every manager has this flexibility, especially when subordinates are unionized, but managers of managers and nonunionized employees do have this job assignment flexibility. For example, I know of department chairpersons at universities who let the top performers have first choice as to courses and schedule times. After the top performers make their choice, the rest of the faculty take what is left. They get stuck with the 8:00 A.M. and 5:30 P.M. time blocks. Someone has to teach at these times and, instead of using a rotation basis for assignment, these department chairpersons assign classes on the basis of meritorious job performance. We will revisit the reward process in Chapter 17.

Superior performance

The end goal of both the coaching and counseling process is superior job performance. This is what we are after. Simply meeting minimum job standards and output will not lead to effectiveness and efficiency. In the private sector, the company who practices minimum job achievement will be eaten alive by competitors. In the public sector, the agency that allows employees to get away with minimum work effort is wasting huge amounts of taxpayer money.

In the "me-decade" of the seventies, this attitude of getting by on the job with the least possible effort is what has seriously hurt the effectiveness and efficiency of many of our organizations in the United States. Our goals should be superior performance, not mediocre performance.

WAYS TO COUNSEL

There are four major ways to counsel subordinates, as shown in Figure 13.2. Each of these ways has its advantages and disadvantages. Competent managers know when and how to use each approach. Let's look at each of these major counseling forms or styles.

Direct

Using the direct counseling process, managers try to diagnose and solve the problem for the subordinate. The emphasis is on the managers telling the subordinates what to do. The advantages of this approach are its speed and reliance on the expertise of the managers. If managers are knowledgeable about the problem affecting the employee, this knowledge can be brought to bear on solving the problem.

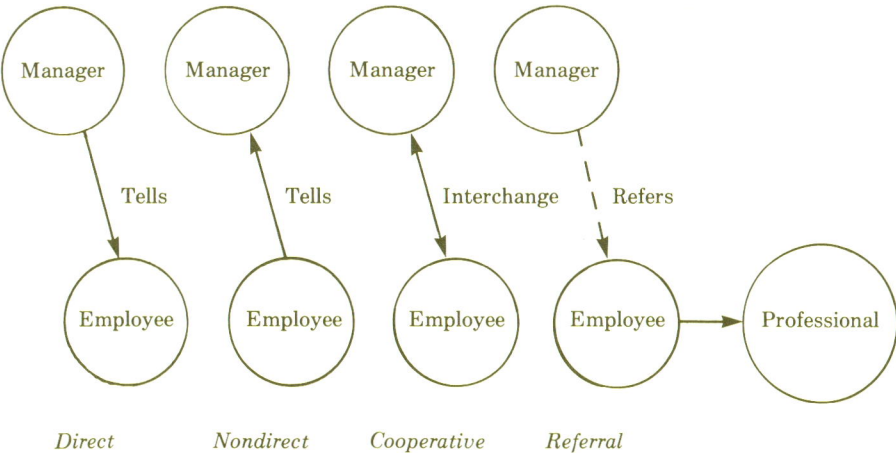

Figure 13.2 Forms of counseling

The primary disadvantage of this approach is that the employee feels little, if any, "ownership" of the solution. The employee simply carries out some action to solve the problem without necessarily understanding why. In other words, the employee may simply go through the motions without any real commitment.

Nondirect

This is client-centered counseling. The primary advantage of the nondirect counseling method is that it relies on the employee to solve the problem. The employee works through the problem and tries to develop the solution. The manager simply serves as a listener, once in a while offering acknowledgment and restatement. (Sometimes this is called "huh-huh" counseling to convey the passive listening role of the manager.) This gives the employee ownership of the solution since he or she has had a direct hand in developing it.

The primary disadvantages of this approach are that it is time consuming and could result in no solution. If the employee can see no way out of the mess, the real need may be for some direct guidance from the manager or a professional counselor.

Cooperative

A true dialogue between manager and subordinate occurs during the cooperative counseling process. Both work together to seek a mutual solution. The client *and* the manager are full partners in the counseling process, sharing the work equally.

The advantage to this approach is that both people involved are viewed as equal partners who *both* must accept responsibility for working out a solution. They each cannot pass the buck. The main disadvantage is that each party can blame the other if there is a failure to reach agreement on the solution to be implemented. Furthermore, there is no way to "force" a solution unless a third party is brought in to mediate differences since neither party is under any obligation to "give in."

Referral

Smart managers recognize when an employee's problem is of such a magnitude that the employee needs to be referred to a professional counselor. Such a counselor could be a professional psychologist or psychiatrist hired by, or on retainer to, the employing organization, or a professional psychologist with a community mental health center. Sometimes the employee can be referred to a clergyman or family medical practitioner.

Often times companies have staffs or people on retainers so that the employee does not have to pay for the counseling service. These firms may also have mental health coverage under their health insurance which pays for most of the cost of counseling services.

In any event, managers should never try to counsel employees with complex or deep-seated emotional problems. Once it is determined that this is the situation, managers should do all that can be done to encourage the employee to seek professional help.

Group versus individual counseling

During the past two decades group counseling techniques have become more widely used. This method has several advantages. First, on a per counselee basis, it is usually a less expensive method of counseling. Second, the method uses group and peer pressures and forces to both support each counselee as well as to help the person work out solutions to problems.

The disadvantages to this approach include gimmickry and lack of individual attention. Gimmickry includes far-out encounter group situations such as primal screaming and birthing. (Under birthing a simulated rebirth usually done with a group nude in a pool of water takes place.) There is very little, if any, scientific evidence that these radical forms of encounter group therapy have any effectiveness whatsoever.

Still, group methods can be effective when a competent group facilitator uses more moderate approaches. Group methods of this type are finding success in prisons, mental hospitals, churches, and universities. Some of the stigma of using psychological counseling is reduced when a person is identified as attending a "discussion" or "learning group" session, as these are often called, instead of "going to the psychologist."

Some do's and don't's for counseling

We need to be aware of a few simple rules to follow in the counseling process to increase its effectiveness regardless of the method used.

1. *Don't try to solve a major personal problem; instead, refer the employee to a professional.* Trying to solve a problem of major magnitude often further complicates the issue.

2. *Don't let a job problem continue without calling it to the employee's attention.* This only serves to tell the employee that either you do not recognize the problem or believe it is not important. If it is important, call it to the employee's attention immediately so action can be taken to correct it. You do not want to create the impression that you condone problem-causing behavior because you are either too afraid or unsure what to do about it.

3. *Don't come across as omnipotent; use tact and judgment.* Keep the employee's interest uppermost. Don't play God by trying to impress and control the employee. Even if direct counseling tactics are used, use them tactfully and in a nonthreatening manner. Playing the role of an all-knowing parent should be avoided. Trust the employee as a partner in the counseling process.

4. *Don't give advice unless you're sure it's correct and appropriate.* Telling an employee to do something or not to do something based upon inaccurate or faulty information destroys your credibility. Be sure you know what you're talking about before you offer advice.

5. *Don't try to solve the employee's problem before you know what the problem is.* Be sure you have worked with the employee to adequately define the problem. Don't jump to conclusions or assume the problem is like others you have encountered on the subject. It may be completely different even though it initially sounds the same.

6. *Don't meddle in personal problems of the employee.* Don't be concerned about an employee's personal problems unless they are affecting job performance. Even when performance is being affected, try not to meddle too deeply in an off-the-job problem. Refer the employee to a professional counselor.

7. *Don't compare the employee's problem with others in the organization. Treat the employee as an individual.* Telling the employee his or her problem

is the same as Bob's, Carol's, Fred's, John's, etc., serves little purpose other than to confirm that the employee is not the only one with the problem. You're there to discuss the *employee's* particular problem, not the problems of other employees.

8. *Try to end on a positive note with a plan of action.* Try to end each counseling session on a positive note. Don't end it by reiterating all of the complex details of the problem. Try to give the employee some tangible course of action that can be taken prior to the next counseling session or at the conclusion of the counseling process.

CONCLUSION

Most managers are not professional counselors, yet all managers must play a coaching and counseling role. Understanding this role and being able to practice effective coaching and counseling techniques in appropriate ways is a key ingredient for successful management. Knowing when and where to refer employees with major problems is also important; and is not a sign of weakness on the part of managers.

A serious concern for the employee as an individual and improving the employee's job performance should serve as the foundation for effective coaching and counseling. Meddling in the personal problems of the employee that do not affect job performance is beyond the scope of the counseling function of the manager. Usually such problems need professional counseling attention.

The organization should support managers in their counseling activities by hiring staff psychologists or employing them on retainers. Training sessions on effective counseling should also be provided to managers.

Since the coaching and counseling function is a specific application of problem-solving behavior, we have only broadly surveyed the coaching and counseling function. There is a great deal of additional material contained in the references at the end of the chapter.

QUESTIONS

1. What percent of time on your job do you spend on coaching and counseling activities? Is this too little, about right, or too much? How do you know?

2. What do you do when an employee comes to you with a personal problem that does not presently affect job performance but could in the future?

3. Which type of counseling do you use most frequently? Why?

4. Does your organization provide professional counseling support for its employees? If so, how could it be improved? If it does not provide this support, why not?

5. Comment on this statement: "Counseling is such a complex process managers have no business trying to counsel employees. Their actions will just muddy the waters and make things worse." Do you agree with the statement? Why or why not?

6. Do managers have a responsibility to try to coach and counsel their *superiors?* Why or why not?

CASES AND EXERCISES

CASE 1: ONE DRINK TOO MANY?

Barry was a payroll supervisor for a large state agency in northwestern United States. He was a dependable, hard working employee who got the job done. Barry had been with the agency for two years and showed much promise for promotion to higher administrative levels in the agency.

On several occasions during the past four months, Ann, Barry's boss, had noticed liquor on his breath after lunch. She said nothing to him about it. His work performance seemed to be as good as ever, but she was concerned that it *could* affect his job performance in the future.

The agency has a rule that states that the consumption of intoxicants and drugs on the job are strictly prohibited. Furthermore, the rule states that anyone in an inebriated state on the job would be immediately suspended without pay for five working days for the first offense and dismissed for the second offense.

Ann does not believe Barry was coming back from lunch inebriated, but she decided to talk with him anyway about his noon-time drinking to "nip the problem in the bud" as she put it. Other employees had noticed liquor on Barry's breath and office gossip had started on Barry's "drinking problem." She was concerned the problem would get worse. After she brought the situation to Barry's attention, Barry made this reply to her:

"It's none of your business, Ann, what I do on my lunch hour as long as I get back to work on time and do my job well in the afternoon. A fella can have a drink or two at lunch if he wants to. People in industry have a three-martini lunch all the time. Furthermore, I am not violating any state or agency rule or regulation.

Please keep your nose out of my personal business. I don't tell you how to run your personal life, so you shouldn't tell me how to run mine. Furthermore, last week, I had lunch with Ken (Ann's boss) and he had two martinis. What do you think of that?"

Questions

1. Should Ann take any action at this point? Why or why not? If so, what action should she take?

2. How does Ann know whether Barry is inebriated or not when he returns from lunch?

3. Suppose Barry starts coming back from lunch five or ten minutes late. How would this affect the situation?

CASE 2: ONLY THE GOOD DIE YOUNG

Just sitting and talking over a serious problem with an employee will have little real effect most of the time on solving a person's problem. Most employees won't admit they have a serious problem and, even if they do admit it, there's not much managers can really do, short of dismissal. They can suggest professional counseling, but how many people will do this even if it's free? There's too much of a negative stigma attached to it.

Furthermore, how many managers really have the time and expertise to spend working with an employee with a serious problem? Counseling can eat up a lot of time. Who's going to get the manager's and employee's work out while they spend time in counseling sessions? Maybe a government agency can tolerate this kind of time wasting activity, but I'll tell you a business can't.

People in business have got to be involved in productive work or profits will be cut. We don't have time to go around holding everyone's hand. People have to stand on their own two feet. Only the strong in business survive. There's no place for the weak. And, let me tell you, government would be a hell of a lot better off if they adopted this attitude too.

Questions

1. With which points made do you agree? Disagree? Why?

2. Does the role of employee counseling differ in a business compared to a government organization? Why or why not?

3. Is the need for counseling a sign of weakness? Explain.

CASE 3: BODY LANGUAGE

"Beverly's got it and she knows how to flaunt it," exclaimed Marsha.

"You know it, and I know it, but does Mr. Rosenberg know it? No way! She's got him wrapped around her finger," answered Sarah.

"She's probably the least competent salesperson in our group. Anyone can have her high sales figures if they had her territory and used her body like she does. When will those guys upstairs realize what little tricks she uses?" said Marsha.

"You're right, Marsha," agreed Sarah. "We could pull off the same stuff if we weren't decent. But who wants to play her games? I want to make it on my brains and job know-how, not on how I swing my hips, flash my eyes, and who knows what else."

"If you ask me, Beverly's really got a problem. She acts like a whore and they love it. She's the worse thing that's happened to women's rights in a long time!" exclaimed Marsha. "She really needs counseling. I think one of us ought to talk with her. I hear she and her husband are on the verge of divorce. I wouldn't put up with her carrying-ons if I were him either. What do you think we should do Sarah?"

Questions

1. Should Sarah and Marsha take any action at this time? If so, what? Why?

2. If no action is taken by Sarah and Marsha, should anyone else in the organization take action? Why or why not? If so, what action should be taken? Why?

3. Are discussions similar to this case harmful to an organization? What might such discussions lead to as far as morale and teamwork are concerned?

EXERCISE: JACK BE NIMBLE

Assume you are in the following situation. Jack is a fifty-six-year-old employee who works for you. He's been with your firm for twenty-two years. Your company has a policy that allows a person to retire with full benefits at age sixty-two, and half benefits at age fifty-eight with at least twenty-five years of service. However, mandatory retirement age is now set at seventy by your firm and a person cannot be forced to retire prior to this age.

During the last five years, you've noticed a gradual decline in Jack's work performance. Whereas his annual job performance ratings once were either good or outstanding, they now tend to be just average. He no longer comes in early and seldom stays late. You surmise he hasn't taken his briefcase home with him in months for evening work. When you ask him to carryout small but important special tasks he always seems to find an excuse why he cannot. Of course, he no longer volunteers for extra work as he once did.

His work does seem to be adequate, however. He is meeting the minimum requirements of the job, but most other employees in your unit far exceed minimum job requirements on a regular basis.

Assume you've decided to have a conference with Jack to discuss this situation. Complete the dialogue that you think would occur by writing in the spaces below.

You: "Good Morning, Jack. I've called you in today to discuss _____

_____

Jack: _____

You: _____

Jack: _____

You (conclusion): _____

Questions

1. What would you hope to be the result of your conference?
2. What counseling measures would you take, if any?

REFERENCES

Anthony, William P., and Anthony, Philip. "More Discipline, Less Disciplinary Action." *Supervisory Management* (September 1972): 18–21.
  Shows how positive discipline should be used as part of the coaching and counseling process.

Argyris, Chris. *Personality and Organization.* New York: Harper, 1957.
  The classic work which shows the problems that can arise when organizations require dependence from independent, mature adults.

Buck, Vernon E. "Working Under Pressure." *Management and Organization Studies* (Autumn 1974): 1–3.
  A good, short discussion of job pressures we all face in our jobs and some things we can do about them.

Burke, Ronald J., and Weir, Thomas. "Organizational Climate and Informal Helping Processes in Work Settings." *Journal of Management* (Fall 1978): 91-105.

Organizational climate influences several aspects of the informal helping process in organizations, including the extent to which problems are disclosed, and the extent to which personal versus work-related problems are disclosed.

Guzzo, Richard A. "Types of Rewards, Cognitions, and Work Motivations." *Academy of Management Review* (January 1979): 75-86.

Alternative approaches to defining types of rewards and what they mean to employees in terms of motivation are discussed.

Kahn, Robert L., and others. *Organizational Stress: Studies in Role Conflict and Ambiguity*. New York: John Wiley & Sons, Inc. 1964.

One source of problems on the job is the stress caused by role conflict and role ambiguity. This book examines the issues involved here.

Lawler, Edward E. "Reward Systems," in J. Richard Hackman and J. Lloyd Suttle, eds. *Improving Life at Work*. Santa Monica, California: Goodyear Publishing Co., 1977, pp. 163-226.

A comprehensive review of reward systems which indicates how important it is for them to be tied to job performance.

Morris, James H.; Steers, Richard M.; and Koch, James L. "Influence of Organization Structure on Role Conflict and Ambiguity for Three Occupational Groupings." *Academy of Management Journal* (March 1979): 58-71.

The structure of a public agency was found to explain variation in role perceptions among professional employees, secretarial/clerical employees, and blue-collar employees working in the agency.

Peterson, James E. "INSIGHT: A Management Program of Help for Troubled People." *Labor Law Journal* (August 1972): 492-495.

Describes a new program of counseling used by several companies.

Reardon, Robert W. "Help for the Troubled Worker in a Small Company." *Personnel* (January-February 1976): 50-54.

The use of community mental health agencies by a small company is explored.

14
How Should a Manager Manage Change and Conflict?

Old habits are tough to break, thought Brent. He was not too sure how far he really could go. He was still feeling his way in his new role.

Brent's position had recently been reclassified from Staff Training Director to Manager of Management and Organization Development. In his old role, Brent was in charge of all training programs for the region. Most of this training was technical in nature, dealing with such things as budget management, contract management, interviewing skills, and equal employment opportunity regulations.

In his new role he was to be in charge of all management and organizational development programs for the region. Programs needed to be developed and offered in such fields as planning, controlling, leadership, communications, and organizational change and development. In his new role, he reported directly to the Regional Director instead of the Assistant Director of Operations where he had previously reported.

This was all new to Brent. On several occasions he had been told by the Regional Manager to "get on the ball and get things going" and to "broaden his horizons." He interpreted this to mean he needed to develop more programs of a managerial nature, but he was not sure which ones were really needed nor how to develop them. He felt helpless and wished he could return to his previous role, but he dared not express this to the Regional Manager. If he did not do something soon he believed his job would be in jeopardy, but he wanted his first few programs to be successful so that he could have credibility in his new position.

Brent's dilemma exemplifies several issues in change and conflict. First, Brent's change in role is producing a conflict situation for him. This creates uncertainty as to what he should do to resolve the conflict. Furthermore, this uncertainty creates insecurity. He faces expectations that are different from those in his previous position, and he is unsure whether he is correctly interpreting these expectations or whether he can fulfill them.

This is a complex situation for Brent and his superior, yet it is one often faced by managers. Competent managers should manage the change process and the conflict which often accompanies it. In this chapter we examine change and conflict processes, and ways to manage them. We pay particular attention to minimizing the disruptive influences of change and conflict while recognizing that both are a natural and necessary occurrence in organizations.

WHAT IS CHANGE?

Change is a fact of life. It is any alteration of the status quo. The only thing we can be sure of is that things will change. It is a neutral concept, neither good nor bad. A particular change, however, can be helpful or harmful to an organization. Change does not have to be new to be change. Adopting something done by others or reinstituting a past practice in the organization is still change, even though nothing new is being tried.

People sit on the horns of a dilemma with regard to change, as shown in Figure 14.1. On the one hand, we desire change because it provides us with new experiences, challenges, and excitement. On the other hand, we desire stability because it provides us with security, certainty, and predictability. Too much change causes chaos; too much stability causes boredom. Finding and maintaining our niche along this love-hate continuum requires almost constant attention.

So we see that people both desire and resist change. The job of managers, then, is to manage the change process so as to maximize its acceptance. Before we can look at some ways of doing this, let's look at the change process itself.

Figure 14.1 The change continuum

Change process

Change involves the process of unfreezing, experimentation and refreezing, as shown in Figure 14.2. First, present behavior and attitudes must be unfrozen. They must be reduced or eliminated. Second, new forms of behavior and new attitudes must be tried out. People experiment with new ways of thinking and acting to see what they like and dislike. Finally, behaviors and attitudes found acceptable are repeated time and time again until they become refrozen as habit.

We go through this process constantly, not only on our job, but also in everyday life. Some of us are more prone to change than others, depending on where we are on the change continuum. Yet, there are some very important reasons why change is often resisted.

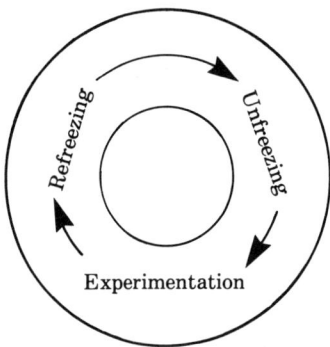

Figure 14.2 The change process

Reasons why change is resisted

There are four major reasons why change is resisted, as we see in Figure 14.3. Let's look at each of these.

Economic reasons. People sometimes resist change because they are concerned about losing their job. A change could result in work restructuring that eliminates their position. This is often why reorganizations and job enrichment programs are resisted.

If the job is not eliminated, there is a chance that work hours or pay could be reduced. Perhaps a person is able to make above the regular wage by working overtime or through commissions. This would be eliminated with a change.

WHAT IS CHANGE? 219

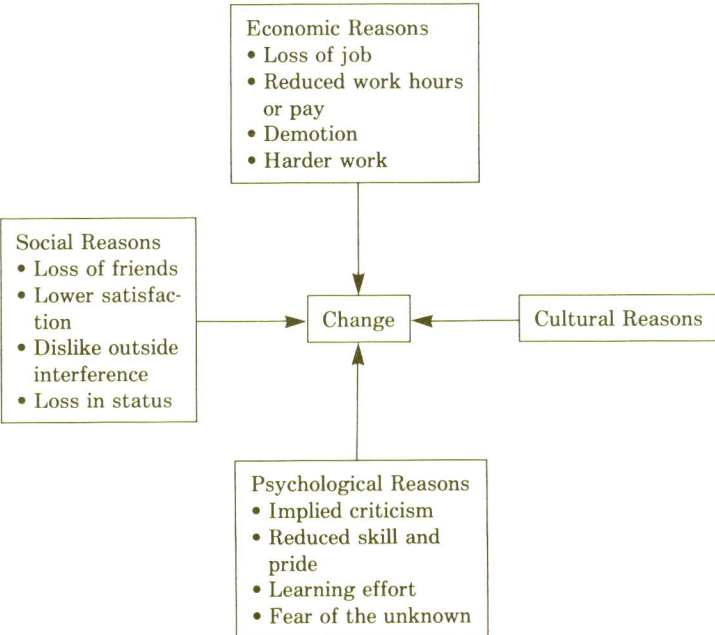

Figure 14.3 Reasons why change is resisted

Also, a person could be demoted or transferred to a less secure position at a lower wage rate. Finally, people are concerned that under a change they could be asked to work harder for the same wages.

Psychological reasons. These reasons are perhaps the most important ones why people resist change. They seem to outweigh all other reasons. First, any change is an implied criticism that the present way of operating is inadequate. Someone set up the present system, and suggesting a change is often interpreted as a personal criticism by this person.

Second, a change may result in reduced skill and pride on the job. We may believe the change results in not only an economic reduction in the job but also a psychological one. Third, any change requires an effort to learn new ways of operating. People sometimes do not want to spend this effort.

Finally, change is resisted because of fear of the unknown. People do not know what to expect of the change. No change can be predicted with 100 percent accuracy. What happens if something goes wrong? Any change involves some risk and some people just don't like to be in a position of risk.

Social reasons. Change often requires breaking present social ties and forming new ones. This can be traumatic, especially for some individuals. This is one reason why frequent employee job transfers are being resisted, not only by the employee but also by the family.

Change can also result in reduced social satisfaction. People may not like fellow employees in the new situation as well as those in the old; there may be personality or other clashes.

Change is also resisted because it often comes about through outside action. People resent outside meddling in their job affairs. They'd like to be left alone. They sometimes resist change because they dislike this outside interference.

When people have not been given a chance to participate in making the change, they resist it. True participation helps people to have a stake in the successful outcome of the change. It also helps them to better understand the change. Participation can bring about commitment if it is used properly.

Change can also result in a loss of social status and prestige in the organization. We all depend on our job for status to some extent, even if it is informal status. Most of us cherish this and don't easily give it up. We resist things that could reduce it.

Cultural reasons. Finally, change is often resisted because of cultural reasons. We may have been reared in a culture where stability and order were valued above all else. Fortunately, most of us reared in the United States have been exposed to cultures and subcultures where change and newness are desirable, although in some sections of the country tradition is valued over innovation.

WAYS OF MANAGING CHANGE

Given this resistance to change, what can managers do to manage change? First of all, managers should realize that they *can* manage change. That is, they should not view themselves as rudderless ships swept along with the current with no control. *Change can be managed,* and the first step for managers wanting to manage change is to believe change *can* be managed. A feeling of helplessness will not lead to effective change management.

Second, managers need to have a clear idea of the change they want to make happen *before* the change is instituted. This is not to say that managers are simply *transmitters* of change made by others in the organization. They do often transmit change, but in transmitting change they can also guide and direct (manage) it within boundaries. Nor are we saying that managers should not buffer, reduce, or deflect some changes. Managing change does not always mean initiating or amplifying it. Sometimes certain changes need to be reduced or redirected.

Having laid out these caveats, let's look at some specific actions that can be taken to manage change.

Make only necessary change

Managers should be absolutely sure that there is a good reason for each and every change. This means that each change should have goals it should accomplish. It also means that a strong rationale should be clearly developed for each change. Change simply for change's sake should be avoided.

Carefully plan the change

Before making any change, carefully plan it out. What is the sequence of steps to be taken? When will they be taken? What will each person's role be in bringing about the change? What are the anticipated results of the change—both favorable and unfavorable? Can we set up some mechanisms now to reduce or avoid the anticipated unfavorable results? All of these questions need answers *before* the change is adopted.

We also need to set up some contingency plans or alternative plans to handle the situation if things do not go as we want them to. We need plans B, C, and D in case Plan A falls through. These alternative plans should be prepared before undertaking the change.

Allow for maximum employee participation

While there are many barriers to employee participation, employees should be allowed to participate in making the change to the extent possible. (Interested readers are referred to Chapters 3 and 4 of my book, *Participative Management,* for a discussion of these barriers and how they can be removed.) Meaningful participation increases commitment and willingness to carry out the change on the part of the employees. This increases employee's ego involvement and degree of felt control over the change.

Communicate, communicate

Communicate the needs, purpose, details, and benefits of the change as openly and honestly as can be done *prior* to making the change. This is an attempt to reduce the uncertainty and fear of the unknown. Not communicating or very selectively communicating will cause the rumor mill to run wild, so managers might as well feed the communication channels with accurate information. This is especially true in very sensitive areas of change such as reorganization, job redesign, or pay.

Use informal groups and key employees as change agents

Managers should recognize the very powerful roles played by the informal work groups and informal leaders in the organization. They can make or break a change. Smart managers know how to use these leaders and groupings to get acceptance and support for changes to be brought about. Sometimes selling three or four key people on a change will convince fifty or sixty others because of the influence and power these few people have.

Use learning principles (behavior modification)

Change requires unlearning old habits and learning new ones. Therefore, learning principles should be used. This means that appropriate desired behavior should be positively reinforced and that undesirable behavior should be punished. It also means people should be provided with a climate that is conducive to bringing out their internal motivation to learn. Distractions should be kept to a minimum. A positive, supportive, helpful, nonthreatening climate should be established.

Learning cues should be provided to help people learn. Perhaps a key slogan (such as "Safety is everyone's business") or signs could be used to trigger appropriate attitudes or behavior. These cues are very important and are frequently used in organizations in safety, fund raising, or new product promotion campaigns.

Work with the union if present

Don't ignore the union when bringing about change, but don't climb into bed with them either. Keep a healthy adversarial relationship. Establish joint committees when appropriate. Negotiate some issues at the bargaining table. Work through some change issues desired while pursuing grievances. But don't ask the union to manage the organization for you. It's not their role and most union leaders do not want it to be their role.

Provide effective leadership for change

Change does not happen automatically. Someone has to be in charge to make it happen—to plan, monitor, and solve problems that come up with it. Certain managers should be given *explicit* responsibility to manage change.

Use appropriate training, development, and orientation programs

People need to be prepared for change. This often means that they need additional training, development, and orientation to appropriately carry out the change. One of the reasons why MBO programs fail so miserably in so many organizations is because they are sprung on the employees with very little employee education and orientation. We would not expect a janitor to operate a tool- and die-making machine without training, and yet, we so often expect employees to put into effect new management techniques, such as MBO, with very little training.

These training programs could be run by in-house trainers or outside consultants. They may include lecture-discussion, role play, videotape, case analysis, gaming, and extensive reading lists as learning methods. Group and individual self-paced learning methods can be used as appropriate. If attitude barriers are extremely difficult to remove, perhaps sensitivity or T-group training could be used. (However, if this method is used it should be used cautiously and under the guidance of a person very experienced in this method. Otherwise, it can do more harm than good.)

All of these methods can help bring about desired change in an effective and efficient manner. But no matter what we do, we still seem to create conflict when making changes. Therefore, we need to also examine this issue since change and conflict are so closely interrelated.

WHAT IS CONFLICT?

Conflict is the competition for scarce resources, ideas, or attention. It occurs when two or more people want the same thing and there is not enough to go around. They are *competing* for what is available.

Conflict is an everyday occurrence in our personal and job life. We wish we could increase our budget, get those two new positions, expand the office, increase our salary, or convince our boss our argument is right. We want the new home or car, more attention from our spouse, a date with the person at the bar whom everyone else is talking with, or more of our teenage daughter's time.

We all have learned to live with conflict, yet we often are not comfortable with it. However, one mark of competent managers is the ability to manage conflict. In this section we examine some types of conflict, causes of conflict, and some ways of managing conflict.

Types of conflict

There are many ways to classify conflict, but, in keeping with our focus on the central role of managers, we use a relatively simple system to type conflict. For our purposes, conflict can be placed into one of three categories: lateral conflict, vertical conflict, or system conflict. Let's briefly look at each of these types.

Lateral conflict. This type of conflict exists when people who have basically the same level of authority disagree as to what or how something should be done. Since these people have approximately the same authority, this type of conflict is often difficult to resolve. However, even though people involved in lateral conflict have similar authority levels, their actual *power* levels may differ. Certain managers have more power than others for various reasons: they may have more credibility, visibility, expertise, or experience, for example. These differences in power will affect how conflict is resolved.

Vertical conflict. With vertical conflict there are a great deal of authority differences between managers in the chain of command. This type of conflict is the classic type found in bureaucratic organizations. How can higher level managers get lower level managers to do specific things? How can lower level managers convince higher level managers that the views and approaches of the lower level manager are correct? Vertical conflict concerns the use and acceptance of authority. Even though this conflict can always be resolved (at least on the surface) by "pulling rank," there are other considerations involved.

These include such things as communication, leadership, and motivation of subordinates. Resolving vertical conflict in an appropriate constructive fashion will enhance communication, leadership, and other skills needed by superiors.

System conflict. This type of conflict occurs when various parts of the organization are not interacting effectively. There is little coordination among units that should be cooperating and not competing. Certain units within every organization must work together if the organization is to survive and prosper. Often this does not happen. For example, the electronic data processing unit should support and assist line management. Personnel should support operating line managers. Sales units must work with billing and accounts receivable units. The list of cooperating units required for effective organizational operations is almost endless.

This cooperation and integration is difficult to achieve in widely dispersed, large organizations. Mechanisms can be set up to help minimize conflict and ensure cooperation among units, but it's not easy. We'll look at some of these mechanisms in the last section of the chapter, but first let's examine the various causes of conflict. If we can accurately pinpoint these causes, we're well on our way to properly managing conflict.

Causes of conflict

There are at least seven causes of conflict, as shown in Figure 14.4. Often two or more are at work in any given situation. Let's look at each cause.

WHAT IS CONFLICT? 225

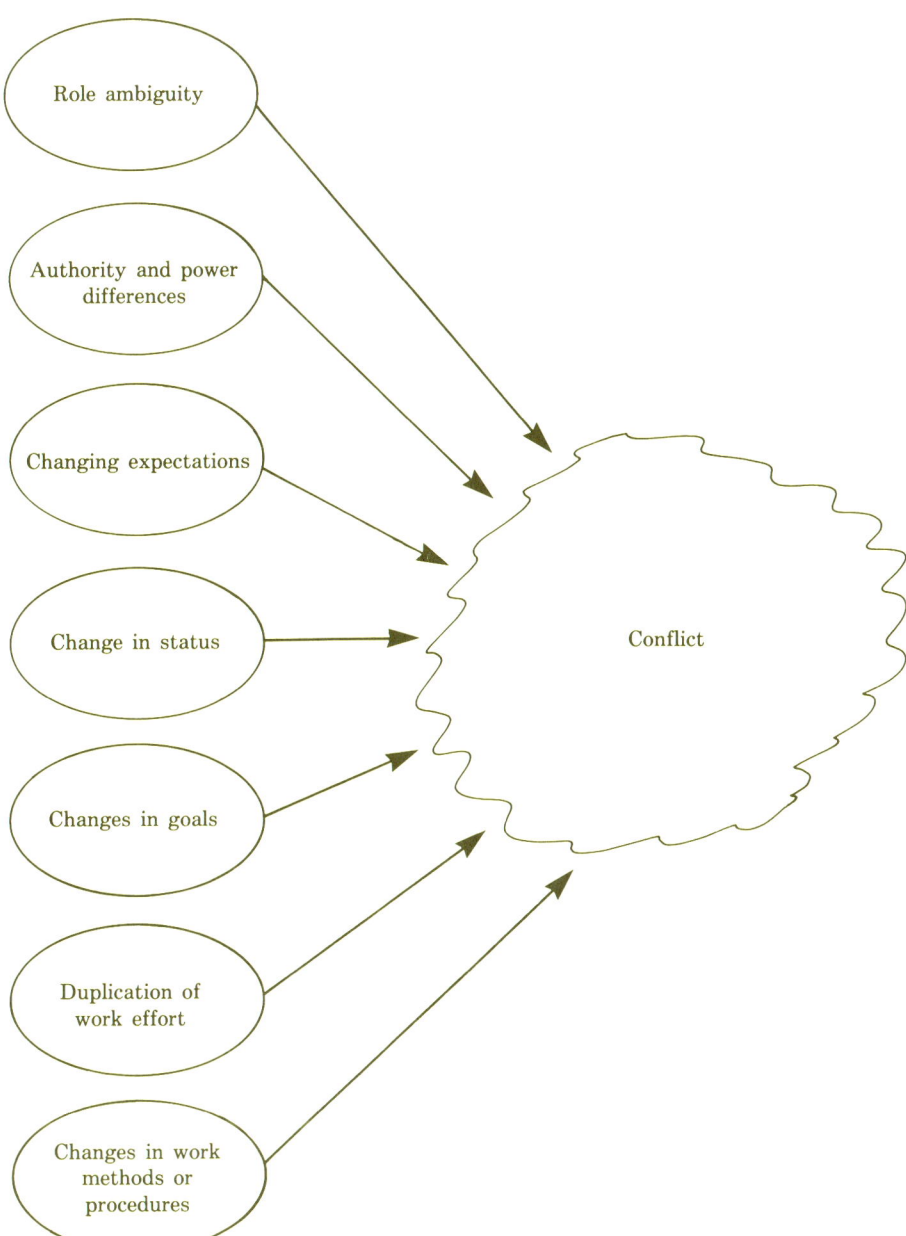

Figure 14.4 Causes of conflict

Role ambiguity. If people are not sure of their role in the organization, there's bound to be conflict. People need to know what they are supposed to do, what their level of responsibility is, to whom they report, and how much authority they have. If these conditions do not exist, roles will be ill-defined, which will lead to role ambiguity, which will lead to conflict.

Authority and power differences. The very fact that a person has power or authority over another person often causes conflict. Most of us do not like to be in a subservient position, but such subservience among subordinates is a fact of organizational life. Minimizing these feelings of conflict that come about because of superior-subservient relationships requires tact, empathy, and good leadership on the part of superiors.

Changing expectations. We need to know what is expected of us. Even once we know this, we need to know changes that come about because we live in a changing organizational environment. Our perceptions need to be similar to those with whom we work. We need consensus-shared frames of reference from which to operate if we are to be able to maintain a common basis of expectations. We also need to be effective communicators so we can inform people as to changing expectations that occur because of changing role requirements.

Changes in status. Our status in the organization changes over time. We pass from being a young turk to a member of the old guard. We are promoted. We are transferred. A new whiz kid is hired and takes over some of our functions. Our boss, on whom we have staked our career, is fired. All of these incidents can cause great changes in our status which, in turn, can cause conflict between us and others in the organization.

Changes in goals. The goals of our organization or unit can cause conflict. We may no longer be committed to the new goals. In fact, we may be very much opposed to them. Furthermore, new goals may be forced on us without our acceptance. We may try to go along with these new goals, but, if conditions get bad enough, we will psychologically tune-out or even terminate our employment with the organization.

Duplication in work effort. "But, I thought she was going to do that." Duplication in work effort (organizational overlaps) can lead to organizational gaps. Important work does not get done because two or more people are assigned the job and each person leaves it up to the other person to carry out the work. These situations cause serious conflict in many organizations. They can be resolved by better defining roles and role expectations.

Changes in work methods or procedures. Developing new procedures or work methods can cause conflict, especially if employees believe they cannot learn the new procedure or feel it to be less efficient than the old. Managers ought to ask employees for suggestions before instituting new procedures or work methods.

WAYS TO MANAGE CONFLICT

A certain level of conflict is good for an organization. Of course, too much conflict can be destructive, but too little can lead to stagnation. Finding and maintaining the right level of conflict is a challenge for managerial competency. There are at least six ways managers can manage and resolve conflict, as shown in Figure 14.5. Each way should be used when appropriate.

Use of power or authority (suppression)

Sometimes managers must pull rank and simply suppress conflict. This probably should be used as a last resort, even though it is the method usually thought of first. This method really does not resolve conflict; rather it just places it under the table only to fester and maybe explode at a later date. Yet, when all else fails, managers may simply have to step in, make a decision, and tell subordinates to "hush" and get back to work.

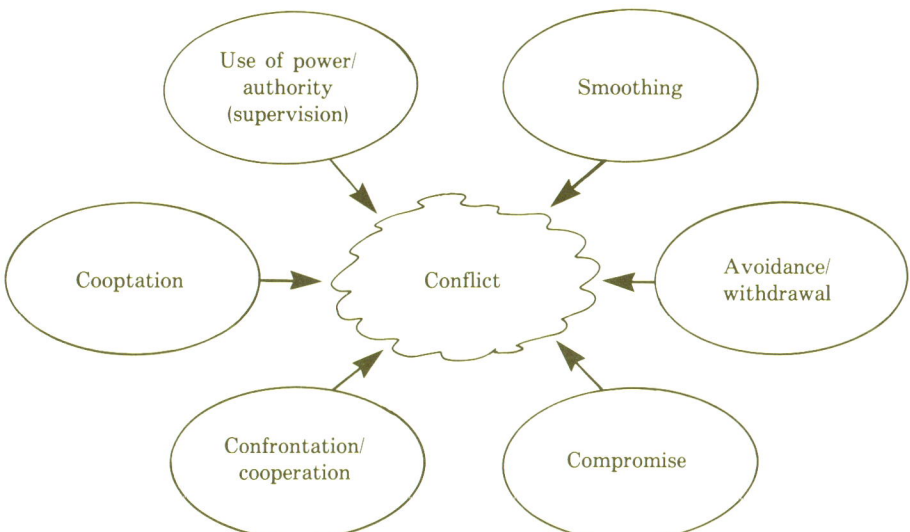

Figure 14.5 Ways to manage conflict

Confrontation/cooperation

The opposite of suppression is getting the conflict out on the table with the parties concerned talking candidly with one another. Confrontation brings conflict to a head in hopes of achieving cooperation. It may, however, lead to a standoff with neither side willing to budge. If the confrontation leads to this, then another method of resolution should be tried.

Smoothing

Counseling often works as a way to resolve conflict. Working with each party separately so as to get them to better understand their needs, wants, and problems can sometimes bring about conflict resolution between the parties.

Compromise

Lyndon B. Johnson was fond of saying, "Come, let us reason together." This is an example of compromise, probably the most commonly used method of conflict resolution. Our political and certainly our collective bargaining systems in the United States rest squarely on this technique. Each party gives up something in hopes of gaining something from the other side. The series of demand and concessions that flow from each party to the conflict situation makes for a stimulating and interesting experience.

Cooptation

Can we absorb a conflicting party? When a larger, more powerful party absorbs a loud, annoying, but fairly weak party, this is called cooptation. This method was commonly used in the late sixties and early seventies by university administrations to absorb vociferous student groups by placing them on committees, etc.

Avoidance/withdrawal

Sometimes one party must simply withdraw from the situation for the conflict to cease. This withdrawal can be done voluntarily or be forced. Parents often separate squabbling children by sending them to their room. Married couples sometimes seek uncontested divorces. Employees sometimes voluntarily quit an organization rather than continually trying to fight to change things.

Using the conflict resolution methods

Each of these six ways should be used by managers to resolve conflict as the situation dictates. We all differ in our own personal styles of management, but I like to start out with compromise first. Can we find some common ground for agreement? If this fails, then smoothing often works as perceptions, expectations, and egos are massaged. From here, confrontation in hopes of achieving cooperation is often used. At least this brings things to a definite head. If the conflict still exists, then I move to cooptation. If this fails, then I move to suppression and then to avoidance or withdrawal as a last resort.

While this sequence seems to work best for me, it may not for you. It depends on the type of employees you have and the situation you face. Also, you may use different methods with different employees. Let experience and judgment guide you.

CONCLUSION

Change and conflict are a fact of organizational life. Competent managers can effectively manage change and the ensuing conflict that often occurs. The ability to live in an ambiguous situation marked by some stress (conflict) is a highly prized skill. Competent managers work at developing this skill.

Change and conflict cannot be avoided, but they can be managed. Like so many other facts of management life, they are not easy to manage. Sometimes we feel like we are being swept along in a current, constantly being banged from one rock to the next. Once we find ourselves in this situation, it is hard to pull ourselves out so we can actually begin to manage change and conflict.

This feeling of helplessness is common, especially for lower-middle and supervisory management levels. After all, these are the people at the bottom end of the organizational totem pole. Yet, we must remember that we are masters of our own destiny. We can take the initiative on certain matters and make things happen. We can influence other people and events, and, to the extent that we can do this effectively, then we can begin to swim out of the stream and begin piloting the ship even if it is only a row boat. At least we are no longer fighting to keep our head above water.

In the next chapter we examine another important managerial skill: political skill. Every good manager is also a bit of a politician. Political skills, which can be misused, nevertheless play a very important role in managerial competency.

QUESTIONS

1. In your opinion, what are the most important reasons why people resist change?

2. What can be done to overcome resistance to change? Which method(s) work best for you?

3. Based upon your job experience, what are the most common causes of conflict you face?

4. Must change always lead to conflict? Explain.

5. What methods of conflict resolution do you most often use? Are these effective?

6. What is your organization's general view toward change and conflict? In your opinion, is this appropriate? If not, can this view be changed? If so, how?

CASES AND EXERCISES

CASE 1: FAT AND HAPPY

The Department of Human Services for a midwestern state has contracted with Dynamic Change Agents, Inc., a consulting group, for a comprehensive organizational development program for the top management group of the department. The department employs approximately 22,000 employees throughout the state, in such areas as mental health and retardation, public health, childrens' services, vocational rehabilitation, and job assistance and employment. The state is lightly industrialized with about 15 percent of the labor force employed in agriculture.

Marsha Manning was appointed Commissioner of the Department three months ago. Marsha has a master's degree in counseling and an MBA from a prestigious midwestern university. She has also worked in the agency for eight years. During the last two years, she was the department's chief legislative liaison officer.

Marsha believed the department was ripe for change. She believed many of the old guard were semi-retired on the job. She felt the department did not attract enough new blood.

She believed the agency lacked innovation. People seemed to be too comfortable with the status quo while there were many unmet client needs begging for attention. Furthermore, legislative and federal audits had recently disclosed some serious problems with several programs, which could become politically embarrassing for the newly elected governor who had appointed Marsha.

Marsha believed that change was something that bureaucrats in the agency avoided every way they could. She also believed the most commonly used method of resolving conflict was through suppression. Managers did not seem willing to confront conflict head on. An "old boy network" seemed to rule that dictated conflict was bad and should be kept to an absolute minimum.

She believed the agency needed to be stirred up and that drastic change was needed; hence, the contract with Dynamic Change Agents, Inc. She has a meeting tomorrow afternoon with the organization and is wondering what plan of attack should be developed.

Questions

1. Can an outside group such as Dynamic Change Agents, Inc., be used to bring about change in a state agency? If so, what conditions must exist? If not, why not?

2. Are government or business organizations harder to change? Why?

3. If you were Marsha, what role could you develop for Dynamic Change Agents, Inc.? What would you hope to accomplish in using them?

CASE 2: EVOLUTION OR REVOLUTION?

Change is an extremely complex and ambiguous concept for most managers. Most of us do not feel comfortable with change. We say we want it, but we really don't. Most of us like structure and a set routine. It makes our job and our life easier. Bringing about change is one of the greatest challenges managers face.

Most managers do not have the skills to bring about change in the appropriate way. Where have they been taught these skills? How can they learn them? This is why so many organizations rely on outside consulting or development organizations to bring about change. But I have little faith in these organizations. Most of the people I meet in these consulting organizations are "flakey," touchy-feely types who are followers of pop-psychology, but know very little about good business practices.

So, where does this leave us? Well, in my opinion, I believe the only way to bring about change is to make it so gradual that people do not know that change is happening. I know this goes against a lot of current thinking on change. A lot of people think fast, revolutionary change is needed in order to get any change at all. I don't agree. Rapid, sharp change just causes too much conflict which becomes very destructive. Gradual change causes much less conflict and can be better managed.

As far as I'm concerned, gradual, incremental change is best. That's the only way to bring about effective change without stirring up a hornet's nest.

Questions

1. Under what conditions would gradual change work better than fast revolutionary change?

2. Do you agree that fast change always causes more conflict than gradual change? Why or why not?

3. Do you agree with this person's belief that most people are comfortable with routine and structure and, therefore, do not want change? What are the implications of your answer?

EXERCISE: HOW DO YOU MANAGE CHANGE AND CONFLICT?

Think back over the past six months to a year on your present job and pick a major change in which you have been closely involved. This change can be in any area of your operations, but it should be one that you had major responsibility to bring about. Answer each of the following questions with regard to that change effort.

1. What were the specific goals to be achieved by the change?
2. What change methods did you use to bring about the desired change?
3. What type of conflict and resistance, if any, did the change generate?
4. What methods did you use to try to overcome or manage this conflict? Were you successful? If not, why not?
5. On the whole, do you believe you were able to reach the goals set for the change?
6. If you had to do the change over again, what would you do differently? Why?

REFERENCES

Barkdill, Charles W. "Organizing for Change." *Michigan Business Review* (May 1972): 1–4.
  The thesis is that change can be profitable as well as acceptable if organizations will free top management to plan for change, follow through on the plan, and motivate the people to accomplish change.

Bennis, Warren. "Organizational Change: Operating in the Temporary Society." *Management Review* (August 1969): 8–14.
  A somewhat dated but still relevant article dealing with the role of organizational change in a dynamic society.

Brooker, W. Michael. "Eliminating Intergroup Conflicts... Through Interdepartmental Problem Solving." *S.A.M. Advanced Management Journal* (Spring 1975): 16–25.
  A good look at ways that can be used to resolve system and lateral conflict.

Goodstein, Leonard D.; Lubin, Bernard; and Lubin, Alice W., eds. *Organizational Change Sourcebook II: Cases in Conflict Management.* San Diego: University Associates, 1979.

A collection of nine case studies that provide indepth analysis on the management of conflict, with issues ranging from international border disputes to personnel grievances.

Kelly, Joe. "Make Conflict Work for You." *Harvard Business Review* (July–August 1970): 103–113.

Written in the typically clear fashion of HBR articles, this piece provides some practical guidance on using conflict as a management tool.

Likert, Rensis, and Likert, Jane Gibson. *New Ways of Managing Conflict.* New York: McGraw-Hill, 1976.

A comprehensive look at managing conflict in business, organizations, schools, and cities using Likert's well known System 4 approach.

London, Jordon. "Consistency of Management in Organizational Change." *Personnel Journal* (May 1974): 363–371.

According to this article, the key to a successful management development program in order to bring about change is continuity, not single programs.

Luthans, Fred, and Martinko, Mark. *The Power of Positive Reinforcement.* New York: McGraw-Hill, 1978.

A good short workbook on the essentials of behavior modification. Especially useful in a workshop situation.

Maccoby, Michael. *The Gamesmen: The New Corporate Leaders.* New York: Simon and Schuster, 1976.

The thesis is that the "gamesman" is replacing the "company man" as the dominant managerial type, especially in high-technology industries; and this fact is resulting in new methods for managing conflict.

Nord, Walter, and Durand, Douglas. "Beyond Resistance to Change." *Organizational Dynamics* (Autumn 1975): 279.

A good review of an organization that had tried several change techniques, all of which were resisted.

15

How Should a Manager Practice Political Skills?

When you come right down to it, management is a political game. Those that know how to play this game get ahead; those that don't never really make it. Oh sure, managers have got to be technically competent; they've got to know what they're doing. But they've also got to be politically astute.

Every organization has a political element. Business organizations are no exception. People vie for position, develop power relationships, work for their own advantage, and so on. These are important actions. Yet, no where are managers taught these skills in business schools. No where are managers formally trained in political survival skills. Good managers learn these skills, but they learn them through the school of hard knocks.

Maybe political skills are not as important as this statement indicates, but they *are* important. And it is true that they are difficult to learn since there is little in the way of formal training in these skills. We try to partially overcome this problem in this chapter by focusing on the necessity of political skills and some of the specific skills managers should practice.

THE INTERNAL POLITICAL ENVIRONMENT

Organizations are made up of people who are constantly vying with one another for power, status, and prestige. People want their way. We saw some of the issues involved here in the last chapter on change and conflict.

This vying for position is what leads to an internal political environment in every organization. Such an environment is a natural element of organizational life. Of course, such vying can get out of hand and become destructive, but a certain amount of politics is natural and should be handled and managed just like any other area of management. It should be made a constructive, not a destructive, force in the organization.

Attempts to completely eliminate the political environment are usually futile. Even Max Weber, the father of bureaucracy, was unable to eliminate the political climate in organizations when he developed his rational theory and method of organization. (However, he did do much to *reduce* the political influence.)

The political environment in the organization should not be the predominant mode. Political skills are not the most important skill or tool of management. Other skills, such as those we have reviewed previously, are more important. When one places too heavy a reliance on political skills, one becomes all form and no substance. Political skills substitute for other managerial skills and competence. It is this occurrence, the predominance of political skills, that has given politics in organizations such a bad cast. They should *not* substitute for other skills, and managers should *not* exclusively rely on them. These are but one set of skills to be used along with other, perhaps more important, skills.

Reasons for political environment

The political environment forms naturally within organizations for several reasons. First, as we indicated, people vie for position. They want room to maneuver so there is much jockeying that goes on. Political skills provide flexibility. They allow for trade-offs and compromising that a strictly rational organization has little room for.

Second, the political environment occurs because people want to increase their power base, status, and prestige. We all want to feel important and to be recognized as being important by others in the organization. We do things to enhance this importance, such as trying to be associated with a competent superior, increasing our staff or budget, being at the right place at the right time with a key idea, or working for a promotion. These are natural occurrences and are okay, unless they lead to apple-polishing. It is at this point that behavior can become destructive since the manager has now developed a cadre of "yea-sayers" who never disagree with the boss. This is dangerous for organizations. Ideas go unchallenged and unquestioned. Excessive loyalty soon becomes the order of the day. Healthy debate is lost.

Third, the political environment exists to cut through bureaucratic red tape. No organization can survive long as a true bureaucracy. It will collapse under the weight of countless rigid rules, policies, and procedures. There are times when this mass of red tape needs to be cut. There are

Catch-22 situations in organizations. The political environment forms as a counterforce to excessive bureaucracy. In fact, Weber expounded the theory of bureaucracy as a way to reduce the internal political environment that so pervaded organizations in his day.

Again there is a danger here. We need policies, procedures, and rules in organizations, but we do not need rigidity. The political environment should not do away with policy and procedure; rather, it should make them livable and workable. The political environment humanizes the impersonal bureaucracy, but should not eliminate it.

TYPES OF POLITICAL SKILLS

Let's take a look at the variety of political skills that can be practiced by managers. A list of these skills appears in Figure 15.1.

Forming coalitions

Sometimes it is necessary to increase one's power base by combining efforts with those of like minds. "In unity and numbers there is strength" is the old axiom at work here. Of course, this is the rationale behind the formation of unions, but managers should also use this tactic when necessary. Combining one's efforts with subordinates or a group of peer managers can be an effective way to bring pressure on a superior. Of course, coalitions should be done above board and people should be openly invited to join. When this tactic is done secretly and behind closed doors, it can be very dysfunctional for the organization as people sneak around from one group to another.

The use of coalitions not only increases the power of individual managers, but it will help convince top level management that it's not "just one or two malcontents raising a fuss." Coalitions demonstrate to others that the concerns are shared by a number of managers.

Furthermore, the use of coalitions in dealing with groups of subordinates demonstrates to them that the organization's management structure has a united and consistent front on an issue. This will help against a sub-

---

• Forming coalitions	• Timing
• Bargaining, compromise, and trade-offs	• Posturing-bluffing
• Lobbying	• Personal visibility
• Use of the media	

Figure 15.1 Political skills used by managers

ordinate tactic of divide and conquer. It will also help against subordinates "whipsawing"—playing one manager against another as children often do with parents.

Bargaining, compromise, and trade-offs

These are probably the most common types of political tactics used. The three are very closely related. We briefly explored them when examining the conflict management process and will look at them in more detail here.

Bargaining, compromise, and trade-offs are really a major subpart of *negotiation* skills. Of course, management groups have been negotiating with unions for years, and we can learn much from this process. But even within management groups, negotiations occur between individual subordinates and superiors, between one management group and another, and between one office or plant and another. Furthermore, negotiations often occur among divisions, product groups, or functional areas. Most often these negotiations occur as various areas try to increase their budget, hiring authority, or physical facilities.

The key point in bargaining and negotiation is to negotiate from a position of strength. You must have something the other person wants. You must be able to give some things up to compromise and trade-off—without completely losing your shirt. Thus, to be an effective negotiator and bargainer, a manager must have a power base and "goodies" that can be traded. Without these, there is little real negotiation. Some of the goodies that can be traded are budget components, physical facilities, key subordinate personnel, ideas, promises, work effort, or support of some issue dear to the other side.

These goodies are traded back and forth among the negotiating parties, much as in bartering, as shown in Figure 15.2. Each side gives up something in hopes of receiving something else of value in return. These trade-offs are done every day, and, from time to time if the scales become unbalanced, we collect our debts or "chits" owed to us. We informally keep track of these in our mind and cash them in as necessary. Most people try to keep from being too far in debt to any one person since this clearly places us in a dependency position. This can cause problems, especially if this person happens to be a subordinate.

Lobbying

Trying to exercise influence—either formal or informal—to convince another party to agree with a particular point of view so as to take action supporting it is lobbying. We see this skill expertly practiced in our legisla-

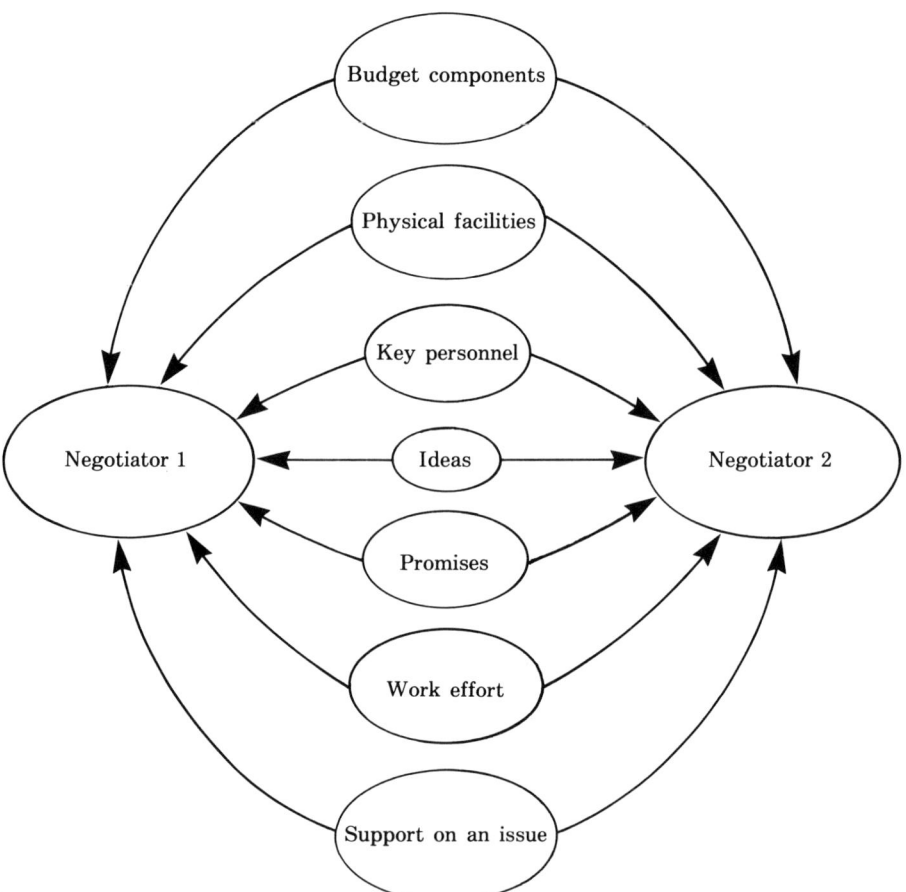

Figure 15.2 Bargaining and negotiating

tive processes at both the federal and state levels. Paid lobbyists representing a variety of interest groups work to convince members of congress and state legislatures to vote a particular way on a particular issue.

Our political system depends on such a process, ensuring that people have a chance to voice their concerns and viewpoints. As long as no one special interest group dominates the process so as to exclude others, then the system is working well. However, if particular lobbyists are able to achieve an extraordinary amount of power because of money, unethical, or even illegal action, the system is not working since other, less powerful groups are prohibited from having significant input to the legislative process.

The same principle holds with organizations. People at all levels should be permitted to lobby for their points of view. They may do this through coalitions, as individuals, or through representatives such as in collective bargaining. Organizations that have effective suggestion systems or open meetings provide a forum for individual or group lobbying.

Unless individuals effectively surface their concerns, little is likely to be done about them. The powers-that-be in organizations must somehow learn of organizational member concerns if members expect action to be taken. Voicing these concerns through direct or indirect lobbying efforts thus becomes an important political skill.

Lobbying is also one of the few effective tools a subordinate can exercise with a superior. Since a subordinate has no authority over a superior, the subordinate has to exercise informal influence to convince a superior to take action. This means the subordinate must lobby by forming coalitions with other subordinates or with managers at the same level of the superior. Occasionally, lobbying with a superior's boss is also necessary.

The use of informal influence through lobbying must be done carefully and candidly. While secrecy should not be the rule, it is also important not to broadcast one's lobbying effort throughout the organization.

Excessive use of lobbying can lead to too much involvement in political processes, such that the daily work of managers takes secondary importance. Managers spend their time going from office to office gaining support for views, and little effort is spent in getting the daily work out.

Use of the media

There are times to leak sensitive information to the press, radio, or TV. Sometimes, as a last resort, managers have to "go public" to get action taken on an issue. This was the situation with Watergate, certain Vietnam War situations, recent corporate bribery cases, and nuclear plant operations disclosures. Such leaks are justified when important action needs to be taken but it is being ignored or even covered up by the powers-that-be in the organization.

Of course leaking sensitive information to the media should be done infrequently and only when all else has failed. The information should be accurate, and the individual or group who goes to the media must be willing to take the repercussions if it is ever found out who leaked the information. Such repercussions could include loss of job, blacklisting, a slander suit, or even a jail term if the material is classified government information. Obviously, such action should not be done lightly. The major benefit of leaking information to the media is to arouse public opinion and censure. If the information is not likely to do this, there is no sense in leaking it.

Some managers try to use the media in another way. Instead of leaking information to them, they use the press as an extension of the corporate PR arm. They flood news bureaus with a blizzard of organizational propaganda, hoping it will get top billing. Thank goodness that the journalistic profession has matured enough so that it ignores most of this ballyhoo! Organizations, thus, are forced to pay for their promotional messages, but at least consumers know it is paid advertisement and not a news item.

All of this is not to say that paid advertising and promotion cannot be effective. They can be. They should be used to get the organization's message across and perhaps to rally public opinion behind some course or issue. In this sense, paid media usage can be a political tool for an organization, but it does not have the same effect that leaking sensitive information has as a managerial tool within the organization.

Timing

A sense of timing is a must for an effective manager. One does not ask for a raise after just losing a major sale. Nor should a manager keep arguing a point if no progress is being made. Let it rest for a while. At the end of a particularly long and difficult day, we do not go to our boss with a major request that requires complex reasoning.

It is difficult to learn how to develop a sense of timing. It comes through experience. One must have a sensitivity about people and events so as to know how to "strike while the iron is hot." There's nothing worse than a cold, stale idea dragged out to be rehashed all over again.

A sense of timing is also necessary when making a phone call, scheduling a meeting, writing a letter or memo, or making an office visit. For example, meetings scheduled at 4:30 P.M. Friday are usually not too productive. A congratulatory memo written several weeks after the good deed has a greatly reduced impact. A returned phone call made two weeks later conveys lack of concern and importance.

We all interpret the timing of a person's actions with much meaning. Therefore, managers must be sensitive as to how others not only interpret what is said or done but also *when* it is said or done.

Posturing-bluffing

"Ask for more than you expect to get. You can always fall back." This major bargaining tactic is a key rule in using political skills. We make demands, even threats, and then pull back from them. We develop positions and "window dressing" only to change later. We go through this maneuvering to throw the other party off stride, to keep them guessing about what we really want. We do this to create confusion so we can keep our maximum flexibility and to appear that we have really given in on an issue.

The use of posturing and bluffing is a prized political skill, but it is the one skill many managers find distasteful. It is a game, no doubt about it. Some managers claim they don't have time to play games because they have so much work to do. But the point is, most competent managers occasionally resort to posturing and bluffing in order to get their way. Often this is done by a superior who does not wish to pull rank. Demands are made and positions are created, only to later seemingly "cave in" to a position the manager wanted originally. For example, a sales manager can tell a subordinate he wants her to sell 120 units per month when he really wishes 80 to be sold. He may tell her he really thinks she should sell 120 per month and that anything less than this would hurt the company. After much haggling and give and take, they may settle on 90 units per month. This is 10 more than the sales manager really wanted originally!

Of course the primary danger in bluffing and posturing is that one has to lie to use it. (Or, as it is called at the Harvard Business School, use "strategic misrepresentation.") One never knows where the other side really stands. All kinds of false fronts are created. Opponents are led down blind paths. Paper barricades and straw men are created only to be sacrificed. You can never really be sure of whose support you have and don't have on any one issue.

Some managers get sick and tired of these silly little games and throw in the towel. In fact, games are often used in the hope that this will happen. However, bluffing and posturing can be effective tools if used sparingly and with good judgment, but, as with other political skills, heavy reliance on these skills makes managers nothing more than blowhards.

Personal visibility

The final political skill we discuss involves enhancing one's personal visibility in the organization. This involves being at the right place at the right time with the right person and the right cause. This means being associated with other competent and respected people in the organization. It also means working in an organizational division generally recognized for its efficient operations and contribution to overall organizational goals, as well as being associated with a progressive and prestigious product or service offering in the organization. We build our reputation and our own visibility in large part based on those with whom we associate. This is not to say we are not judged for our own personal competence, but we are also judged to some extent based on those with whom we associate in the organization.

It is also important for managers, especially new managers, to do something to gain personal visibility in the organization. Excelling in one's area of expertise on the job is the best way to gain visibility, but there are other ways. For example, being appointed to a special task force that will make a presentation to a division V.P. or a regional director is an excellent way for managers to enhance visibility. This visibility is important since it is easy for new managers in large organizations to get lost in the shuffle.

As with other political skills, managers must be very careful in using visibility as a tool. For example, do *not* become known as a name dropper or braggart. Let actions speak for you. There are times, however, when you should inform others of your accomplishments to ensure that they know what you are doing. Often this occurs during the performance appraisal process, but it could also occur through publicity when receiving a special award, or through casual conversation with a superior.

WAYS OF USING POLITICAL SKILLS

As you no doubt noticed, the theme that pervades the use of political skills is one of *caution*. Heavy reliance on these skills, especially when they are used to substitute for other important management skills, creates the impression that one is all fluff and no substance. Such reliance should therefore be avoided. Also, one must be very careful of ethical and legal pitfalls when using these skills, especially when "strategically misrepresenting" facts or situations.

Given these problems, how then should managers use political skills? They should be used as icing on a cake is used—to enhance and complement the taste of the cake itself; to add visually pleasing characteristics; to add beauty, grace, and art to the cake. Icing should not drown out the flavor of the cake, nor should it "dirty" the cake with unnecessary bric-a-brac. A good cake is still good without the icing, but the icing makes a good cake even better. However, icing won't make a bad cake good.

So it is with political skills. Artful use of these skills will not make a poor manager a good one, nor will these skills necessarily "dirty" an ethical manager. As with other managerial skills, political skills can be used unethically and illegally, but they need not be. We will look at these issues later in the book.

CONCLUSION

Let's summarize some basic do's and don't's in using political skills, as shown in Figure 15.3. First, don't place too heavy a reliance on political skills at the exclusion of other skills. Second, be mindful of ethical and legal traps when using them. Third, recognize that some organizations are more political than others and that the skills, therefore, are more appropriately practiced in some organizations while frowned upon in others. Fourth, try to

1. Do not rely too heavily on political skills.
2. Watch for ethical and legal problems.
3. Assess the political climate in the organization.
4. Practice the skills honestly and openly.
5. Do not use them in place of basic competency.
6. Do not use them viciously.
7. Retreat and admit defeat when necessary.
8. Try to achieve a nonzero sum game.

Figure 15.3 Guidelines for practicing political skills

practice the skills in an open, honest, and candid fashion. Avoid secrecy, gossip, and back-stabbing.

Fifth, don't use political skills at all unless you are first a competent manager in your field of expertise. Like icing on a cake, political skills don't make a bad manager good. Sixth, don't use the skills to completely break down your opponent. Show mercy and kindness, and allow others to save face. Don't kick people while they're down. While the use of political skills is a game, let's not make it a vicious game.

Seventh, know when to retreat or give in. Admit defeat or to being outmaneuvered when they occur. Don't be a poor loser, and don't make excuses and rationalizations. Go on to the next "battle." Eighth, try not to always have a zero-sum game. Don't try to win at someone else's expense. Instead, try to create a nonzero sum game, conditions where both parties gain, even though you might be able to gain more than the other party.

If managers practice political skills with these guidelines in mind, it should minimize the common criticism of politics as being a dirty business.

QUESTIONS

1. Do political skills really have any place at all in profit-motivated companies? In government organizations? In religious groups? Explain your answers.

2. Which political skills do you believe to be most important? Why?

3. What problems seem to most often hinder the practice of political skills? Why do these usually occur?

4. Under what conditions would the practice of political skills be clearly inappropriate? Why?

5. How are political skills generally practiced in your organization?
6. What political skills do you generally use? Why?

CASES AND EXERCISES

CASE 1: THE SHORT END

"He simply cannot deal in a political environment," said Ken. "He just doesn't represent us well with higher management. We continually get the short end of the stick."

"I know. I agree, Ken," replied Nancy. "We need a shrewder manager."

Ken Wears and Nancy Javitz were discussing their boss, Jack Thornberg. The two of them plus six other engineers work for Jack in the engineering department of a medium-sized metal fabrication firm.

"Jack seems to be fairly competent," continued Ken, "but he lacks bargaining and negotiation skills. Unless he fights for us, we'll get the leftovers. It's easy to forget about a staff group stuck over to the side and to just fund line operations. But if we don't get a good budget we can't do good work, and if we don't do good work, it will soon show in equipment breakdowns and poor products."

"I wish Jack were more like Mark Alletti," said Nancy. "He really fights for his people over there in R&D."

"Well, Nancy, I think Mark goes a little overboard. He does fight well and he does seem to do okay budget-wise, but I'm not sure of his basic managerial competence. He is just a blowhard, P-R type with little substance," replied Ken.

"Sometimes I think that's the best type; when you're in a political position you need a political person," stated Nancy. "I think you've got to measure a person by results and, let's face it, Mark gets results—more so than Jack does for us."

Questions

1. In the final analysis, should managerial effectiveness be based on results accomplished? If you answer yes, does this mean Mark is more effective than Jack, even though Ken and Nancy agree Mark is not as competent as Jack? Explain your answer.

2. Do resource allocation decisions in organizations tend to be heavily influenced by political considerations? Why or why not?

3. As subordinates, what action, if any, should Nancy and Ken take now? Why?

CASE 2: DIRTY POLITICIANS

I have very little respect for politicians and for the political process itself. I think Watergate showed us the real side of politics. Not only is it a dirty business in the national, state, and local governmental political arenas, it's also dirty in business organizations. Politics is politics no matter where it's practiced and it's always a dirty business. It's a dog-eat-dog situation. Someone must always lose at someone else's expense. I think Colson was right—politicians will step over their grandmother if they have to. There are no nonzero sum games in politics.

The political solution is seldom the best solution. There usually is a better way to solve a problem. People only resort to a political solution when they're so incompetent they cannot do anything else. When people become political they spend so much time huddling, holding caucuses, and covering their butt, they never get any work done.

In my opinion, politics should be avoided by competent managers. If managers are truly competent, there is no need for politics. It just leads to vicious gossip and innuendo and, in the long run, it will ruin an organization.

Not only should managers not practice political skills, they must keep their subordinates from practicing them also. All managers would be better off learning how to do their jobs better rather than trying to cover up their incompetencies through politics.

Questions

1. With which points made by this person do you agree? With which ones do you disagree? Why?

2. In your opinion, does this person understand what is meant by political skills?

3. Might the type of organization affect whether this person is correct or incorrect? Explain.

EXERCISE: WHAT POLITICAL SKILLS DO YOU PRACTICE?

Listed in Figure 15.4 are the political skills we discussed in this chapter. In this exercise you are asked to rate the *relevance* of each political skill to your job, using a 1 through 5 scale as follows:

5—Greatest relevance
4—Relevant
3—Somewhat relevant
2—A little relevant
1—Not at all relevant

Political Skill	Relevance to Job (1-5 scale)	Situation Where Appropriate	Situation Where Inappropriate
Example: Forming coalition	3	Budget increase for department	Counseling an employee
Forming coalition			
Bargaining/ bluffing			
Lobbying			
Use of the media			
Timing			
Posturing-bluffing			
Personal visability			
Others			

Figure 15.4 Political skills in practice

In the second two columns, you are asked to briefly describe a situation where it would be very appropriate to use the skill, and a situation where it would be clearly inappropriate to use the skill on your present job. An example of the first skill is shown.

REFERENCES

Chernich, William N. *Coalition Bargaining*. Philadelphia: University of Pennsylvania Press, 1969.
   While focused on coalition bargaining between unions and management, there are some good insights on the coalition forming process that apply to the skill of managing.

Giffman, Erving. *The Presentation of Self in Everyday Life*. Garden City, New York: Doubleday & Co., 1959.
   Presents material dealing with political skills and impression management necessary for living and for success in organizations.

Gouldner, Alvin W. "Cosmopolitans and Locals: Toward An Analysis of Latent Social Roles." *Administrative Science Quarterly* 2 (December 1957): 281–292.
   This classic article describes the two basic orientations employees and managers take. The cosmopolitan identifies with the profession and the local with the organization.

Harragan, Betty L. *Games Mother Never Taught You*. New York: Warner Books, 1977.
   Even though this is a survival manual for women managers, it contains much information of interest to all managers on how to play the political game in organizations.

Maccoby, Michael. *The Gamesman: The New Corporate Leaders*. New York: Simon & Schuster, 1976.
   A very popular book that explains how the skills of the "gamesman" are more valued today over those of the "craftsman," "jungle fighter," or "company man."

Ross, Robert O. *The Management of Public Relations*. New York: John Wiley & Sons, 1977.
   A comprehensive examination of the analysis and planning required for an organization to maintain good external relations.

Strauss, Anselm. *Negotiations: Varieties, Contexts, Processes and Social Order*. San Francisco: Jossey-Bass, Inc., 1978.
   A model for negotiations is presented that applies to business arrangements, labor relations, and international diplomacy. Model is applied to specific cases in Part II of the book.

Thompson, Victor A. *Modern Organizations*. Tuscaloosa: University of Alabama Press, 1977.
   Chapter 7, titled "Dramaturgy," presents an excellent discussion of the roles we play in organizations and the political skills we use.

Whyte, William F. *The Organization Man*. Garden City, New York: Doubleday & Co., 1957.
   The classic book on organizational conformity and the political skills required for survival.

16

How Should a Manager Manage Time?

Schedule: Monday, May 14

Open morning mail	23 min.
See Les about lunch meeting	7 min.
Monday morning staff meeting	1 hr.
Review meeting notes, type up minutes	15 min.
Interview job prospect	30 min.
See Sam about new sales campaign	30 min.
Luncheon meeting	1½ hr.
Executive committee meeting	1½ hr.
Dictate letters and memos	45 min.
Read and study R&D report	1½ hr.
Check with Sid on Chicago trip and meeting	25 min.
Review tomorrow's work load and rest of week. Take material home.	1¼ hr.
Evening Work: Prepare cost alternatives on Bolger project	2 hr.

This is an actual schedule from a manager's desk pad. How does this schedule look to you? Does it indicate that this person knows how to manage time? Would you like to have a schedule like this?

Let's take a closer look. First, the schedule ends with 11 hours and 45 minutes of work for the day. (This includes a working lunch.) If this is a regular schedule for this individual, it is too long. No manager should work regularly more than eight or nine hours a day. Remember the first and cardinal rule with time: It's not how *hard* you work, it's how *smart* you work. Regular work days over eight hours cause fatigue and reduced effectiveness in most managers.

Second, what is presented is technically not a time schedule; it is a *time budget*. If it were a time schedule, times of day would be stated instead of time allocations.

Third, the daily work schedule should reflect priorities. We cannot tell if this is an effective schedule because we do not know what the priorities should be on the job this person holds.

Fourth, this schedule apparently allows no time for slack. What happens if an unexpected meeting is called? When will this person answer phone calls? What happens if a meeting exceeds its allotted time? What happens if a crisis arises? Every time schedule/budget should have some slack built into it. No schedule should be so tight that *every* minute of *every* day is programmed in advance.

Fifth, what are the chances of this person sticking with this schedule? Ambitious schedules often are not met. Making up the schedule then becomes an exercise one goes through either to impress others or to impress oneself. While such a person has good intentions, the intentions are left unfulfilled.

Given that there are these problems with the preceding schedule/budget, it still could be modified so that it becomes an effective way for managing time.

TIME AS A RESOURCE

Earlier in the book we said that time could be viewed either as a resource or a constraint. We're going to change that approach now and say that competent managers *should* view time as a precious resource. There are only twenty-four hours in any one day and, therefore, there is a finite limit to time. In this sense, it is a constraint, yet we must make the best use of what we have. That is, we should not waste time just as we should not waste any other resources. Thus, time is more than just a constraint to actions; it is also a resource that should be used wisely.

Time can always be made for the things we really want to do. This statement is true not only in our personal life but also on our job. So many of us feel constrained and hemmed in, yet we are the masters of our own destiny. We can make things *happen* if we move aggressively and wisely. It may take some careful planning and some skillful use of political skills, but we can maneuver ourselves into positions where we want to be. Of course, we need to know where we want to be first; that is, we need *personal* goals. We also need to have some idea how we can realistically achieve these goals.

A conscientious effort on understanding ourselves and our goals will pay handsome dividends in the future.

The other key point on time as a resource is that competent managers do *not* let others manage their time for them. If you do not manage your time, someone else will. Your time is a scarce resource that is in much demand by others who will manage your time if you let them. Therefore, you really have no choice in managing your time. It *will be* managed—either by you or by someone else.

PRIORITIZING GOALS AND ACTIVITIES

In the chapter on setting goals, we discussed the issue of priority. We discussed the "must-do," "should-do" and "nice-to-do" categories for prioritizing goals. We also indicated that these priority categories were related to how closely the goals helped us to achieve our unit's purpose.

The same argument can be made with regard to time management. If you are doing something that is not ultimately leading to achievement of a priority goal, then you should not be doing it. We ought to be able to ask ourselves at the end of each day how much of our time and effort was wasted. How much time did we spend in unproductive activities? How much was spent in activities directed toward low priority goals? There will always be some time spent this way each day, but it shouldn't be a large amount—say no more than 10 percent of the day. We must not lose sight of our priorities and those activities which lead to their accomplishment.

Setting priorities in a job is a highly personal activity that each manager must perform. It involves an analysis of superior, subordinate, and peer manager demands and requests. Some questions that must be addressed in setting priorities are listed in Figure 16.1. These are reviewed elsewhere in the book. The point to remember is that setting priorities is very important for time management and involves most of the skills and knowledge areas we have already discussed.

---

1. What is the purpose of our unit and of our organization?
2. What are the major objectives I am trying to accomplish?
3. Who are we trying to serve?
4. What are the important functions in my job?
5. Will my actions lead to better service or product?
6. Am I acting efficiently and effectively?
7. What does my boss expect of me?
8. What do my subordinates expect of me?
9. What do my peer managers expect of me?

Figure 16.1 Key questions to ask in setting priorties

WAYS OF MANAGING TIME

Six key ways of managing time are listed in Figure 16.2. These are very important tools and concepts that managers should understand and use in order to be effective managers of time. These are not always easy to practice. Sometimes it requires a rather hard-nosed attitude, but as with any other resource, we try to protect it and use it efficiently. We do not let others freely spend our money for us; nor should we let others freely spend our time for us.

On the other hand, we should not be selfish. We should not be unwilling to give our time when it is truly needed for priority items. A selfish attitude will be interpreted by others as uncooperativeness. People will say you are just out for yourself and not for the organization. Of course, no matter what you do or how well you cooperate, some people will always say this. Don't worry about them; rather, be sure that key people with whom you work don't feel this way about you. Of course, if you have a history of solid performance and output, let your record speak for itself.

Forecast and plan for contingencies

Usually the better we can forecast the future and develop contingency plans, the better able we will be to manage our time. Most people who have trouble managing time always seem to be moving from one crisis to another. They have trouble closing the "planning loop." That is, they may know where they want to go and how to get there, but they never seem to reach these goals. They get sidetracked—things come up that push them off course.

The key, then, is to forecast effectively. Can future conditions be forecasted accurately? Do we know what major interruptions we are likely to have? Can we forecast demands and requests of superiors, subordinates, and peer managers? And, if we can do these things, can we set up alternative plans that can be followed if conditions change? Can we develop alternative scenarios that are likely to happen and be prepared to deal with each?

---

1. Forecast and plan for contingencies.
2. Develop both project and personal schedules.
3. Delegate.
4. Assist others to manage their time.
5. Manage interruptions.
6. Manage meetings.

Figure 16.2 Key ways of managing time

The key, then, to closing the planning loop is good forecasting and contingency planning. We addressed these issues in more depth in the chapter on goal setting.

Develop both project and personal schedules

We should have two types of schedules in order to manage our time effectively. Each should be related to the other. First, we need *project schedules*. What are the steps that must be accomplished by what dates in order to ensure accomplishment of the objective or project? These schedules tend to cover several weeks, months, or years.

We also need *personal schedules* of our daily work. These should be related to project schedules, but personal daily schedules will address several projects in various stages of completion. Of course these will be of a shorter time frame than project schedules, even though some busy managers plan their work days several weeks, or even months, in advance. The schedule/budget presented at the beginning of this chapter would be an example of a daily work schedule if times of day were added to each activity block.

The use of a daily calendar pad such as "Week at a Glance" is enormously helpful in planning daily work and in helping one to stick with it. It also serves as a log of activity at the end of the quarter or year.

Most busy managers use a secretary to help plan appointments, meetings, and other items on the daily work schedule. If your secretary assists you, it's imperative that the secretary know your priorities and time preferences so that proper scheduling is done. Remember that the secretary is to *help you* manage your time, *not* manage your time for you.

Another helpful hint for developing personal daily work schedules is to use a "do list." Keep a pad handy at home, while traveling, or at work to jot down items to do when back at work rather than trying to remember them. This little hint can be very helpful in preventing things from falling through the crack. (You might wish to use a cassette recorder in addition to or instead of a pad, not only for dictating while away from the office, but also for the "do list.")

Delegate

There is no way managers can effectively manage time unless delegation is practiced. Lack of delegation will cause managers to never have enough time.

The act of delegation falls under the general topic of "Participative Management." Managers unfamiliar with this topic will want to read one of the fine books or articles on it listed at the end of this chapter. Figure 16.3 shows the essential steps for effective delegation. Managers are most afraid

WAYS OF MANAGING TIME 253

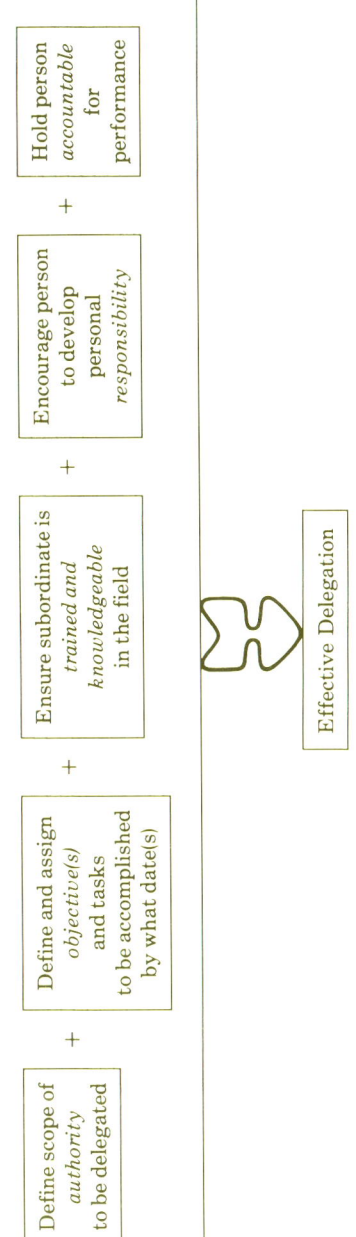

Figure 16.3 Requirements for effective delegation

to delegate because they fear either loss of control or that the project or task will not be carried out effectively. This need not be so if each of the boxed items in Figure 16.3 is followed. Let's briefly examine each of these.

Define scope of authority. Managers *share* authority with subordinates when delegation occurs. Authority is not abrogated by managers; a piece of their total authority is carved out and shared with subordinates. This is why it is absolutely essential that managers clearly state exactly what part of the authority is being shared. We do not want confusion here, which is evidenced by such statements as, "Well, I thought you were doing that" or "I didn't know I had the authority to do this." Both superiors and subordinates should have a very clear understanding of the boundaries of authority being shared.

Define and assign objectives and tasks. Subordinates not only need authority, they need to know what they are supposed to do with it. They need to know the objectives they are to accomplish and the tasks they are to carry out. Managers need to work with subordinates to *mutually* work these out and then to reduce them to writing.

Ensure trained and knowledgeable subordinates. It's hard to delegate when you have incompetent people working for you, but if you face this situation, can't you do something about it? Can the people be trained and developed? Can they be transferred to another unit? Can they be terminated? Many managers complain that they would delegate more if the people below them could handle delegated duties, yet these same managers do nothing to improve the ability of those below them.

Encourage subordinates to develop personal responsibility. Managers cannot make subordinates responsible. Responsibility is a personal obligation to carry out duties to the best of one's ability and in accordance with organizational directives or guidance. Since responsibility is a personal obligation, managers can only encourage subordinates to develop this sense of responsibility, they cannot *make* subordinates have it. To encourage subordinates to develop this sense of responsibility, managers should first delegate a minor task. Once superiors are convinced that the person has the responsibility to carry out this task, greater and greater tasks can be delegated up to the limit desired. Of course, superiors should always be available to provide coaching and counseling skills as needed.

Hold person accountable for performance. If we expect delegation to work, we must be willing to hold subordinates accountable for the performance of the task or objective. Accountability is the requirement that subordinates report in an appropriate form to superiors for the performance of an assigned duty or task. It also implies that the person will receive sanctions—rewards or punishments—related to how well the assigned duty was carried out.

If managers conscientiously practice these five steps, they will find that delegation will be effective, and that it will significantly reduce their time in carrying out duties that should rightfully be performed by others.

Assist others to manage time

Helping your subordinates, peer managers, and, yes, even your superior to manage their time is a requirement for effective time management. This does not mean you plan their day for them. What it does mean is that you encourage them to manage their time wisely, and in such a manner that it does not continually disrupt your day.

Subordinates. Encourage subordinates to solve their own problems. Prompt them to plan their own work day, then let them alone so that they can carry it out. Have them come to you only when they face serious obstacles they cannot solve. Try not to lay emergency crisis after crisis on their shoulders.

Peer managers. Be aware of other managers who continually come into your office to shoot the breeze, as well as other managers who do not have enough to do. Associate yourself with other competent managers and ask for their help only when you really need it. By the same token, don't make a pest of yourself with your fellow managers.

Superior. The real problem here is when you work for an inept superior. You must manage this person's time or they will ruin your career. Often you find yourself covering for this person, redoing the work they failed to do correctly, or doing the work they simply fail to do at all. This can be a serious burden on you since you end up doing two jobs—your's and your boss'. Try to set an example of good work habits. Encourage your boss to set priorities, and tactfully suggest ways that he or she can improve management style. If all else fails, ask for a transfer or quit. Don't ruin your career and your health working for someone who is incompetent.

Manage interruptions

Learn the fine art of saying "no." There are occasions when we must tactfully say no, even to our superior. If you always say yes to a request or demand from a superior, you will implicitly convey the impression that you don't have enough to do. This will lead to even more piling-on of the work from above, especially if you do a good job on the tasks assigned.

Tell a superior that if you take on an additional task you won't be able to accomplish certain tasks already assigned. Spell them out. State your priorities. Perhaps you simply have to say no. Don't be afraid to go to your superior's boss if you have to, to make your no stick.

As far as interruptions from subordinates and peer managers go, make it clear that you are available in your office only for certain hours during the day for them to see you. Set up a daily time when you *can* be interrupted. Unless an extreme emergency arises, stick to this time. At other times, tell them no, you're too busy. They'll soon get the message. You'll probably be called uncooperative and obstinate, but let your competent performance speak for itself.

One other major interruption that makes it difficult to properly manage time is telephone calls. Don't answer or respond to the phone if you are talking with someone in the office. Set aside a specific time each day to return phone messages and return them *only* during this time unless it's an emergency. Have your secretary or assistant screen and handle as many calls as possible. Keep calls short. Ask an assistant or secretary to place calls for you, especially long distance ones. Do use the phone instead of a letter or a meeting if you can because it *is* faster.

Interruptions are very costly since not only is time spent away from the task at hand, but there is also time wasted as one shifts gears and trains of thought—first to handle the interruption and second to get back on track with the initial work at hand.

Manage meetings

Meetings can be very productive investments in the use of time, or they can be major time wasters. However, following a few simple guidelines can turn meetings from time wasters to time investments. These guidelines are shown in Figure 16.4. Let's briefly look at each guideline.

Determine whether a meeting is really needed. Before you call a meeting, ask yourself, "Is the meeting really needed?" What do you hope to communicate in the meeting? Can this be communicated another way more effectively? Consideration here should also be given to regularly scheduled ver-

> 1. Determine whether a meeting is really needed.
> 2. Determine the purpose and objectives of the meeting.
> 3. Develop and circulate a meeting agenda.
> 4. Facilitate and manage group discussion.
> 5. Keep an accurate record of meetings and distribute minutes.
> 6. Evaluate the effectiveness of each meeting.

Figure 16.4 Guidelines to enhance meeting effectiveness

sus ad hoc meetings. Ad hoc meetings have the major advantage of meeting only when there is business to transact. Since they are ad hoc, however, it may be difficult to get people together when needed because of schedule conflicts. Regular meetings have the advantage of getting people together since the meeting is preprogrammed into the schedule. The major disadvantage, however, is that there may not be a need for the meeting.

One compromise solution some managers have found effective is to have a regularly scheduled time for the meeting, such as 1:00–2:00 P.M. Mondays, but to cancel it in advance if there is not sufficient business to transact.

You also need to determine if you really need to attend a meeting called by someone else. If you don't need to go, don't go.

Determine the purpose and objectives of the meeting. This guideline is closely tied to the first. Don't have a meeting unless you have a clear idea of what you hope to accomplish. Meeting purpose usually falls into one of three categories: (1) Information Dump meetings are meetings where the person who called the meeting (the chair) tries to convey information to the participants. (2) Problem-Solving Conferences concentrate on using the meeting participants to focus on and try to solve a problem or set of problems. (3) Clear the Air Conferences are where participants are given the chance to let off steam by discussing any issue that affects them.

Develop and circulate a meeting agenda. Every meeting should have an agenda developed and circulated to participants *prior* to the meeting. The agenda should not only contain the order of business, but it should also contain the purpose and objectives of the meeting. Attached to the agenda should be any documents that will be discussed at the meeting. This will give participants the opportunity to study the documents prior to the meeting. In most cases, participants should be given the opportunity to provide suggestions on the items for the agenda.

Facilitate and manage group discussion. Except in the information dump type of meeting, the chair must manage the group discussion. This means discussion must be facilitated—people should be encouraged to offer their views. It also means that long-winded blowhards need to be shut off, and people talking about irrelevant subjects must be brought back on course. The chair must walk a tightrope between coming down too hard on the irrelevant talkers and not stifling the good comments.

Some managers set a maximum time limit of one hour for any meeting held. They even provide uncomfortable or sometimes no chairs so that participants don't settle in for a long stay. These managers feel that making participants a little uncomfortable will keep the discussion crisp, clear, and to the point.

Keep an accurate record of the meeting and distribute minutes. How often have you heard comments such as, "Didn't we decide that last time?" or "I thought you were assigned that task at our last meeting." These comments reflect an inadequate record and distribution of meeting minutes to participants and other interested parties. Minutes should be clearly written, short, and to the point. Every meeting should have minutes without exception.

Evaluate the effectiveness of each meeting. Was the meeting really necessary? Were the purpose and objectives of the meeting achieved? Were members on time and did the meeting flow well? Was discussion fruitful? Are additional meetings needed? If jobs are to be done, were people assigned specific tasks to carry out and were they given deadlines for accomplishment? Do you have a way to follow up actions that are to be taken as a result of the meeting? These are the major questions that should be addressed after every meeting. The person who called and/or chaired the meeting is responsible for evaluating it. The results of the evaluation should then be used in planning future meetings.

CONCLUSION

We've taken the approach in this chapter that competent managers view time as a resource, not as a constraint. As a resource, managers should spend time just as they spend any other resource—*very* carefully. However, in attempting not to waste time, managers must be careful that they do not project the image of being uncooperative or selfish. It's important to strike a balance on the continuum between letting other people manage your time for you and selfishly guarding all of your working minutes.

Competent managers manage time by doing at least six activities: forecast and plan for contingencies, use both project and personal schedules effectively, delegate properly, help others manage their time effectively, manage interruptions, and manage meetings to make them effective investments of time.

How we spend our time tells others a lot about our priorities. Our time is our career and, indeed, our life. Thus, time management is a real challenge for all of us.

QUESTIONS

1. In your own job, is time a resource or a constraint? Why do you feel this way?

2. Of the ways to manage time, which way(s) do you most often use? Are there other ways you use not listed in the chapter?

3. Why do managers often not delegate very much? Do you delegate enough in your job? Does your boss delegate enough to you? Explain your answers.

4. On the whole, how would you evaluate the meetings you attend? If they can be improved, how?

5. Is your boss a good manager of his or her time? How does this help or hinder you in your job?

6. If you had time to add or expand on just one activity in your work day, which would it be? Why? Why don't you have enough time for it now?

CASES AND EXERCISES

CASE 1: TIME ONE MORE TIME

"Jim, if I've told you once, I've told you a hundred times, you've got to do a better job of managing your time. You spend too much time on unimportant matters and you let too many things fall through the crack. You just seem to be disorganized. Are you using a desk calendar to map out your days?"

"Yes, I am, Larry. I'm trying to manage my time. I just get so many interruptions."

"Tell 'em to go to hell. Don't let 'em push you around. Assert yourself. Tell people you're too busy when you are."

"But I don't want to appear uncooperative. I want to help people when they ask me."

"Yes, but don't let them distract you. Look, I'm your boss. I'm the only one you really need to please. I try to leave you alone so you can get your work done. Don't take on so many projects that you never get any of them done and done right. You're spread too thin."

"Yeah, I feel like that sometimes, Larry. But I believe we've got to work as a team and when Dot, Don, and Ray (peer managers) ask me to help them I feel that I should. Also, when Martin (Larry's boss) asks me to do something, I feel I should."

"Well, Martin ought to go through me first before he asks you to do anything. Next time he asks you, tell him to see me first. As far as Dot, Don, and Ray go, don't help them until you've got your own work done first."

"I know, Larry, I know. But that's tough to do. Sometimes I need their help on projects and if I tell them no, they'll likely tell me no when I need them. Furthermore, since we've added that annual peer evaluation process, I don't want them to get a bad view of me. They'll really put it to me in peer evaluation."

"Jim, forget about peer evaluation. It's *my* evaluation of your performance that really counts. The point is, your performance is falling off and your career could be in jeopardy unless you get a better hold on your time. Try to do better."

Questions

1. What factors seem to be contributing to Larry's perception that Jim cannot manage his time properly?

2. Do you believe Jim really is not managing his time effectively? Explain your answer.

3. Do you agree that Jim should be primarily concerned with pleasing Larry? What are the implications of your answer?

CASE 2: NO TIME TO MANAGE TIME

Sure I'd like to manage my time better. Who wouldn't? We all can do a better job with our time. Each of us can improve, but how can a person manage time when new and unexpected demands are always being made on one's time? Take my job for example—every month after the executive committee meets, there always seem to be new demands or new wrinkles thrown at me.

I keep getting curve balls. These demands are totally unexpected. I know forecasting and contingency planning should help, and I do try to do this, but there are so many new and unexpected contingencies each month, there is just no way I can anticipate them.

When you come right down to it, I don't manage my time at all. My time is managed for me. I've got my own job to do, as well as respond to the executive committee each month. After they meet, I lose the entire week doing their crap. This puts me a week behind in my job and I never catch up. When am I to manage my time? I don't have time to manage time. I'm not about to tell the Executive Committee "no." I'd be fired if I did.

Questions

1. What evidence is there that this person has a poorly defined or structured job? How does this affect one's ability to manage time?

2. Are there certain jobs in an organization that are just naturally crises-response oriented? What, if anything, should be done about these jobs?

3. Is it possible to forecast even unexpected events? Explain.

EXERCISE: HOW DO YOU MANAGE YOUR TIME?

The purpose of this exercise is to determine how you actually use your time and how you can better manage it.

The first step for improving the use of your time is to determine how you are presently using it. Once this is done, then you can determine ways to better manage your time. Pick a typical week in your job and keep track of how your time is *actually* spent in fifteen-minute blocks. Then for each activity block examine the following (summarized in Figure 16.5):

1. Was this activity scheduled (planned) by you in advance? (Did you have control over how you spent this period or did someone else determine this activity at this time for you?)

2. Toward what objective were you working during this period? Was it a high priority objective? Did you make any progress?

3. In what managerial functional categories did your time usage fall (e.g., planning, organizing, controlling, staffing, problem solving, leading, rewarding, communicating, etc.)? Try to develop a summary at the end of each day for total minutes by category.

4. Are you using your time efficiently and effectively? If not, what specific measures can you take to improve the management of your time? You may wish to review the suggestions in the chapter.

Date:_____   (Use a separate sheet for each day.)

	Actual Activity	You Control?	Objective to be Reached	Management Function Practiced	Was this Effective?	Improvement Action?
7AM						
715						
730						
745						
8AM						
815						
830						
845						
9AM						
915						
930						
945						
10AM						
1015						
1030						
1045						
11AM						
1115						
1130						
1145						
12N						
1215						
1230						
1245						
1PM						
115						
130						
145						

	Actual Activity	You Control?	Objective to be Reached	Management Function Practiced	Was this Effective?	Improvement Action?
2PM						
215						
230						
245						
3PM						
315						
330						
345						
4PM						
415						
430						
445						
5PM						
515						
530						
545						
6PM						
615						
630						
645						
7PM Evening						

Figure 16.5 Time log and evaluation sheet

REFERENCES

Aayres, Robert U. *Uncertain Futures: Challenges for Decision-Makers.* New York: John Wiley & Sons, 1979.
 This book presents the major qualitative and quantitative trends that will affect business from sociopolitical and demographic factors to economics and technology. Helpful for those whose job is so changeable that time management is extremely difficult.
Anthony, William P. *Participative Management.* Reading, Mass.: Addison-Wesley, 1978.
 A summary of participative management techniques, exercises, and cases. Includes a comprehensive bibliography.
Anthony, William P. "Managing Effective Meetings." *Personnel Journal* (August 1979): 547-550.
 A comprehensive article that sets out the procedures and techniques that should be followed in order to effectively manage meetings.
Armstrong, J. Scott. *Long-Range Forecasting: From Crystal Ball to Computer.* New York: John Wiley & Sons, 1978.
 Synthesizes important research in management sciences, economics, and psychology to offer a comprehensive guide to all aspects of long-range forecasting needed to plan long time frames.
Chambers, John C.; Mullich, S. K.; and Smith, D. D. *An Executive's Guide to Forecasting.* New York: John Wiley & Sons, 1974.
 A problem-oriented management guide that provides a general discussion of forecasting, including all major techniques, applications, and considerations. Helpful in time management.
LeBoeuf, Michael. *Working Smart: How to Accomplish More in Half the Time.* New York: McGraw-Hill Book Co., 1979.
 A practical guide to time management that provides many suggestions on organizing one's worklife around realistic goals.
Mackenzie, R. Alec. *The Time Trap: How to Get More Done in Less Time.* New York: McGraw-Hill Book Co., 1972.
 A short practical look on time management that includes discussions not only on managing you own time, but also the time of your subordinates and your secretary.
Moss, Leonard. *Management Stress.* Reading, Mass.: Addison-Wesley, 1979.
 One of a series of six books on occupational stress in the Addison-Wesley series, this book deals with how to handle stress that often comes about in jobs with severe time management pressures.

17
How Should a Manager Provide Incentives and Rewards?

"They can't pay me enough to do this job."

"I'd work for this company even if they cut my pay in half, I love my work so much."

"It's just not fair. I work twice as hard as Laura and yet we both are paid the same rate."

"I'm just working long enough until I can retire, then the fun will begin."

"Money in itself has no value; it's what you can buy with it that counts."

"I like this job; the harder I work the more money I can make."

Each of these statements reflect a different view of a very important aspect of work: how we value money and other rewards we receive from working.

We saw in the chapter on coaching and counseling that part of a manager's skill and responsibility is providing rewards and incentives. In this chapter, we take the perspective that the effective practice of this skill is a requirement for competent management. Providing rewards and incentives is not something that can be shoved off to the personnel department; it's the responsibility of *every* manager and cannot be delegated. It is true, however, that personnel or another staff group can assist and support managers in providing rewards and incentives, but they cannot do the job for line management.

The skill of providing rewards and incentives is the last of the essential skills we examine for competency in management. We take the individual manager's perspective in this chapter when examining rewards and incentives, and are only tangentially concerned with the details of wage and salary administration from a personnel perspective.

PURPOSE OF REWARDS AND INCENTIVES

We all work because we expect to get something out of it. This something is usually money, but often it is much more than this. We may work because we find our job very satisfying, we may enjoy the security provided through our job—especially health and retirement benefits, or we may have social and status reasons for working since our job may give us social acceptance and respect from our coworkers and neighbors.

When working, we trade our time and effort for these rewards. If we feel the rewards do not match the time and effort put forth, we will reduce or increase time and effort to try to bring them into balance with our rewards. If rewards get substantially out of balance with time and effort, we'll likely look for a new job.

The feedback we receive from working is not all positive. We also receive *negative sanctions* when we work, including tension, frustration, boredom, anxiety, fatigue, anger, unhappiness, and pressure. When these negative sanctions outweigh the positive rewards we receive for a job, we will try to secure another job.

This leads us to the twofold purpose of rewards and incentives. First, rewards and incentives must *attract* employees, and second, they must hold or *keep* employees from leaving. Besides this double purpose, rewards and incentives have subsidiary purposes. These purposes include (1) spurring employees to higher levels of productivity, (2) rewarding employees for doing a good job, (3) providing a dependable workforce, (4) contributing to national employment security, and (5) keeping employee discontentment and friction to a minimum.

Role of managers

What is the role of managers in the reward and incentive system? In most organizations, personnel departments exist to assist managers in administering a fair and effective reward and incentive system. The key word here is *assist*. Managers are still responsible for administering the system and should never abrogate this responsibility to personnel.

What does this mean for managers? It means that the reward and incentive system should be designed with significant input from line managers so as to accomplish the organization's goals. Second, it means personnel should provide line managers with guidance and support when they (line) administer the system. Third, the system should not be so restrictive that line managers have to continually run to personnel for an interpretation or an exception. Fourth, the clerical and daily administrative aspects of the system (payroll, record keeping, etc.) should be handled by personnel, not by line management. Fifth, personnel should help line managers in explaining the system to employees. And, sixth, the system should be flexible and amenable to updating as the needs and goals of line managers change.

Personnel and line management must work as partners in the design and management of a reward and incentive system. If either party ignores the other, the system will not be effective or efficient.

THEORY OF REWARDS AND INCENTIVES

In this section we briefly review the underlying theory of good reward and incentive systems. Figure 17.1 examines four such theories. Adherence to the tenants of each of these theories will help ensure an effective reward and incentive system in an organization.

Behavior modification

A good reward and incentive system should positively reinforce behaviors we want repeated and negatively sanction those we do not want repeated. This means that an employee should be rewarded for performing well. This will encourage the employee to repeat such behavior. The reward could consist of a salary bonus, praise, letter of commendation, or promotion. The reward should come soon after the outstanding performance to have maximum effect. Also, it should be something actually desired by the employee, not something the organization or management *thinks* the employee might want.

Goal-path theory

Employees will undertake behavior that they think will lead them to a desired goal. That is, they will follow a path that takes them to their desired destination. Management's responsibility, therefore, is to help employees follow the proper paths to the proper goals—ones that will not only satisfy the employee, but will also satisfy the organization.

- Behavior modification/positive reinforcement
- Goal-path theory
- Expectancy theory
- Equity theory

Figure 17.1 Four theories of an effective reward and incentive system

Sales commissions, for example, play this role. The salesperson wishing to maximize income must sell a lot of products. Each time a product is sold (path), the salesperson earns a commission (goal). Each time a product is sold, the organization earns income and a contribution to profit.

The lack of a tie-in with rewards and incentives is one of the biggest problems in governmental operations. There is little, if any, reward or incentive for doing good work. Goal-path theory plays a minimal role in government at this time, but this could change. Civil Service reform at the federal level will enable a Senior Executive Corps to earn bonuses for outstanding work. The Florida legislature also recently enacted a similar measure. These actions could lead to the day when governmental managers have clearer cut paths to follow to reach both personal and organizational goals. As it stands now, for many government managers, the only game in town is CYA—a game not conducive to superior performance.

Expectancy theory

Employees need to have a reasonable expectation that performance *will* lead to the desired goal. If they expect the goal is unrealistic and will be difficult to achieve no matter how hard they try, it will have little effect to spur performance. If they do not desire the goal, it will have little if any effect as a reward or incentive.

Employees must want the goal, see it as reasonably attainable, and see how the effort they need to undertake will lead to the goal. If any one of these three things is missing, the goal will not have much effect as a reward or an incentive to action.

Equity theory

The final theory that must be followed in designing a good reward and incentive system is equity theory. Employees must view the system as fair and equitable, but this does *not* mean that everyone receives equal rewards. It means that people are rewarded commensurate with their effort, skill, and output.

In order to have equity, employees must be able to understand the system in use. This simple fact has killed more incentive pay systems than any other reason. Many systems are so complex and sophisticated that employees (and most managers, for that matter) cannot understand them. This leads to much carping and complaining, which eventually sinks the system. Thus, the KISS principle should be followed here if the system is to be easily communicated and understood.

Equity theory works like this: each of us compares our effort/output and rewards with the effort/output and rewards of significant others. As shown in Figure 17.2, if we believe that we are working harder and produc-

THEORY OF REWARDS AND INCENTIVES 269

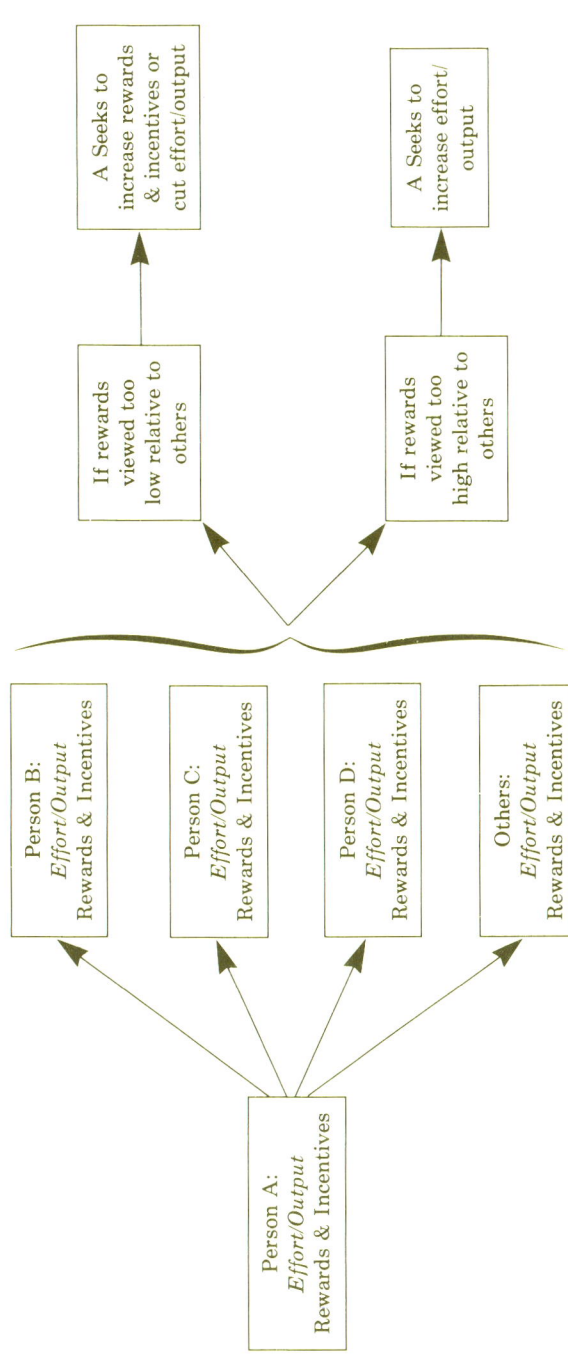

Figure 17.2 How equity theory works

ing more than others around us and are not being rewarded for it, we will either try to increase our rewards and incentives or cut back on our effort until an equitable balance is reached in our opinion. Conversely, if we feel we are being overpaid relative to others, we will increase our effort/output until a balance is reached. Sometimes in this second case, there may not be any increase in output, even though we increase effort; it just takes us longer (more effort) to produce the same output. We make others think we are working harder, even though we may not be, because we want them to think we really are earning our salary.

Notice that equity theory only has meaning in relation to others with whom we are working who are doing similar work. We must have a meaningful comparison group. In order to prevent feelings of inequity is why many companies keep salaries a secret, especially if they do not have a rational, objective basis for the salary and reward system.

The key principle on which equity theory rests is that meritorious performance shall be rewarded far more than average performance. This is a key principle that should pervade any effective reward and incentive system. If we ran a race, we all would not expect to receive the gold medal once the race was completed. We would expect to receive the medal in relation to where we finished. Of course this assumes that effort and performance can be controlled by the employee. If this is not the case, then it is difficult to relate rewards to performance. This is why so many production workers are paid an hourly rate, no matter how they perform. On assembly lines, the work is often *machine-paced* and the individual employee has little, if any, control over the amount he or she can produce.

WAYS TO REWARD AND PROVIDE INCENTIVES

The number one principle to keep in mind when using rewards and incentives is: if the reward or incentive is tied to performance, it will motivate employees. The whole reason we want an effective reward and incentive system is to attract and keep good employees. We want a productive workforce. We want our reward and incentive system to be a tool to lead to higher productivity. Thus, when designing a good reward and incentive system, managers must ensure that the system helps the organization reach its performance goals.

There is a variety of rewards and incentives that can be used. Our purpose is not to exhaustively examine each type—that chore is better left to a book on wage and salary administration or one on compensation management (see references). Rather, we want to highlight the key rewards and incentives that can be used by managers to encourage superior performance from employees.

For our purposes, rewards and incentives are broken up into two major categories, as shown in Figure 17.3. These two categories are financial and nonfinancial. Prudent managers and prudent organizations use both types of rewards in a comprehensive and logical manner rather than relying on one type at the exclusion of the other.

Financial

Three basic types of financial rewards are available: time payment, incentive payment, and security payment. Let's briefly look at each.

Time payment. Perhaps the most common type of financial reward is time payment. This payment usually takes one of two forms: an hourly wage rate with provision for higher payments for overtime, or a weeky, monthly, or annual salary. Even though this is the most common form of payment, it does *not* reward output or performance. Reward is for time or input. Presumably, of course, a person is producing while putting in time, but this isn't always the case.

Of course, an annual salary increase can be viewed as a reward for performance if it is *significantly* above the rate of inflation for the previous year. If it is not, then it will not be viewed as a reward for performance, but rather as a maintenance payment to keep the *real* wage the same (money wages adjusted for inflation).

The advantages of time payment are that it is simple, provides security for employees as long as at least minimum performance is achieved, and is

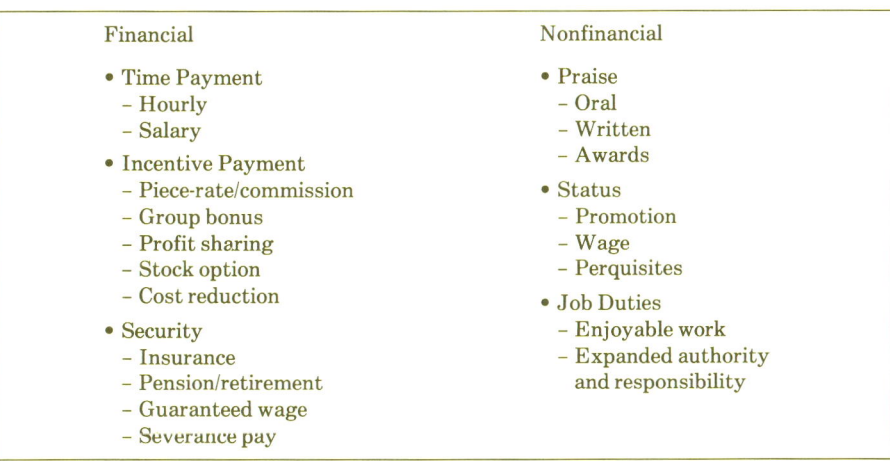

Figure 17.3 Categories of rewards and incentives

easy to administer. It is especially good to use when it's very difficult to distinguish output among individual employees or among groups, or where the work is machine-paced.

Incentive payment. Financial payments directly tied to performance are widely used usually in conjunction with a base hourly or salary wage. These can be viewed as motivating factors by employees if they understand the incentive system, desire the money provided, believe the system is fair, and believe management won't jack up the requirements to earn the incentive.

Piece-rate incentives pay the employee so much money (usually in cents) per piece produced, provided each piece meets accepted quality standards. A sales *commission* is similar to piece-rate, except the employee is paid a specified amount of money for each unit sold. Piece-rate and commission directly tie individual effort and performance with the financial reward earned.

Group bonus systems are used when work output is determined by group effort rather than individual effort. That is, this incentive system is used when the output of the group can be measured, but the individual output of each employee is difficult to determine. The group shares in the reward.

Profit sharing incentive plans involve the entire organization. The employees share in the profit *if* the organization makes one. The most serious disadvantage here is the delayed nature of the reward (usually only provided annually) and the fact one unit may have had a super year even though the company failed to make a profit. That unit would *not* receive the financial incentive since the organization did not make a profit.

Additionally, both profit sharing and group bonus plans tend to be very complex and are not easily understood by employees.

Stock option plans allow employees to purchase a specified number of shares during a specified time period at a share price *below* market. The company pays the difference in price. The employee receives both dividends and stock appreciation, as well as the entire proceeds of the sale of stock after some minimum time period if the employee chooses to sell.

Initially, stock option plans were made available only to a few select, higher level managers, but today they are becoming increasingly more common for middle level, supervisory, and nonmanagerial employees. Sears is a good example of a widely shared stock option plan. This incentive makes the employee an owner of the company. It gives the person an extra stake in the company and an extra incentive to see it prosper. Sometimes this incentive is lost if the employee owns a minute portion of outstanding shares, or if stock value and dividends drop through no fault of the employee. The incentive might also lose much of its meaning if it entirely substitutes for other incentives such as piece-rate, bonus, or commission. Furthermore, some companies actually use the stock option plan as the basis for the retirement plan. This could be dangerous because of a lack of a diversified portfolio of investment for earnings for retirement payment.

Cost reduction savings plans can be used where there is no profit, but there are operations or production costs which have been reduced below some previously agreed upon level by management and employees. Two popular examples of cost reduction plans are the *Kaiser plan* and the *Scanlon plan*. Even though each plan is slightly different, both rely on sharing the costs saved between the employees and the company when a specified quantity and quality of production is met at a cost below that initially agreed to by both parties.

Cost reduction or savings plans hold great promise for not-for-profit organizations such as governmental agencies. A variation of such a plan serves as the backbone of the bonus system for the Senior Executive Corps of federal government managers. Perhaps by using this system, a bonus system that rewards outstanding performance in government will finally be developed.

Security payment. Almost all organizations provide rewards that are geared more to maintain employee security than to reward outstanding performance. This package of rewards is very important for attracting and holding employees, even though it doesn't do much to motivate them.

Almost all organizations provide either a partially or wholly paid premium group health insurance plan for employees. Dental, mental, and outpatient coverage are becoming increasingly more common as part of these plans. Also included as part of the insurance plan are death insurance benefits.

Pension and retirement plans with a wholly or partially paid employer contribution are also very common. These plans often allow for early retirement below age sixty-five, vesting rights to recover any amount plus interest paid in by the employee, and maintenance of a similar or slightly reduced health insurance plan after retirement. Also, more common in this age of inflation are retirement plans that provide an annual increase in payment which is tied to the rise in inflation.

Guaranteed annual wages through a guaranteed minimum annual salary or hours worked, or through supplemental unemployment benefits (SUB), is very common today in cyclical manufacturing, such as the auto industry. Since workers are regularly laid off during annual model changeover or during economic recessions, the United Auto Workers union was successful in bargaining for and obtaining a SUB package for employees that pays almost a regular weekly wage when SUB is combined with unemployment compensation. This guarantee of wage is an important tool for financial security for employees in cyclical industries.

Severance pay is provided when employees are terminated by the organization. This pay is designed to provide employees with some financial security for a short period of time until they find a new job. Often this amount only equals a few weeks of pay.

Nonfinancial

Three basic types of nonfinancial rewards are available to management: praise, status, and the assignment of job duties. Let's examine each of these.

Praise. Not only should verbal praise be used liberally (but only when justified), but written praise should also be used to reward employees. A letter of commendation or congratulations for a job well done can do much to lift an employee's morale, especially if copies are given to higher level managers in the organization and placed in the employee's permanent file. Praise gives visability and recognition. It lets the employee know that management officially recognizes and is appreciative of employee performance.

Awards, such as service pins, a paid vacation, a plaque, or other tangible item, can provide meaningful evidence to employees of a job well done. Awards have their greatest impact when presented before a large body of coworkers and superiors, such as at an awards banquet, and are fully publicized in the organization's newspaper or newsletter. One potential danger in using awards or praise is their use at the exclusion of other rewards. After all, a service pin does not put bread on the table. Praise and awards should not substitute for other rewards, but should complement them.

Second, the praise or award should be something desired by the employee. Some employees do not desire these, especially if they have low trust levels of management. The issue of *credibility* is critical. Employees must believe that management really means it when praise and awards are offered.

Status. Desired by almost all employees, status can take the form of a promotion (new job title), a wage level, or certain *perquisites* provided to employees.

Promotion usually brings more money, a more responsible job, and increased visibility. But the new job title itself and the fact that a particular employee is promoted over others connotes a special kind of status in and of itself. Therefore, even if the financial increase or new job duties associated with the promotion are not high, the mere fact a person was promoted will have a certain amount of status associated with it.

A wage or salary also has status connotations. For managers to know that they are the highest paid in the group or received the largest raise has meaning beyond the dollars involved. Prestige, recognition, and status all are conveyed by a high wage.

Perquisites are the little extras that go with a job or position. These could include such things as a private office, private secretary, use of the company airplane, use of an exclusive recreational facility, a company car and chauffeur, dining rights at the executive dining room, tuition payments for children, and so on—the list is almost endless. These perqs convey much status to employees since they are usually limited to an exclusive few. Of course, they often carry a real financial value as well. The use of perqs seems to be increasing since salary increases are so often completely eaten up by taxes and inflation.

Job duties. If job descriptions are not too narrowly defined and if a union does not severely restrict management's authority in assigning work, then the actual assignment of job duties can be used as a reward.

We are all familiar with the poor army private who is assigned KP as a form of punishment. By the same token, more desirable tasks can be assigned to individuals as a form of reward. For example, some academic department chairs allow the outstanding professors in the department to have first choice on courses taught and class times. Those whose performance is not as high are then assigned courses and class times not desired by the high performance group. Someone has to teach at undesirable times; it might as well be the low performers.

A second way job duties can be used as a form of reward is by expanding an individual's scope of job authority and responsibility. In other words, allowing a person to increase the opportunity to perform more responsible activities and to grow and develop in the job can be an effective reward. New challenges, when mastered, become satisfying experiences. Of course, if the organization significantly expands the individual's job duties and responsibilities, then an increase in pay should also be provided.

CONCLUSION

Since rewards mean different things to different people and since our desire for particular rewards changes over time, managers and organizations should make a variety of rewards available to employees. Reliance on any one type of reward exclusive of others is a dangerous course of action. Instead, an integrated system of rewards should be developed by the organization.

Managers should use rewards liberally, but only when justified by performance. Creating the impression of stinginess is not good for the manager or the organization. Employees must feel that they will be rewarded and *significantly* rewarded when their performance warrants it.

276 HOW SHOULD A MANAGER PROVIDE INCENTIVES AND REWARDS?

Finally, managers cannot cop-out of or rationalize away their responsibility for providing rewards by saying it's the job of the personnel department. While personnel should assist in the design and administration of the reward system, the primary responsibility for rewards rests with line management.

QUESTIONS

1. What is the primary reward you experience on your job? Why do you feel this way?

2. Examine and explain each of the statements at the beginning of the chapter.

3. In your opinion, does your organization provide a good range and variety of rewards to employees? In which area(s) is your organization the weakest? Can anything be done about this?

4. How much authority do you have for rewarding subordinates? Why? Is this enough authority? If not, what can be done about it?

5. Are perqs unfair to those who do not receive them? (That is, should they be made available to everyone in the organization who has good performance rather than an exclusive few?)

6. What rewards do you believe managers will want in the future? Why?

CASES AND EXERCISES

CASE 1: LET'S HAVE A PARTY!

Bev was excited. The gardenias were just lovely and the little lapel rosebuds would add just the right touch for the retirement coffee. She knew Ron, Jill, Jack, Jay, and Charles would appreciate the extra effort she expended in planning this year's affair. The coffee, punch, cookies, and cake were all ordered and everything was set.

Bev, forty-five years old, had worked with Semitech since the company was founded twenty-two years ago. She was administrative assistant to Hal Ferrelli, Department Head, Marketing: Commercial Group. She enjoyed her very responsible job, and she saw a continued successful career with the firm. She ultimately hoped to be executive secretary to the Chief Operating Officer.

Bev very much enjoyed getting other secretaries and even a number of managers involved in planning the social gatherings she has developed on her own over the years. In addition to the annual retirement reception, she planned and helped host the annual welcoming reception for new managers in marketing, the Christmas party, and the summer picnic. None of these activities are an official part of her job description and no one has ever told her to perform these tasks, yet she finds them among the most rewarding in her job. She very much enjoys people and loves parties and social gatherings.

Planning parties requires much extra work. While Bev can do a lot of it during normal work hours, she often must work on her own time without pay to complete the planning. However, when she is asked to work overtime with pay on her regular job activities, she almost always refuses, claiming that it interferes with her family and leisure time.

Some of the younger secretarial personnel, and especially the younger women managers the company has hired over the past couple of years, very much resent Bev's social planning activities. They believe her actions further the stereotype of women employees, thereby preventing women from obtaining more responsible managerial roles not considered traditional "women's work."

Bev's boss is also becoming somewhat concerned since she seems to be spending more and more time on these activities each year. While her normal work performance has not been affected, Hal is concerned that the company's internal auditors will call a halt to the practice and give the department unfavorable publicity with top management. However, he had not said anything to Bev yet, and probably won't since he knows she enjoys these activities so much. He must admit that she does plan a great party.

Questions

1. Are social relations and relations with coworkers satisfying rewards for most people? Why or why not? If you answered yes, why do you think they were not listed and discussed in the chapter?

2. Should Hal take any action at this time with Bev? If so, what should he do? If not, why not?

3. If you were a female secretary or manager working at this company, what would be your attitude toward Bev? Would it be different if you were a male? Explain your answers.

CASE 2: REWARD IN GOVERNMENT?

I agree that a manager should use a variety of rewards for employees. I also agree that the manager cannot delegate the necessity to reward to a personnel department. But I work in a large agency for the federal government. What can I do? We have a civil service system that pretty well spells out most rewards—pay, promotion, time off, health benefits, retirement, etc. I am one of thousands of managers. All I can do is go by the book. I cannot violate civil service rules.

Furthermore, most of the rules are so difficult to understand, I hesitate to interpret them myself. I must ask the Office of Personnel Management people to interpret them for me. Once you do this, you're letting them make the decisions for you, but I really have no choice.

Of course, in government, the number one thing we have to offer in the form of a reward is job security. That's why people go to work for the government anyway. Oh sure the pay's good now—at least at most levels—and there are opportunities for promotion. But have you ever heard of anyone getting laid off, let alone fired, who worked for the federal government? It may happen occasionally, but it sure is not nearly as common as it is in private industry. If government attracts the type of person interested in security, how effective can other rewards be anyway?

I know changes are being made. The federal Office of Personnel is replacing the Civil Service Commission. A Senior Executive Corps is being developed. Some states are also taking these actions. These senior managers will not have civil service security protection, but they will be eligible for bonus and extra promotions based on their performance. This could change the reward system in government, especially if these changes are made at the middle management ranks. Of course these changes could also lead to the return of the spoils system if adequate controls are not instituted and enforced.

As things stand now, I as a government manager can do very little to really reward others. Most are only interested in job security and the civil service rules tie my hands in using other rewards.

Questions

1. Is the reward system less flexible in government than in private industry, from an individual manager's perspective? Explain your answer.

2. Do you agree that the number one reward of concern to most government managers is security? Why or why not?

3. What rewards could this manager use on his or her own?

EXERCISE: HOW DO YOU REWARD?

In Figure 17.4 the various forms of reward and incentive are presented on the left side. The purpose of this exercise is for you to assess your use of each reward in your organization. Using a scale of 1 through 5, with 5 being very often and 1 being not at all, assess the frequency that each statement at the top applies for each reward. In the last column, explain if any changes need to be made in how this reward is used.

Type of Reward	You Control the Use of this Reward	Frequency of Use of Reward	Serves as Real Incentive for Output	Can be Used in a Flexible Way	Has Real Meaning for Most Employees	Explain any Need for Change
Hourly pay						
Salary						
Piece rate/comm.						
Group bonus						
Profit sharing						
Stock option						
Cost reduction						
Health ins.						
Pension/ret.						
Guaranteed wage						
Severance pay						
Oral praise						
Written praise						
Awards						
Promotion						
Perqs						
Enjoyable tasks						
Expanded resp.						

Scale: 5 – Very often
       4 – Often
       3 – Sometimes
       2 – Seldom
       1 – Never

Figure 17.4 Assessing reward use

REFERENCES

Beier, Emerson. "Incentive of Private Retirement Plans." *Monthly Labor Review* (July 1971): 33–41.
  A good look at how retirement plans can be used as more than a security device.

Dearden, John. "How to Make Incentive Plans Work." *Harvard Business Review* (May–June 1972): 58–66.
  Some practical, sound advice on how to construct and administer an effective incentive pay system.

Dunn, J. D., and Rachel, Frank M. *Wage and Salary Administration: Total Compensation Systems.* New York: McGraw-Hill, 1971.
  A comprehensive text on the design and administration of wage and salary systems that should be of particular interest to personnel managers.

Fox, Harland. *Top Executive Compensation.* New York: The Conference Board, Inc., 1974.
  A good review of various forms of compensation frequently used to reward top executives.

Goodman, Paul S., and Friedman, Abraham. "An Examination of Adam's Theory of Inequity." *Administrative Science Quarterly* 16 (1971): 271–288.
  A very good summary and critique of equity theory that contains most research on the subject.

Henderson, Richard L. *Compensation Management: Rewarding Performance in the Modern Organization.* Reston, Va.: Reston Pub. Co., 1976.
  Emphasizes the reward aspect of compensation as it relates to job performance.

Lawler, E. E., and Porter, L. W., "Predicting Managers Pay and Their Satisfaction With Their Pay." *Personnel Psychology* 19 (1966): 363–373.
  A somewhat dated but still relevant examination of the managerial pay issue.

Lawler, E. E. *Pay and Organizational Effectiveness.* New York: McGraw-Hill, 1971.
  A comprehensive review of the relationship of pay systems to various measures of organizational effectiveness.

Mahoney, Thomas A., ed. *Compensation and Reward Perspectives.* Homewood, Ill.: Richard D. Irwin, Inc., 1979.
  A collection of articles that covers all aspects of compensation and reward, from labor supply to using rewards as motivational tools.

Roch, Milton L., ed. *Handbook of Wage and Salary Administration.* New York: McGraw-Hill, 1972.
  A good collection of papers dealing with many practical aspects to consider in designing and administering a wage and salary system.

Part IV
Avoiding Managerial Pitfalls

Up to now, we have been examining the actions competent managers should take. We now focus on some activities competent managers should avoid. In particular, we are interested in seeing how competent managers avoid the fatal mistake—the killing mistake that ruins a career.

Often, this fatal mistake is something initially viewed as relatively minor. However, as time goes by, the mistake takes on added importance, which makes it a critical event. For example, the very serious consequences that developed from the relatively minor break-in at the Watergate apartments led to ruined careers for Nixon, Haldeman, Erlichman, and others associated with the Nixon administration (as well as national trauma). Actions taken to cover up the relatively minor event came to have more serious consequences than the event itself.

Managers often face situations where a minor event leads to major consequences. We often get ourselves into these fixes gradually, sometimes without realizing it. Only after it blows up in our face do we realize how serious things have become. Often it is then too late to do anything about it.

What are some pitfalls that competent managers should avoid? What are the managerial *incompetencies?* In Chapter 18, we examine some common mistakes that should be avoided when performing the day-to-day, routine work of managing. In Chapter 19, one of the most common mistakes of managers in large organizations is examined—adopting the bureaucratic mind-set. Legal and ethical problems faced by managers and ways to avoid and resolve them are the subject matter for Chapter 20. Finally, in Chapter 21, we look at how managers can keep a proper professional career perspective.

These incompetencies discussed are usually difficult to avoid. There are many pressures on managers to do things that are *not* in their best professional interests as managers. Explicit consideration of these pressures and recognition of the conflict that they develop is important for any manager wishing to maintain competence.

18
What Are Some Common Managerial Mistakes?

"I really need that report by noon Tuesday, Meg. Will you be able to do it by then?"

"Ben, I don't think so. I told you three weeks ago I doubted if I would have time to work on the report. Remember, I told you I would help out if I could but not to count on me for too much work."

"Yeah I know you said that, Meg. But at the time I thought Jerry would be able to fill in. Yesterday he told me he couldn't help on it, so I'm left hanging. I've got to get this to Mr. Tomkinson by 5:00 P.M. Tuesday, so I need the material from operations by noon. If you don't help me I don't know who I'll get and I sure can't do it myself."

"I guess you're really in a bind, Ben. I wish I could help you, but I've got so much else scheduled. I'm really booked up."

"Oh, you can't let me down, Meg. I really need your help. Don't leave me hanging like this!"

(Pause) "Alright, Ben, I'll do my best to get it to you. I don't know when I'll do it. I'm already planning on working Thursday and Friday nights on another project that is due, and I had planned a weekend camping trip with my family but I guess I can cancel it. I'll do my best."

Ben is not Meg's superior, but works in a staff position in the organization. Meg is under no official responsibility to meet his request. Meeting his request will cause Meg to (1) postpone the completion of another project required in her job, and (2) cancel a weekend camping trip. If you were Meg, would you have agreed to Ben's request? Did Meg make the right decision?

It depends. Does she owe Ben a favor? Is Ben very powerful in the organization? Are her husband and family tolerant? Is her other project more easily postponed? Perhaps Meg did make the correct decision, but she may have committed a fatal mistake for two reasons. First, time will be taken away from her primary responsibility—her other project that is due. Second, agreeing to Ben's request might label her as a soft touch. Perhaps Ben and others will ask her for additional work in the future because "you can always count on good ole' Meg to come through for you in a pinch." In other words, the competent, busy people tend to get busier because they are agreeable and do a good job. This is fatal and can ruin managerial effectiveness. We cannot be all things to all people. We cannot have so many projects going that we soon find we cannot do a good job on any of them. Yet, it is *precisely* the competent managers who are asked to do more because they can be counted on.

So competent managers sit on the horns of a dilemma. Their competency causes them to be asked to do more, yet, at some point, being asked to do more will eventually lead to incompetency. Finding the place on the continuum between doing all that is asked and doing very little is a very real challenge. In this chapter we examine some of these issues and ways to resolve them.

THE ACTIVITY TRAP

One of the most common managerial mistakes made is falling into the activity trap. The activity trap means that managers become more concerned with actions than accomplishment; more concerned with inputs than outputs; more concerned with process than product, and more concerned with details than the bottom line. This is not to say that actions, inputs, process, and details are not important; they *are* important, but *not* as important as accomplishments, outputs, product, and the bottom line. Effort should never substitute for performance. The only reason we are interested in actions, inputs, etc., is because we hope they will lead to results and performance.

Perhaps an analogy will make this point clearer. Suppose I ask you to clean the hallway floors on your floor in your office building by 5 P.M. tomorrow. At five the next day, I inspect the hallways and see you only have fifteen feet or so cleaned of one hallway. I notice that you are using a tooth brush and a cup of water to clean the floor. I say, 'You haven't cleaned the halls like I asked you to." You respond by saying, "I've been really working hard. My arms and shoulders are sore, my back aches, and my knees are killing me. I'm exhausted. I've used up three toothbrushes and ninety-two cups of water. I've really been working hard."

Yes, you have been working hard. Much time and effort has been expended, and you're sore and tired, but you have not achieved the desired result—and that is what really matters. It's not how hard you work, it's how *smart* you work that matters. You've fallen into the activity trap.

It's pretty clear in this example that the means have substituted for the ends. However, it's not always so clear in managerial jobs when this has happened. It's easy to lose sight of the goals and to start focusing on activities without making sure they are leading to desired goals. After all, it's by performing daily activities that we reach goals. Daily activities should and do occupy our time. They are tangible. They are what we *do* on our job, but they are *not* the reason for our job. They are only means to the end. Reaching goals, accomplishing results, achievement, performance—these are the reasons why we are employed.

Why managers lose sight of goals

Why is it that so many managers lose sight of goals and fall into the activity trap? Figure 18.1 lists the major reasons. Let's briefly look at each.

Daily activity grind. We perform daily activities at work: talk on the phone, dictate or write letters and reports, talk in meetings, read letters and reports, counsel employees, etc. All of these activities should have a purpose or reason for doing; that is, each activity should have a goal associated with it. Sometimes it's difficult to see how countless activities performed during the course of a day are each tied to a specific goal. Even if we are very goal conscious, we will perform some activities that have no goal associated with it. How many of us have helped out a fellow employee with a problem when the action had absolutely nothing to do with the goals *we* were supposed to reach in our job? Therefore, we know that not *all* activities will always be goal-directed, so we make exceptions. But to what extent does making this allowance for some activities keep us from making other allowances for other activities? Soon we may neglect to ask ourselves the relationship for each activity. The exception has now become the habit. We've fallen into the activity trap.

• Daily activity	• Fear of failure
• Measurement problems	• Lack of goal direction from the top
• Small cog in big machine	• Effort rewarded, not output rewarded

Figure 18.1 Reasons why managers fall into the activity trap

Measurement problems. Probably the most common reason for managers to fall into the activity trap is their concern for being unable to measure output in their job, unit, and organization. We can easily measure output on an auto assembly line: how many cars or components were produced? But how is the output of education measured? How do you measure the output of a design engineer or a research chemist? What about a social worker counseling clients? These service delivery or service supporting fields are more difficult to measure, but they *can* be measured as we saw in the chapter on goal setting.

Managers must be concerned with developing better ways to measure output and performance. This means explicitly defining standards that define desirable output. It also means searching for indicators of performance. For example, if a manager simply tries to answer the question, "How do I or my unit know when we've really done a good job?" the groundwork for measures of key results will be developed. This, then, should lead to development of goals and objectives.

So, managers with hard-to-measure outputs should not throw in the towel. This will lead them into the activity trap. When it's difficult to measure outputs, we tend to focus on inputs instead. We become more concerned with the time and effort put in (was he here on time?; did he punch the time clock?; did she work hard?), rather than the results or output produced.

Small cog in big machine. Some managers fall into the activity trap because they do not see the connection between what they or their unit do and what the organization produces. They view themselves as a very small part of a very large operation. Consequently, when they are asked to define output, their response is often, "I assist X department in doing so and so," or "We are in a support capacity, so it's hard to tell exactly what we do," or "What we do is such a small part of this organization, they wouldn't even miss us if we ceased to exist."

These comments more reflect a lost sense of purpose or mission than an inability to define output. Managers in these organizations are unable to integrate their units' work activity and sense of purpose into the organization's purpose. It is for this reason that defining organizational purpose and the purpose of each succeeding level in the organization is so important. Unless this is done, it is very difficult for managers of units far down in the organization to see how they tie in with the larger organization.

Suppose you are a manager who finds that you are in an organization where no role and purpose statement exists for the organization and its major units. What can you do? At a minimum, you can get your employees together and mutually work out a purpose statement for your unit. You can also encourage your superior to do the same. You can assist peer managers to do the same, and you can order subordinate managers to do likewise for their units. At least through these efforts, purpose statements will be developed for units with which you must deal on a daily basis.

Fear of failure. Working toward measurable goals gives managers accountability. Superiors, subordinates, and the manager can all see if goals were accomplished at the end of a particular period. Accountability brings feelings of success when goals are accomplished, but it also brings feelings of failure when they are not. Thus, the fear of failing can lead managers to avoid writing and working toward measurable goals.

Usually, this fear of failure is greatest when managers believe that they have very little control over achieving the desired objectives. Managers do not want to—and should not—be held accountable for the achievement of objectives over which they have little control. This is understandable, but this fact should not be used as a blanket excuse. It is usually possible to carve out or define that portion of a goal or objective over which managers *do* have some control. This should be done and the objective restated in this form so that a clear objective does exist. To the extent that this can be done, the fear of failure will be reduced.

Lack of goal direction from the top. Some managers fall into the activity trap because they maintain that it's impossible to set goals when their bosses do not set goals. "When my boss is not interested in defining goals, how can I be?" is a common question.

As we saw in the chapter on goal setting, even though it is easier to set goals when it's done at higher levels in the organization, it is not necessary that higher level goals exist for unit goals to be set. Again, as in defining purpose, managers can call subordinates together to define goals for the unit. Superior and peer managers can be encouraged to set goals. Subordinate managers can be told to do so for their units. At least the people with whom managers must work will have a sense of goal-directed behavior.

Effort rewarded, not output rewarded. In some organizations the primary focus for rewards is on effort and other inputs. It's the old "look busy" syndrome. This often occurs because higher level managers feel threatened by high performing junior members of the organization. It's also caused by tradition if, in the past, the organization has not been concerned with reaching measurable goals. This old style of management emphasizes subjective measures of performance such as attitude, appearance, loyalty, demeanor, and so on. These hard-to-measure, subjective input factors are difficult to tie in with actual performance results, but it's these results that really count.

When the reward system—promotions, salary increases, etc.—are geared to subjective input measures, managers have little incentive to focus on outputs.

All of these reasons can cause managers to fall into the activity trap. However, there are two additional issues we must examine before we look at ways to avoid these common managerial mistakes.

PERFORMING NONMANAGERIAL WORK

Early in this book the point was made that if managers did not perform managerial work, it would not get done. The first and foremost responsibility of managers is to manage. One of the most common management mistakes made is doing the work of others. Managers should not perform operative work; instead they should plan, organize, control, lead, motivate, communicate, reward, and so on. Managers should avoid the actual carrying out of the task being managed. Doing nonmanagerial work not only means managerial work will not be performed, but it also is another reason why managers might fall into the activity trap.

To avoid performing nonmanagerial work means managers must *delegate*. Delegation is passing down authority to carry out a task to a point in the organization as close to the actual performance of the task as possible. Managers who liberally practice delegation in an organization will create a *decentralized* organization. Authority for job performance will be placed down in the organization where tasks are to be performed.

Even though we discussed delegation in Chapter 16, it is such an important management concept (yet so difficult to practice) that we examine it again here in greater depth.

Delegate, don't abrogate

Managers are often afraid to delegate authority to subordinates because they view this as *abrogation*—giving up authority. When authority is delegated, it is *shared* by the superior and subordinate; it is not given up. Superior managers carve out a specific part of their authority and share it with subordinates. This is shown in Figure 18.2.

During delegation, the following steps should occur:

1. The manager determines whether the subordinate is willing and able to handle the authority to be delegated.

2. The manager next ensures that the subordinate will assume the personal obligation to perform the delegated task. This is called *responsibility*.

3. The manager then holds the subordinate *accountable* for the performance of the task. By the same token, the manager does not give up ac-

PERFORMING NONMANAGERIAL WORK   289

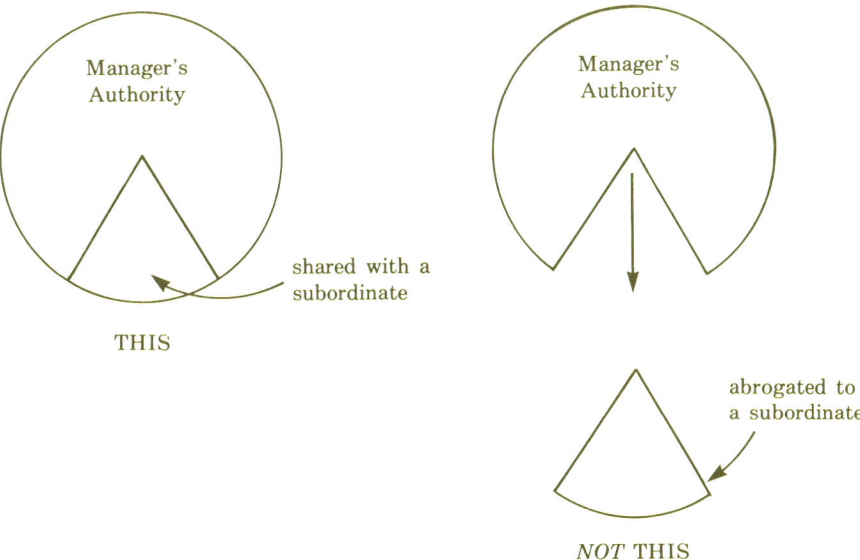

Figure 18.2 Delegate, don't abrogate

countability to a superior, but instead is held accountable for the task. (Technically, the manager is held accountable for making a proper delegation.) Accountability is the requirement to report, in whatever form, to a superior on the extent to which a task was completed.

For delegation to work best, authority should equal responsibility in order to hold a person accountable. We should not hold someone accountable unless they have the authority *and* responsibility to carry out the task, as shown in Figure 18.3. Responsibility cannot be delegated. It is a personal obligation that a person has to perform a task to the best of one's ability. Managers can do things to encourage a person to practice responsibility—such as provide rewards or training—but managers cannot make someone responsible. If a person is irresponsible, authority should not be delegated.

Figure 18.3 Effective delegation

Factors that increase delegation

How can managers increase delegation? How can managers delegate more in order to avoid doing nonmanagerial work to avoid the activity trap? Figure 18.4 shows factors that increase the amount of delegation possible. Let's briefly examine each of these.

Trained and competent subordinates. If subordinates are not trained or competent in their area of job responsibility, then they should be trained, transferred, or terminated. Managers who have incompetent subordinates will not be able to delegate and will end up doing their work for them.

Subordinate desire for autonomy. The more subordinates like to work without close supervision, the easier it will be to delegate to them. This desire for autonomy can be enhanced through on-the-job as well as off-the-job development programs. Competent managers try to develop their employees so they can take on added authority and duties as they grow professionally on the job.

Highly motivated subordinates. Managers do not motivate subordinates. Motivation is an internal process or drive to action. However, managers can create conditions—incentives, counseling, etc.—to encourage subordinates to be self-motivated. To the extent that this can be done by managers, delegation can be increased.

Clear organizational policies and procedures. Delegation must occur within guidelines. These guidelines are provided through clear, current, and explicit policies and procedures. This does not mean that policies and procedures must be voluminous and extremely detailed—they should not be. It does mean policy and procedures should exist to provide guidance for subordinates in carrying out delegated authority and duties.

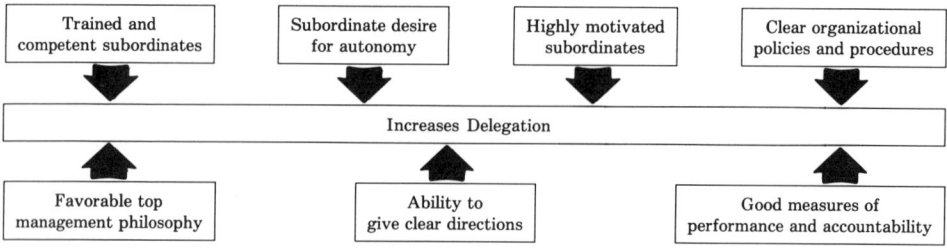

Figure 18.4 Factors that increase a manager's ability to delegate

Favorable top management philosophy. Like so many other things in management, delegation is enhanced when managers at the top of the organization fully support it. We often tend to manage as we are managed. If top managers delegate and encourage subordinates to do so, chances are that more delegation will be practiced far down the organization. This is not an absolute requirement for delegation, however. Managers can still practice delegation even though it is not actively encouraged by top management; its practice is just not as easy.

Ability to give clear directions. For delegation to occur, managers must be able to adequately outline the task to be done to subordinates. Delegation does *not* mean subordinates are turned loose to do their own thing. However, in giving adequate direction, superiors must be careful not to get into all of the nitty-gritty details of a task. Let the subordinates decide these issues. Direction should be clear and explicit, yet not so detailed that it stifles the subordinates.

Good measures of performance and accountability. It's easier to delegate when you can track and measure performance. This way, managers can determine if the task is actually being accomplished within the specified time period. Clear-cut goals and objectives, as well as standards (benchmarks) to be accomplished by the subordinate, greatly enhance the ability to delegate authority.

If subordinates are highly motivated, competent, desire autonomy, and can work toward clear-cut goals within broad policy guidance and direction, it becomes very easy to delegate. Managers will then be able to focus on the essential managerial work and avoid the activity trap.

SAYING "YES"

Perhaps this section should be titled "the fine art of saying 'no' " because that is our focus here. We saw earlier in the chapter that busy, competent managers tend to get busier because they are asked to do more. Many competent managers commit a serious mistake by saying "yes" too often. This will eventually lead to a dispersion of work effort such that objectives will either be accomplished at a minimal level, or worse yet, will be completely ignored.

Overcommitting oneself is a dangerous managerial action that should be avoided. The old sayings "Don't bite off more than you can chew" and "Don't promise more than you can deliver" are pertinent here. People count on us when we take on more work. Our failure to carry through on this work not only hurts our reputation for competence, but it also hurts those who have depended on us. They now are delayed and either must wait longer, find someone else to do the work, or do it themselves. In any case, the work will not be accomplished as efficiently and effectively as it could be.

While managers must be careful not to overcommit, there is a danger to saying "no" too often, as we've discussed elsewhere in the book. It can lead to being accused of being uncooperative. Hence, managers must walk a tightrope between being too cooperative and not being cooperative enough. This is, indeed, a difficult chore, but it can be done.

The risks of saying "no"

What can happen to you if you say "no"? Every manager must answer this question. Can you be terminated, demoted, or transferred? Will you lose all consideration for raises and promotion? Will your job be redefined so that you have less authority, power, and prestige? Will your pay be cut? Will you lose budget, subordinates, or facilities? Will you be viewed as being uncooperative? Will you have trouble getting others to help you when you need it? How powerful is the person you say no to? All of these questions need to be answered prior to saying "no." But these answers must be weighed against the costs of saying "yes." These costs can be greater than those of saying "no," as we indicated.

Let's now turn to some ways to recognize and avoid these common managerial mistakes that we've been examining.

WAYS TO RECOGNIZE AND AVOID MANAGERIAL MISTAKES

How do we know when we are falling into the activity trap? How do we know when we are doing less managerial work and more nonmanagerial work? When should we start saying "no" more often? These are indeed difficult questions to answer and no one can answer them for you, but there are certain cues to look for. Figure 18.5 summarizes these cues through a series of questions you should periodically ask yourself. After you answer each of these questions, determine which of the questions seem to be giving you the most trouble. Focus on those and try to pinpoint the cause for these difficulties. Then try to remove the cause by: (1) practicing delegation, (2) saying "no" more often, (3) focusing on clear-cut goals rather than inputs, and (4) performing managerial not nonmanagerial duties. Managers who conscientiously practice these actions will be well on their way to avoiding the common managerial mistakes faced in daily routine activities.

CONCLUSION

In this chapter we've examined some common managerial mistakes to be avoided in order to maintain management competency. These mistakes are the type that are easy to make as managers get caught up in the daily rou-

1. Do I seem to be doing a lot of "wheel spinning"—working hard but accomplishing little?
2. Am I putting in excessively long hours?
3. Do I end up doing my subordinates' work for them?
4. Have I lost sight of the goals in my job?
5. Am I a soft touch and afraid to say "no"?
6. Do I seem to jump from one project to another without really completing them properly?
7. Do I promise more than I can deliver?
8. Do I frequently miss deadlines?
9. Am I usually late for meetings and appointments?
10. Do I feel like the office will fall apart if I take a week or two off for vacation?
11. Do I face a horrendous set of problems when I return to the office after a few days' absence?
12. Is my calendar always so full that I have no free time in the job to think and reflect?
13. If my boss asked me what I had been able to accomplish during the past year, what would I say?

Figure 18.5 Questions to aid in recognizing managerial mistakes

tine of their jobs. They are the type of mistakes managers drift into often without knowing it, rather than the serious, one-time "smoking gun" types of mistakes that can easily end a manager's career. Even so, it is essential that managers recognize and avoid these mistakes if they expect to maintain *their* competency and effectiveness.

In the next chapter we examine a problem that is a particularly common nemesis to managers in large organizations—the bureaucratic mind-set. This management problem comes about as managers struggle to cope with the myriad set of rules, procedures, and policies found in centralized, bureaucratic organizations, be they business or government. Like the problems examined in this chapter, managers usually slip into the bureaucratic mind-set without realizing it. Therefore, avoiding this very grave incompetency becomes a real challenge for competent managers.

QUESTIONS

1. Are you caught in the activity trap? How do you know if you are or are not? If you are, what can you do to get out of it?

2. What, if any, are the reasons why you hesitate to delegate to subordinates? What can you do personally to get subordinates to accept more delegation?

3. What can a manager do with incompetent subordinates and claims that they cannot be fired, transferred, or demoted because of various organizational rules?

4. Even though performance and output are rewarded, should not effort also be rewarded? Shouldn't a person also be given some reward for trying? Explain your answers.

5. Do you believe your superior delegates enough to you? Explain.

6. What should you do if you find yourself with unequal amounts of authority and responsibility?

CASES AND EXERCISES

CASE 1: THE TEAM PLAYER

Frank Donello was Public Works Manager for Crescent City. He was appointed one year ago by Mayor Louis Ferrari. Frank managed six subordinates whom he was able to appoint with confirmation from Mayor Ferrari. One of his subordinates was Sally Jay, director of the city's CETA program. Sally was a recent MBA graduate of a state university located near Crescent City. Frank viewed her as a competent employee, knowing he could count on her to do a job right and on time.

On two or three occasions over the past six weeks, Sally had mentioned to Frank that she was concerned about being able to maintain her high level of performance. Although they had not discussed the issue in depth, Frank had briefly told her that she needed to be sure she scheduled her work properly and try not to take on more than she could handle. He also told her to delegate liberally to her Deputy, Budget Manager, and Compliance Manager. She indicated she thought she had done all of this.

Therefore, Frank was shocked when Sally entered his office this morning with her letter of resignation. At first he refused to accept it, only to change his mind when she became quite adamant about it. Finally, he told her he would accept it conditionally, but wanted her to take the rest of the day off and think about it until 9 A.M. tomorrow at which time they would meet again.

The matter seemed so urgent that Frank decided to talk with Mayor Ferrari about the issue. CETA is an important program for the city, employing about 1,000 low-income people at an annual total budget of approximately $10,000,000. Besides that, the program was "politically visible," and Frank believed the resignation of its director so quickly could embarrass the city administration.

"Come on in Frank," the Mayor invited. "Have a seat. How's tricks?"

"Not so good," answered Frank. "Sally has submitted a letter of resignation."

"Well, I don't think that will be a problem. We can replace her. I haven't been that happy with her work anyway," stated the Mayor.

"What do you mean?" asked Frank.

"Well, she really can't seem to get it all together. Several reports I've asked for lately are at least two weeks overdue," the mayor said.

"What reports? You mean you've asked her for reports?" exclaimed Frank.

"Sure, I do it all the time and she usually does a damn fine job—except lately," answered the Mayor.

"Gee, I wish I'd have known about this earlier, Lou. I've been giving her a lot to do also. I had no idea you were asking her to do things for you," said Frank.

"Oh, I thought you knew. But no matter, she's gone and we can get a good replacement. I've got several people in mind," observed the Mayor.

"Wait. It might not be that easy. Where are you going to find a black woman with Sally's credentials and competencies? This could be embarrassing for your administration," indicated Frank.

"Well, yes, I suppose it could, but I wasn't that pleased with Sally anyway. Sure she did good work, but sometimes I think she was more concerned with pleasing those people than with pleasing me. Some of the 'radical' speeches she's made—I don't know. She didn't seem like a team player to me. She seemed like she had her own way of operating. Why, do you know on this last report, she actually said that she would not be able to get it for me when I needed it? Can you imagine that, telling the Mayor no!" exclaimed the Mayor.

"Well, Lou, I must take some of the blame here. I did not know you were asking Sally to do things for you. Had I known, I wouldn't have asked her to do so much for me. She never said anything to me about this, although she did mention she thought it might be hard to maintain her level of performance." stated Frank.

"Forget it Frank, we'll get someone else. I want a team player this time who will do what I say. This CETA thing is too important to handle otherwise," concluded the Mayor.

Questions

1. Should Sally have said "no" to the Mayor? What factors should you consider in making this judgment?

2. If you were the Mayor, would you be so willing to let Sally resign?

3. What action could Frank and the Mayor have taken to prevent Sally's resignation? What responsibility did each have? What responsibility did Sally have toward the Mayor, Frank, and the clients CETA serves?

CASE 2: IF YOU WANT IT DONE RIGHT, DO IT YOURSELF

Would you rather have something done right the first time or would you like to have it done three or four times to get it right? I would rather have it done right the first time. This is why I usually do the really important things myself. Sure, a manager can delegate minor details to a subordinate, but the really important things can not be delegated. After all, if things are screwed up, it's the superior's head that will roll, not the subordinate's. The superior is always ultimately accountable.

I realize that in following this philosophy a manager risks falling into the activity trap, but I think the risk is worth it. In the long run, doing important things instead of delegating them will save the manager time since messed up actions won't have to be done over again.

Of course if managers had competent, motivated subordinates, more could be delegated to them. But my experience is that subordinates very often are not that capable. I've worked in both government and business, and usually a manager cannot choose subordinates, nor can they be easily transferred or terminated. I'll be darn if I'm going to stake my career on incompetent subordinates. If they screw up, my career will suffer, not theirs.

Every competent manager works long, hard hours. Sixty- and seventy-hour work weeks are common among all of the managers I know who get things done. This is as it should be; after all, we should not be afraid of hard work. Anything that is really worthwhile takes much time and effort anyway.

Questions

1. Do you agree that most managers have little say as to who will be working for them? Explain.

2. Do you agree that most competent managers put in sixty- to seventy-hour work weeks? Should or should they not put in such a long week?

3. Can *major* decisions or actions be delegated? Explain.

EXERCISE: WHAT COMMON MANAGERIAL MISTAKES DO YOU MAKE?

We often slip into common managerial mistakes without realizing it. The purpose of this exercise is to identify, explain, and remove common mistakes that you might be committing. Pick a typical three-day period on your job. Log all of your activities during this time using the Time Log sheet from Chapter 16. Then complete the chart below (Figure 18.6) to see what mistakes you've made and how they can be removed.

Mistake	Specific Incidents During Period	Which Incidents Could Have Been Avoided?	Specific Way to Prevent Mistake in the Future For Each Incident
Doing Subordinates' Work for Them			
Carrying Out Actions Without Specific Goal			
Taking on Extra Work Which Reduces Effectiveness			
Working More Than 8 Hours/Day			
Suboptimization— Achieving Less Than Desired Goal			

Figure 18.6 Common managerial mistakes

REFERENCES

Flory, Charles D., and Mackenzie, R. Alec. *The Credibility Gap in Management*. New York: Van Nostrand Reinhold, 1971.
  Examines the issue of believability in management actions and points out that the loss of credibility is a serious obstacle to management success.

Lakein, Alan. *How to Get Control of Your Time and Your Life*. New York: Signet, 1973.
  A down-to-earth book on time management that covers managing time on and off the job. The assumption is better time management will lead to fewer management mistakes.

McConkey, Dale D. *No-Nonsense Delegation*. New York: AMACOM, 1979 (paper).
  A highly readable, straightforward presentation on the guidelines to be followed to achieve effective delegation.

Moment, David, and Fisher, Dalmar. *Autonomy in Organizational Life*. Cambridge, Mass.: Schenkman Publishing Co., 1975.
  Examines how individuals can maintain their autonomy and independence in organizations. Greater autonomy can lead to greater delegation.

Oates, Wayne E. *Confessions of a Workaholic.* New York: World Publishers, 1971.
   A rather humorous personal view of a common management mistake —working hard instead of smart.
Steinmetz, Lawrence. *The Art and Skill of Delegation.* Reading, Mass.: Addison-Wesley, 1976.
   An excellent, short book with exercises on ways to increase one's ability to delegate authority.

19

How Should a Manager Avoid the Bureaucratic Mind-Set?

"But I've already been to the Registrar's Office and they sent me here."

"Maybe you ought to check up at the Dean's Office then."

"The Dean's Office is of no help. They sent me to the Registrar's Office."

"Have you talked with your advisor?"

"No. He's never in."

"Did you try to catch him during his office hours?"

"No, I have to work then."

"Well I don't know what I can do to help you. You say you've been upstairs to the Dean's Office, but have you tried the Dean of Students Office across campus?"

"Yes, last week. They couldn't get me in the class either. In fact, they sent me to the College Dean's Office. Look, I need this course to graduate. As department chairman, you've got to let me in. If I don't graduate this summer, I'll lose the job I have lined up this fall."

"Did you talk with the instructor?"

"Yes, he'd let me in if there were more chairs. But there aren't and the fire code won't permit anyone standing.

"You're right. Well, I'll petition the Dean's Office and see if we can waive the course requirement. We should know something in two weeks."

"Two weeks! Then it will be too late to add another course. I need to know now in case I cannot get it waived so I can add another."

"I'm sorry, but I can't tell you anything for two weeks. It takes that long to process these requests."

The old bureaucratic shuffle is alive and well. How many of us have gone through a similar routine while in college? Students, like most clients or customers of large organizations, often share the same Catch-22 fate. Why is this? What causes managers to adopt the bureaucratic mind-set? What can be done to avoid the bureaucratic shuffle?

BUREAUCRACY DEFINED

Several decades ago in Germany, Max Weber developed the bureaucratic system of organizing and managing. He saw it as a vast improvement over the then present way of operating. Instead of reliance on nepotism, personal friendships, ill-defined policy and procedure, informal power relationships and politics, organizations would be governed by a group of professional managers selected solely based on their competency who would work under a rational system of authority, accountability, policies, and procedures. The system would vastly improve the haphazard, political system then governing organizations with a rational-legal one.

Weber certainly did not envision the negative connotations the term *bureaucracy* would take on over the years. But such a connotation now envelops the term almost to the extent that it smothers its basic tenets which are, indeed, useful guidelines to follow in organizing. Let's look at each of these important tenets espoused in the pure Weberian form of bureaucracy.

Tenets of Weber's bureaucracy

The major tenets of bureaucracy as developed by Max Weber seem reasonable for the most part. They are summarized below.

1. Law or administrative regulations establish fixed and official authority and duties for organizational positions. Individual managers do not decide for themselves what authority they have in their jobs or what they should do. The official, formal organization establishes this for them.

2. There is a firmly ordered system of levels of authority in an organization whereby there is supervision of lower level offices by higher level offices. There is a hierarchy of structure with decreasing amounts of authority as one goes down the organization chart.

3. Written documents (files) are used as the basis of managing an office. That is, procedures, rules, policy, and precedent are reduced to writing and are expected to be followed.

4. Managers are competent experts in their field and have adequate training prior to taking the position. This idea serves as the foundation for a professional management staff.

5. Managers devote all working time to carrying out the official duties of the position. These duties are not secondary to some list of unofficial or political set of duties.

6. Managers follow stable, general rules when managing that are exhaustive and which can be learned by the office holder. While the rules are general, they are complex and stable; yet they are learnable by the incumbent.

7. Holding a managerial position is a "vocation" and is not to be exploited for personal gain through bribes, favors, etc. Loyalty is to the position and organization and not to any one person or group of people.

8. Holders of management offices enjoy a social esteem bestowed by society.

9. Lower level managers should be appointed by higher level managers.

10. The position of the office is held for life. Tenure for life is granted to office holders.

11. Managers receive a regular fixed salary and old age security through a pension.

12. Managers follow a career in the organization moving up in the organization from positions of lower authority to ones of higher authority as qualifications and seniority dictate.

Even though Weber developed these tenets primarily for governmental organizations, his writings indicate he believes they apply as well in business organizations. Furthermore, his tenets have been widely adopted in business organizations.

One can see that the effect of these tenets was to reduce the amount of personal whim and wish of individual managers in the operations of organizations and to replace it with a logical, formal system of *official* authority. This system of official authority would operate year after year, regardless of who "peopled" the management positions in the organization. The effect of this change is to reduce the amount of personal flexibility allowed in organizations. Carried to its logical conclusion, the *formal official organization replaces the informal unofficial organization* under Weber's bureaucracy. It is precisely this fact that has led to the commonly held popular connotations of bureaucracy.

Popular connotations of bureaucracy

Today when we hear the term *bureaucracy* most of us think of the following:

1. Large centralized organizations.
2. Explicit, complicated, and detailed rules and procedures that must be followed ("red tape").
3. Rigidity and slowness of action and response to problems.
4. Impersonal treatment of employees and customers/clients.
5. Very slow communications ("hardening of the organization's arteries").
6. More concern with process and procedure than goals, output, and performance.

These connotations are pretty accurate in that they do pinpoint the ills of a bureaucracy. Weber never did deal with two primary issues regarding organizational life so prevalent today: (1) the organization's ability to cope with change, and (2) the need to focus on objectives.

Need to cope with change. At the time Weber wrote his theory of bureaucracy, the assumption was made that organizations existed in a relatively stable world. The change that was occurring in the organization's outside environment could be handled by the organization by insulating itself from the outside environment. It was thought that the organization could thicken and seal up its *boundaries*—points of environmental contact—to keep the changing environment from interfering too much with internal organization pressures.

Of course, we know today that this is a very dangerous action for an organization to take. Isolation from the environment has been the reason for the demise of many organizations, both business and governmental ones. We know today that effective organizations interact with their environment and change when environments dictate such change. Business organizations lose the favor of the customer if they fail to do this, and government organizations lose the ultimate approval of the voter. Organizations are ultimately justified on the basis of their ability to serve some need in society. If this need changes and the organization fails to change with it, the organization risks its very survival.

This need to cope with change requires flexibility, good internal communication, and fast decision response times. Bureaucracies are hard pressed to meet these requirements.

Need to focus on output and objectives. The second deficiency with the bureaucratic organization is the very low priority given to goal achievement. Process is emphasized more than content. Inputs are stressed over outputs. The key question in bureaucracies becomes, "Were all rules and policies followed by a manager in carrying out authority?" instead of "Did the manager achieve the desired goals?" As we've seen throughout this book, managers in organizations must focus on this latter question in order to be competent.

THE BUREAUCRATIC SHUFFLE

The obsession with following rules, policy, and procedure over all else leads managers to dance the "bureaucratic shuffle." The bureaucratic shuffle is the old run-around, carefully packaged in much red tape, that is commonly presented to employees and the customer/clients of organizations. It's what the hapless student experienced in the incident at the beginning of this chapter.

Why do managers practice this action? Why is the bureaucratic shuffle so common in large organizations? There are several reasons, as shown in Figure 19.1. Let's look at each of these.

CYA

Sometimes managers think the best way to protect themselves from an embarrassing situation or personal criticism is to follow each and every rule explicitly down to the last comma, semi-colon, and period. At least if things fall apart they'll be able to claim they followed organization policy on the issue. Any policy or procedure needing interpretation or judgment is shunned like the plague. These managers usually have been burned in the past and they practice CYA to ensure that they are not burned in the future.

Not knowing policies and procedures

In organizations that have a policy or procedure to handle any conceivable event, it becomes quite difficult for managers to learn all of them. These policies and procedures are usually quite voluminous and almost impossible to know thoroughly. Consequently, managers practice the old dictum, "When in doubt, mumble." Employees, clients, and customers are given the old run-around because no one is really sure what to tell them.

Buck passing

When managers are afraid to make a decision, they pass the buck, hoping that someone else will make the decision for them. Decision making requires taking some risk. Managers in large bureaucratic organizations usually do not like to take this risk; furthermore, they often are not encouraged nor rewarded for doing so.

Centralization is usually a fact of life in bureaucracies. This means that most decisions are made only at the top of the organization. This increases the time for decision responses, as important decisions are bucked up the chain of command for a response. The response is further delayed since top managers can only do so much in a work day. This centralization is especially bad in bureaucratic organizations facing a very fast changing environment. By the time a decision is finally made in these organizations, the environment has changed again so that the decision, finally made, is no longer applicable.

- CYA
- Not knowing policies and procedures
- Buck passing
- Lack of personal concern for client or employee
- Loss of sight of goals

Figure 19.1 Reasons for the bureaucratic shuffle

Lack of personal concern for clients/customers and employees

The impersonal attitude created by the bureaucratic form is easily transferred by managers to the employees and the people (clients/customers) served by the organization. People are no longer treated as individuals with unique problems and interests. Everyone is made to fit the same standard mold, and to follow the same rules and regulations—regardless of their unique situation. There is no room for exceptions. Most of us detest this, above all else, when dealing with the bureaucratic mind-set. We want to be recognized and treated as individuals. If we ask why we have to do something a certain way, we are usually given the answer "because it's policy" with no further explanation. Managers say this because they don't want to take the time to tell us why it's policy, or because they really do not know why it's policy and are afraid to ask.

Managers who regularly deal with employees, such as those in the personnel office, or with clients/customers, such as counselors in a state welfare agency, develop a sense of *personal detachment* as a defense mechanism in order to survive. The problems of the employee or client are not allowed to penetrate the managers' protective skin. Significant major problems of the employees become routine daily problems of the managers handling them.

Managers develop this sense of personal detachment so that they can survive in the organization. They cannot become too personally involved because they want to sleep at night. They cannot take on the burdens of the populace. Yet, this sense of personal detachment often results in treating people simply as numbers or as case files, not as human beings. It prevents managers from giving individuals the personal attention they so often need.

During a recent research project, I had the opportunity to interview counselors and their managers at a large human services agency. For the most part, these individuals start their jobs with the agency as sensitive, personally concerned employees with a strong helping attitude. After six months on the job, their attitude changes to one of cold detachment. They become controllers and enforcers, making sure all clients follow rules and regulations to the letter in order to receive assistance payments. People are referred to as case numbers. These counselors claim that agency rules and regulations, plus their desire to preserve their own mental health, gradually push them to this approach. In effect, they have become desensitized to the problems of the clients they are serving. Their supervisors have similar attitudes.

Loss of sight of goals

So often, bureaucratic managers are at work just to put in time. They are the first ones out the door at 5:00 P.M. They live from one weekend to the next, all the while counting the number of years left until they retire. Their whole life revolves around off-the-job activities. A job is simply a necessary evil.

These individuals have lost all sense of meaning in their work. They've lost sight of work goals. They are the glum-faced paper pushers and rule enforcers so common in large bureaucratic organizations. They gloat over being able to tell people they cannot do certain things that might violate "policy." Instead of working toward constructive goals, they adopt a negative attitude designed to thwart action.

All of these reasons contribute to the bureaucratic mind-set and the bureaucratic shuffle. While organizations should have some elements of a bureaucracy, they should not become hamstrung by it. Organizations need policies, procedures, and rules, but they do not need a pretzeled web that strangles performance and output. There is no easy answer to this dilemma, but one major series of actions that should never be overlooked by an organization is the *humanization* process.

HUMANIZING ORGANIZATIONS

The concept of bureaucracy was developed to make organizations more rational and formalized. The intent is to reduce the amount of personal variation permitted, yet this process can lead to certain ills identified in the previous section. Thus, the dilemma: how can organizations develop formal, rational ways of operating without fostering the bureaucratic mind-set which treats employees and customers/clients as things, not human beings?

Humanizing the organization means that the organization designs and uses systems to protect human dignity in the organization. It means that employees and customers/clients are treated as individual human beings. It means that policy, procedure, and rules are flexible and allow for exceptions. How is this brought about? What methods can organizations use to achieve humanization?

Organization development

Most of what organizations do to achieve humanization falls under the concept of *organization development* (OD). Organization development is a process of examining and renewing organizations to ensure that goals, structure, policies, procedures, and rules are current and flexible. Some authors call the process *organizational renaissance* to reflect the rebirth or renewal aspects of this process.

Inherent in the OD process is *change*. Most efforts in OD are directed toward bringing about desired change in the organization. This change is usually focused on goals, structure, policy, etc., but it can also focus on the attitudes, roles, and emotional health of members of the organization. In this sense, it tries to restructure and redirect members' ways of thinking and acting.

OD usually occurs in some type of training and development format using an internal or external consultant. The consultant acts as a *change agent* to help the organization identify and bring about the desired changes in the organization. In this sense, the change agent is a catalyst for action. The role of the change agent and of the OD process is diagrammed in Figure 19.2. Let's look at each of these steps in the process.

Problems/issues are experienced. Usually a need for change comes about because people in the organization experience some problem, issue, or conflict. Perhaps goals are not being met, decisions are not being made, communication gaps are occurring, or product/service lines are becoming stale. Managers with power and authority in the organization see these problems and decide to do something about them. If these problems are large enough

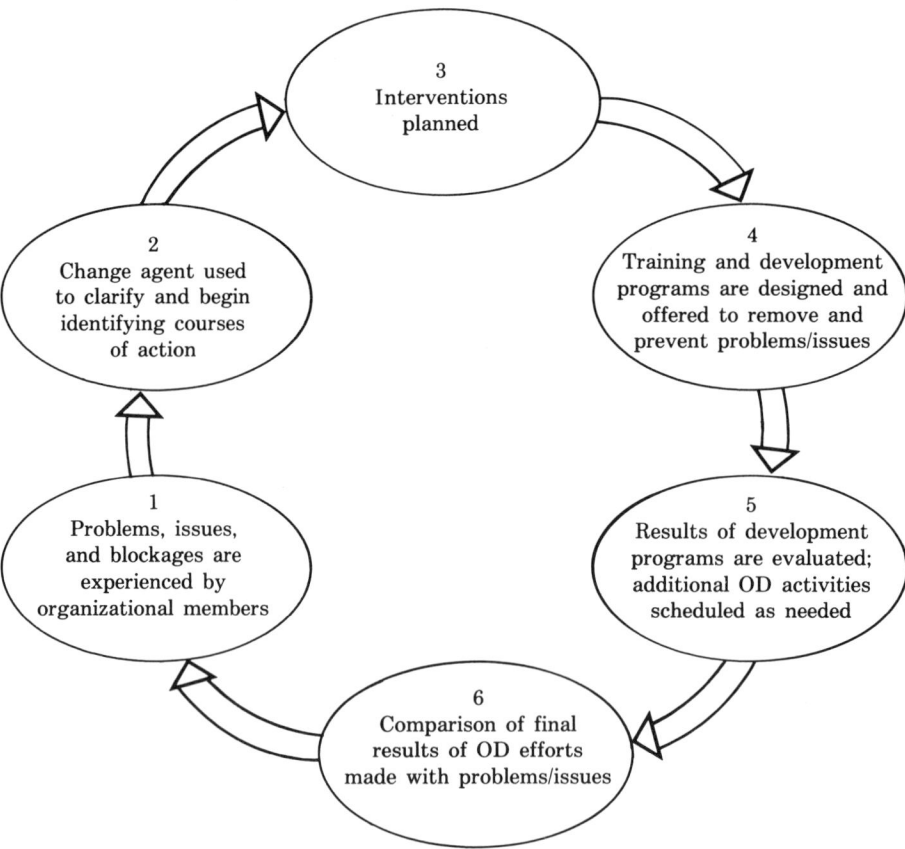

Figure 19.2 An overview of the organizational development process

and cannot be handled through the application of routine managerial problem-solving processes, then the use of a change agent is called for to break the bureaucratic shell preventing problem solution.

Use of change agent. Many organizations today employ internal OD consultants as full-time employees in a separate division of the organization. If these individuals have a high degree of autonomy and power in the organization, they can effectively perform the role of a change agent. Of course, most organizations still use external OD consultants as change agents, even if they have their own, since these people bring a fresh outside viewpoint to the issues and have a wider variety of previous OD experience on which to draw.

It's important that competent OD change agents be used and that they are given a specific charge and enough autonomy to do the job properly. It's also important for the change agent to have direct access to the CEO of the organization or the CEO's designee. This gives the change agent the credibility which is so essential for proper functioning.

Interventions planned. Working with the organization's top management and other key personnel in the organization, the change agent specifically identifies key problems/issues or roadblocks and plans specific actions to remove them. The identification of issues/problems usually comes about through an organizational assessment or audit, which is a systematic way to determine key issues via interviews or mailed questionnaires to a sample of organizational members. Some of the common questions asked of organizational employees in an audit are presented in Figure 19.3. Answers to these questions are supplemented with information from reviews of performance data for individuals and units, as well as reviews of policy and procedure manuals and memoranda.

1. Do you feel any time pressures on your job?
2. What are the three most serious limitations in your unit?
3. What are the three greatest strengths in your unit?
4. If you were the CEO (or other high official), which issues of the organization would you address?
5. What would you do to resolve each of the issues identified in #4 above?
6. What role should training and development play in resolving the important issues in your unit and in the organization?
7. How well are you able to perform the management functions in your job?
8. How can your organization's image with clients/customers be best improved?

Figure 19.3 Questions to aid organizational assessment

Once the issues are defined, a series of structured learning experiences are established to help the employees identify and build solutions to remove the problems. These experiences can be held as workshops, seminars, conferences, or on-the-job problem-solving sessions using a variety of learning and change techniques.

Training and development sessions offered. The planned series of developmental experiences is conducted by competent OD and training specialists from inside and outside of the organization. For the developmental effort to have its maximum effect, a systematic series of coordinated activities over a period of time should be offered rather than one-shot, one- or two-day training sessions. Also, it is important that actions on the job reinforce what is learned in the developmental sessions and that the sessions deal with actual on-the-job issues. This type of relationship, as shown in Figure 19.4, will help to overcome the blockage of training transfer so common in training and development programs. (We will examine some specific types of developmental programs that can humanize the organization later in the chapter.)

Evaluate initial OD effort and plan new ones. The OD effort should be an ongoing activity with varying levels of intensity over time. In other words, some OD activities should always be going on in some units, but periodically more intensive activities are needed that have wider impact in the organization. OD is not something that can be taken off the shelf for a

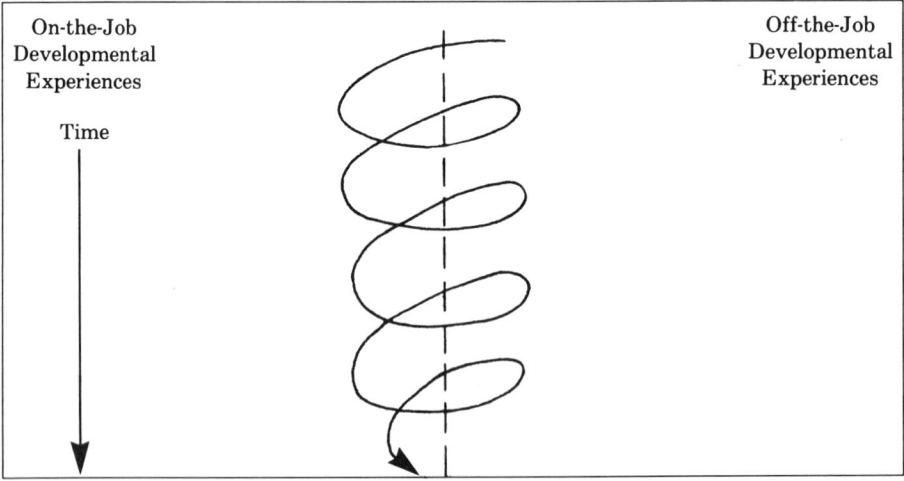

Figure 19.4 Ideal relationship for developmental experiences

month or two every other year if we expect it to have any real impact on the organization.

For OD to have the greatest impact, the results of the various activities need to be assessed against the problems/issues previously identified. Has the development effort made any real impact in removing the actual problems/issues identified? Why or why not?

Comparison of final results of OD effort with desired goals and problems to be resolved. Even though ongoing evaluation of the program is necessary, a major evaluation of the entire program should occur at least once every two years. This comprehensive assessment and evaluation of the entire OD program is necessary to keep the program relevant to the needs of the organization and to keep it from turning into a mini-bureaucracy—the exact ill the program is designed to cure.

Now that we have briefly examined the overall OD effort that can be used to humanize organizations, let's look at some specific ways that the OD program can be integrated with other actions to reduce the bureaucratic mind-set.

WAYS TO AVOID THE BUREAUCRATIC MIND-SET

Adopting an integrated, systematic OD program is one of the best ways to try to avoid the bureaucratic mind-set, but there are others. In this section, we briefly discuss some specific OD programs, as well as some other actions that an organization and its managers should take. These actions are summarized in Figure 19.5.

- Adopt a comprehensive OD program
- Promote and otherwise reward only on the basis of competency
- Bring in new blood—avoid inbreeding
- Keep red tape to a minimum
- Fire incompetent managers
- Keep goals at the forefront

Figure 19.5 Ways to avoid the bureaucratic mind-set

Adopt a comprehensive OD program

As we saw in the previous section, this is probably the most important action to take to avoid the bureaucratic mind-set. Figure 19.6 shows some

Off-the-Job Methods	On-the-Job Methods
• Sensitivity/encounter group training	• Expanded responsibilities
• Trans-actional analysis	• Job coaching
• Knowledge/concept training in management	• Job rotation
• Communications workshops	• Survey feedback sessions and problem-solving conferences
• MBO workshops	
	• Modeling/internships

Figure 19.6 Some common OD programs

common OD approaches. Because of space limitations, these are not discussed here; however, references at the end of the chapter have comprehensive discussions of each of these types of programs.

Promote and reward based on competency

Rewarding competent managers who have a solid record of performance will do much to discourage the narrow-minded, pencil pusher bureaucrats in the organization. Employees will see that bureaucratic behavior does not pay off and they will be discouraged from doing it. Of course, using competency as the basis for reward means that managers will be expected to take risks. They cannot hide in the protective bureaucratic cocoon. Risk means a chance of failure. Thus, organizations emphasizing competency and risk-taking must provide a safety net for those managers who will occasionally make a mistake. The organization needs to support its managers.

Bring in new blood

Organizations need a continual inflow of new ideas to avoid the bureaucratic mind-set. This inflow should not only occur at the entry level jobs, but also at higher level positions with greater authority. This is not to say that a promotion from within policy should not be used; it should be. But it should be blended with an outside hiring policy to ensure a wide variety of backgrounds, experiences, and perspectives are brought into the organization. Organizations who fail to do this risk inbreeding, stagnation, decay, and usually death.

Keep red tape to a minimum

Practice the KISS principle when writing a policy, procedure, or rule. Don't overcodify everything that goes on in the organization. Allow room for managerial flexibility and judgment. Permit exceptions without destroying the policy or rule. Develop short cuts around the bureaucracy without violating procedure.

Fire incompetent managers

Organizations—even governmental ones—should not tolerate incompetence. Incompetent managers should either be terminated or transferred to a position where they can do no harm. Managers who make an occasional mistake are not incompetent. Instead, I'm referring to managers who have the hard-headed bureaucratic mind-set and simply cannot perform. Even in governmental organizations these will be a dying breed if the Senior Executive Service in the federal government and in many of the states becomes more widely implemented.

Keep goals at the forefront

Unit and organizational goals should always be kept visible if bureaucratic ills are to be avoided. Working toward and being measured against specific desired results will keep managers from losing their perspective and drifting into the bureaucratic mind-set.

CONCLUSION

The ills of bureaucracy are not easy to avoid in large organizations. These organizations need the benefits of bureaucracy—rational structure, policy, and procedures—but their managers do not need the ills—the bureaucratic mind-set, bureaucratic shuffle, impersonal detachment, and other ills bureaucracy often brings.

These ills of bureaucracy gradually creep into any large organization. A conscientious, ongoing organizational development program will do much to reduce the problems of bureaucracy. Promoting on the basis of competence, bringing in new blood, keeping red tape to a minimum, firing incompetent managers, and keeping goals visible will also help to reduce the adverse consequences of bureaucracy. But even all of these actions will never completely reduce all of the ills of a bureaucracy. There will always be a few people in even the best managed organizations with the green eye shade, pencil-pushing mentality who find great comfort in the bureaucratic cocoon. In the future, however, these people should be fewer and fewer in number.

QUESTIONS

1. Are there a large number of managers in your organization who have the bureaucratic mind-set? If so, what causes this?

2. Does your organization have an organizational development program? If so, is it successful in significantly reducing the ills of bureaucracy? If your organization does not have an OD program, do you know why?

3. With what specific points, if any, laid out by Weber in his bureaucracy do you disagree? Why?

4. Can large organizations ever really become humanized? Explain your answer.

5. Won't a promotion from within policy ultimately lead to inbreeding, even if outside people are occasionally brought in at higher level positions? Explain your answer.

6. Do you know any OD specialists? What is your candid opinion of their capabilities?

CASES AND EXERCISES

CASE 1 PAYDAY SURPRISE!

"I'm sorry, Jessie, but today is not a payday. We do not have any paychecks," informed Sarah.

Jessie's heart sank. "What do you mean? It's been two weeks since the last payday."

"Yes, but, every year at this time we go three weeks between paychecks. Then you'll get a pay check for two weeks in a row. This happens every summer when we go from one fiscal year to the next," explained Sarah.

"Fiscal year? What do you mean?" asked Jessie.

"It's the way we keep our books," answered Sarah. "We in the payroll department have to conform with the rest of the company on this policy. It's always been this way since I've been here. In fact, weren't you here last year?"

"Yes," replied Jessie.

"Well, this happened last year, but I guess you don't remember do you, Jessie?" asked Sarah.

"No," answered Jessie.

"Well, at any rate we do send out notices to all employees in May and early June reminding them of this one week delay at the end of June. Maybe you didn't get one?"

"What am I to do now? I've got bills to pay this week. My family needs food," replied Jessie.

"Have you tried the credit union?" asked Sarah.

"No, but I'm up to my neck in hock to them now. They refused me a loan just last week," responded Jessie.

"Well, how about a small loan from a bank?" quizzed Sarah.

"Are you kidding? If I can't get more money from the credit union, no bank is going to give me any!" exclaimed Jessie.

"Well, I can loan you a few bucks to..."

"No, that ain't enough and you're probably short too," interrupted Jessie. "I don't know what I'll do."

"Let me call personnel and one or two other people. Maybe we can work out an emergency loan," volunteered Sarah.

After a phone call to personnel and one to a vice president of the company, Sarah replied, "Well, Jessie I'm sorry, there's no way we can loan or advance you the money. It's against company policy. They suggested you try the credit union."

Jessie left the office very disappointed. He knew he couldn't ask his fellow maintenance workers for a loan. They would be strapped almost as tight as he. And the credit union was out of the question.

Sarah felt very strong sympathy for him, but she believed there was little she or anyone else could do. The company had always had this delayed check policy at the end of the fiscal year—at least for as long as the thirteen years she had worked there. Even though she wanted to help, she didn't think there was much she could do as payroll clerk. Thank God, she thought, at least there were only a few employees with Jessie's problem that came to see her each summer.

Questions

1. If more employees experienced Jessie's problem each year, do you think the company would find a way to change its payroll policy? Would it matter if these employees were higher paid, skilled professionals, and managers? That is, does one have to have power to buck the bureaucracy? Explain your answers.

2. Does Sarah have any additional responsibility to Jessie beyond that which she has shown? Why or why not?

3. If you were Jessie, what, if anything, would you do now? What would you do if you were Sarah? Why?

4. If you suggest that Jessie turn to the state or county for assistance payments, what implications are there for a society that uses public monies to correct inadequacies in corporate policies?

CASE 2: DOG AND PONY SHOWS

It sounds nice to say that we want to humanize organizations, but let's face it, it's almost impossible to do. Most of the ways to humanize revolve around organizational development techniques. OD techniques usually involve training. It's been my experience most management training never "takes." The people go off to a two- or three-day workshop and go back to their job doing the same things they were doing before they left.

People come to training and development sessions with either one of two expectations. First, some attend expecting to be entertained. They want a dog and pony show. They want to enjoy the training, laugh, and generally have a good time. Learning something is a very low priority to them, if it exists at all.

The second type of expectation some people bring with them is that they are looking for a savior. They expect the training and development session to solve all their job problems for them. They want the magic answer, the Rosetta stone.

So here's the dilemma: on the one hand you've got participants looking for an entertaining dog and pony show and on the other hand you've got participants who want the answers to all their problems in two or three days. In either case, the conscientious training and development specialist will not be able to fulfill the expectations. At best, the OD specialists can give the people some tools to solve job problems and begin working with them to structure some solutions, but the specialist cannot solve the problem for them. They must do that. Furthermore, if the OD consultant concentrates on entertaining them, they'll learn very little. A seven-hour program will consist of one or two hours of content and the rest will be comedy filler.

So where does this leave us? It tells me that humanizing an organization will never occur unless the people in the organization want to be humanized. If they are bureaucrats and like being bureaucrats, bureaucrats they will remain. An OD specialist cannot come in and work wondrous miracles that will change an organization over night or even over a year.

Questions

1. Do you agree with this person's perceptions as to why people come to a training and development session? Do you believe they might have expectations other than the two identified?

2. Is it true that "humanizing an organization will never occur unless the people in the organization want to be humanized"? If an organization is made up predominantly of bureaucrats who are comfortable, can it ever be changed? If so, what is required?

3. How can the blockage of training transfer between what goes on in a training session and what is practiced on the job be dealt with to reduce the blockage?

EXERCISE: ARE YOU LIVING IN A BUREAUCRATIC JUNGLE?

In this exercise you are asked to indicate the extent of your agreement with a series of forced-choice statements coded as follows: SD—Strongly Disagree, D—Disagree, A—Agree, SA—Strongly Agree. Please circle the appropriate number for each statement that honestly represents your views and experiences in your present organization. There is a scoring key at the end of the exercise.

	SD	D	A	SA
1. In our organization, following the proper procedure or rule seems to be more important than achieving the goal or objective.	1	2	3	4
2. Because of the service/products we offer, it's really too difficult to set measurable goals.	1	2	3	4
3. It seems that for any possible condition that could arise, we have a policy or procedure developed to handle it.	1	2	3	4
4. People seem to get promoted based on how hard they work, not on what they actually achieve.	1	2	3	4
5. When a subordinate comes to me with an idea, the first thing I do is to check organizational policy on the issue before proceeding.	1	2	3	4
6. We seem to have many policies for which I see no valid reason.	1	2	3	4
7. If our customers' or clients' needs and demands change rapidly, we seem unable to meet them rapidly.	1	2	3	4
8. It seems that every decision around here is made at the top of the organization.	1	2	3	4
9. If I broke the chain of command by going to my boss's boss with an issue, I would be in deep trouble.	1	2	3	4
10. I cannot write a letter or memo in this organization without first having it cleared by my boss.	1	2	3	4

		SD	D	A	SA
11.	If an employee (who was not my subordinate) came to me with a unique job problem, I would not spend much time to help resolve it if it meant my own work output would be delayed significantly.	1	2	3	4
12.	Every organization should have at least three important manuals for daily use: a personnel manual, a financial manual, and an operations manual.	1	2	3	4
13.	I am seldom given the opportunity to attend meaningful management education and development programs.	1	2	3	4
14.	On the whole, most managers in this organization have little real personal concern for their fellow employees.	1	2	3	4
15.	If one of my subordinates came in ten minutes late one morning, I would say something to the person about it regardless of whether the person was a good or poor performer because a rule is a rule and must be enforced firmly.	1	2	3	4
16.	There are very few exceptions to our policies and this is as it should be since most people wanting an exception don't have a valid excuse.	1	2	3	4
17.	Ordering a piece of office equipment, such as a desk, requires several approvals in the organization and usually takes at least several weeks.	1	2	3	4
18.	Reimbursement for my travel expenses usually takes at least several weeks.	1	2	3	4
19.	Customers or clients of our organization don't seem to be able to get a fast resolution of their concerns or complaints.	1	2	3	4
20.	My superior and I seldom discuss and resolve ways of handling problems; basically, most decisions are made for me and I do what I'm told.	1	2	3	4

Add numbers circled in each column and add totals.

__+__+__+__

=_____

Key:

    70–80=You work in a heavily bureaucratic organization.
    60–69=Your organization is rather bureaucratic.
    50–59=Your organization has some ills of a bureaucracy.
    40–49=Your organization has only a few ills of bureaucracy.
    30–39=Your organization is free of bureaucratic ills.
    20–29=Your organization may be too unstructured and may need more structure, policies, and procedures.

If you scored 60 or above on this instrument, what has been your role in perpetuating this bureaucracy? Can you change your role? If so, how?

REFERENCES

Bowers, David G., and Franklin, Jerome L. *Survey-Guided Development I: Data Based Organizational Change.* San Diego, Calif.: University Assoc., 1977.
    This is the first of three volumes published in 1977 which addresses the issue of changing organizations using data collection procedures for diagnosis and change in the organization. Vol. II is a manual for consultants using the technique, and Vol. III is a manual for training with the package.

Burke, W. Warner, ed. *The Cutting Edge: Current Theory and Practice in Organization Development.* San Diego, Calif.: University Assoc., 1978.
    Contains nineteen readings of the OD '78 Conference which gives the state of the art of OD as of 1978.

Fordyce, Jack K., and Weil, Raymond. *Managing With People: A Manager's Handbook of Organization Development Methods.* 2nd ed. Reading, Mass.: Addison-Wesley, 1979.
    Offers detailed procedures for undertaking the management of change, plus guidelines and methods for managing the improved effectiveness of an organization's human resources.

Galbraith, Jay. *Organizational Design.* Reading, Mass.: Addison-Wesley, 1977.
    Examines new ways to design and structure organizations in order to minimize the adverse consequences of bureaucracy.

Henderson, A. M., and Parsons, Talcott, eds. and trans. *Max Weber: The Theory of Social and Economic Organization.* New York: Free Press, 1947.

A readable translation of Weber's bureaucratic theory. Weber is very difficult to read if translated verbatim. This book edits his work as well as translating it to make it more readable.

Mansfield, Roger. "Bureaucracy and Centralization: An Examination of Organizational Structure." *Administrative Science Quarterly* (December 1973): 477–88.

The coming death of bureaucracy has been a recurrent recent theme in management literature. This article finds this to be premature. Implications are made for the continued successful use of bureaucracy in the future.

Pfeiffer, William J., and Jones, John E., eds. *A Handbook of Structured Experiences for Human Relations Training.* Vols. I–VII. San Diego, Calif.: University Assoc., 1973–79.

These handbooks of cases and exercises are issued regularly by Pfeiffer and Jones of University Associates. Most exercises and cases deal with problems in small group or one-on-one interpersonal relations.

Warren, Malcom W. *Training for Results.* Reading, Mass.: Addison-Wesley, 1979.

Treats training as a system and includes charts and checklists to serve as planning and evaluation guides, as well as numerous examples of different approaches to the training system.

White, S. E., and Mitchell, T. R. "Organization Development: A Review of Research Content and Research Design." *Academy of Management Review* 1 (April 1976): 57–73.

An integration, synthesis, and critique of current OD evaluations which focus on content and design of the studies.

Woodcock, Mike, and Francis, Dave. *Unblocking Your Organization.* San Diego, Calif.: University Assoc., 1975.

Written for practicing managers and those who teach management practice, the book includes sixty-three activities for dealing with organizational blockages and a questionnaire for use in assessing organizations.

20

How Should a Manager Avoid Legal and Ethical Pitfalls?

"Janice, does Ron know that he dated his retirement papers for June 7?"

"Yes, Jeff, I believe he does."

"Does he know he'll lose his retirement check for June? He should have dated his retirement May 31."

"But his contract extends through June 7. Technically he is paid through June 7, Jeff."

"Well, yes, I guess so. Why don't you just go ahead and redate the papers for May 31? I'm sure Ron would appreciate it."

"Oh no, I couldn't do that."

"Look Janice, Ron worked here for over twenty years. He was a vice president. This is the least the company can do for him. Go ahead and change it. No one will know. Certainly *I* won't say anything. I'm sure Ron will appreciate it. It means the difference of $700 to $800 to him."

"No Jeff, if you want them changed you come over and change them yourself or have Ron come in. I'm not doing it."

Poor Ron. Poor Janice. Is it fair for a manager like Jeff to put Janice, a secretary, in this type of position? Should Janice make the change Jeff has requested? Does Ron know anything about this?

This incident is an example of countless situations where managers must decide an ethical or legal question. It also shows how managers sometimes involve subordinates and others in the organization in ethical dilemmas. The issue of properly resolving ethical and legal dilemmas has always been an important one for managers, but it has become increasingly more important since the Watergate trauma and society's increasing demands for accountability from its organizations. Properly resolving these ethical and legal dilemmas, then, is a requirement for competent management. Failure to resolve this issue properly can be a very serious mistake, which may well spell the end of a career.

In this chapter we examine the legal/ethical dilemma faced by managers. We are concerned both with areas of conduct that border on unethical behavior, as well as those that might be clearly illegal. Specifically, we deal with the common temptation managers face to slightly bend a law, rule, or policy or selectively interpret a procedure to make things go a little more smoothly.

ETHICS, MORALS, AND SOCIAL VALUES

Every society has a commonly accepted standard of conduct that guides the behavior of its citizens. Such conduct also guides the behavior of people in organizations. Most of these standards are unwritten; they appear in the culture of the society. However, many of the standards are written and appear in the form of a constitution, legislation, and court rulings. In this section we discuss many of the unwritten rules and guidelines that serve as the basis for ethics and morals. In the next section we examine the legal issues that arise from the written codification of social standards and rules.

Social values and norms

Ethical behavior arises from social values and norms. *Social values* are basically held beliefs of a society which are widely shared by people in that society. Words like *brotherhood, peace, love,* and *freedom* come to mind as examples of social values in the United States. These words represent concepts that are abstract and rather vague to most people. Yet their vagueness is precisely what allows the vast majority of people to "buy into" them—each of us can interpret these values in our own way so that we feel comfortable with them. In this way, values are the cement that hold a society together.

Values serve as the basis for norms. *Social norms* are commonly accepted ways of behaving or not behaving in a society. They are standards of behavior that grow out of specific values. Norms serve to make certain values operational. An example of some common social values and the norms associated with them is shown in Figure 20.1. Note that each norm is more specific than the value. Also note that a value serves as the basis for more than one norm. Of course, there are many more values and norms than those depicted in Figure 20.1.

Values sometimes conflict with one another. Is peace more important than patriotism, for example? This was a critical value issue during the war

Example Values	Example Norms
Democracy	Vote on Election Day Participate in campaigns
Brotherhood	Help others in need Be kind to others
Patriotism	Celebrate the Fourth of July Learn country's history
Work	Everyone should work for a living Hard work never killed anyone
Affluence	Owning a home is desirable Purchase of status symbols is acceptable
Peace	Try to settle an argument without fighting Our country should never be an aggressor in war

Figure 20.1 Social values and social norms

in Vietnam. Resolving conflicting values usually requires the development of a priority. A priority listing of values from most to least important is very difficult to get widespread agreement on. This, coupled with the abstract nature of values and difficulty of defining them, can make for much conflict in a society during times of stress. We are seeing further stress caused between the values of conservation and affluence now because of the energy shortage. We believe in both values in United States society, and yet we may be asked to value conservation more than affluence in the future.

Values, norms, ethics, and morals

These values and norms of a society give rise to ethics and morals. Ethics and morals are a personalization of the values and norms of a society. They rest on the values and norms, but they reflect the way an individual internalizes the values and norms.

For example, one value we have in society is *honesty*. A norm that flows from this says that one should accurately represent information in any type of oral or written report; in other words, one should not lie. Yet, how many people slightly alter income tax returns because they think they can get away with it and "everybody else does it"? This action may very well be illegal and certainly it is unethical behavior.

Thus, a person's moral code and personal standard of ethics rests on society's values and norms, but morals and ethics will deviate somewhat from the values and norms because of the way people *selectively* interpret society's values and norms.

LEGAL ISSUES

Society also attempts to codify its values and norms to some extent through law. These laws are passed at the national, state, and local level by legislative bodies elected to represent the interests of constituents. Law is also made, however, through executive action (issuing of rules and procedures by regulatory bodies, heads of state, etc.) and by the courts. Courts make law when setting precedent. Most *common law* in a country is law established by precedent. Law also exists in federal and state constitutions. Courts further refine the intent of constitutions when interpreting cases in light of them.

Most values and norms are *not* codified. While we seem to have a plethora of laws in this society, which do attempt to codify values and norms, most people learn and follow cultural values and norms because it's what they've been taught to do. In other words, our cultural institutions interpret, refine, and pass on to the members of society the society's values and norms. These institutions include the family, schools, and the church. Thus, family-rearing practices, educational policies, and religious teachings and documents also serve as the basis for ethical and moral behavior. Our laws play an important part, but so do our social institutions.

The relationship between social values, norms, institutions, ethics, and morals is shown in Figure 20.2.

Sometimes laws conflict with family practices, sound educational policy, or religious teachings. Some questions which show these conflicts are presented in Figure 20.3. These are difficult questions to resolve because there is much variance of opinion as to what *the* correct answer should be. Some actions are prohibited by certain religious teachings, but are permitted by law (e.g., abortion), while other actions are permitted and encouraged by religion, but constrained by law (e.g., liability for good Samaritan practices).

Furthermore, the teachings of one religion will conflict with those of another. For example, some religious groups use mind-altering drugs during services, while many religions totally prohibit the use of such drugs. Some

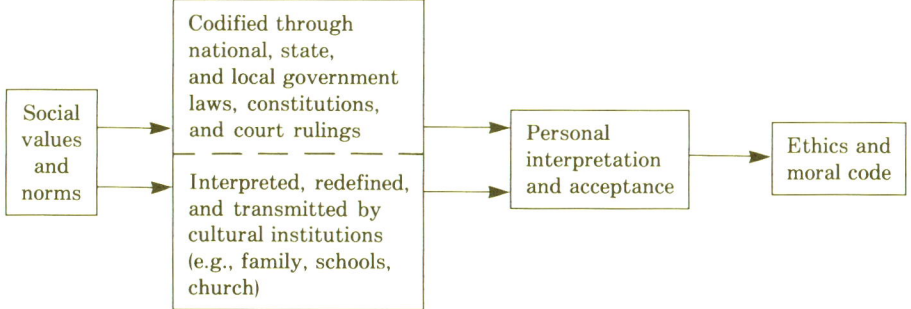

Figure 20.2 Basis for ethical and moral codes

groups forbid dancing, others have no prohibition. Some require weekly church attendance, others do not. Some require strict adherance to dietary rules, others have different rules or no rules on diet. There is no way the state can codify all religious teachings with these conflicts unless the state decrees one official religion that all will follow, such as was recently done with Islam in Iran. If this were done, then the religious code could be incorporated into national law. (This is unlikely in the United States and would require a constitutional amendment.)

In addition, the laws in a society will often conflict with one another. In some states, counties, or cities, the sale of liquor is prohibited, but in most states it is permitted. Some states and local subdivisions allow the sale of marijuana of a certain amount (or at least treat it as a misdemeanor offense) but other states treat it as a felony. Prostitution is permitted in at least one state (Nevada) but is prohibited elsewhere. The list is almost endless; however, when local or state law conflicts with federal law in the United States, federal law will prevail.

1. Should abortion be illegal?
2. Should children be compelled to attend school until they reach some age?
3. Should prayer be permitted in public schools?
4. Should the sale of distilled spirits (liquor) be prohibited?
5. What is pornography?
6. What is the legal liability of someone who tries to help someone in need (Good Samaritan Laws)?
7. Should gambling be prohibited?
8. Should the smoking of marijuana be prohibited?
9. Should men and women have equal rights under the law?

Figure 20.3 Questions showing conflict

The point is, what is considered right (legal) in some parts of the country is considered wrong (illegal) in other parts of the country. Those who believe in ethical absolutism find this a difficult phenomenon with which to deal. They believe something is either right or wrong—it should not vary from county to county, state to state, or religion to religion.

It is this variance in law and in ethical and moral codes from state to state and from religion to religion that causes so many problems in moral and ethical behavior.

Absolutism versus relativism

In law and especially in ethics, the trend today has been toward *relativism* or *situational ethics*. This means that what is legal or illegal, what is right or wrong, and what is acceptable or unacceptable varies from state to state, from religion to religion, or even from person to person—it all depends on the situation. There are very few things that are *absolutely* wrong all of the time. Even the taking of another person's life is allowed under certain circumstances. In time of war it is permitted, some states kill murderers, and in most states it is permitted in self-defense (justifiable homicide). So the answer to the question, "Is the taking of another human being's life always wrong?" is no; there are some circumstances when it is permitted, indeed, even encouraged (as in time of war).

It is this situation of legal, moral, and ethical relativism that opens the door for various individual interpretations as to what is right and what is wrong. For example, most of us would agree that it is wrong to lie. Yet suppose someone came to your door with a gun asking if your spouse were home. Suppose he or she were home, would you say so or would you lie, hoping the person would go away so you could call the police? If you were sheltering Jews in Hitler's Germany and a member of the Gestapo asked you if there were any Jews in your home, would you say "yes" knowing it would mean almost certain death for them? Most of us would lie in both of these instances because we place the safety and value of human life above telling a lie. In other words, the appropriateness of lying is relative; it is not absolute.

PERSONAL RESPONSIBILITY

It is this issue of relativism that presents managers with the dilemma of legal, ethical, and moral behavior on the job. If certain acts are not always wrong, when *are* they wrong? Should each manager be able to apply personal standards to determine when something is right or wrong? How selectively should managers be permitted to interpret social values and norms? Can laws be interpreted selectively? What about organizational rules and policies—can they be selectively interpreted? Are acts of others in the organization okay to copy even if they violate company policy (e.g., it's okay to cheat on your expense account because everyone else does it)?

These are not easy questions to answer, but most of us believe that there is a line that separates behavior which is clearly appropriate from that which is clearly inappropriate on many issues. In other words, as we see in Figure 20.4, there is a boundary or parameter that separates clearly wrong from clearly right behavior, but there is a large gray area that many managers hold to be relative. For example, most managers would agree that killing another person to get promoted is wrong. Most would also agree that paying someone an agreed upon wage for work performed is right. But what about cheating on expense accounts when everyone else does it and when travel reimbursements do not fully reimburse for travel costs incurred? This last issue would probably fall in a gray area open to selective interpretation by individual managers.

Clearly Wrong Behavior	Gray Area	Clearly Right Behavior
Example: Killing someone in order to be promoted.	Example: Cheating on expense account when everyone else does it and travel costs not fully reimbursed.	Example: Paying someone agreed upon wage for work performed.

Figure 20.4 Boundaries of behavior

What, then, is an individual manager's personal responsibility? We can identify at least six areas of responsibility, as shown in Figure 20.5. Below we examine each of these. In the final section of the chapter, we examine some actions managers should take to avoid legal and ethical pitfalls.

Responsibility to self

In the final analysis, a manager must be responsible to self. A manager who successfully avoids or resolves legal and ethical issues will have a clear conscience. Each of us must be able to live with ourself. Each of us has a personal standard of moral conduct, and we should try to live up to it.

Responsibility to profession

Management is a profession, even though some would disagree with this statement. As a profession, it has certain standards of behavior associated with it. These professional standards, while perhaps not as clearly articu-

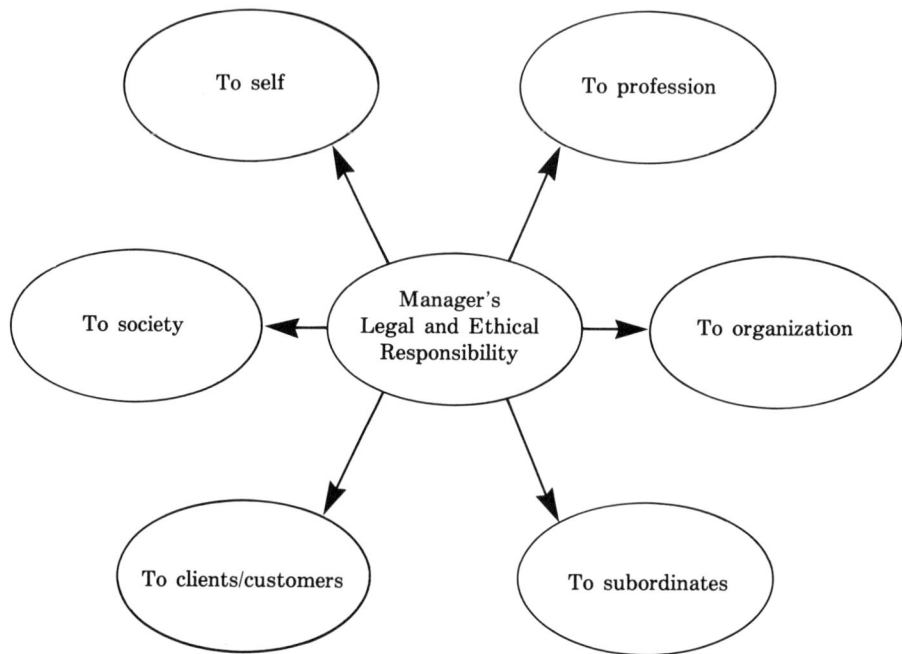

Figure 20.5 Legal and ethical responsibilities of a manager

lated nor as widely held as those in medicine or law, nevertheless are there. Perhaps as management becomes more widely recognized as a profession, professional codes of conduct will become more widely developed and accepted. Still, managers have a personal responsibility to live up to standards of appropriate management conduct.

Responsibility to organization

Every organization has policies, rules, and standards of conduct which it expects all employees in the organization to follow. Some organizations clearly spell these out in written form; others hold them implicitly. Either way, managers have a responsibility to live up to the standards of conduct expected by the employing organization. When one works for an organization, one implicitly accepts these standards as part of the employment contract.

Responsibility to subordinates

Managers have a heavy responsibility over the professional lives of their subordinates. Their superior position over subordinates gives them much power. This power should not be abused. Subordinates, for example, should not be ordered to do something illegal or unethical. Managerial responsibility to subordinates should guide management decision making involving subordinate action. Without this responsibility, management power and authority is subject to much abuse. Responsibility tempers the abuse of power.

Responsibility to clients/customers

Organizations exist solely for the reason of satisfying some need in society. This need derives from the customer or client group being served. As guiders of organization action, managers have a responsibility to see that customer/client needs are met in an efficient and effective manner. In business, this means the needs should be satisfied at a reasonable profit to the firm consistent with normal accepted business standards. In government and other not-for-profit organizations, it means that these needs are to be met consistent with legislative intent in the most efficient manner possible since taxpayer money is being spent.

To society

Managers in all types of organizations are in a position of social trust. Managers are responsible to society for legal and ethical performance. This social responsibility not only encompasses the fruitful and efficient use of society's resources (energy, people, raw materials, etc.) and the protection of the environment, but also extends to responsibilities to family, government regulatory agencies, and the unfortunate or disadvantaged. It also includes respecting the laws and mores of foreign countries if the organization is working in a multinational environment.

Balancing responsibilities

Balancing personal responsibility to each of these "constituents" is very difficult. Do I violate a law when asked to do so by my company? Should I work weekends on a regular basis even though it severely depresses my family? Do I offer bribes to foreign nationals even if it is an accepted business practice in certain countries? These are extremely difficult questions to answer and no one except the individual manager can answer them. Yet they *must* be answered. Answering them involves each manager weighing the importance of the responsibility to each area so an appropriate choice can be made.

While specific answers to each of the above questions and others dealing with conflicting responsibilities are not provided in this chapter, we can examine certain acts that every manager should follow to avoid or resolve legal and ethical dilemmas.

WAYS TO AVOID LEGAL AND ETHICAL DILEMMAS

Six broadly based courses of action for avoiding or resolving legal and ethical dilemmas are shown in Figure 20.6 and are discussed below. While these may appear to be rather simplistic, most managers will find that following these few courses of action will go a long way toward resolving moral and ethical dilemmas.

Never knowingly break a law

Managers should never knowingly violate a law if they expect to avoid or resolve legal and ethical dilemmas. While ignorance of the law is of little excuse, at least the managers' motives are excusable even though the action is not. Thus, managers have a responsibility to inform themselves of the law and then follow it.

Set an example for others

Managers should set a good example for subordinates. If subordinates see their superior undertaking some questionable action, they will be more likely to believe that such action is acceptable in the organization. Subordinates look to superiors as models of behavior. Managers have a responsibility to provide a good model.

Know and follow organizational rules and regulations

It is incumbent upon managers to learn and follow organizational rules and regulations. This is expected as part of the employment contract. Also, this knowledge is required in order to set a good example for others in the organization.

Enforce organizational rules and regulations

It is up to the managers to enforce organizational rules and regulations. If managers do not enforce them, no one else will. Rules and regulations have as much actual authority as the intensity with which they are enforced.

• Never knowingly break a law	• Enforce organizational rules and regulations with subordinates
• Set an example for others in the organization	• Adhere to the responsibilities of the profession of management
• Know and follow organizational rules and regulations	• Observe standard cultural norms for behavior

Figure 20.6 Ways to avoid or resolve legal and ethical dilemmas

Adhere to responsibilities of the management profession

Certain standards and practices for professional management should be followed by managers. This means ethical factors should be considered when making decisions. When writing reports, letters, and memos, the truth should not be distorted. The interests of owners, customers, and subordinates should be represented fairly and accurately. Stockholder or taxpayer monies should be spent wisely.

Observe standard cultural norms for behavior

The standard cultural norms of decency, honesty, integrity, forthrightness, and so on should be followed as a matter of course in everyday management activity. Granted, people differ as to the specific meaning of these terms, but most everyone agrees that fellow human beings should be treated as individuals with a sense of dignity, no matter what their status is in life. Managers often have many pressures placed on them to ignore this simple standard of human decency as they struggle to beat out a competitor, or struggle to get to the top in promotion battles. Yet remembering these normal cultural standards will do much to help avoid or reduce ethical dilemmas.

CONCLUSION

Properly avoiding or resolving legal and ethical dilemmas is one more hallmark of competent managers. Managers who ignore these issues or violate legal and moral codes do so at great risk to their personal life and career. The days of trying to get away with something questionable by covering up are gone in this post-Watergate era. Demands for accountability from our organization's managers—in both business and government—have never been greater. The role of the media and of governmental investigatory bodies has never been more activist. Even corporate stockholders are taking a closer look at the actions of corporate officers. Members of boards of directors are being held personally liable for decisions they make.

Competent managers welcome this challenge for accountability. They realize that holding people accountable for responsible legal and ethical performance should ultimately improve management effectiveness and should reduce the amount of nonproductive work in the organization that sometimes goes on in trying to cover up illegal and unethical actions. While adding another dimension to management competency, more strict attention to legal and ethical issues should make our organizations better places in which to work.

In the next and final chapter of the book, we expand on some of the ideas introduced in this chapter as we explore the way managers should keep a proper career perspective. In making career decisions, managers must balance obligations to themselves, to their organizations, and to their families. The way they resolve ethical and legal issues will also impact on their career, as we've pointed out in this chapter. Finally, career decision making involves the issue of individual evaluation, training, and development which have yet to be adequately addressed in this book.

QUESTIONS

1. What has been the most important legal or ethical issue you have ever faced as a manager? Why was this so important? How did you resolve it?

2. Is it okay not to follow company policy or procedure if your superior and others in managerial positions do not? Explain your answer.

3. What responsibility do you have to report others in the organization who:
   a. break an organization policy or rule?
   b. break a law?
   c. encourage others to break a policy or a law?

   If you believe you have a responsibility to report others in any of these categories, would you do so even if it might cost you your job? To whom would you report these individuals?

4. Internal auditors are often placed in the role of enforcing certain rules and regulations in the organization that deal with financial matters. What responsibility do you have in your present job to cooperate with internal auditors in your organization? What conflicts have you experienced with them? How have you resolved these conflicts?

5. How have you adequately balanced the responsibilities shown in Figure 20.5? That is, what is the priority listing you use? Does it work?

6. Suppose you were asked by your superior to lie to cover an error made by your superior. List the factors you would consider in deciding whether or not to go along with the request.

7. What role should a person's religious beliefs have in the everyday conduct of a managerial job?

CASES AND EXERCISES

CASE 1: A CONFLICT OF INTEREST

No purchasing agent shall take a gratuity in any form from a present or potential supplier. This refers to items of significant value such as cash, gifts, travel, lodging, etc. Any purchasing agent who does not follow this policy shall be subject to immediate disciplinary action which may include termination. This policy is necessary to ensure that our organization make purchase decisions solely on the basis of price, quality, quantity, service, timeliness, and other factors associated with the product or service being acquired.

J. R. McMillan
Vice President, Purchasing

"Did you see this new policy, Fred?" exclaimed Wilma. "Who do they think they're kidding?"

"Yeah, it's horrible isn't it?" answered Fred. "It's virtually unenforceable."

Fred and Wilma are purchasing agents with Protex, Inc., a textile manufacturer located in the southeast. The firm recently adopted the above policy statement on gratuities for purchasing agents. Up until now, the firm did not have a written policy on the subject, although it was generally understood that purchasing agents were not to become "too cozy" with suppliers, as J. R. McMillan, the Vice President for Purchasing often said.

The formulation of a written policy on gratuities was largely precipitated by the case of Homer Miller. Homer had been a purchasing agent for Protex for twenty-three years and was considered one of the best agents the company had. During the past four years, Homer had frequently used a condominium in Florida provided, at no cost to him and his family, by Trucktransit, Inc., a major truck transport company the firm had used for over ten years. During the first year, Homer and his family used the condominium only once, but during the last three years, they had used it a total of eleven times. Homer was the only Protex purchasing agent permitted by Trucktransit to use the condominium. This upset some of the other Protex agents who complained to Mr. McMillan.

What really brought the issue to a head, however, was Homer's use of the company credit card to charge travel expenses to and from the condo. He claimed them as business expenses since he claimed he met with Trucktransit officials while staying at the condo.

This also upset other Protex agents since they believed Homer and his family were getting regular vacations to Florida at company expense. McMillan's initial action was to warn Homer not to charge the expenses of his family on these trips and to document any business transactions with Trucktransit prior to charging off his personal travel expenses. Homer refused to do this at first, but after a disciplinary two-week suspension from duties with pay by Protex, he agreed he would do so in the future.

Several months passed since Homer resumed duties with Protex when Mr. McMillan noticed he had once again traveled to the condo with his family at Protex expense. When confronted with this, Homer said he was a bit short of cash, but fully intended to reimburse the company at a later date.

In the meantime, other agents heard of Homer's latest trip and complained loudly to McMillan that they should be accorded the same privileges with their respective suppliers. Seeing that the situation was causing much discord among the company's agents and was about to get out of hand, McMillan fired Homer and issued the policy prohibiting gratuities.

"Boy, old J. R. has gone overboard on this policy," continued Wilma. "I wonder if having a supplier pick up our lunch tab falls under this?"

"How about Christmas gifts? I sure enjoy that case of bourbon I receive each year from Wellswood. I hope I don't have to give that up," remarked Fred.

"Yeah, a policy like this sure is going to make it tough for this company to hold on to its good purchasing agents. You know what's going to happen—if they try to enforce the policy strictly it will drive everyone away. If they don't try to enforce it, it will be meaningless and we'll have more 'Homer Miller' situations. It's a shame how one person can ruin things for the rest of us," concluded Wilma.

Questions

1. Is a policy such as the one stated at the beginning of the case good for a firm to have? How would you modify the policy, if at all?

2. Should the company have taken less or more stringent action than was taken with Homer Miller? (Should he have been fired earlier? Should he have been fired at all?) Why or why not?

3. Do you think the company will be able to enforce its new policy on gratuities? Why or why not?

CASE 2: CHRISTIAN COMPASSION

It seems to me that the very qualities needed to get ahead in business are at direct odds with the teachings of the Christian religion. Christianity teaches cooperativeness, business teaches competitiveness. Christianity teaches forgiveness, business views people who forgive as weak. Christianity places a low priority on material possessions, business emphasizes material rewards. Christianity teaches compassion, yet a businessperson needs a cold heart to survive.

These differences were recently shown to me in the case of Jerry, who had been with our firm for twenty-seven years. He was a good employee, although his productivity had slipped some during the past two years. He was fifty-eight years old, four years away from retiring at full benefits with the company, when he was asked to resign. His resignation four years early meant he could only collect 50 percent of his full retirement benefits under our pension plan. Do you think this company would keep him on? No sir, not this firm. All this company is interested in is making a buck. Anything for the almighty dollar. Drive, drive, drive! Meet that competition!

Jerry was a good worker. He did his job well, he just didn't do it as well as he once did. He still got out the work, though, and I'd say he was just a bit below average on performance. Would this company have compassion for the guy and move him to a less demanding job? No sir! Did this company consider Jerry's feelings when they asked him to resign? Nope, they just cut him off free and clear. Jerry was devastated. Here's a guy fifty-eight years old with two kids still in college and zap!—he's out on the street. Who's gonna hire him at his age? The poor guy will never get a job. Washed up at fifty-eight with at least fifteen to twenty years left to live.

The worst thing is that there's no law against this. The Age Discrimination Employment Act prohibits discrimination on the basis of age, but how can Jerry prove this? Let's face it, his performance had fallen off some. He was fired for not performing as well as the company thought he should and as well as he had in the past.

Even though Jerry's case really hit home since he's a close personal friend, there are countless other examples that show that business is anti-Christian. It's screw your brother whenever you can to get ahead or make a buck. People are expendable. Where's human dignity? Where's compassion? There's no place for these qualities in a business. It's the almighty dollar which rules—not God.

Questions

1. Do you agree that the teachings of Christianity are at odds with the actions required for successful business behavior? For success in a not-for-profit organization? Explain your answers.

2. If you were in a position in this company to make a decision on Jerry, what would you have done, given what you know about Jerry's performance? Why?

3. Should government prohibit actions, such as that faced by Jerry, through a law or regulation? Why or why not?

EXERCISE: WHAT IS YOUR ETHICAL QUOTIENT?

Listed in Figure 20.7 is a series of statements summarizing various situations managers commonly face on the job that might raise an ethical or legal question. Using the scale, rate each situation as to its likely ethical or legal impact. In the second column indicate whether you have ever engaged in the activity listed. Finally, in the last column indicate whether your activity was consistent or inconsistent with the way you rated the situation. For example, if you rated something as definitely illegal, but did it, it would be inconsistent behavior. An example is provided at the beginning of the list.

Scale: I/U = definitely illegal and unethical
I = illegal; maybe unethical
U = maybe illegal but definitely is unethical
MU = maybe unethical; not illegal
NU = neither unethical nor illegal even though it may violate company policy

Example	Illegal/Unethical?				Ever Do?		Consistent?	
	I/U	I	U	MU	NU	Yes	No	Yes	No
Making a personal phone call on company time.				✓	✓		✓	
1. Making a personal phone call on company time.								
2. Filing a fake travel reimbursement voucher.								
3. Falsifying a job application form.								
4. Asking a secretary to run a personal errand on company time.								
5. Misrepresenting features of a product or service to a customer or client.								
6. Accepting a gratuity from a supplier.								
7. Giving a subordinate a higher than deserved rating for merit raise or promotion purposes.								
8. Denying someone a job who is qualified but whom you just don't like because of their race.								
9. Asking a secretary to type a personal letter for you on company time.								
10. Placing a personal long distance call on company WATTS line.								
11. Copying a personal item on company copier during company time and not paying for it.								
12. Bringing home company tools, equipment, supplies, etc., for personal use.								
13. Billing company for personal use of company car.								
14. Using company letterhead and envelopes for personal correspondence.								
15. Charging postage fees to company for personal correspondence.								

	Illegal/Unethical?					Ever Do?		Consistent?	
	I/U	I	U	MU	NU	Yes	No	Yes	No
16. Recommending someone for a job you know who is not qualified.									
17. Falsifying time cards or asking others to do same.									
18. Charging personal items on company credit cards and not reimbursing the firm.									
19. Writing an undeserved, glowing letter of recommendation for a subordinate in order to get rid of him or her.									
20. Doing personal work on company time.									
21. Falsifying attendance records.									
22. Recording higher than actual miles traveled for travel purposes.									
23. Taking a client to dinner.									
24. Giving a client or customer a Christmas present worth more than $10.									
25. Coming in late to work or leaving early without permission.									
26. Taking a long nonbusiness lunch that exceeds normal lunch time by fifteen minutes or more.									
27. Telling someone they've done a good job when they haven't.									
28. Leaking a company secret to a competitor for remuneration.									
29. Buying your superior a Christmas present worth more than $10.									
30. Having a subordinate do a report and taking personal credit for it.									

Figure 20.7 Ethical legal question sheet

REFERENCES

Baumhart, Raymond C. "How Ethical Are Businessmen?" *Harvard Business Review* 39 (July–August 1961).

A somewhat dated but still insightful discussion of a survey of business managers done around 1960 which shows that business managers desire to improve business behavior but that it takes a very strong stand from top management on the issue to bring about improvement.

Carr, Albert Z. "Is Business Bluffing Ethical?" *Harvard Business Review* 46 (January–February 1968): 143-158.

Points out that the ethics of business is more like those found in a poker game than those found in society.

Gwirtzman, Milton S. "Is Bribery Defensible?" *New York Times Magazine* 5 (October 1975): 19ff.

A good discussion of multinational companies paying off foreign nationals for sales, special favors, and so on.

McCall, David B. "Profit: Spur for Solving Social Ills." *Harvard Business Review* 50 (May–June 1973): 46-52.

This article shows the positive role of the profit motive in society and contends that business will not solve society's problems until the solutions are made profitable to business managers.

Nicholson, Edward A.; Litschert, Robert J.; and Anthony, William P. *Business Responsibility and Social Issues*. Columbus, Ohio: Charles E. Merrill, Inc., 1974.

A book of original text and controversial articles on various social and legal issues for business, including civil rights, pollution, consumerism, abuse of power, and personal social responsibility of managers.

Sawyer, George C. *Business and Society: Managing Corporate Social Impact*. Boston: Houghton-Mifflin, 1979.

Comprehensive treatment of various social impact issues for business organizations. Takes a managerial approach.

Schmidt, Warren H. *Organizational Frontiers and Human Values*. Belmont, Calif.: Wadsworth Publishing Co., 1970.

A superior anthology of articles that deals with various value issues in organizations. Articles by John Lindsay, Eric Trist, Robert Tannenbaum, and Sheldon Davis are especially insightful.

Smith, Robert M. "Company Control Over Internal Ethics is Urged." *New York Times* (November 1975).

Ways to better establish, monitor, and enforce ethical systems of behavior within corporations are discussed.

Sulton, Francis X.; Harris, Seymor E.; Kaysen, Carl; and Tobin, James. *The American Business Creed*. New York: Schocken Books, 1962.

A somewhat dated but still valuable analysis of the foundation creed which underlies the capitalistic system as practiced in the United States.

21

How Can a Manager Keep a Proper Career Perspective?

Suddah Corporation
Memorandum

To: J. R. Jenkins, Controller
From: Bill Board, Accounting Supervisor
Subject: Promotion Recommendation for Frank N. Stein
Date: July 16, 1979

This is to highly recommend Mr. Frank N. Stein for the position of Assistant Controller with our company. Frank has worked for me for three years. He is a very conscientious, highly motivated employee with a strong sense of dedication to the company.

Frank carries high professional standards as an accountant. His work is accurate and is done on a timely basis. He is able to handle and solve problems on his own and only under exceptional circumstances does he ask me for assistance.

Frank's work habits are excellent. He is always at his work place on time in the morning and often works through lunch. On numerous occasions he has stayed past 5:00 P.M. to finish up work as needed.

If there is additional information I can furnish you, please call me.

The next day on the phone:

Mr. Board: Mr. Jenkins, did you receive the letter I sent to you yesterday on Frank Stein?

Mr. Jenkins: Yes I did, Bill. It's a good letter of recommendation.

Mr. Board: Well ignore it. I *had* to write it.

Mr. Jenkins: What do you mean?

Mr. Board: Well, Frank is an excellent accountant, but he would not make a good assistant controller, at least not yet in his career. Frank asked me to write him a letter of recommendation so I had to do it. But, in all honesty, I can't recommend him for the job. He is just not ready. He's a good accountant, but I'm not sure he would make a good manager.

Mr. Jenkins: Why didn't you tell Frank all that?

Mr. Board: Well I thought about that, but I didn't know how he'd take it. He is a good accountant and he really wants the assistant controller's job. Besides that, I've given him several extra assignments in the past. He's always been so willing to help out when I needed him. I'm afraid his attitude would change now if I didn't recommend him. So you can see I *had* to write the letter, but I really didn't mean it.

Managers have two major responsibilities in career planning: they must manage their own career, and they must assist subordinates in managing their career. The example just shown raises a number of questions. First, does Mr. Board really have Mr. Stein's interest in mind, or does he have his own in mind? That is, does he not want Stein to get the job because Stein is doing such a good job for him that he doesn't want to lose him? Second, why is Mr. Board unwilling and/or unable to confront Stein with a candid, honest discussion of Stein's career progression? Third, does Board really want the job for himself? Fourth, if Mr. Stein is not now ready for the position, is someone else ready for it in the company, and what is Board doing to help prepare Stein for future positions?

The situation depicted in this incident is rather common in organizations. It shows several things. First, superiors often let their own job ambitions cloud or interfere with their subordinate's. Second, many superiors do not have frank, honest, career planning discussions with subordinates; yet this is one of a manager's most important responsibilities. Also, some managers lie about subordinate capabilities, thus placing themselves in a moral/ethical morass. Next, managers are required to appraise subordinate performance, but often do not do this accurately or fairly. And last, managers have a responsibility to develop subordinates for future job openings in the organization since most organizations promote from within.

CAREER PLANNING AND LIFE-SPACE GOALS

In our society, a person's career is a central focus of life. We tend to relate to others in terms of their job and career. For example, when you meet someone you do not know at a party, how often do you ask, "What do you do?"

We tend to peg people based on their job. Maybe we should not do this; maybe we should relate to others just on the basis of their being an individual human being; but, regardless, we do relate to people this way.

This means that any career decisions we make must be made in view of what we want out of life. We express this concept in terms of *life-space goals*. These are our personal goals for family, religion, civic responsibilities, leisure time, and education. Our career decisions should be consistent with our goals in these other important areas. In fact, if they conflict with these other goals, we usually are very frustrated and dissatisfied. We are all familiar with the busy executive who has no time for spouse and family. This can lead to divorce, alienated children, and mental trauma for all concerned. There are other examples: some individuals are so bored with their job they must "party hardy" every weekend to relieve job frustrations; others have jobs that so dominate their personal life that they have no leisure time pursuits; still others try to do too much—they have a demanding job and are very active in civic, religious, and educational organizations and soon burn out.

This balancing of career goals with life-space goals occurs throughout our entire career. We do not do it only at the point of choosing a career, although we should do it at this time. We also should do it as we move through our career from one job to the next. We need to periodically reassess our career, relative to what we want out of life. People who fail to do this on a regular basis are usually the ones who experience a *mid-career or mid-life* crisis between ages forty-five to fifty since, for the first time, they realize they're really not getting out of life what they vaguely believed they wanted. Periodic reassessment of career and life-space goals with appropriate adjustments can help prevent this mid-career crisis. We'll examine this issue more later in the chapter. Let's first turn to an examination of the career planning process.

The career planning process

Figure 21.1 shows us how the career planning process should work. Let's look at each of these steps.

Self-assessment. The first step in the career planning process is self-assessment. We must know our interests, aptitudes, aspirations, and abilities before we can even begin thinking about a job and goals. There are many aids to help us in our self-assessment. For example, we can take personality and intelligence tests. We can complete interest inventories, such as the Strong Vocational Interest test. Personal counseling from guidance counselors is also helpful. Reviews of high school or college courses that we found interesting can help us to narrow our specific interests. The point is, we must know ourselves before we know what we want or can do.

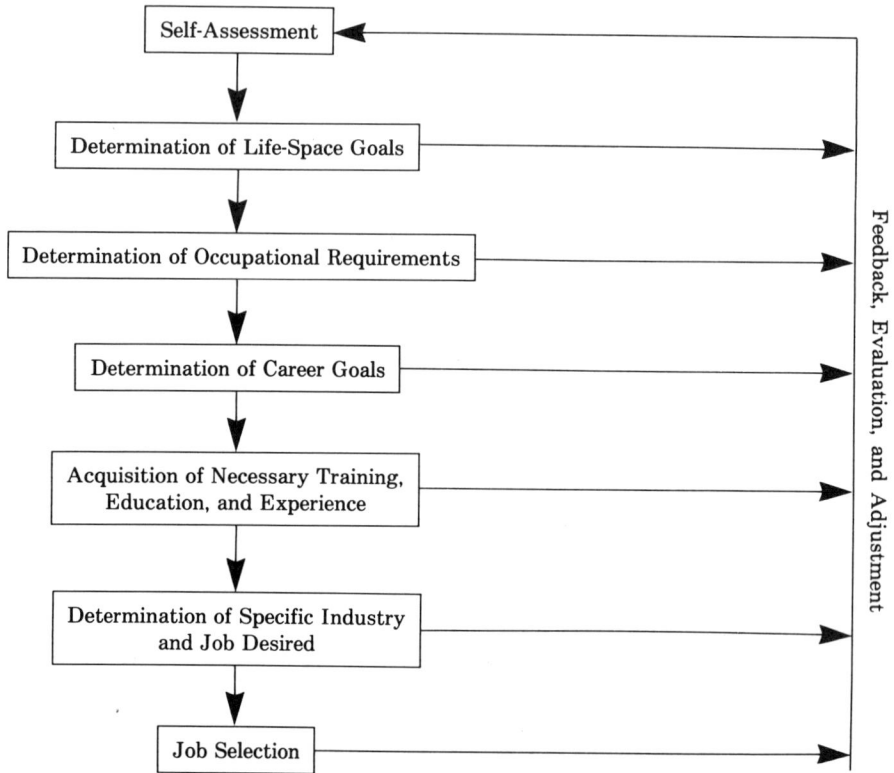

Figure 21.1 The career planning process (Adapted from William P. Anthony and Edward A. Nicholson, Jr., *Management of Human Resources* (Columbus, Ohio: Grid, 1977), p. 159.)

Determination of life-space goals. As we saw earlier, we cannot be concerned about job and career goals until we have some idea of the things we want out of life. We must assess our goals in terms of family, church, civic responsibilities, education, and leisure time. Often this can be done to some extent based upon what we learn though our self-assessment. But we must carry this a step further through discussion with parents, siblings, spouse, trusted friends, and professional counselors. The decision we reach here will always be a compromise. We never get all we want out of life, nor are we able to be all things to all people, as we've seen in previous chapters.

Determination of occupational requirements. Once we know ourselves and what we want out of life, we can begin exploring various occupations and careers to find those most consistent with our desires. For example, if we want a balanced life with substantial civic, religious, and leisure time activities, we probably would not become a practicing physician since this work involves long hours and on-call duties. Or, suppose we want a job with a lot of challenge, strong promotional possibilities, excellent salaries, high levels of autonomy, but low security; we would probably want to work for a small to medium-sized company rather than a government agency.

There are many sources of career information, including published sources such as the *Dictionary of Occupational Titles* compiled by the U.S. Department of Labor. Also, there are specific books and pamphlets published on various occupations such as physician, attorney, sales, electrician, secretarial, etc. Of course, it also helps to talk with individuals in each of these occupations to see what their experiences have been.

Determination of career goals. Now we come to the crux of the career planning process: what specific goals do you want to accomplish in your career? This is very difficult to answer, but it involves answering the questions shown in Figure 21.2. Answering these questions is not easy. It requires careful, time consuming analysis, yet, if careful analysis is done in the first three steps of the career planning process, a person should be well on the way to answering the questions in this step.

1. What starting salary do you want?
2. What fringe benefit package do you desire (e.g., insurance, pension, etc.)?
3. Where do you want to live?
4. How fast do you want to be promoted?
5. How much job autonomy and responsibility do you want?
6. How important is job security to you?
7. Are you willing to be transferred periodically to different locations?
8. Do you really enjoy working with people?
9. What is the highest management position you ultimately hope to reach?
10. Do you want to do something that has a strong "social impact" (e.g., social work, counseling, etc.)?
11. Do you wish to work on a commission or incentive payment basis?
12. By retirement, what will be important to you?
13. Are you planning on switching careers during your lifetime?
14. Do you like work which requires physical activity?
15. How large a workforce would you like to manage?
16. How much budget authority do you want?
17. Do you want a career with fixed or flexible work hours?

Figure 21.2 Questions to determine career goals

Once these questions are answered, then specific career goals can be established. A list of career goals for a recent MBA graduate is shown in Figure 21.3. Note the specificity of these goals. Note also the person will be able to measure whether the goals have been accomplished. Finally, also note that some of the goals are short term, while others are long term.

Sometimes people resist actually writing out a list of career goals because they do not believe they necessarily will be able to meet them. They also believe that luck plays such an important part in determining one's career that achieving career goals is beyond their control. However, just because goals are written down does not mean they cannot be revised as conditions change. Also, while being in the right place at the right time to seize a key opportunity is often important, this does not necessarily happen by accident. We *can make* our career opportunities. We *can* do things to help ensure that we are in the right place at the right time. Remember the key principle we discussed in the chapter on goal setting—if you don't know where you want to go, any road will take you there. Thus, without career goals, how do we know what kind of a career we want and what we hope to achieve?

Acquisition of necessary training and education. If we have occupational requirements and our career goals, we can go about acquiring the necessary training, education, and experience to help us reach these goals. Most people are well on their way to an education or even have completed it before they finalize career goals, as we saw with our MBA example in Figure 21.3. Yet, even this person will likely have to acquire additional education to meet these goals. Good managers never cease to learn. Much of this learning takes place on the job. Much of it also occurs through short courses, seminars, and workshops. One does not have to attend formal college credit courses to obtain an education. Acquiring needed education and determining career goals is an interactive process.

---

1. Obtain a job at a slightly higher than average starting salary for MBA's in 1980 dollars (e.g., at least $20,000 annual salary).
2. Enter an organization with a fast-track training program for MBA's.
3. After four years of general management training and work, specialize in field of personnel management with emphasis in EEO administration.
4. Locate in metro area in southeastern United States.
5. Within twenty years be a vice president for personnel or human resource management at a salary of at least $50,000 in 1980 dollars.
6. After twenty-five years, retire from company and go into personnel consulting work.

Figure 21.3 A list of career goals for a recent MBA graduate

Determination of specific industry and job desired. At this point, the career planning process becomes fairly specific. What type of industry do you want to work in (e.g., electronics, automobile, steel, rubber, agriculture, education, health, etc.)? What specific type of job do you desire (e.g., salesmanager, personnel assistant, engineering supervisor, production superintendent, market research director, buyer, etc.)?

This part of the career planning process requires a conscious choice and a commitment. For example, "I want a sales job in the computer software industry" reflects the choice made at this stage in the process. Notice, however, that this choice is not made until the person has first gone through the first five steps of the career planning process.

Even though this specific choice is made and does require a commitment, it does not mean we cannot change our mind if something better comes along. The choice is not cast in concrete, but at least an initial choice is made. Of course at the other extreme, this does not mean that we make a choice and a commitment only to change it the next day, and then again the next, and the next, and so on. There is a happy medium between too much and not enough flexibility.

Job selection. This is even a more specific choice than that made in the previous step. Here we actually choose the specific job in a particular organization that is desired. Usually at this point we have several offers and select the one that we believe will best enable us to meet our individual career goals.

This job selection decision occurs periodically throughout a career. It's made whenever we consider a promotional opportunity, after termination, and after resignation. It's made when we learn of another job opportunity than the one now held. Yet, each time this choice is made, we should rate the potential job offer against the criteria developed in each of the previous six career planning steps. This is necessary in order to keep a proper career perspective.

A caveat

Do managers actually go through these seven steps in planning a career? Can managers become obsessed with the career planning process so that they are compulsively evaluating their career all the time? That is, how much attention should be devoted to the whole idea of career planning? It is true that people can become so compulsively obsessed with their career that they continually question whether a right choice has been made. At some point, one must choose a job and go with it. Yet, competent managers who get ahead do devote conscientious effort to planning a career. They do not ignore this important process or somehow think "things will automatically work out for the best" with no attention on their part.

Few managers probably go through the process in as much detail as indicated here. They probably consider the factors involved, but not in the neat order presented in this chapter, and they may not actually write out factors for each step. The point is, some systematic consideration of career planning issues is necessary if managers hope to keep a proper career perspective.

CAREER PATHING AND PERSONAL DEVELOPMENT

As we saw earlier in the chapter, competent managers are concerned with developing their own careers *and* those of their subordinates. They do not leave career development up to chance. It's a planned management action carried out for a definite purpose.

Personal development should coincide with career plans. In other words, once an individual determines a career plan using the steps in the previous section of the chapter, it is necessary to lay out a development plan. This development plan specifies the on-the-job and off-the-job developmental experiences that will lead a person through a career plan. This whole process of laying out a career plan and the necessary supporting developmental experiences is known as *career pathing*. Each person in the organization should have a career path—a route to follow that enables the desired developmental experiences to be obtained so to reach career objectives. Personal ownership of a career path is very important in order to keep a proper career perspective. The absence of such a path leads us back to the old maxim—if you don't know where you're going. . . .

A person's career path should be realistic. It should reflect a person's interests, abilities, and aptitudes. If the path is too ambitious, it will lead to frustration; if it is too easy, it will lead to boredom. Because of this need for a realistic career path, it is doubly important for a person to do a thorough self-assessment and to spend adequate time and effort in determining life-space goals prior to developing the career path. The assessment process does not stop here; rather, it is an ongoing process.

Evaluating and appraising performance

Managers have a very important responsibility to evaluate and appraise their own and their subordinate's job performance. Even though a thorough self-assessment is carried out, performance must be assessed periodically to ensure that accurate judgments are made about interests, capabilities, and aptitudes. These factors change over time. Requirements of jobs also change over time. For example, compare what is required to be a data processing manager today with what was required even just ten years ago.

Thus, evaluating and appraising your own performance and that of subordinates is very important. The process involves five steps, as shown in Figure 21.4. Let's briefly examine each step.

Observe performance. Managers must periodically observe performance of subordinates either directly or indirectly. Data about performance must be objectively obtained in some fashion, by actual observation or by having the subordinate provide data orally or through written reports.

Managers must also obtain data on their own job performance. This can be done by reviewing personal output or performance on the job. Here, just as with subordinates, it is important to be as objective as possible in gathering job performance data.

Compare with objective standards. Once job performance data are obtained, they must be compared with objective standards of performance previously established for the job. For example, if a salesperson sells one hundred units a month, this would be compared with the standard set for the job, which might be ninety units per month.

This step assumes that it has been possible to previously establish these standards for job performance. In some jobs this is difficult to do, as we discussed in the chapter on goal setting. Yet, without predetermined, objectively-set standards of job performance, it is very difficult to control the personal bias that so often pervades the appraisal and evaluation process.

These job standards are also required of the manager's job. The manager should know the performance standards required in the job in order to do the job properly and in order to self-appraise and evaluate performance.

Evaluate performance relative to standards. After actual performance is compared with desired performance as specified by standards, an evaluation is made. Some questions to be answered here are: Was the performance higher than specified? Was it lower? How much deviation, if any, exists? Why does this deviation exist? Was the deviation caused by the job incumbent, the superior, or by other factors? A job performance diagnostic sheet,

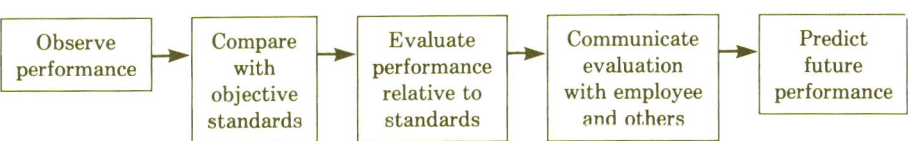

Figure 21.4 Steps in evaluating and appraising performance

shown in Figure 21.5, can help organize the answers to these questions. (A separate sheet would be completed on each significant deviation from performance expected and probably should be completed when performance is higher than expected.) Of course, it is important for managers to go through this process themselves as well as to do it for subordinates.

Communicate evaluation with employee and others. We evaluate and appraise performance for several reasons:

1. To provide a basis for a reward such as a merit salary increase
2. To determine candidates for promotion
3. To use as a basis for a career path
4. To determine what corrective action must be taken to improve performance
5. To use as a basis for possible disciplinary action

Our focus in this chapter is with number three above. The evaluation and appraisal process has so many other uses that it is essential the results of the process are not only accurately communicated with the person being evaluated, but also with others in the organization who are in a position to

```
Name_____
Department_____
Period Covered_____
Performance Variance (briefly explain relative to standard expected)_____
```

Reason for Variance	Action (if any) to correct
Subordinate's role:	Subordinate:
Superior's role:	Superior:
Circumstantial (other factors):	Organization:

Figure 21.5   Job performance diagnostic sheet

make a judgment or recommendation about the employee. This is not a startling fact or revelation, but it is surprising how many organizations ineffectively communicate these evaluations, not only to individual employees, but also to others in the organization who need to know.

Most organizations require managers to have a performance evaluation interview with subordinates. Often, these are awful. Either they lightly gloss over inadequacies in performance and turn out to be fluffy congratulatory episodes, or they dwell too heavily on inadequacies and end up generating a heavy load of antagonistic feelings between superior and subordinate. Making these sessions ones of *dialogue* and *diagnosis* that focus positively on the future is what is required for them to be effective. The appraisal interview is not to be a blame session nor a bull session; instead, it should be an important communication and problem-solving session.

Furthermore, the results of the appraisal should not just rest in an employee's personal file, never to be consulted. They should be made available to others in the organization who have the responsibility for making some of the judgments about the employee's future.

Predict future performance. This leads us to the last step in the evaluation and appraisal process. We are primarily interested in appraising and evaluating a person's performance because we intend to make some decision about the person's future. There is some danger in using past performance to predict future performance because conditions that shaped the performance in the past might be different from those conditions affecting performance in the future. A good salesperson may not be a good sales manager. An accountant may not make a good accounting supervisor, and an accounting supervisor may not make a good controller.

Thus, we have to make a judgment as to how well past performance will predict future performance. This judgment must be made not only for subordinates but also for ourselves. In making this judgment, we might as well be as honest as possible. There is no sense in fooling our subordinates or ourselves. Inaccurate predictions about future performance simply to get a promotion will likely lead to much job stress and frustration as we or our subordinates find out we cannot adequately handle the new assignment.

These, then, are the five steps involved in the performance evaluation and appraisal process. This process is central to career pathing and needs to be tied to the development process.

Personal development

None of us wants to be a manager who claims to have twenty years of experience but who, in reality, has one year repeated twenty times. We want to continue to grow on our job. We want to develop and sharpen our skills and abilities and to learn new ones. This continuing personal development is a requirement for managers in order to maintain competency.

We saw in a previous chapter that development involves learning and that this learning can and should occur through both on-the-job and off-the-job learning experiences. Too often, managers do not have a proper balance between these learning activities. They weigh one more heavily than the other. A proper balance of on-the-job learning experiences tied with off-the-job short courses, workshops, seminars, and conferences is best. Also, for these learning experiences to have maximum impact, they should be tied to a person's career *plan*. When this happens, the career *path* becomes operational: the plan is tied with developmental activities so that a path for advancement is laid out.

This responsibility for career pathing requires serious attention on the part of each manager. It is not something to be shoved onto the personnel department, although they do have a role to play. Line management is responsible for career pathing for themselves and their subordinates, and should receive support services such as testing, counseling, job opening notices, etc., from personnel. But they should not expect personnel to carry out the career pathing process for them. This responsibility cannot be abrogated to someone else.

BALANCING LIFE-ROLES

Let's look at one last issue required to maintain a proper career perspective. As we go through our career, we juggle the various roles we must play. As we saw at the beginning of the chapter, our career is a central life focus for us in the United States, but it isn't the only thing we do. In addition to being an employee and a provider, we also play other roles. For example, in addition to being a professor, I am also department chairman, husband, father, son, uncle, nephew, grandson, neighbor, voluntary association board member, swimmer, jogger, student, consumer, fisherman, football booster, college alumnus, church goer, consultant, and writer. Some of these roles are more important than others, and most of the time there is very little conflict among them. However, these roles are *not* static. Roles change as we get older and progress through our career. The changing nature of these roles causes changing demands that have to be met in each role. As these demands change, we must make sure that the demands of our career are consistent with the new demands in our other roles.

In other words, just because we have reached a balance between career and life-space goals at an early point in our career does not mean that we can now ignore this balancing process. In fact, if we expect to maintain a proper career focus, we must periodically assess our career position relative to our life-space goals on a frequent and regular basis. Only by doing this will we be in a better position to avert a surprise mid-life career crisis.

CONCLUSION

Managers are responsible for their own personal development, and in assisting subordinates with their development. This responsibility should not be taken lightly nor should it be abrogated to others in the organization.

Maintaining a proper career perspective is analogous to a train staying on the proper track: the best, most efficient train is worthless if it keeps going in the wrong direction. So it is with managers. Without a career path, the most competent, effective managers are virtually useless if they are not on the proper track. Their competencies are simply being wasted in behavior that is unproductive not only to the employing organization but also to the manager.

In this book we've examined what it takes to be a competent manager today. We've looked at the knowledge base and skills required for managerial competence. Of course, no book of this length can give a complete and thorough analysis of each and every concept we've raised. In fact, that is why additional references are provided at the end of each chapter. It is so important for a manager to have a life-long learning attitude about management. The only way this will happen is if it is built into a manager's career path. A career plan integrated with appropriate development activities will greatly assist managers in maintaining management competence.

QUESTIONS

1. Evaluate your organization's career planning process. Is enough attention given to the developmental activities required to ensure proper career pathing?

2. Evaluate your organization's evaluation and appraisal process. Is this process appropriately linked with the career pathing process?

3. Do you have a career plan? If you do, are you following it? If you do not, why haven't you developed one?

4. In your opinion what is the most important step in the career planning process (Figure 21.1)? Why?

5. How would you resolve the issues presented in the incident at the beginning of the chapter?

6. Have you worked with each of your present, immediate subordinates to help them to develop a career plan? If so, are you satisfied with the process? If not, why haven't you helped to develop such plans with them?

CASES AND EXERCISES

CASE 1: PROMOTION BY SURPRISE

Harvey Kowalski was flabbergasted. He had just read in the company newsletter that Jerry Sevorini had been promoted to Divisional Vice President for Transportation. What surprised Harvey was that he thought Jerry was about to be fired!

Harvey and Jerry began employment with Buyright, Inc., on almost the same day ten years ago. They had almost the same educational and experience background prior to joining the firm. Both had previous experiences in retailing and both had joined Buyright because of its very promising future in discount department store sales.

Harvey and Jerry had entered the firm's management development program together and both had been promoted to department managers and then assistant store managers at about the same time. But that's where their careers parted. Jerry became a store manager and now a vice president, while Harvey still remained an assistant store manager.

What amazed Harvey was that Jerry hadn't been canned by the company. During the past year and a half, the store Jerry had managed had lost money during four of the six quarters. Previously the store was a moneymaker for the company. Harvey thought sure that Jerry's poor performance would put him out in the street. He decided to call Jerry and rib him about his newest success.

"Hey, Jerry, I see the Italian Stallion has the big job now," exclaimed Harvey over the phone. "How does it feel to be a big shot?"

"Not bad, Harvey, not bad at all. Say it's good to hear from you again. How's the family?" asked Jerry.

"Fine, fine. We're doing great. When do you start your new job?" asked Harvey.

"Oh, I started Monday. It's great. You should see my office. And, boy, you should see my secretary—what a body!" exclaimed Jerry.

"Boy, some turkeys have all the luck. Here I am still an assistant manager. How'd you do it Jerry?"

"Well, Harv, ole' buddy, you just got to know the right people. That, plus being in the right place at the right time is the key to getting ahead in this company," explained Jerry.

"I guess so. I didn't even know you were in the running for a V.P. position," commented Harvey.

"Neither did I, Jerry. It came as a complete surprise to me. I came to work one day and got a call from old Claude...."

"Old Claude!" interrupted Harvey. "You mean the old man himself called you?"

"That's right. The big chief himself. He asked me if I wanted to take over Lou's job and I told him sure. I mean, what could I say?" responded Jerry.

"Wow, I guess. Well, that's great. Think you'll be able to handle it?" asked Harvey.

"Sure, nothing to it. I've got a good assistant and a super secretary. I'll tell you it sure beats managing that damn store. This will be a piece of cake," said Jerry.

"Jerry, I don't know how you did it. I thought your store was going down the tubes."

"It was, Harv, it was, but that was because of the recession, so I guess that didn't matter. Ole' Claude can recognize talent, huh? Well, give my best to your wife and kids. We'll have to get together next time I'm in Portsmouth. Bye," concluded Jerry.

"If that don't beat all," thought Harvey. "Some guys have all the luck. Here I sit with a well thought-out career plan and good performance and who cares? It sure hasn't helped me any. Old Jerry just wings it and look where he is. I guess I better start looking around because it's obvious this company doesn't give a damn about me."

Questions

1. How *should* the career planning process be tied to the promotion process? How *is* it often tied to it in reality?

2. Do you agree with Jerry that "knowing the right people and being in the right place at the right time" is often the key to getting ahead? If you do agree, how should this affect the way you plan your career?

3. Speculate as to why Jerry was promoted even though the store he was managing had lost money four out of six quarters.

4. If you were Harvey, what else would you have asked Jerry in your phone conversation with him?

5. If you were Harvey, what would you do now?

CASE 2: WORKED UP

The first time I really sat down and looked at my career was two months ago. Oh sure, I had briefly given it some thought from time to time, but I never really sat down and asked myself if I was happy doing what I was doing. I never really thought that I *should* be happy in my work. "A job is a job" was what I always thought. I felt I had to take the best opportunity that came along whether *I* wanted it or not. That's the way one gets ahead, right?

Wrong. I'm miserable. Here I am, forty-eight years old, and what future do I see for myself? It's mighty dim, I'll tell you. Don't mistake me, I've got a good job. Most people would love my salary and position, but I don't. I don't like it for several reasons. First, who gives a damn whether we sell 10,000 more widgets next year? What effect does that have on the whole scheme of things? How will humanity benefit? Damn little. The company stockholders will do okay because of increased dividends, but so what? Ten years from now no one will know or care whether we sold 10,000 or 30,000 more widgets.

Second, what good does making a lot of money do when you can't enjoy it? I work long hours, seldom see my family, and half of what I make goes to Uncle Sam. That, plus inflation, continually eats away at my pay. I'd be better off at a lower paying job that gave me more time with my family. Let's face it, the really important things in life are free anyway.

My only daughter graduated from high school Sunday. This fall she enters college away from home. Do you know the last time I had a good talk with her? I think it was when she was eight years old after our dog died. The last ten years are gone. I'll never be able to replace them. She grew up before I knew it and she'll soon be gone. Were those last ten years worth the money? Was all that business travel really necessary? Did I really have to work those evenings and so many weekends? What has it gotten me? Money, a good job, prestige—but are those really important?

I've got at least seventeen years of work ahead of me. I still have a son at home who is about to enter high school. I don't want to make the same mistake twice, but what can I do? If I ask for a demotion, they'll think I'm looney or incompetent. I'll probably be fired. If I quit, I'll lose most of my pension and stock benefits. I'd have to start all over with a new company and I have no guarantee I wouldn't be in the the same boat two years from now that I'm in now. I feel trapped.

Questions

1. Why do you think this person is in this dilemma? What could have been done to prevent it?

2. What should this person do now? Why?

3. Do you know anyone who has experienced a similar mid-career crisis? How was it resolved?

4. Does this person's employing organization have any responsibility to prevent or resolve problems such as this one?

EXERCISE: WHAT IS YOUR CAREER PLAN?

In this exercise you are asked to complete the seven steps in the career planning process. This is probably the most difficult exercise in the entire book. Most likely, it will take a considerable amount of time and several sheets of paper, but it should have a good payout for you. Use the information generated in this exercise to design a career path that helps you carry out your career plan.

Step One: Self-assessment. Describe your abilities, interests, skills, and aptitudes as briefly as possible. Review any interests, aptitudes, or intelligence tests that you may have taken. Review courses and jobs you've held that you found interesting and satisfying as well as those you found boring and dull. Make a listing of your skills, interests, aptitudes, and abilities.

Step Two: Determination of life-space goals. What do you want out of life? How do you want to relate to spouse, children, parents? What civic role do you wish to play in your community? What religious responsibilities do you desire? What do you wish to do in your leisure time? Try to develop a brief list of specific goals in each of these areas.

Step Three: Determination of occupational requirements. What occupations interest you? What does it take to be successful in these occupations? How similar are these occupations to your interests, aptitudes, abilities, etc.? How similar are these occupations to what you are doing now? How easy would it be for you to meet the requirements of these occupations? Try to list at least three occupations and their major requirements.

Step Four: Determination of career goals. Now tie in information from steps 1, 2, and 3 to write specific career goals for the next year, five years, and fifteen years. Be as brief and as specific as possible. Are these goals realistic?

Step Five: Acquisition of necessary training, education, and experience. What specific types of training, education, and experience will you need so you can reach your career goals? How and when will you go about getting this education and experience? Develop a list and time table.

Step Six: Determination of specific industry and job desired. In what industries would you like to work? What types of jobs will enable you to reach your career goals? Will these jobs require the education and experience you outlined in step 5? List these industries and job titles.

Step Seven: Job selection. What specific jobs should you be looking for? Do you now hold a job that helps you meet your career goals? If not, how easy would it be for you to change jobs? List the criteria for an ideal job if you could design one. Do you know of such a job? How closely does your present job match this list of criteria?

REFERENCES

Bostwick, Burdette. *Finding the Job You've Always Wanted.* New York: John Wiley & Sons, Inc., 1977.
> Subjects covered include preparing for a job search, resumé preparation, interviewing, negotiating salary and benefits, assessing the job and company, and assessing your future.

Figler, Homer. *Overcoming Executive Midlife Crisis.* New York: John Wiley & Sons, Inc., 1978.
> The author explains how to develop a personal program for making the mid-life period a time of growth, productivity, and self-fulfillment. Can assist in preventing or resolving mid-life crisis.

Holland, John L. *Making Vocational Choices: A Theory of Careers.* Englewood Cliffs, N.J.: Prentice-Hall, 1973.
> An excellent discussion of the theory behind the choice process in careers. Brings to bear pertinent psychological, sociological, and economic theory.

Hopke, William E. *The Encyclopedia of Careers and Vocational Guidance.* Chicago: J. G. Ferguson Publishing Co., 1972.
> A good compendium of careers and advice for making career decisions.

Jennings, Eugene E. *Routes to the Executive Suite.* New York: McGraw-Hill Book Co., 1971.
> A thorough examination of various career paths that enable one to move up the organization to higher level management jobs.

Kaufman, H. G. *Obsolescence and Professional Career Development.* New York: AMACOM, 1974.
> Keeping oneself current and learning to live with the knowledge explosion is the theme of this book. Some practical ways to learn through working are presented.

Lorsch, Jay W., and Barnes, Louis B. eds. *Managers and Their Careers.* Homewood, Ill.: Irwin-Dorsey, 1976.
> A fine collection of articles describing various aspects of the career planning process for managers.

Shertzer, Bruce. *Career Exploration and Planning.* Boston: Houghton-Mifflin, 1973.
> A guide to the career planning process with discussions of various career planning activities.

Stewart, Nathaniel. *The Effective Woman Manager: Seven Vital Skills For Upward Mobility*. New York: John Wiley & Sons, Inc., 1978.
Reviews the skills of planning, coordinating, delegating, evaluating, problem solving and decision making, allocating time, and training and guiding.

Index

Index

Aayres, Robert, 264
Abrogation, 288
Absolutism, 324
Accountability, 287
Ackoff, Russell L., 184
Action, 188
  by default, 102
  steps, 140
Activity trap, 284
Advertising, 70
Aldag, R. J., 126
Alexis, Marcus, 183
Anthony, Philip, 214
Anthony, William P., 62, 150, 200, 214, 264, 336
Argyris, Chris, 214
Armstrong, J. Scott, 264
Assessment, 139
Avoidance/withdrawal, 228

Bargaining, 237
Barkdill, Charles W., 232
Barnes, Louis B., 354
Baumhart, Raymond C., 336
Beardsley, Monroe C., 33
Behavior modification, 267
Beier, Emerson, 280
Bennis, Warren, 232

Blackwell, Roger, 79
Blau, Peter, 113
Bluffing, 241
Bostwick, Burdette, 354
Bottom-up approach, 135
Bowers, David G., 317
Brainstorming, 174
Brief, Arthur P., 126
Brooker, W. Michael, 232
Brownstone, David, 34
Buck passing, 303
Buck, Vernon, 214
Budgets, 10, 142
Bureaucracy, 300
Bureaucratic
  mind-set, 300
  system, 300
Burke, Ronald J., 215
Burke, W. Warner, 317
Buying behavior, 66, 68

Career
  pathing, 344
  planning, 338–339
Carr, Albert Z., 336
Carrol, Archie, 113
Carroll, Stephen J., 150
Chambers, John C., 264

360 INDEX

Change, 40, 217, 218
  agent, 306
Chemers, Martin M., 166
Chernich, William N., 246
Clear the air conferences, 257
Clients, 64, 168
Coaching, 40, 203
Cognitive dissonance, 190
Communications, 38, 186
  barriers, 188
  electronic, 194
  media, 239
  nonverbal, 194
  oral, 193
  skills, 38
  written, 193
Competition, 73
Compromise, 228, 237
Conferences, 257
Conflict, 223
  causes, 224
  lateral, 223
  managing, 40
  resolution, 228
  system, 223
  vertical, 223
  ways to manage, 227
Consensus conferences, 106
Consideration, 152
Constraints, 52
Consumer needs, 70, 168
Contingency
  framework, 152
  planning, 10
  theory of management, 97
Controlling, 11
Cooptation, 228
Coordination, 134
Corrective action, 144
Cost reduction, 273
Costanzo, Philip R., 166
Counseling, 40, 203
  cooperative, 207
  direct, 206
  group vs. individual, 208
  nondirect, 207
  referral, 208

Credibility, 274
Cultural
  institutions, 22
  values, 22
Culture, 22
Customers needs, 4, 28, 64
CYA, 303

Davis, Keith, 94, 113, 200
Dearden, John, 280
Decentralization, 288
Decisions, 177
  controlling, 11
  directing, 11
  job design, 10
  making, 37
  organizing, 10
  planning, 10
  resource allocation, 4
  short run, 176
  staffing, 11
Decoding, 188
Degreene, Kenyon B., 62
Delbecq, Andre L., 183
Delegation, 288
Demand, 98
Design, 10
Dictionary of Occupational Titles, 341
Dill, William R., 62
Directing function, 152
Domain, 55
  consensus, 55
Drucker, Peter F., 19
Dunham, R. B., 126
Dunn, J. D., 280
Durand, Douglas, 233

Economic system, 23
Effectiveness, 5, 158
  managerial, 5
Efficiency, 5
  managerial, 5
Electronic communications, 194
Emery, F. E., 62
Empathy, 38
Employee orientation, 153
Employees, 4

Encoding, 187
Engle, James, 79
Environment
   components of the outside, 21
   constraints and opportunities, 52
   and market, 21
   people in, 4
   relevancy of, 53
   scoping of, 57
   sources of knowledge about, 57
   task, 53
Equity, 268
Ethics, 321
Evaluation, 42
Exchange theory, 98
Expectancy theory, 268
Expectations, 98

Feedback, 107, 188, 191
Festinger, Leon A., 200
Fiedler, Fred, 166
Fiedler's contingency factors, 153
Figler, Homer, 354
Financial rewards, 271
Flory, Charles, 297
Fordyce, Jack K., 317
Forecast, 139
Fox, Harland, 280
Francis, Dave, 318
Franklin, Jerome L., 317
Friedman, Abraham, 280

Galbraith, Jay, 317
Gantt Chart, 121
Gardner, George, 201
Giffman, Erving, 246
"Giver," 98
Glueck, William P., 19
Goal
   appropriateness, 5
   displacement, 135
   multigoal effort, 115
   need for, 84
   organizational, 25, 115
   setting process, 135, 136
   variables, 156
Goal-path theory, 267

Goodman, Paul S., 280
Goodstein, Leonard D., 233
Gorton, Carruth, 34
Gouldner, Alvin W., 113, 247
Government, 4
Grapevine, 192
Green, Thad B., 201
Group bonus, 272
Guaranteed annual wages, 273
Guest, R. H., 127
Gustafson, David H., 183
Guth, William T., 183
Guzzo, Richard A., 215
Gwirtzman, Milton S., 336

Hands-on (dirty hands) syndrome, 28
Harragan, Betty L., 247
Harris, Seymor E., 336
Hatch, Richard, 201
Henderson, A. M., 317
Henderson, Richard L., 280
Hill, Norman C., 47
Hodge, B. J., 62, 150, 201
Holland, John L., 354
Homans, George, 113
Hopke, William E., 354
Hudson Institute, 15
Human resources information system, 108
Humanizing process, 305
Humble, John W., 150
Huse, Edgar F., 47
Huseman, Richard C., 113

Ideation, 187
Immediate superior, 101
Initiation, 152
Incentive payments, 267, 272
Influence process, 152
Information dump, 257
Inputs, environmental, 5
Integration, 134
Internal political environment, 234
Ivory-tower syndrome, 29

Janis, Irving L., 183
Jennings, Eugene E., 354

Job, 120
 consensus, 171
 description, 10, 101, 106, 171
 duties, 275
 enrichment, 115
Jones, John, 318

Kahn, Herman, 15
Kahn, Robert L., 215
Kaiser plan, 273
Kaufman, H. G., 354
Kaysen, Carl, 336
Keller, R. T., 126
Kelly, Joe, 233
Kerr, Steve, 166
Key personnel, 27, 89
Key products and services, 90
Knippen, Jay T., 94
Knowing, ways of, 121
Knowledge, 121
Knudsen, Harry R., 47
Koch, James L., 215
Kollat, David, 79
Koontz, Harold, 19
Kotler, Philip, 79

Lakein, Alan, 297
Lau, James B., 47
Lawler, Edward, 215, 280
Lawrence, Paul R., 62
Leader
 position power, 154
 variables, 155
Leader-member relations, 153
Leadership, 37, 158
 skills, 152
 style, 152
Le Bocuf, Michael, 264
Ledger sheet, 97
Legal issues, 322
Life-space goals, 339
Likert, Jane Gibson, 233
Likert, Rensis, 233
Litschert, Robert J., 336
Lobbying, 237
London, Jordon, 233
Lorsch, Jay W., 62, 354

Lubin, Alice W., 233
Lubin, Bernard, 233
Luthans, Fred, 233

Maccoby, Michael, 233, 247
Mackenzie, R. Alec, 297, 280
Maier, Ayesha A., 47
Maier, Norman R. F., 47, 183
Manage, 3
Management
 audits, 107
 by crisis, 4
 financial, 8
 human, 7
 information, 8
 information system, 144, 194
 by objectives, 137
 operations, 119
 philosophy, 55
 physical, 8
 of resources, 7
Management Information Exchange, Inc., 33
Manager, effective, 5, 27
Managerial
 effectiveness, 5
 efficiency, 5
 ineffectiveness, 4
 skills, 36
 work, 3, 116, 288
Managing
 change and conflict, 40, 220
 time, 251
Mandates, 132
Mansfield, Roger, 318
Manszka, Robert M., 95
Marcus, Alexis, 183
Market, 2–3
 segmentation, 69
Martinko, Mark, 233
Maslow, Abraham, 79
Maslow's need hierarchy, 71, 97
Matrix organization, 118
McCall, David B., 336
McCarthy, E. Jerome, 79
McConkey, Dale D., 94, 297
McCormick, E. J., 126
Measures of leadership effectiveness, 158

Media, 39, 239
Mediating technology, 118
Meetings, 193, 256
Member variables, 156
Mentor, 89
Mintzberg, Henry, 33, 183
Mitchell, T. R., 19, 318
Moment, David, 297
Moore, P. G., 183
Morals, 321
Mores, 22
Morris, James H., 215
Morrisey, George L., 95, 150
Mosman, Charles, 34
Moss, Leonard, 264
Motivators, 70
Mottice, Homer J., 33, 201
Muddled thinking, 190
Mullich, S. K., 27
Multinational relations, 24
Mutual goal setting, 135

Nadler, G., 126
Needs, 97
  consumer, 71
  ego and esteem, 72
  love and belonging, 72
  Maslow's hierarchy of, 71, 97
  physiological, 71
  safety and security, 72
  self-actualization, 72
Negative sanction, 267
Negotiation, 237
Newstrom, John W., 95
Nicholson, Edward A., 336
Nonfinancial rewards, 274
Nonmanagerial work, 116
Nonverbal communications, 194
Nord, Walter, 233
Nordland, Rod, 33
Norms, 22, 320
Nystrum, Harvey, 184

Oates, Wayne E., 298
Objectives
  for MBO, 139
  long, intermediate, and short-range, 15
  must-do, 14
  nice-to-do, 14
  organization-wide, 13
    efficiency, 13
    product/service mix, 13
    profitability, 13
    satisfied customers, 13
    satisfied employees, 13
  organizational, 4
    priorities of, 13
    setting, 132
    should-do, 14
    time frames for, 15
    types of, 13–14
Odiorne, George S., 150
O'Dohnell, Harold, 33
Operations
  analysis, 119
  management, 119
Oral communication, 193
Organ, Dennis, 113
Organization, 25
  chart, 10
  design, 10
Organization development, 305
  goals, 25, 115
  inputs, 5
  matrix, 118
  objectives, 4
  outputs, 4
  policies, 27
  procedures, 27
  products and services, 26
  project, 118
  purpose, 25, 139, 286
  structure, 10, 27
  ultimate rational, 13
Organizational
  assessment, 307
  audit, 307
  gap, 136
  objectives, 12
  overlap, 136
  renaissance, 305
  tradition and heritage, 56
Organizing, 10
Opportunities, 52

Outputs, 5
Overcommitment, 291
Owners, 4, 24,

Parsons, Tolcott, 317
Peer managers, 28, 105
Performance, 171
Perquisites, 275
Personal
 responsibility, 324
 visibility, 241
Peterson, James E., 215
Pfeiffer, William J., 318
Physical noise, 190
Physiological needs, 71
Piece-rate incentives, 272
Pierce, J. L., 126
Pietri, Paul H., 201
Planning
 contingency, 10
 horizon, 133
Policy, 27, 87
Political
 skills, 41
 system, 23
Porter, L. W., 280
Position, 120
Positive reinforcement, 267
Posturing, 241
Praise, 274
Precedent, 107
Pricing, implications for management, 69
Problem employee, 202
Problem solving, 38, 171
 conferences, 257
Procedures, 27, 87
Products, 90
Profits sharing, 272
Project organization, 118
Promotion, 70
Psychological noise, 190
Public, 24, 28
Purchasing agent, 65
Purpose
 multipurpose, 115
 organizational, 139
 statements, 82
 unit, 139

Raia, Anthony P., 95, 150
Raisinghani, Duru, 183
Ratio, input-output, 5
Reardon, Robert W., 215
Receiving, 188
Reif, William E., 95
Relativism, 324
Request, 98
Resources, 7
 basic, 4
 decisions, 9
 financial, 8
 human, 7
 information, 8
 physical, 8
 time, 9, 249
Responsibility
 balancing, 327
 to clients, 327
 organizational, 326
 personal, 325
 professional, 325
 to self, 325
 to society, 327
 to subordinates, 326
Reward, 42, 267
 process, 267
Richards, Max O., 19
Roch, Milton L., 280
Rochel, Frank M., 280
Rokeach, Milton, 184
Role ambiguity, 226
Rosenberg, Jerry M., 33
Rosenberg, Larry, 79
Ross, Robert, 247
Rothman, Stanley, 34
Rumor, 192

Sahoner, Bertron, 80
Salem, Allen R., 47
Samuelson, Paul A., 79
Sawyer, George C., 336
Sayles, Leonard, 166
Scanlon plan, 273
Scenarios, 174
Schedule, 142
 personal, 252
 project, 252

Scheduling, 121, 252
Schmid, Clavin, 201
Schmid, Stanton, 201
Schmidt, Warren, 336
Schnachel, Harry S., 34
Schuler, Raudall S., 47
Scoping, 57
Security rewards, 273
Selective perception, 190
Selective rejection, 191
Selective retention, 190
Self-actualization, 72
Services, 90
Severance pay, 274
Shannon, Claude E., 34
Shaw, Marion F., 166
Shertzer, Bruce, 354
Shrode, William A., 201
Sims, H. P., 126
Situational ethics, 324
Situational framework, 152
Skills, 36
Smith, D. D., 264
Smith, Robert M., 336
Smoothing, 228
Social norms, 320
Social values, 320
Staffing, 11
Standards, 143
Stanton, William J., 80
Status, 274
Steers, Richard M., 215
Steinmetz, Lawrence, 298
Stewart, Nathaniel, 355
Stock option plans, 272
Strauss, Anselm, 247
Structure, formal and informal, 10, 27, 86
Structuredness of the task, 154
Subordinates, 28, 103
Sulton, Francis X., 336
Superiors, 28
Szilagyi, A. D., 126

Taguirir, Renato, 183
"Taker," 98
Tannenbaum, Robert, 166

Task, 28, 120
  environment, 53
  identity, 156
  orientation, 153
  technology, 116
  variables, 156
Taylor, F. W., 126
Technology, 23, 118
  intensive, 118
  long-linked, 118
  mediating, 118
  subsystem interfaces, 118
  task, 116
Theoret, Andre, 183
Theory of rewards and incentives, 267
Thompson, James D., 63, 127
Thompson, Victor A., 247
Through-puts, 5
Time
  budget, 249
  managing 41, 251
  payment, 271
  resource, 249
  variables, 156
Time and Motion Study, 120
Tobin, James, 336
Toffler, Alvin, 63
Tosi, Henry, 150
Trade-off, 237
Transmission, 188
Trist, E. L., 62
Turkovich, R., 63

Uhl, Kenneth, 80
Ultimate rational, 13
Unit, goals, 3
Unity of purpose, 134
"Unk-unk" situations, 29, 173
Utility, 66
  balancing, 67
  form, 67
  place, 67
  quality, 67
  quantity, 67
  time, 67

Verbal skills, 190
Voich, Dan Jr., 34, 201

Von de Ven, Andrew H., 183
Vroom, Victor, 113

Walker, C. R., 127
Warren, Malcolm, 318
Weaver, Warren, 47
Weber, Ross A., 19
Weil, Raymond, 317
Weir, Thomas, 215
White, S. E., 318

Whyte, William F., 247
Wilson, Charles Z., 183
Woodcock, Mike, 318
Woodworth, Robert T., 47
Work
  effort, 10
  managerial, 116, 288
  methods, 118
  nonmanagerial, 116, 288
Written communications, 193